Letting Your Heart Sing

Letting Your Heart Sing

A Daily Journal for the Soul

By Deborah Tyler Blais

CAPITAL
BOOKS, INC.
Sterling, Virginia

Capital Books, Inc.
P.O. Box 605
Herndon, Virginia 20172-0605

ISBN 1-892123-49-5 (alk. paper)

Library of Congress Cataloging-in-Publication Data

Blais, Deborah Tyler.
   Letting your heart sing : a daily journal for the soul / by Deborah Tyler Blais.
     p. cm.
  ISBN 1-892123-49-5 (hardcover)
   1. Spiritual journals--Authorship. 2. Devotional calendars. 3. Blais, Deborah Tyler. I. Title.
BL628.5 B53 2001
291.4'32--dc21

                              00-068913

Printed in the United States of America on acid-free paper that meets the American National Standards Institute Z39-48 Standard.

First Edition

10 9 8 7 6 5 4 3 2 1

Contents

FIRST MONTH: IDENTIFYING THE PROBLEM

SECOND MONTH: MOVING INTO THE SOLUTION

THIRD MONTH: HEALING WITH GOD, SELF, AND OTHERS

FOURTH MONTH: DISCERNING YOUR DIVINE PURPOSE

FIFTH MONTH: EXPANDING LOVE

SIXTH MONTH: EMPOWERMENT

SEVENTH MONTH: TO THINE OWN SELF BE TRUE

EIGHTH MONTH: NURTURING YOUR SOUL

NINTH MONTH: BUILDING STRENGTH AND COURAGE

TENTH MONTH: DEEPENING YOUR VISION AND CONNECTION WITH SPIRIT

ELEVENTH MONTH: MANIFESTING YOUR DREAMS

Introduction

Dharma—My Little Angel

Nearing the lake on that warm September morning, I heard a tiny mewing sound. My first inclination was to ignore the cries. *I've been through enough lately,* I thought; *I can hardly take care of myself.*

Three months earlier, at age thirty-seven, I had been diagnosed with breast cancer. Because the cancer was in more than one place, the doctor had recommended a radical mastectomy. It was scheduled for later that same month. I still remember the shock and denial I felt when I overheard my husband, Gary, telling someone on the phone, "She's probably going to lose her breast." Those words seared through me like a knife. *No. No!* I cried silently to God, *I'm too young for that.*

A few weeks later, while I was recovering from the mastectomy, the surgeon called with more bad news; "The cancer has spread to your lymph nodes. Chemotherapy offers the best chance for survival." All I could do was sit there stunned, thinking, *Oh God, I'm going to die.*

I was terrified of dying. Many of my friends draw comfort from their beliefs about the afterlife or reincarnation. But I had trouble blindly believing in things I couldn't see or touch. I wanted proof. I prayed to God to show me the truth about death.

With the fear of dying in my heart, I decided to take part in an aggressive clinical trial that included a combination of high-dose chemotherapy and a five-year follow-up with a hormone blocker.

The chemotherapy wiped me out completely. Even with the antinausea drugs, I was sick every time. Two months into the treatment, it was all I could do to get dressed and keep a little food down every day. In addition to working, my husband was doing his best to care for the house and me. Wonderful as he was, it was hard on both of us. I was irritable and lonely most of the time. This short walk to the lake was my first time outdoors in a while.

Meow! Meow! The insistent pleas continued.

No, I really can't care for an animal right now, I thought as I passed by. Suddenly, ear-splitting shrieking and squawking filled the air. Four blue jays were dive-bombing the bush where the mewing sounds were coming from. Shooing the birds away, I ran and looked under the bush. Standing on wobbly legs was a tiny, three-week-old orange tabby, with bright blue eyes, mewing his little head off. Gathering him up into my arms, I headed to the lake in hopes of finding his owner or convincing someone else to take him home.

The wind whipped all around us as the shaking kitten cuddled close, still scared to death. We sat together by the lake trying to find him a home. After asking a number of people and finding no takers, I decided to take him home temporarily until I could find him a home of his own. Still feeling exhausted from the chemo, I spent most of the day on the couch with the little kitty curled up on my chest purring. Later that evening, as my husband was leaving to go to a meeting, I asked him to take the kitten with him. "Try and find him a good home," I said, placing the kitten in a box. Little did I know, my heart had already been stolen.

An hour later, I beeped my husband. "Have you found him a home yet?" I asked.

"I was just giving him to someone," Gary replied.

"Don't," I said without hesitation. "Bring him home. I need him."

When Gary and the kitten returned home, the little orange tabby curled right back up on my chest like he'd never left.

For the next week, while I was bedridden, Dharma and I were constant companions. He just loved snuggling, sometimes trying to get right up under my chin. He didn't even notice my lack of hair or uneven chest. It felt good to love and be loved so unconditionally.

I chose the name Dharma because in India it means, "fulfilling one's life purpose." Cancer research has shown that finding and following one's bliss or purpose supports the immune system and increases chances of survival. For me, I hoped this would include my two deep-seated desires: writing and being of service to others. Dharma's name reminded me of that intention and so much more.

As a result of chemotherapy and the hormone blockers I would soon be taking, childbearing was out of the question. My husband and I had been trying to have children for years, but now it was final: *we could not have children.* My heart was heavy, suffering so many losses at once. Dharma licked my tears and helped bring out the nurturing side of me.

Arriving home from my biweekly doctor visits, I immediately picked him up like a baby and carried him around the house with me. I even carried him to the garage while I did laundry. We were inseparable. With Dharma around, I wasn't so needy and grouchy with Gary. And boy, did Dharma purr loudly! It was so comforting hearing and feeling the love he expressed so freely.

As he grew fighting, biting, and clawing furniture became his favorite pastimes. We have a fenced-in back yard, so when he got too wild for me, I would let him play out back to play.

Dharma also loved chasing butterflies. Last spring, I planted purple Porter's Weed specifically to attract them. The whole backyard, with its multitude of colorful butterflies, was one big playpen for Dharma. I don't think he ever caught any, but I spent countless afternoons sitting on the back porch watching Dharma live his bliss. So free. No cares. My spirit soared as I watched him live his life so fully, and decided it was time that I do the same.

Late that December, I scheduled my final reconstructive surgery and let my office know I would be back to work in February.

Then, three days after my final surgery, the unthinkable happened. Escaping from the backyard, Dharma was hit by a car and killed instantly. My life, too, seemed to end at that moment. I was devastated, and no one, not even Gary, could console me. I sat there on that same couch where

Dharma and I had shared so much love and cried and cried for hours. "Why, God, why?" I asked in desperation. I wanted to turn back time and never let him outside. I couldn't accept that he was gone. It just wasn't so. With all my might, I willed it not to be so. And still it was so.

Finally, Gary asked, "Do you want to see him?" Although I had never wanted to see a dead animal in the past, I answered, "Yes." Gary then wrapped Dharma in a towel and placed him in my arms. I held him and wept. We decided to bury him in the backyard by the Porter's Weed.

While Gary dug the hole, I held Dharma one last time, telling him all he meant to me and how much I loved him. I thought back on all the gifts he brought me in the short time he was with me: unconditional love, laughter, a playful spirit, a reminder to live fully, and a sense of my life's purpose. My husband said, "You know, I believe Dharma was sent by God to help you through a very rough time. Now that you're through the worst of it, it's time for Dharma to move on and help someone else."

"Do you really think so?" I asked, wanting so badly to believe it was true.

"Look at the timing," Gary said, "You hadn't been to the lake in months and the one day you venture out, you find Dharma blocks from our house in dire need of help, and in rescuing him, you get rescued as well. He was your little buddy just when the chemo side effects were at their worst. When your immune system was so weakened that you couldn't be around people, Dharma was there. He stayed in bed with you all week that first week when you were so sick. Then, as you got better, he became more playful and brought you hours of smiles and joy. And now, literally days after your final surgery, when you are well on your road to recovery, he's gone. All of this can't be a coincidence. There's definitely a reason he was put in your life when he was and also taken out when he was. He was your little angel."

"Thanks," I said, letting my husband's healing words wash over me.

Watching Dharma lying so peacefully in my arms, I got the much-needed answer to my prayers about death. I realized that he would go on in me forever, the same as I would in the lives of everyone I touched. I believe Dharma gave his life so that I might know peace. When Dharma died, I was awakened spiritually. I am no longer afraid of dying. Through Dharma, God showed me there is nothing to fear. There is only peace. And love.

We buried him at the foot of his butterfly bush and on his headstone I wrote, "Dharma—My Little Angel." Now, whenever, I sit on the back steps, I see Dharma chasing butterflies for all eternity.

Dedication

Three years have passed since Dharma died. While I miss him terribly, this book is testimony that he lives on. As I live my bliss and encourage others to do the same, Dharma's life has a ripple effect, spreading outward into an ever-increasing circle of changed lives.

Although Dharma can never be replaced, God saw fit to place another little orange tabby into my life. Six months ago Karma adopted me, and we've been inseparable ever since. Karma, like Dharma, is not happy unless he is curled up on my chest, right up under my chin. Now I've had cats all my life, but never any like these two; their personalities are one and the same. And just like Harley-Davidsons have a distinct, patentable sound, so do Dharma and Karma.

My husband believes that when two souls, bound by an intense love, are separated, the connection is so strong that one soul finds its way back to the other. I still don't know "truth" in that area, but it feels like I have my little angel back.

As to my health, I am happy to report that I am one of the 2.6 million women recovering from breast cancer. My gratitude is tinged with sadness though, because so many have not survived. However, if Dharma taught me anything, it's that we do go on—forever—in the hearts of those we've touched.

So although this book is about *living* your bliss, it is dedicated to all of the women who lost their lives to breast cancer and to all of the lives touched by theirs.

May God's love shine through these pages, helping us all live the lives we are meant to live.

With special thanks to my earthly angels:

- My husband, Gary, for his love, admiration, and unwavering belief in me
- My mom for guiding me to the writing class where I met my mentor
- Tom Bird for his invaluable guidance and insightful tools
- Mary Ann Gibavitch and my agent, Robbie Anna Hare, for birthing *Heart* with me
- Noemi Taylor and Kathleen Hughes for allowing me to let my heart sing
- Alec Courtelis and Lawrence LeShan, Ph.D., for pointing the way
- Susan Fawcett, Helen Duncan, Erica Jordan, and Lorraine Varese for their valuable input
- All of my friends and family for their encouragement and support, especially the members of my Thursday night Bliss Group: your light is astounding

How To Use This Book

My own nature is, at times, thirsty and insatiable, devouring new information; wanting to reap benefits with lightning speed. Other times, I am content to take a long, leisurely stroll with a good friend, enjoying the beauty of the journey.

With your own nature in mind, you can use *Letting Your Heart Sing* in a variety of ways. You can use it as a daily companion guide and read a story a day over the course of the year, doing the suggested daily actions as you go along. You can read it straight through as though it were a novel, then go back and use it as a daily guide, doing the actions the second time around. Or somewhere in between—reading a few stories at a time, doing whichever actions you are drawn to. All methods work. Whatever the pace, keep to the road, for there is much richness along the way.

Because this journey of *bliss* is such a personal one, the choice of how to read and use this book is best left up to the individual. Let Higher Wisdom guide you toward what you need.

Experiential in nature, *Letting Your Heart Sing* is most beneficial when the readings are combined with the actions. Transformation takes place over time, and whether the effort is daily or occasional, rigorous (disciplined meditation or calling someone you haven't spoken to in years) or gentle (walking barefoot in the grass or listening to your favorite songs) is, again, up to the individual. The more adventurous bliss seeker might randomly select stories to read and actions to take.

Ideally, you will want to have a special journal (a *Bliss Journal*) on hand to record valuable insights and dreams, to brainstorm, or to assist you in moving through any blocks or resistance that crops up as you begin *letting your heart sing*.

As you embark on this intimate journey of the spirit, remember, there is a gift in every story and transformation in every action—take as much or as little as you like.

Follow your heart and enjoy the journey.

- For possible inclusion in a future *Letting Your Heart Sing* book, feel free to send stories to my e-mail address, **LetYourHeartSing@aol.com**. Let me know how this book is influencing your life and helping you *let your heart sing*.

First Month

Identifying The Problem

It's Now Or Never

*W*hat in the world would provoke someone to get up at 5:30 A.M. and write for two hours before going to a 9-to-5 rent-paying job, especially when they like the job and it provides a more than adequate living? What exactly!

Well, that is what my writing did to me. It provoked me into living large. It refused to let me off the hook. I had no choice but to open up to a bigger vision of what my life could be. When you find your heart's desire, it is like that. It just sort of takes over, and you have no say in your own life anymore. I am not a morning person; getting up at 5:30 A.M. was the last thing I wanted to do. I kicked and screamed for as long as I could. But the desire to write was so strong that ultimately I surrendered. Best decision I ever made.

Six years ago, when I was taking a drawing class at a local university, the teacher spoke of a book called *The Artist's Way*. I did not pay much attention because I was not an artist. I was only taking the course for fun. A year later, my creative writing teacher recommended the same book to help remove writer's block. I thought to myself, *I have tons of ideas. I am not blocked.*

My teacher spoke so highly of the book that he piqued my interest. Then he mentioned that one of the main exercises was to write every morning, free-associating on paper until you filled three pages. Well, that is all I needed to hear. *I already get up early to exercise and meditate before work. I will be damned if I am going to wake up even earlier for anything!*

A few years passed, and along came that wake-up call I did not put in for: breast cancer. Early on, I realized I was going to have to make radical changes in my life if I was to beat this disease. By a series of what I call "*Godincidences,*" I was led to a book called *Cancer as a Turning Point* by Lawrence LeShan, Ph.D. It spoke of building up your immune system through exciting your body, mind, and spirit about life.

Within weeks, I reawakened to my long-buried dream of writing a book (I had been writing for newsletters and magazines for some time, but fear and time constraints always kept me from *really* going for it). Now here it was, as clear as day, what I really wanted to do.

I began tentatively by keeping a journal of my spiritual and emotional experiences in dealing with cancer. Feelings, gripes, goals—everything—hit the paper. Then, an idea for a book about cancer emerged.

Within a few months I was struggling horribly with fears and doubts. *What do I have to say that has not already been said? Who am I to think I can do this?* And on and on. All it took was one person displaying a lukewarm reaction to my writing and I would close up. After about two months of torturous attempts, I stopped writing.

Then one day a friend mentioned *The Artist's Way*. This time I did not balk. Having just finished five grueling months of chemotherapy, I was now willing to get up at whatever hour and do whatever.

I picked up the book.

Ah, the desperate become sweetly willing.

And so I was. The still small voice inside of me that *knew* there was a deeper purpose for my life would not stay quiet a moment longer. Over the next few months, that voice became deafening.

So, now I write. I can't *not*.

When you find and follow your bliss, it will be like that for you, too. We are each born with our unique purpose imprinted on our very souls. When the time is right, it forms into an idea . . . then a yearning . . . then a burning desire. When that happens—get out of the way—because nothing can stop it. Just hang on for the ride of your life!

Today's Action | If you were told you had only one year to live, what would you want to do or accomplish to experience perfect peace when night falls for the final time? One way to find this out is to ask what regrets you would have if you learned your life would end today.

Write about the relationships that need mending, activities that you want to participate in, books that you want to read, classes you want to take, places you want to visit, dreams you want to live. Do not worry about time or money. Just write.

Dream A Little Dream

The many wounds and losses suffered during our lifetimes have caused many of us to close our hearts, not daring to risk anymore, reasoning *If you do not allow yourself to be vulnerable, you cannot experience loss or failure.*

Personally, I have spent most of my life playing it safe. With safety we may have security, but rarely do our hearts soar. My wake-up call came in the form of a lump in my left breast in the spring of 1995. Today, I thank God for it because it was what I needed to awaken fully from my slumber. Under the illusion that I had all the time in the world, I put off living many of my dreams. Lack of time, lack of money, lack of motivation, and lack of courage kept me from fulfilling my divine purpose.

I believe each of us was put on earth for a special purpose. We each have a unique purpose that no one else can fulfill. What a tragedy if I lived my entire life and was never fully awake to my true purpose.

Deep inside each of us is a song in our hearts waiting to be sung. Mine had been buried for so long that it took a serious illness to shake me up enough to be willing to admit it was there. By recounting my own journey, I hope to inspire others to find the courage to live their dreams without needing life-threatening wake-up calls to do so.

The first month of this journey is about awakening our spirits and revealing our true hearts' desires. As the year unfolds, we will develop the courage necessary to realize our dreams, one step at a time. This journey is not for the weak willed. It takes great courage to put ourselves first. It takes great courage to heal our wounds and forgive. And it takes great courage to honor our truth and to *live* our truth.

The path to authenticity and blissful living is *through*. We must move *through* our fears, *through* our doubts, and *through* our excuses to experience the freedom and joy that await us on the other side.

During the next year, allow me to guide you as I have been guided, for there is strength in numbers. Daily, there will be inspirational quotations, experiences to share, and actions to take.

Many times since beginning on this path, I have wanted to turn and run in the opposite direction—back to safety—back to the security of life before dreams. However, once your dreams are awakened *there is no turning back*. So be forewarned!

Having said that, let me also say that this is a very gentle and loving path. Each step forward brings bursts of self-esteem and enlightenment to carry you on to the next level of growth and awareness. If friends can embark on this journey with you, so much the better. Form a *Bliss Group* as a means of creative and emotional support while you move toward your dreams. This support can be in person, on the telephone, or via the Internet.

Or if you choose, venture out on your own, using this daily companion guide for encouragement, remembering that you are never really alone.

More and more, you will come to know just how true that is.

Today's Action | Make a list of some of your favorite "feel good" songs and begin listening to them. They can be songs from your childhood, your adolescence, or later in your life. Just any songs that make you smile when you think of them.

Torn . . . I'm All Out Of Faith

Remember when you were a child and saw your first butterfly up close? How about when you climbed a tree and could see really far—I mean blocks and blocks away? Remember the day they took the training wheels off, and you rode a two-wheeled bicycle alone for the very first time? How about the time your dad took you fishing, or your mother baked a cake and let you lick the bowl?

Do you remember your first real loss? Mine was a calico kitten named Amanda. She was a present for my eighth birthday. I was a big girl now and could finally be entrusted to take care of my very own pet. My family raised German shepherds and always had dogs, never cats. We had two shepherds at the time, Katherine and her son, Gerlich.

Because Amanda was so tiny, I always locked her up in my room whenever we left the house. One day, we were leaving for church and I could not find Amanda. My mother yelled from the car, "Come on, we're late." Desperately, I searched for Amanda, ignoring my mother's pleas.

Insistent, she finally came to the door and said, "Leave the cat. She'll be fine."

I don't remember a word they said in church. All I thought of was getting home to Amanda as soon as possible. I ran into the house and stopped short as I turned the corner of our living room. Amanda's lifeless body lay at the foot of the stairs. One of the German shepherds had killed her, probably by playing too rough.

My eight-year-old heart was crushed. I ran from my mother as she tried to comfort me. Neighbors came outside to see what all the commotion was as I wailed on the sidewalk for my kitten. I hated my mother for making me go to church. I hated Gerlich who I knew killed her. I hated God for not protecting her while I visited Him. In fact, it was on this day that I decided God didn't exist. Or if He did, I did not want anything to do with a God who could allow something like this to happen.

Most of all, I hated myself. I blamed myself for what happened: *If I had just found Amanda or if I had stood my ground and not gone to church until I found her.*

Amanda's death altered the course of my life. Any connection I might have had with a higher being was severed the moment I discovered that she'd died. In my mind, there was no point in being a good little girl if this was what happened when you were. This one incident changed all the beliefs I had held up until that moment. As my beliefs changed, so did my actions. This occurred over time, and I realized it only in hindsight. Some of our greatest wisdom and healing takes place in hindsight.

Daydream Believer

What did you want to be when you grew up? As a child, I wanted to be a ballerina, a teacher, a stewardess, or a rock star. At the age of fifteen, mesmerized by Ayn Rand, author of *Atlas Shrugged* and *The Fountainhead*, I wanted to be a writer. By the time I was seventeen, I wanted to counsel troubled teens, since I no longer felt I was one. (Little did I know things were not to be peaceful for quite some time.)

Early on, Gary wanted to be an astronaut, a baseball player, or a cowboy like John Wayne. Later, he looked up to the tough guys in his neighborhood. This admiration led him down a dark path that lasted more than twenty years. Neither of us regrets our poor choices, though. They led us to where we are today, and for that, we are grateful.

Think back. What were your dreams? Did you spend hours fantasizing about your future: who you were going to marry, how your names would sound together, how many children you would have, what your career would be?

I did. I remember lying at the beach, losing myself in romance novels for hours, dreaming—planning my escape. Unburdened by adult responsibilities, my time was my own. Sometimes I used it unwisely and shoplifted or skipped school, but mostly I floated about in my dream world. In this world, I was happy, adored, rich, and famous. *The Millionaire* knocked on *my* door and the story always ended with, "*. . . and they lived happily ever after.*"

Oh, to be young and carefree again. No worries, no bills to pay, no grown-up responsibilities. To be like little Dharma, frolicking in the backyard, chasing butterflies without a care in the world.

7

Open Your Eyes

Letting Your Heart Sing is an experiential way of life, not an intellectual one. Part of you knows that there is more to life than being a responsible, good person. These daily stories are meant to awaken your childlike spirit from its slumber.

Our souls long for less hectic days, yet we forget that life is more than gathering the latest modern conveniences, attending the right functions, or being on the right committees. Sometimes we are so busy that we scarcely notice how chaotic our lives are. Our children are so busy that even *they* need appointment books.

8

Letting Your Heart Sing inspires, engages, and disarms you, expanding your vision to a deeper possibility for your life. Allow *Letting Your Heart Sing* to be your cheerleader, encouraging and guiding—ever so gently. On good days, it will lift you up in celebration of your accomplishments. On discouraging days, it will be that soothing friend assuring you: *You can do it. Believe in yourself. Try one more day, one more way.*

Over the years, I have faltered many times. I have asked myself *Who do I think I am?* I have told myself *I can't do this. I'm not talented enough, educated enough, or disciplined enough.* I have even sneered to myself, *Who am I kidding?*—only to have someone read one of my stories and tell me how much it helped them. When I am at my lowest, just the right inspiration or motivation comes along. I always get exactly what I need, right when I need it.

I trust the divine plan, that wonderful purpose and plan for each of our lives.

At first, I could not imagine an interactive Universe or creative energy responding to my every need. However, my experience has shown me that when you stretch out of your comfort zone and reach for your dreams, the Universe responds—big time!

My concept of a God or Higher Power today is not just that of a loving, caring being, or a creator. For me to trust God, without reservation, God *must* be the kind of power that would not awaken a dream in my heart without giving me the means to carry it out. I need to know that I am supported every step of the way. And that is exactly what has been happening.

Every day, in every way, the Universe encourages my dreams in the form of positive feedback and open doors. I am constantly assured I am on the right path. There is no doubt anymore, only faith.

Time Has Come Today

Daily, thousands of commuters fill up every spare moment of their lives with their need to be productive. Juggling cell phones, beepers, laptops, and appointment books, we have no time for the truly important things. What are we all running from?

What would happen if all of us just stopped—if we turned off our computers, TVs, and beepers, unplugged our telephones, didn't charge our cell phone batteries, but sought instead to recharge our spiritual batteries? What would happen indeed.

Thank God for Cancer. The big "C" stops most people dead in their tracks. It certainly got my attention. At thirty-seven, I consider it a blessing to have gotten a wake-up call when I did. Cancer helped me re-evaluate my priorities by asking myself, "How do you want to spend the time you have left?"

It doesn't have to be that way. We don't have to wait for a life-threatening illness to wake us up. We can wake up right now. In this moment. Yes, this one.

In *this* moment, it is late in the day and all is quiet. No television. No mental chatter. No opiates of busyness or constant noise. Just the stillness of the moment.

In the still, quiet moments, life asks questions we dare not ask—*Why are we here? What is the meaning of life? Is there a God? What happens when you die?*

What if the answers scare me? Scarier still, what if I never ask the questions? What if I just go through the motions, numb to who I really am and to my greater purpose? Or what if I know my heart's desire, but remain too scared to follow it?

To truly listen to our hearts, we must first become quiet. It is impossible to hear our heart's song above the clamoring of today's fast-paced world. When our hearts stop, so does our time on earth. None of us knows when that last moment will be.

We need to ask, "If this were my last day on earth, is this how I would want to spend it?" Take time to think about that today.

In the silence of the late afternoon, the ticking of a distant clock reminds me . . . *Don't waste me.*

Reach Out In The Darkness

Although it is possible to find and follow your bliss alone, it is far easier if you seek guidance and accept help. The path can be rocky and treacherous, but a guide who has traveled the path before knows the terrain and can lead you through safely.

The first two years after finding my bliss, I traveled alone, not daring to speak my desire out loud. Occasionally, the small voice inside let my dream slip out to some unsuspecting stranger, but mostly my path was solitary. I used only books to guide me. That was fine in the beginning, but it is infinitely easier having a real person as a guide.

As a budding writer, I sought out a published author whose style I admired and asked him to tutor me. He agreed, and each week he shows me ways to open myself up and deepen my writing. I have grown tremendously under his tutelage.

All it took was that first step of asking.

Just as professional football players wouldn't dream of playing football without a coach, I too do much better with expert guidance. As my teacher helps me develop and hone my skill, I share my experience with others. My first coaching position was with a retired man named Joe.

For years, he wanted to write, but, like me, his fears and insecurities kept him from picking up the pen. Joe and I spent our first week together overcoming objections and circumventing excuses. He had an endless list of reasons for why he could not write, even for ten minutes. I told him to call me back in thirty minutes, *after* he wrote for ten minutes about anything at all.

Joe called me back with the excitement of a six-year-old riding his bike for the very first time. He told me he felt exhilarated and wondered if his breathing medication was working properly. I had to laugh out loud. The little boy in him was so excited, but the adult was still scared to death.

It helps me so much to help Joe, more than he'll ever know.

Today's Action | Who could help you on your path? Who has what you want or is ahead of you right now? Pick up the phone, yes, the phone, and call them. Ask them to be your *Bliss Mentor* or *Coach*.

Seek the guidance and support for which your heart longs, but is afraid to ask. If someone says "No," ask someone else. Many people would love to help themselves by helping you.

Dear Mr. Fantasy

Joe devours books, educational channels, news shows, and anything else he can get his hands on. Now there is nothing wrong with learning, but sometimes we will use absolutely anything to avoid our heart's calling.

Joe's busyness was definitely keeping him from his dream of writing a short story.

Because I would never ask anyone to do something I was unwilling to do myself, I suggested to Joe that we both abstain from television for a week. I did this via e-mail. It took four rounds of messaging, "I have to watch the Atlanta Braves. I never miss their televised games. And *Seinfeld*—there're only a few more shows left before it ends *forever*! I *always* go to sleep watching *Letterman* and I *always* have my morning coffee with *Regis and Kathie Lee*," before Joe conceded.

He was going through withdrawal before the set was even cold. To alleviate Joe's anxiety, I suggested he tape a few hours of the shows that meant the most to him and watch them the following week. I told him, "We could wean ourselves from the TV over a period of time, but sometimes to truly effect change, a radical approach is necessary."

Joe, a practicing alcoholic at one time, now sober for more than thirty years, knows the value of going cold turkey, so he agreed.

Addicted nonetheless, Joe knows the exact minute he can go back to television next week. Again, I have to chuckle because I know both of us will find the week very challenging.

Sometimes you have to go nuts before you get sane.

Today's Action | Is addiction keeping you from doing things you really want to do? What habit stops you in your tracks when you think of giving it up for one week—reading, exercising, watching TV, shopping, working overtime, working on the computer, or talking on the telephone? To what lengths will you go for your dreams?

Abstain for one week from anything you think you might have a problem with. This may kick up intense emotions, so have tools handy such as your *Bliss Journal* or your *Bliss Group* to help you.

Angel

Cheerleaders are as important as coaches are in the game of life. Fortunately, I have quite a few. They read my stories and give me encouragement and support or constructive criticism, depending on my need. And God always knows exactly what I need, right when I need it.

Last year, two women were instrumental in helping me get this book off the ground. Deborah, my spiritual cheerleader, assured me, "God is *so* excited about what you are writing. I just know he is working through you." Now how can someone not write when they have a cheerleader like that in their corner?

Susan, an accomplished writer and poet, is my sounding board. She shares her beginnings with me and holds my hand as I ride the emotional roller coaster of life as a writer.

This year, a new woman, Debbie, became my guiding light. And God definitely had a hand in our meeting.

It was 7 P.M. on Friday evening, and I had just gotten home from a horrible day at work. I was so overwhelmed that I had actually broken down in tears at a gas station on my way home. Moreover, I had not touched my manuscript in two months. It was during this low point that the stranger from Texas called.

Astonished by the similarities in our lives, we could not get off the phone. Our names were the same, we were about the same age (I was thirty-seven and she was thirty-eight), we both had stage II breast cancer, we both had had mastectomies and chemotherapy, and neither of us could have children. All of that, in and of itself, is a lot of coincidence, but what propelled her to call a stranger halfway across the country is what makes this truly a "*Godincidence,*" and that is *how* she found her breast cancer.

Debbie was lying on the floor playing with her new puppy when she felt a lump in her breast. She had had a mammogram ten months earlier with perfect results, but instinctively knew something was very wrong as she lay on the floor, feeling the hard lump in her breast. A biopsy later confirmed what she already knew: she had breast cancer.

If it were not for that little puppy, Debbie might not have found this fast-growing cancer for quite some time. Amazingly, her puppy's name is *Dharma*.

A few months later, a friend of Debbie's gave her the issue of *Angels on Earth* magazine, where a condensed version of "Dharma—My Little Angel" appeared, telling her, "You *have* to read this."

Afterward, Debbie debated all week whether to call information and get the number of the woman in Florida with whom she had so much in common. Finally, on that Friday when I was so stressed out from work, she made the call.

We talked for over an hour. I helped her feel less alone, and she helped me see how much my writing helped others (sometimes I cannot see it). Debbie now thinks of me as her "angel on earth." Trust me, it is mutual: within a week, I started writing again.

My little angel, Dharma, moved me so much that I shared his story with others. Through that sharing, I became someone's angel. That person unwittingly became mine. Here, Debbie, in the middle of her chemotherapy treatments, called me for hope and ended up giving me more hope than she will ever know.

Today's Action | Who are your earthly angels? Who has a calming effect on you? Who listens intently and really hears you when you express a concern? Who can be counted on in a pinch? Who wields their honesty with kindness? Who makes your heart smile?

Make a list of *Bliss Cheerleaders*—people who are unconditionally supportive of your endeavors.

13

That's What Friends Are For

I am so used to being in control that I find it hard to ask for help. And harder still to receive it. This stems from feeling unworthy of someone's time or love. I thought I had worked through this, but something happened recently that showed me otherwise.

Shortly after I asked Deborah to be my *Bliss Cheerleader*, she asked me to sponsor her. Initially, I wanted to say yes. However, because I tend to take on too much, I checked with my sponsor, Patricia, first.

Patricia looks like an angel with her porcelain skin, flowing hair, and angelic smile, and loves and guides me as only an angel could. Patricia said, "Isn't it interesting that as soon as you are in a position to receive, you feel compelled to give."

After this insight, I knew I needed to tell Deborah no, even though I was afraid we would lose touch if I didn't have a significant role in her life.

Although wonderfully supportive of my writing at first, Deborah moved shortly afterward, and we drifted apart. I was sad at first, but have since learned that people come into and leave our lives exactly when they are supposed to. Just like Dharma did.

Shortly after Deborah moved, Debbie called from Texas. With us, the miles didn't matter, and we became fast friends. I give her hope that she can beat cancer, and she, in turn, is one of my biggest cheerleaders, always encouraging me to keep writing.

14

Today's Action | Pick two people you can call on for support and encouragement as you reach for your dreams and ask them to be your "*Bliss Cheerleaders.*"
Identify exactly what you need from your *Bliss Cheerleaders*. Then ask for it. Do you want them to remind you of your dreams and encourage you to follow them, or will you feel guilty if you are off track? Do you want helpful feedback or a just good listener? Discern and ask.
Allow someone to give to you for a change.

We Are Family

My *Bliss Group* is a unique group of eight other women who support me most by allowing me to be who I am at any given moment. We bring our honesty, vulnerability, hopes, dreams, fears, and anger to the group, and are accepted exactly as we are.

Nine women, ranging from twenty to fifty years old, meet every other Thursday for purposes spiritual in nature, but far beyond our limited understanding. Each night we let each other in a little more, and in doing so, we heal.

Angel, with all her biker bravado, brings a vulnerability deeper than anyone can imagine. Twenty-year-old Gina's innocence brings us in touch with the beautiful child within each of us. Sari brings her pain, physical and emotional, leaving it at our doorstep as the healing balm of unconditional love washes over her. Hilda shares with us her deepest fears as she walks through each one, including her panic about learning to drive again at forty-three.

Our only grandmother, Terry, brings her warm heart and soothing nature. Lorraine's excitement about the group is as contagious as is her love of life. Life's questions loom large for Maggie as she tries to figure out whether to become a nun or quit smoking, helping us all to lighten up. And Patty, our newest addition, wants so much to fit in and for us to like her. Little does she know, she already does and we already do.

Me, well, I just open my heart and home and give us all a safe place to blossom.

Today's Action | Deep inside each of us is the desire to know and be known. A *Bliss Group* can be just what you need to nudge you along in the direction you long to go.

The group can help you reach a goal, battle procrastination or sloth, or address anything else that is preventing you from accomplishing your goals. Ask for what you need, then be prepared to give and receive freely.

The group can be all men, all women, or a mixture of both. The members can all be writers, people with similar creative goals, or a mixture.

My group is very diverse. Some members are in creative fields, others are in business, and some are students. The specifics do not matter: all that does is that they have dreams they want to live. Something mystical and magical happens when like-minded people join together for mutual aid.

Living In The Material World

Addictions such as vegging out in front of the TV, playing on the Internet, and reading are just a few of the ways I avoid living consciously. Housework and busyness are two other avoidance techniques I gravitate toward when I am avoiding my bliss. I don't want you to think I'm some kind of neatnik; I'm not—not by anyone's standards. But I have become adept at straightening, organizing, filing, boxing, and storing things. A book about simplifying your life finally got me to stop holding on to things. Now I do my best to deal with whatever mail or information comes my way immediately, throwing out or recycling the rest.

I clean out my garage and closets every January, giving things to charity or to people in need. Because I know I now have a certain time set aside for this specific purpose, I can let go of my internal urgings throughout the year to organize, sift through, or rearrange things.

I have also almost completely stopped using credit cards. I found myself making too many impulsive purchases that I later realized I didn't want or need. I realized that the fewer things there are in my life, the less there is to clean, repair, organize, or store.

Gary and I both enjoy our pared-down lifestyle. It frees up our time and resources for things we both love, such as traveling.

Hawaii, here we come!

Clearing debt and clutter makes room for more abundance and freedom in our lives.

In these quiet spaces—in between the gathering of possessions—we find our center: the center of our beings that knows there is more to life than the way we have been living. It is from *this* place that we find our bliss.

When we stop doing and learn how to just be—we find out who we really are. It was in the quiet, stillness of the morning that the writer within me emerged.

Today's Action | Shed the excess possessions in your life. Create more room for dreams. Start with one drawer, one closet, or one room. Begin giving away things you no longer use. Tackle one small area a week until done.

Next, curb impulse buying by leaving your credit cards at home or using a debit card instead. As your desire to gain material possessions lessens, your financial freedom increases. You'll find you are freer to live the life you really want, instead of trying to afford the life you have or gain the one you think you want.

With A Little Help From My Friends

One day, I found myself with a day off, a dream of writing in my heart, a belief that this was something I was destined to do, and a burning desire to do anything but.

I was flitting about the house doing my usual "busy" routine when I ran out of things to clean and organize. When I pulled out the ironing board and realized I would rather iron than write, I knew I was in trouble. I did two things right away.

First, with the money we were saving from purchasing less, I hired a housekeeper to clean the house every other week. Best fifty dollars I ever spent! I turn the house over to her care and do only the bare necessities myself. I also enlist Gary's help in everything I do, "Honey, can you help me cut vegetables? Would you mind unloading the dishwasher while I fix dinner?" Knowing his help affords me more time and energy for my writing, Gary is usually eager to lend a hand if I am specific in my request and open-minded about when things get done.

Next, I hired a professional writing coach to guide me in my writing endeavors. "My dreams deserve my financial backing" is no longer just an affirmation from *The Artist's Way*, it is a reality. I am accountable to someone whose sole purpose in my life is to assist me in achieving my goals. Transcending my fears, my laziness, my procrastination, and my excuses, I am now *doing* what I always wanted to. When the artist is ready, the helpers appear.

17

☀ Today's Action | Whether it's achieving goals, career or relationship changes, or making time for a hobby, enlist other people's support and expertise in all of your undertakings. Make time for living your dreams.

Somewhere Out There

Two weeks before my cancer was diagnosed, someone said, "The only thing constant is change." At the time, I thought: *My life is perfect right now. I want everything to stay exactly the way it is.*

Oh, what I would have missed if the Universe had listened. I had no idea what I would have to go through to get where I am, but if given the choice, I would not accept my breast back for anything in the world—not if it meant giving up my heart's desire.

At one time, my heart's desire was to have children. In fact, when I found out I couldn't have children, I pulled away from God and sunk into a deep depression. No one knew I was depressed, not even me. It wasn't the cover-your-head-stay-in-bed kind of depression, but the move-so-fast-you-don't-have-time-to-think-straight kind.

Life didn't make sense anymore, and there was no reason to go on living if I couldn't have children. It took years to come to terms with this, but by the time I was diagnosed with cancer, Gary and I were traveling a great deal and really quite happy. We had adjusted. And I kept busy—so very, very busy.

One of the ways I kept busy was through sponsoring women in my Twelve-Step program. Sponsorship is a lot like mothering. You guide and shape people's lives in meaningful ways. But it didn't fill the void. My heart ached every time I saw a baby or a pregnant woman. At thirty-seven, I still had a glimmer of hope that some day, some way, I would become a mother. Then came cancer.

When the recommended treatment took away the option of pregnancy permanently, I told Gary, "It feels as if the door is being slammed shut."

Very quietly, he said, "I think the door has been closed for a while now."

My heart stopped as the truth of his statement hit me. The dream of being a mother died a very quiet death.

However, what emerged was a whole new dream, one buried even longer than the dream of motherhood. My *true* heart's desire is to be part of the birthing process, to pass on some of me. Writing. Creating. Birthing.

I realize I can have many dreams; some will come true, and some won't. Others lie dormant . . . waiting. Divinely inspired circumstances brought me to my bliss. And I propose that this book did not land in your hands by mistake. There is a spark somewhere deep in your innermost recesses, waiting for the right moment to ignite. Possibilities abound. We need only awaken to the truth of who we really are, then find the courage to *be* who we really are.

Darn That Dream

In 1991, I saw *Defending Your Life*, with Meryl Streep and Albert Brooks. In the movie, everyone's life is reviewed on Judgment Day, and the criteria for going to heaven is, "Did you live courageously?" If fear motivated your life, you got a "do over" and went back to earth.

A chord was struck even then. *I knew I was not living authentically.* I skirted challenges that would have pushed me beyond my comfort zone.

On the surface, I was happily married, satisfied at work, and had many friends, but deep inside, I felt like a fraud. Never quite able to put my finger on what I was feeling, I just stayed busy. But something was very *dis*-satisfying.

Then, in the fall of 1995, after seeing the movie *Something To Talk About*, with Julia Roberts and Dennis Quaid, I figured out what was wrong: *my life's work.*

Julia Roberts's character trained horses at her father's stable. Her dream was to be a veterinarian, but she was too afraid to go for it. She took the easier, softer way. Not until she was losing her marriage did she begin living by her own lights.

When Julia's character admitted that she didn't want to get to the end of her life wishing she had done things differently, I realized that I, too, hid out—too afraid of failure and rejection to really go for it.

In the field of accounting for more than twenty years, with the same employer for ten, I had become very comfortable. Although I am good at what I do, it is unchallenging and certainly *not* my bliss. Why should that matter? Well, it matters because I felt I was living below my potential and not in accordance with the divine plan for my life.

Bottom line: I thought and lived small out of fear.

That is why Julia Roberts's character moved me so much. I was where she was, in the "in-between place"—after my wake-up call, but before I began living my truth. It is a very painful place, but sometimes a very necessary one to pass through.

It was a powerful moment when I realized I could move toward my dream—right now: I could write today.

Until then, I was always waiting—until I retired, won the lottery, or had enough courage to quit my job and live on peanuts until I made it—you know the starving artist bit. Instead, I found that if you put one foot in front of the other and don't give up, the Universe finds a way to make it happen.

It can't *not*, because the Universe *itself* planted the seed.

| Today's Action | List five things you secretly want to do, but something stops you. |

Lean On Me

Where are your energy sources? Mine is the ocean. Luckily, I live just a mile from Hollywood Beach. For years however, I took it for granted. When I got sick, I realized I took many things for granted: my health, time, nature, my husband, family, friends, and even my cats. I rarely found time or energy for the things I loved most.

Toward the end of my chemotherapy treatments, out of necessity, I had to find things that replenished my spirit instead of leaving me feeling drained. I had given to others for so long, I had forgotten how to receive. I had to retrain myself.

A week after my mastectomy, my friend Deborah drove me home from my mother's, while Gary followed in his car. The cats had thrown up on the bed and the sheets needed changing. I couldn't use my left arm, but that didn't stop me from trying to help Deborah make the bed. Finally, she said, "Sit down already. I know how to make a bed." Since there are no chairs in our bedroom, I sat on the floor, feeling helpless.

Learning how to receive took time, but my family and friends were wonderful. They sent cards, left jokes on the answering machine, brought me fresh fruit and vegetables, and drove me to my doctors' appointments. Everyone was so thoughtful, and I felt so unworthy.

Where does that unworthiness come from? Why does it take a serious illness for us to see how loved we are? Even then, I felt frustrated and guilty about having to rely on others. Yet I was told it was an honor to be able to return the love they had received from me over the years.

In my weakened state, the strength of my family and friends' love lifted me up and helped me heal.

One way to begin living the life you've always wanted is to allow others to love you. Allow them to help you. Don't wait for a life-threatening illness to receive the gift of love. Think how much you enjoy doing thoughtful things for others. Allow them the same pleasure. Put your needs out into the Universe and enjoy receiving for a change.

Giver and receiver alike are equally blessed. You are worthy of love. You are worthy of someone's time and attention. We all are. Open up and receive all of God's abundance.

Today's Action | Spend thirty minutes at your energy source. Then, once filled, ask for the encouragement, financial support, child care, or prayers you need. Whatever you need, ask for specific help or assistance. Ask God. Ask others. Ask and ye shall receive.

Nothing's Gonna Stop Us Now

When I started writing, it was only safe to do it in a journal, with no real purpose in mind. I broke myself in slowly to the greater possibilities. Now, I write with a specific goal in mind: publication and leaving my day job. I do the necessary footwork: get professional guidance, seek representation, and write daily.

Writing is my priority, and *nothing* comes before it. Well, that's not completely true, I do pray and feed my cats before my morning writing session, but that's it. The point is, I started. You must start, *where* doesn't matter, as long as you start. My vision grows in direct proportion to the actions I take.

Today, I go to any lengths to live as I believe God intends. God would not put this intense a desire in my heart if he did not mean for me to reach for it.

For years, I stayed so busy helping others that I couldn't dream. I was too exhausted. I believed I was doing God's will: serving others. I *was* doing the right thing, and I enjoyed much of it, but I overdid it—always helping others tend their gardens, while mine was overgrown with weeds.

Recently I learned that if I but *live* my own heart's desire, a desire placed there by God, I will help others simply by virtue of living authentically. I had no idea God's will for me could be so grand.

When I made the decision twelve years ago to turn my will and life over to God's care—a God I was just beginning to trust—I was afraid God would send me to the outer reaches of Mongolia. I just knew God's will would include *camping* and *bugs* in some remote part of the world. I assumed serving God meant sacrificing your life as Mother Teresa did.

It turns out that the God of my understanding wants for me what I want for myself. My highest vision for myself is God's will for me. God simply wants me to live my heart's desire.

My bliss is God's will for me. By living it, I am at peace. When I put pen to paper I connect with myself, God, and others in a way I never imagined possible. I completely lose track of time. In fact, when I write before going to work, I set an alarm clock, so that I'll stop in time for that rent-paying job of mine.

Peace of mind is the goal. Love is the answer. Writing fills my heart and brings me peace of mind. When I am honoring this truth, I am in a state of bliss.

22

Today's Action | Pull some weeds by listing activities you engage in where you totally lose track of time. Painting, writing, needlepoint, playing with children, dancing, or gardening—what do you lose yourself in so completely that hours can pass before you realize it?

Seize The Day

When *Dead Poet's Society,* starring Robin Williams, came to theaters, everyone loved it because it spoke to our hearts. It gave us permission to live the lives we envisioned, not ones filled with obligations or others' expectations. If you only had one day to live, how would you spend it?

Well, today is that day. Tomorrow is not for certain, so begin with this day.

Carpe diem!

Here's my ideal day:

At sunrise, I ride my bicycle to the beach, kick off my shoes, and dive into the ocean for a swim. Afterwards, I write for a while under my favorite palm tree. Mid-morning, I meditate to the sound of waves lapping against the shoreline. Then I top off the morning with a salad, followed by a Haagen Dazs® strawberry ice-cream cone—not the low-fat kind—*the real thing*.

After lunch, Gary joins me for walk on the beach. We end up at a secluded beach and make love in the surf just like the scene in *From Here to Eternity*. Then we head back to our house to spend some time with family and friends. By now I've built the small backyard waterfall that I had always dreamed of having, and we listen to the water cascade over the rocks as the sun sets in the late afternoon sky.

As evening falls, Gary and I take a nap and then enjoy a scrumptious dinner, topped off with crème brulee, sprinkled with fresh raspberries, done to perfection. Life is good.

Then, it's back to the beach for a romantic moonlight stroll before we return to our lovely little house, where my husband puts on the tape I made of all of "our songs," and we dance to "Have You Ever Really Loved A Woman?" "Unchained Melody," "Our House," and "I've Got You Babe."

We close the evening listening to "Amazing Grace" sung by Judy Collins, and our eyes well up with tears as we look into each other's eyes.

Thankful for this special day together, we fall asleep, with me lying in the crook of Gary's arm as he says, "Perfect fit."

Today's Action | Plan your perfect day. Then go live it. If you can't do the whole day, start by bringing aspects of your perfect day into your everyday life.

The Wall

"The path I have chosen now has led me to a wall . . . It rises now before me, a dark and silent barrier between all I am and all that I would ever hope to be."

Many times, in order to live our bliss, we need to remove the blocks standing in our way. These blocks can be past traumas, current wounds, toxic relationships, or our own fears and doubts. Whatever the block, it can be removed with a simple tool designed specifically for this purpose by my coach, Tom Bird. Tom uses this process of "tearing down the wall" with hundreds of writers to deepen their writing and flush out any unresolved issues. "The Cards" remove any blocks standing between writers and their writing.

Because I help people recovering from addiction, co-dependency, cancer, and other issues and illnesses, I have used the tool with a wide range of people and found it will work with anyone, regardless of their dream. The premise is the same: this simple tool will "trick" your left brain, your logical, critical side, into going to sleep so that you can access anything hidden in your subconscious that is blocking you.

With Tom's permission, I will explain the process. Start with a stack of three-by-five-inch index cards. Relax for a few minutes, create a space where you will not be disturbed, and stack the index cards in front of you, blank side up. Free associate by writing one word on each card, working up to one thought per card. Flip the cards over as quickly as possible. Whatever thoughts come up write them down—judgments of this exercise, grocery lists, memories, fresh ideas—whatever. Just write them down.

One woman wrote "blank" on her first card and "card" on her second one. My first day on the cards began like this: teaching . . . trusting . . . learning . . . oh . . . I . . . get . . . it . . . I . . . am . . . beginning . . . to . . . jump . . . into . . . the . . . fire . . . will . . . I . . . ever . . . stop . . . sorting . . . controlling . . . organizing?

Do not drive yourself nuts deciding when to flip to the next card, just do so as quickly as possible. When in doubt, flip. Better to flip too often than not often enough.

As the days go by, the speed of your thoughts flows faster and faster to the point where whole phrases and sentences are flying out of you on to the cards. More words end up on each card with each passing day. Keep flipping to the next card as soon as the next thought begins.

At times the cards became a conversation with an unknown source; other sessions not much happened. Writing for an hour each day, I found the last fifteen minutes of each session were usually the most powerful. The critical left side of my brain lost more control each day I spent working with the cards. More and more, my subconscious was allowed to emerge. By the end of the first week I knew without a doubt I was meant to be working with the cards.

By then, the pace increased tenfold, and everything rushed to the surface. On my sixth day, whole phrases poured out of me. I wrote: *the lessons that came with my losses were well worth the price* . . . your hands already look different—don't they? . . . yes . . . *I knew something was up—but did not realize exactly what . . . or that it was all connected . . . so if the rain represents all of this for me does it represent the same for others?* . . . for some yes—most no . . . I mean different things for different people . . . for the harried workaholic—whose eyes are not yet open—it is just another obstacle to surmount (at this point I tried to cross out surmount and write overcome) . . . I said surmount . . . *yes you did* . . . I meant surmount . . . you do not know what it means . . . so you put in another word . . . you will do that from time to time . . . but in time you will learn and become more comfortable with the process . . . trust Tom . . . he has been there and he knows what he is talking about . . . see you stuck with it and now you are beginning to see how the cards truly work . . . your left brain is supposed to be in the background . . . but you have let it take over . . . it is time for you to tap into your own wellspring of power—where "I" reside.

Deep right-brain work such as this is best done first thing in the morning, and setting aside an hour is ideal. However, any time of day will work, and as little as thirty minutes is effective. Depending on how much has been suppressed and for how long, this process may last a few weeks. Buy more cards as needed.

Anywhere from three to seven weeks should do it. The beauty of this process is that once you have dealt with something on the cards, while in a right-brain state, you are done with it. This tool is so powerful that it can accomplish in weeks what normally might take years to move through. I know of at least three women who have dealt successfully with memories of childhood sexual abuse, freeing them to move on with their lives.

One woman, after years of seeing only the negative in her life, now has a balanced picture of her childhood, which continues to reframe her present.

Do not worry about knowing when you are finished with the cards. As Tom says, "Once you are done, you are done—and you will know it."

| Purchase 1,500 index cards and start working with them tomorrow, writing one word/thought per card as fast as you can, free associating without editing. Do not obsess on whether a card contains more than one thought or that a thought you took three cards to write could have been written on one card. Just turn to the next card as quickly as you realize you are on to the next thought. The point is to lose control—to enter into a right-brain creative state.

Continue daily for at least three weeks, longer if necessary. Remember, any resistance you feel is coming from your left brain, which is determined not to lose control. Just say, "Thanks for sharing," and continue working with the cards. Trust the process. You will not regret it.

Don't Fight It

A ton of resistance kicks up when you stand on the brink of your dreams. Mine was: *I don't need to do the cards. I've already done the "Morning Pages" as laid out in* The Artist's Way. *I've been through the Twelve Steps and done my inventory many times. I've been in therapy and already processed everything I need to.* Chances are that you, too, have been on a path of personal growth for some time now. The index cards are not a repetition of, nor do they negate, the work you've already done. They are an enhancement to and deepening of that work. Again, trust and surrender.

My resistance continued:

Environmentally aware, I avoid waste and recycle as much as possible. Writing only one word per card offended my sense of duty to the trees, *Why waste all that paper?* I wrote anyway. I trusted that by removing my blocks, I would be much more useful to the entire planet.

I'm cheap. Call it frugal, call it sensible, call it whatever you like, but spending an hour on the cards the first day, I went through hundreds of cards. I added up what it would cost me if I continued at that pace and thought, "I can't afford this." Money flew out of my pockets faster than my thoughts flew onto the cards!

My practical side said: *Cut up blank paper and use that—it won't cost as much.* I reminded myself that this was my critical, left-brain side talking and that I was worth real index cards. I affirmed, "My dreams deserve my financial backing," and wrote anyway.

During the four weeks I spent on the cards, my beliefs about money, my self-worth, and my dreams changed dramatically. Each week I used the cards, it became more evident I was willing to do whatever it took to live authentically and pursue my bliss, no holds barred!

I realized it's up to me to create whatever I need to facilitate my growth. It's up to me to *make it up*. The Universe will work with me, but I have to believe in myself enough to manifest what I need. Whether that means working more, borrowing, selling something, bartering my time or talent—I must be willing to do what it takes to go where I want to go.

The cost of cards wasn't the problem, but rather my *belief* about my worth and my dream's value. The cards fleshed out these issues and more. Everything that surfaced healed.

In just a few short weeks, I realized that this was one of the most effective tools I had ever used.

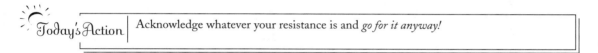

Today's Action | Acknowledge whatever your resistance is and *go for it anyway!*

Broken Wings

The cards fleshed out many painful childhood memories.

My father teased me mercilessly as a small child. His singsong chant, "Borax, Borax," short for Deborah, rings in my ears to this day. From taunting me to put my finger in his fish tank of piranhas, to dangling me over the alligator pit at the Serpentarium, my father could always be counted on for a tear or two. He didn't mean to be cruel, but the big macho hunter and fisherman in him didn't know how to be gentle and caring with a little girl. From as far back as I can remember, we were at odds with each other.

My parents divorced when I was a baby, and I saw my father a total of a few weeks every year—on holidays and an occasional odd weekend. I always tried to win his love and never felt as if I got it.

My deepest wounds roared to the surface of the index cards. I was seventeen and very excited about going to college. Then my mother told me that she could not afford to send me and that I needed to ask my father for financial support if I wanted to go. My father was a huge bear of a man and the very thought of asking him scared me half to death. However, I wanted to go to school so badly that I went to see him.

Sitting in his living room, I stammered out the words, "Dad, I . . . I want to go to college, I think I want to be a psychologist." He looked at me as if I was crazy, and asked, "What in the world for?" "I . . . I think I can help troubled teens." Without skipping a beat he replied, "I'll be damned if you think I'm going to spend a fortune on college, while you take a bunch of meaningless courses trying to figure out what you want to do with your life."

"It is just junior college . . . I don't think it will cost too much," I responded, eyeing the thick pile carpet.

"Why should I send you to college when you are just going to end up like her," motioning to the kitchen where my stepmother was, "barefoot, pregnant, and in the kitchen!"

Feeling hurt and rejected, I left and never brought up the subject again. The message I internalized was, "Don't reach so high. You're not worth my time or money. You'll never amount to anything." My self-esteem was crushed, and it took a long time to bounce back from that one.

For a few semesters, I tried to manage on my own, but it wasn't long before the easy money I made selling health club memberships persuaded me to drop out of college. My lack of direction and lack of belief in myself eventually led me down the self-destructive path of drug and alcohol abuse. It was ten years before I turned my life around and developed faith in my own abilities.

The other crushing event of my young adulthood was when it was time for me to marry. My father had sold his business and gone through all of the proceeds. When I asked if he could help with the wedding, he said he couldn't. So my mom bought my wedding dress and my fiancée and I charged everything else.

Later, I asked my father to give me away, and he said he wasn't sure he could come. When it was obvious he wasn't, I asked my two brothers to walk me down the aisle. They did, and it was wonderful, but it always hurt that my father wouldn't at least attend my wedding.

It was especially hard to accept after having watched him throw my stepsister a huge wedding and walk her down the aisle. I had always clung to my childhood dreams that one day that would happen for me, too. But it was not to be.

| Thinking back on your early years, is there someone who teased you or let you down— someone who did not have faith in you, or caused you to lose faith in yourself? On the cards, flush out any old wounds that still smart when you touch them.

My Father's Eyes

For many years I carried the pain of my father's words and his lack of belief in me. I'm sure he just passed down the messages he got from his father. However, as a young, impressionable woman, I believed what I thought he believed about me. It wasn't until I sought help for my addiction and co-dependency that I healed from these old wounds.

After I'd been in recovery about a year, my father's sister, Bobbie, sat me down and without being too hard on my grandfather, told me what it was like to grow up with a father who didn't know how to show love except by providing for his family. I was able to step into my father's shoes and feel what it must have been like for him as a little boy, never getting the love he needed, never measuring up to his father's expectations. My aunt's bird's-eye view into their childhood helped me in opening my heart to his wounds.

Now, I understand those macho walls he put up, why he felt he had to tear other people down, even his own children. I understand why he was threatened by my dreams, having compromised his own a long time ago. Today, I know my father loved me. He just didn't know how to show it.

Although we were never close, by the time my father died, we had made our peace. In fact, as he hung up the phone in what turned out be our last conversation a few weeks before his death, he said, "I love you." It's a memory I will always treasure.

Two years later, I went back to college. It took three-and-a-half years to earn a two-year degree, but graduating with highest honors was one of the high points of my life. It may have taken a while, but I *earned* that degree. I think my father would have been very proud of me. I know I was.

How I feel about me is so much more important than how others think or feel about me. As Erica Jong once said, "I no longer personalize rejection. I realize the way people treat me is much more of a reflection on them than it is of me."

It has taken time, but I now have the strength and courage to live by my own lights. Today, *no* dream is out of reach.

29

Break On Through . . . To The Other Side

Forgiveness heals both the person being forgiven and the one forgiving. My anger tied me to my father and to my stepfather in negative ways for years and blocked me from having healthy relationships with other men.

While my father used words and animals to tease and terrorize me, my stepfather preyed on the budding young woman I was becoming. From the time I was around ten, my stepfather was sexually inappropriate with me. By the time I was thirteen he was turning me on to marijuana and trying to get me to have sex with him. It got so bad that by the time I was fifteen, I stopped coming home from school because my stepfather worked nights at his auction gallery and was home alone in the daytime.

30

A school counselor became concerned when my grades plummeted, and my absenteeism skyrocketed. The counselor stepped in, and everything that was going on in our house came to light. My mother confronted my stepfather and kicked him out when he didn't deny it.

A year later we all moved into a new house together for a fresh start. Within months, my stepfather was doing even more drugs and brought his girlfriends right into our home. I resented him and I resented my mother for putting up with his behavior.

Finally, my mother took on three jobs so she could leave my stepfather. And leave him we did. However, the scars of living with someone addicted to drugs took their toll, and eventually I became addicted to cocaine and alcohol myself.

My own recovery process started when I got off the party circuit, put down the chemicals, and began living a life based on practicing spiritual principles, including forgiveness of others. For a long time I felt the things my stepfather did were unforgivable and was too confused to even understand my mixed emotions toward my mother. It took time to work through these feelings.

Today, I know what happened wasn't right. And although I do not condone the things the adults in my life did, in my heart of hearts, I do forgive them. Forgiveness is a process, not an event. But learning to forgive the seemingly unforgivable brings peace.

My father and stepfather were not well men, and my mother lived in a constant state of denial. The two most important men in my life died at early ages due, in part, to their addictions. My mother, however, is alive and well today, having found a spiritual path of her own. She was even gracious enough to go into therapy with me a few years ago to help bring closure to some of these old wounds and memories.

Occasionally I still wonder, "What *was* she thinking?" But for the most part, I know she did the best she could with the tools she had at the time. Her father was an alcoholic, and her own mother traveled a great deal. We are all products of our environment, but I believe the cycle can stop with us. Just as addiction affects the whole family, so does recovery. Today, nearly everyone in my family is in recovery or on a spiritual path of some kind. It is wonderful to be part of a life-affirming cycle, instead of a life-destroying one.

Today's Action | Tell the truth about your family today, either on the cards or to a trusted friend. Whether it's someone who has been through something similar, an older relative who has a broader perspective, or therapy, seek out whatever you need to help heal the past.

Open your heart and allow forgiveness to melt any long-held resentment, first by acknowledging the pain, anger, or sadness. Then ask yourself if possibly the person who hurt you was harmed by another at some point. With compassion in your heart, see into the other person's heart and know they must have been doing the best they could with the tools they had at the time.

The Storm Is Over

The road forward is also the road back. I wish it weren't so, but it is. I can't move forward into living fully unless I am willing to embrace the past.

When I started writing this book, I worked with the index cards, accessing my right brain, my creative side, allowing me to speak the truth without the internal critic's input. I knew what I wanted to write. However, once I started writing on the cards, only the past came up.

At first I thought I was ridding myself of blocks and didn't pay much attention. Two, three, four, and more days passed, and all I wrote about were memories from my childhood—painful memories, things I had not thought of in years and didn't want to. It took four days of writing all around my stepfather's sexual advances toward me before I faced what happened.

The memories came flooding back: the terror I felt leaving my bedroom when *he* was home, the awkwardness of running into *him* in the hallway, the shame of admitting how absent my mother was. I hate remembering my past and the things it led to. Often, I wish I had had a perfect childhood. But the truth is, I didn't. And I can't live authentically today unless I am honest about yesterday and its effects on me.

It wasn't until I removed these roadblocks that I was able to truly live my bliss of writing. My father's judgments got in the way. My mother's unavailability left me with major self-worth issues: *Wasn't I worthy of her time? Am I worthy of my dream?* And my stepfather's addiction to pills and his sexual advances greatly altered my path in life.

With the cards, I learned I am a road that leads both ways: to the past and to the future. But the only way to travel this road is to feel the gravel beneath my feet each day. Acknowledging the past frees me of it, releasing its effects on me. No longer controlled by people, circumstances, or substances, today I am free to be whomever I choose. I stand tall, knowing everything happened for a reason. By facing the past, I am free to embrace the future.

Today, I am whole, complete, and perfect. There is no shame or judgment in me. I have faced and released my demons.

32

Today's Action | Take time today to look at any area of your past that needs a voice. Allow the younger versions of you to tell the truth about anything they need to. Be courageous and face any remaining demons. The truth will set you free.

Walking On Broken Glass

I found I couldn't love deeply until I had hated deeply. I had to get really mad at my father, my stepfather, and my mother before I could be free of my anger. I also found it was okay to be angry with God. God can handle my anger. And God can help me to the other side where freedom lies.

The healing didn't happen overnight, but I kept at it until I moved through my anger. Eventually, I was freed from the bondage of my resentments and all they held me back from being. I don't know if the fact that my fathers aren't alive made the process easier or harder, but I discovered that any healing or act of courage I have with another man helps me to heal with my fathers, and vice versa.

Every time I see a father holding his daughter on his lap or walking his daughter down the aisle at her wedding, my father and I heal. What any one man does for his daughter today heals fathers and daughters everywhere.

Today, Gary and I have a very loving, healthy marriage. Considering where we came from, that is amazing.

My mother and I are very close. We both accept the past and live fully in the present. Because of all the emotional work we have done over the years, she is no longer the absentee mother, and I'm not longer the bad little girl acting out her pain.

In fact, my mother's house is near my office, so I spend a few nights there each month, visiting with her. Today, my mother takes great pleasure in making me a nourishing breakfast of oatmeal, fresh fruit, and tea, mothering me in ways she never could when I was a child.

Spiritually, I have healed as well. I no longer blame God for all the horrible things that happened to me. When I shed my victim cloak, a beautiful, empowered woman emerges. And oh, how I love her.

This is the woman I've always wanted to be—free-spirited, vibrant, funny, glowing, joyful, and at peace.

The journey to bliss can be very rocky at times, especially when you're barefoot and walking on broken glass.

Miraculously, feet heal, and the journey continues. Sometimes it's all an uphill climb, other times you're flying downhill at the speed of light, and still other times it's a quiet stroll.

Whatever the pace the scenery is always fantastic.

Today's Action | Figure out who in your family of origin you need to heal with. One way to tell is to look at your current relationships with men and women. Generally, there is a correlation between your issues with your father and your present relationships with men. The same holds true with any unresolved issues with your mother. If you have difficulties with one sex or the other, look back to the original mother or father figure in your life and flesh things out on the cards.

33

We're Not Gonna Take It!

Our biggest enemies are fear and doubt. These blurts, or critical inner voices, tell us to give up before we start. If we find the courage to reach for the stars, they quickly remind us: *It is too far. You'll never reach that goal. You might as well quit now. Who do you think you are, anyway?* Our internal critic, the saboteur, our negative side, hates the unknown and wants to be in control—always.

Its motto is safety at all costs—even if it kills me. The fearful one says: *Stay at the unfulfilling job. Stay in the dull marriage. Don't expect too much. Don't dare to dream. Don't get too excited, you'll only be let down.* The doubter says: *I don't know . . . we might get hurt. We might make a mistake. We might get laughed at. We might not measure up. We might fail.* So I stay. I stay in my secure little life, afraid to change.

For years I listened to those voices and, without realizing it, I stopped trying. I stopped risking. I settled. On the surface things seemed fine, but inside I felt like a fraud. I felt like more of a failure than if I had actually tried something and failed. I felt inauthentic—that is what I felt!

Somewhere deep inside, I knew the truth. I knew I could do more, be more, give more, and I was worthy of receiving more.

There are no limits except the ones I place on myself.

Rising up above my wounds, I see the stars are not as far away as I thought. They *are* within my grasp.

Hope is on the horizon and that still small voice says: *Maybe . . . just maybe, I can.*

Today's Action | Flesh out on cards all the negative things you say to yourself or have heard from others. Become aware of the internal critic's messages. This is the year we slay the dragon!

Shattered Dreams

One of the things that came up on the cards was my inability to have children.

I thought I went through that dark night of the soul five years ago when Gary and I quit seeing infertility experts. I shut down, pulled away from God, from people, and from life in general. I didn't grieve the loss; I just closed my heart. Then when the cancer came and chemotherapy and tamoxifen closed the door for good, I cried a lot—but was too focused on saving my life to really sit with the feelings.

Along came Dharma, who, by allowing me to mother him, opened my heart. When he died, the floodgates opened. But it wasn't until I wrote on the cards, from the deepest recesses of my soul, that the anguish of not having children surfaced. Up until then, it was more of an intellectual acceptance. Writing on index cards shuts off your analytical mind so completely that what comes up is as raw as it gets. My heart ached with desire and sadness over what would never be.

The cards allowed the pain of my shattered dreams to surface and heal. I have come to accept the fact that I am not meant to be a mother in the traditional sense. I have also learned there are many ways to give birth and to be a mother. And so I write and I sponsor and I hug my kitties. In my heart I know everything is turning out exactly as it is supposed to.

With this knowledge comes deep peace.

Today's Action | Write about any regrets, losses, shattered dreams, or unresolved issues on the cards today. Get into a relaxed state and ask, "Help me see what needs to be healed." Then let the pen take over.

35

Why

Another painful loss I didn't fully grieve until it came up on the cards was the loss of my breast. Again, when deciding on a course of treatment, it was a matter of—*just do whatever you have to—I want to live.* Two years after my mastectomy, while working with the cards, a memory surfaced from a very long time ago.

As a child, I lived in Miami Shores, a small suburb of Miami. It was a nice, quiet neighborhood with a five-and-ten-cent store, a bakery, and a movie theater all within walking distance of my house. The drugstore had an old-fashioned soda fountain that served root beer floats, banana splits, and milkshakes. A few times week, I walked along NE Second Avenue to the center of town, to get a milkshake or go to the movies, sometimes with friends, sometimes alone.

One day, as I was walking along NE Second Avenue, a man drove by and shot me in the chest. The bullet went right through my breasts, killing me.

Obviously, this never happened, but I had the thought and fear of it happening many times, as a young girl. The fear plagued me so much that I stopped taking the direct route to town. I was afraid it was a premonition and imagined every man that drove down Second Avenue had a gun, ready to pull on me. These were not nightmares, but my waking thoughts. Thoughts and fears I didn't remember having until they showed up on the cards.

In an instant the connection was made—here, nearly twenty-five years later, a *man* cut off my breast, and I almost *died*! All of sudden I wanted my breast back. I wanted more time to decide. I wanted to undo the surgery. I hated men! There, I said it. Oh, my God—no, I don't. I have a wonderful surgeon. He hugs me hello every time he sees me and lets me call him at home when I need to.

But the thoughts and feelings flew unedited onto the cards: *I want my breast back!!!* After writing that, I just laid my head down next to the cards and cried.

This time I got it. I really got it.

After this gut-wrenching writing session, I was miraculously more at peace than at any other time in my life. I don't know if I had a premonition, or if I was just self-conscious about my budding breasts. But no matter—yes, they took my breast—*but I didn't die*! I'm here. I'm alive.

And I've befriended men. Even though I was hurt and abused by men when I was a child, that is not the case now. Today, the men in my life are loving and supportive. They are here to help, not hurt me. So much healed with that connection and release.

Today's Action | Write about childhood pain, fears, memories, and nightmares. Use the cards to process anything that stands out for you as a child. Keep writing until it's all out. Remember, when you deal with your memories in this deep, right-brain state—you are released from the prison that they held you in, *forever*. You are free. *Free!* Free at last. Free at last.

I Got The Power

As I step out on that ledge, ready to take that first leap toward my dreams, a barrage of feelings kick up.

Some days I feel confident. *I know* I can do this. I believe it's my destiny and God's will for me. I know my deepest heart's desire is to write. To write in a way that is helpful to others—honestly and from my heart. I believe God's will or the greater plan for my life includes my deepest desires. I trust this—now—in this moment.

Other days I feel small, incapable of taking even the tiniest step toward my dream. Fear paralyzes me—I dare not dream. Doubts undermine my confidence. Sloth keeps me in bed watching TV all day. My people-pleasing side takes care of everyone else first, and if by chance there is any time leftover, *maybe* I'll do something for me.

Today, I acknowledge and embrace my negative, fearful side. It's okay. It's normal. Many successful writers say the majority of writers are just like me—at times confident—at times filled with doubt.

Susan, a successful writer of English textbooks and poetry, has been earning a wonderful living writing for more than twenty years. At times, even she thinks she won't ever write anything good again—that her previous success was a fluke, even though all evidence proves the opposite.

Another writer, my writing coach, has published a dozen books and still occasionally suffers from doubts and negative self-talk. The point is, they both keep writing.

I speak with Tom and Susan frequently because both are farther down the road that I wish to travel, and it is comforting to know I am not alone with my doubts. This knowledge gives me the courage I need to move forward.

It's a wonder any of us ever achieves any measure of success with all that goes on between our ears. But we do. And each time one of us embraces our fears, we pave the way for the next person to do the same.

Today, it's my turn—*I've got the power* to write *through* my fears and doubts.

Today's Action | Speak to someone today, a mentor, a peer, or a friend—anyone who can help dispel some of your doubts and fears. Let them in. You'll find you are not as different as you thought. You are not alone. Use that energy to propel you forward. *You've got the power.*

Suspicious Minds

At times, I envy other people's success, especially those who write books similar to mine. I judge them mercilessly: *There is a mistake. He's not speaking from his heart. He's too detached. He hasn't even experienced a life-threatening illness; how can he possibly write about dying? She's not clear enough. She's too wordy, too highbrow; too fancy for my taste. This one doesn't go deep enough, that one doesn't do it the way I would.* And so on, ad nauseam.

Bottom line: anyone with a book in print is farther down the road than I am and must be doing something right. And the real bottom line is that they are putting themselves out there, risking, following their dreams. It takes courage to intimately share yourself through the written word. Once you're published—it's out there for all to see.

I once heard it said, "No work of art is ever really finished, but at some point, you must find a stopping point."

Later, if you change your position, your earlier, unenlightened views are still there for all to see. This applies to anything: photography, music, painting, sewing, or a business idea. Additionally, you run the risk of someone not agreeing, not appreciating, or just plain not liking your labor of love.

38

My fears *could* hold me back from following my dream, but they don't. I've learned that if I don't put myself out there, I miss my own opportunity to live authentically, and I miss the possibility of touching another soul. If the words stayed in my head, and the notebooks remained in the closet, you would not be reading this. My words would be like the tree falling in the forest where no one is: sound not heard in a void.

To move forward, I must trust.

Someone is waiting for my gift, just as someone is waiting for yours. I move beyond my fears and doubts and use my blocks to build steps, steps I can climb up and out on. I write honestly, from my heart, trusting God will speak through me. I share my fears, comforting others with the knowledge that they are not alone. As one of us gets stronger, we all do.

Today's Action | Risk. Risk feeling jealous, envious, or afraid. Risk imperfection. Risk and do it anyway. Do the one thing you are scared of doing. You know what it is. Ask God, the Universe, your Higher Self, whomever, for the courage to *do* that which you must do.

Puff, The Magic Dragon

Today I draw my trusty sword . . . er . . . pen and slay the evil dragon lurking in my mind. Illusory or real, it doesn't matter. Today I explode the drawbridge, severing my connection with my negative, fearful, doubting side—empowering my creative, trusting, believing side. Today, words turn the evil dragon into *Puff, the Magic Dragon!*

I write, as fast as I can, all the affirmations I have needed to hear my whole life. Starting with what I wanted to hear from my parents, God . . . and from myself today:

You are beautiful. You are the child we always wanted. We will treasure and protect you. You are safe. We love you. I love you. You can come to me. I will always be here for you. Here, let me do that for you. You are so smart. You are so creative. You are so brave. We are so proud of you.

You are My precious child and I will never forsake you. I created you in My image and you are perfect exactly as you are. You do not need to earn My love—it is unconditional. When I watch you live your life—I am smiling inside. I see your heart and it is beautiful. I have a wondrous plan for you. All you need do is look into your heart. What makes your heart sing? What would you truly love to do? Where does time cease to exist for you? That is your bliss. That is My plan for your life. Your own heart's desire *is* My will for you. Together we will find a way for you to live it. *Never* give up hope.

I am enough. I have everything I need within me. It is okay to be where I am. My feelings are valid. It is safe to dream again. I am here for myself. I have friends and family that love and support me. I know there is a higher source of energy and love that created me and is with me on this journey. I am okay. I can do this. I *am* doing this. I can be all I ever wanted to be and more. The possibilities are endless. Everything is fine. I can do anything I set my sights on. Trust. With God all things are possible.

Open your heart. It is safe to love again and to dream again. Relax in My arms and know that all is well.

Today's Action | Write everything you need to hear from your parents, God, and yourself. Do not think— just write, fast and furiously. Allow the healing words to wash over you. Puff! Like magic, the dragon is gone!

Second Month

Moving Into The Solution

Tomorrow . . . Tomorrow Is Only A Day Away

The irreducible minimum.

*S*ometimes we get stuck. We don't want to begin or think we can't. We may need a little jump-start. *The irreducible minimum.*

A little old man from Ireland spoke of being immobilized by fear. He said, "What is the very least you could do and still be moving forward? That's *the irreducible minimum.* Do it."

Break down whatever you are afraid of into baby steps. Maybe the whole ball of wax is too much. What *are* you willing to do? Break it down until you find an action you are willing to take. Then do it.

Let's say you want to be a writer, but it is still a dream held in the confines of your mind. Pick up the pen and write today. If you are not willing or ready to do that—buy a notebook and pen today and write tomorrow. If, when tomorrow comes, the fear is still there, just put the notebook and pen out on a desk you've cleared and say, "I am prepared to start tomorrow."

By now, you've had a few days where the fear was in charge, but you took action anyway. That's the key: take some action, any action that continues to move you in the direction you want to go.

Continue doing *the irreducible minimum.* Open the notebook and write one sentence. It doesn't have to be profound or on any specific topic. It can simply be, "I am not ready yet," or "I am scared." Just write one simple sentence. Don't write more unless you want to.

You'll find you can feel the fear and do it anyway.

This principle works in any situation where fear, sloth, or procrastination threatens to do you in. I have used it in recovery with people who are afraid to take the dreaded Fourth Step inventory. I've used it with people who are afraid of driving a car, calling someone they're afraid to call, straightening out their finances, making restitution, changing jobs, or ending an unhealthy relationship. Whatever the circumstance, those three words—*the irreducible minimum*—are incredibly powerful.

41

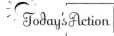 Today's Action | Today, do *the irreducible minimum* on whatever you know your next step is to be, but where fear has kept you from it.

Let's Get Physical

Ten years ago, when I began my spiritual journey, I dove into my new way of life headfirst, and that was all I focused on. Twelve months later, I realized I had not exercised all year. I felt fat and flabby and promised myself I would exercise—tomorrow. For months I procrastinated. Then, finally, I remembered *the irreducible minimum*.

The best thing about this principle is that you don't even need to do enough to accomplish your goal, just enough to get moving in the right direction. My biggest excuse when it came to exercise was that I was concentrating on my *spiritual* growth, and I didn't have time for *physical* concerns. Then *the irreducible minimum* kicked in.

I started with five half sit-ups and five leg raises. Now that's not enough to accomplish any results whatsoever, but it got me moving and it took less than one minute. I did that little bit every morning. If I wanted to do more, let's say eight, I did. If not, I didn't.

Eventually, I worked up to ten minutes of exercise. From there it gained a momentum of its own. And here I am, eleven years later, still maintaining some form of physical activity on a regular basis, as well as my commitment to my spiritual growth.

42

Today's Action | Pick one area of your life you want to change and are willing to take some action. What is the very least you can do and still be moving forward? Do it.

Someday Soon

I applied *the irreducible minimum* to my writing. I dabbled for years, but never pursued my writing on a regular basis. Then, that fateful summer when I was diagnosed with cancer, my life jumped into high gear. All of a sudden, I didn't have all the time in the world. I began writing.

I wrote to save my life. I wrote to deepen the quality of whatever life I had left. I was no longer comfortable thinking in terms of: *When I retire I'll* . . . having no idea if I would wake up tomorrow, much less see retirement.

At thirty-seven years of age I woke up. All I have is today and don't want to waste any more days.

Practicing *the irreducible minimum*, I bought a book about recovering your creativity and did the suggested exercises. I wrote daily for six months.

Then I faltered.

Little things, such as the initial rejection of Dharma's story, had the power to send me into a tailspin.

Then, a man who now lives in the Philippines gave me an audiotape of Natalie Goldberg, a wonderful Buddhist writer. Natalie spoke of building your writing muscles through "writing practice" by writing ten minutes on any topic at any time of day or night. Over the next few months, I developed my writing muscles.

Next came another right book, then the perfect seminar. Each time I got stuck, something was placed into my life to keep me moving in the right direction. That man from the Philippines was in my life only a few short weeks, but he left behind a pearl of wisdom that kept me going for months. Every step I took strengthened me for the next.

There is a time for books and seminars, a time for putting pen to paper. At each juncture I am ready for the next. It's like that. Trust and keep moving forward.

Today's Action | Trust and take the next right step.

Goin' Mobile

When I began living my bliss, there were many roadblocks, most put there by me. Doubts, worries, and fears cropped up all the time, causing me to get stuck. If I stayed stuck long enough, paralysis set in. This could last for days, weeks, even months.

From this I gleaned it's best to *keep moving*. Keep moving toward your dream—no matter what.

The most painful experience I had during the last few years was not losing a breast, or my hair, or throwing my guts up during chemo, or even my childhood memories.

It was the emotional pain I experienced when I was not writing.

It's the *resistance* to action that causes pain, not the action itself.

Many tricks kept me moving: Affirmations, rewards, support systems, being held accountable to others, sayings such as, "Oh, what the heck, *go for it anyway!*"

When I realized how important movement was, I made a list of things that keep me moving toward my dreams.

Here's my list:

- Call my *Bliss Mentor* or *Coach*

- Work with the index cards

- Listen to my *Feel the Fear and Do It Anyway* tape by Dr. Susan Jeffers

- Listen to my *If You Can Talk, You Can Write* by Joel Saltzman

- Call one of my *Bliss Cheerleaders*

- Re-read highlighted portions of *The Artist's Way* by Julia Cameron and Mark Bryan

- Re-read highlighted portions of *Do What You Love, The Money Will Follow* by Marsha Sinetar

- Share my fears, doubts and insecurities with my *Bliss Group* and affirm the opposite

- Take a walk to clear my head and get me grounded

- Do *the irreducible minimum*

- Pray

44

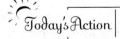

Today's Action | Make up your own list of things that keep you moving—things that move you into the solution.

Teacher

Who had a profound impact on your life? A teacher? A parent? An older sibling? Someone you admire but have never met?

Who shaped you into the person you are today? Who inspired you? Encouraged you? Believed in you and helped you believe in yourself?

Pick one of these people and write them a letter thanking them for the difference they made in your life. Tell them of your goals, your dreams, your plans, and how you are working to change your life. Express your gratitude for all they have done.

Some of the positive influences in my life are:

My second-grade teacher, Mrs. Newell, for helping me to feel useful

My fourth-grade teacher, Mrs. Wood, for being kind to me

My fifth-grade teacher, Mr. Kevorkian, for helping me feel special

Helen Keller and her teacher, for their perseverance

My seventh-grade creative writing teacher, for praising my writing to the class

My ninth-grade teacher, Mrs. McCreary, for encouraging me with my writing

My ninth-grade counselor, Mr. Greenberg, for noticing something was wrong

Ayn Rand, for writing with such depth and passion

Gammy, my great-grandmother, for passing on her love of the English language

My mom, Elaine, for her courage and generosity

My grandmother, Jackie, for her strong will and thoughtfulness

My Aunt Bobbie, for passing on her love of books

Bill Wilson and Dr. Bob, for starting Twelve-Step recovery

Jimmy K. and Lois W., for continuing it

My husband, Gary, for being my rock

Linda McCartney, for her personal courage and commitment to the planet

Arthur Ashe, for his dignity and grace

Melody Beattie, Shakti Gawain, Natalie Goldberg, and Julia Cameron, for leading the way for me as a woman and as a writer

Jimmy Carter, for his commitment to Habitat for Humanity, his vision for the planet, and his own efforts toward world peace

Oprah Winfrey, for the difference she is making in the world

My sponsors—especially Patricia—who all did more than they could ever imagine toward making me the person I am today

Tom Bird, without whom this book would not have been written

Mary Ann, for her unwavering encouragement and editing skill

There are so many people lighting the way, beacons in the night, shining brightly to keeps us from losing our way. It's impossible to thank them all, but we can start.

Today's Action | Express your gratitude in a letter to someone who has made a difference in your life. Then pass it on. Be willing to be a light for someone else.

A Day In The Life

Linda McCartney died of breast cancer today. She was diagnosed with cancer the same year I was.

Now here is a woman who lived her bliss. She had a wonderful thirty-year marriage to a man who adored her, four children, and a successful career in photography. She joined her husband on stage regardless of what critics said because she obviously enjoyed the life they shared.

She gave her time and energy to many worthy causes and cared deeply about the planet, particularly animals. At fifty-six, Linda McCartney had lived a rich and rewarding life, yet still it seems she was taken from us too soon. It's sad when someone so vibrant passes on.

Upon hearing the news, my mother said, "Well, I know she was a vegetarian, but that was mostly because of how she felt about animals, maybe she wasn't as health conscious as I thought."

My mother, a breast cancer survivor herself, was trying to make sense of why someone seemingly doing all the right things would die an untimely death. I do the same myself. Someone else recently said to a friend of mine, "You can't have colon cancer, you aren't resentful," implying that colon cancer is caused by resentment. This line of thinking really irks me. I wish we would stop blaming ourselves for getting cancer or judging others when they do.

Yes, some of us knowingly contribute to our illness with our lifestyle choices. And others have unresolved issues that may be toxic to their bodies, but sometimes, bad things happen to good people or rather what we perceive to be bad. When I get concerned about death, my husband asks, "What if dying is really a birth into the next life?" We honestly don't know. We may never make sense of why someone doing everything right would die young. We want so much to understand, to control the uncontrollable.

We think if we eat right, exercise, don't smoke or drink, if we do everything we are supposed to, we can stave off death. But we can't. Each and every one of us will die. The only thing we have control over is the quality of our life. We can choose to live as Linda did, fully in the moment, or not. The choice is up to us. We can be proactive regarding our health and make life-affirming choices or not. The choice is always up to us.

My mother and I mourn Linda McCartney's passing and are sad for her husband and children. But one thing is for certain, the world is a better place for her having lived, and that, more than anything, is what I want to be true about me.

Today's Action | Review your life. Do you have any regrets? Can you do anything about them? If not, let them go. Have you lived fully? Made a contribution to society? What is still left undone? What dreams are, thus far, unlived? What relationships need mending? Is the world a better place for your having lived?

Dreams

In the four years since my diagnosis, many people have died from cancer. One such person had a tremendous impact on my life.

In February 1995, I took my grandmother to hear Dr. Bernie S. Siegel give a talk because she just adores him. He was speaking to a predominantly elderly crowd on his new book, *Love, Medicine, and Miracles*. I listened, somewhat detached, since little of what he said seemed relevant to a healthy young woman such as myself. (Funny, that perception changed two months later when I found a lump in my breast.)

After Bernie finished speaking, he introduced Alec Courtelis, a successful developer, who designed one of my favorite places—a shopping center in South Miami called "The Falls."

The Falls Shopping Center is built around a series of cascading waterfalls, wooden landings, and huge, flat rocks, creating a tropical paradise in the midst of an urban shopping center.

Mesmerized whenever I go there, I often watch the crystal-blue water pour over the rocks, rolling down to the next level, wondering, "What kind of person would design such a beautiful shopping center?"—obviously someone who shared my love of waterfalls.

During my meditations, when I create my "sacred place," it looks exactly like "The Falls," only set in a rainforest instead of a shopping center.

Knowing waterfalls connected us, I listened intently as this innovative developer told his story. Diagnosed with pancreatic cancer months earlier, he was told he only had a few months to live and to get his affairs in order. Alec sank into a deep depression. That is, until Bernie's message of laughter and joy as a means to wellness touched his spirit and moved him into the solution.

Wanting very much to live, Alec underwent traditional treatments and alternative therapies alike. At one alternative center, Teri Amar's Institute for Mind-Body Health, Alec was guided to Lawrence LeShan's book, *Cancer as a Turning Point*, where he learned that a person could improve their immune system by doing what they love, enabling them to live a longer, healthier life.

Until then, Alec had devoted most of his time to his business. He never took the time to ask, "What is important to *me*? What are *my* dreams?" Now, what mattered most were his loved ones, not the business to which he had given most of his waking hours.

A spark was ignited and a forgotten dream awakened. Alec wanted to build a dream house on the water for himself and his family. The spark turned to fire, and the fire set a passion ablaze in his heart.

A few months later Alec broke ground on his dream home.

Today's Action | If the doctors told you to get your affairs in order, what would that mean to you—your financial affairs or your spiritual ones? Flesh it out on the cards.

I Believe…You'll Never Walk Alone

Alec Courtelis lived three years longer than the doctors said was possible, but more importantly, they were the richest years of his life.

When I heard him speak that Saturday, he exuded such joy and love, his presence so powerful, his message so inspirational, that I personally went to thank him for speaking, still having no idea I was there for me, not my grandmother.

Four months later, days after my own cancer diagnosis, I asked my mother, "Do you think it would be okay for a stranger to call Mr. Courtelis—I *have* to find out more about his path?"

My mother replied, "They are hardly strangers. I installed the carpet in the Courtelis's previous home and am working with them on their dream home right now."

She called Mrs. Courtelis, got the information I needed, and I immediately made an appointment at the Institute for Mind-Body Health. Fear of dying consumed me. If the cancer didn't get me, the fear would.

Dr. Gregory Lecklightner recommended I read *Cancer as a Turning Point* to discover my dreams. It was hard to admit aloud, but I knew right away I wanted to be a writer. I love telling stories and instilling hope in others with my sharing. I have no shortage of ideas, but with little discipline or self-esteem, my early attempts fizzled.

However, persistence pays. Here I am, almost four years later, still writing.

To me, the sequence of events that led me to find my bliss is nothing less than astonishing.

First, I take my grandmother to hear Bernie Siegel talk of healing cancer through laughter, all the while unaware of the cancer growing in me. Then, the dreamer in Alec Courtelis awoke the dreamer in me. Finally, when it became imperative I learn more about Alec's path, I find my own mother knows the Courtelis family professionally. I was one phone call away from finding my bliss.

I guess there is a plan for my life. Funny how it took this specific series of events for me to find it. God certainly found an interesting way to stretch my wings and make me fly.

Thank you, Bernie. And thank you, Alec.

Today's Action | Pay attention to the synchronicity of the Universe responding to your dreams. Be ever on the lookout for *Godincidences*—the little coincidences that let you know how very much God cares about you and your dreams.

Is It Written In The Stars?

There were so many losses the year I entered the world of cancer. After years spent working with the terminally ill, Teri Amar, head of the Institute, where I went for cancer psychotherapy, died from a fluke respiratory ailment. Carmen, the first breast cancer survivor I spoke with after my diagnosis, died from a recurrence shortly after I finished my treatments, leaving behind a husband and two small children. Barry, a member of my cancer support group, died from a blood clot while fighting lymphoma. Eric, my law firm's accountant, died of brain cancer at the age of forty-two, leaving behind a wife and two small children. He was diagnosed with cancer two months after I was and died before I returned to work seven months later. Within the span of six months four people I knew, died—two suddenly. It was a very scary time for me.

What is this precious thing we call life? A gift from God? A span of time? A learning experience?

Living blissfully means prioritizing, asking, "What is of value to me?"

Many people, myself included, spend too much time living vicariously through others. Whether the vehicle is TV, books, movies, computers, spouses, or our children—sometimes we lose our center and let life pass us by.

My husband likes to watch sports, news, and TV dramas. I like spiritual shows, sit-coms, and an occasional television movie. Between us, the TV is on a lot . . . too much, in fact. Last week we decided to withdraw from our passive life and engage more actively in life: We turned the television off.

By the end of the week, we were like a couple that had just quit smoking cigarettes: constantly on edge. Personally, I think every family needs at least one sane person; a couple should never go through withdrawals at the same time. Somehow, we survived.

Actually, we enjoyed the slower pace of less technology. Watching less television and using the computer less gave us more time for walks to the lake, reading, and relaxing in a more fulfilling manner. I found myself longing for quiet days on a farm or lazing in a hammock. Not that I dislike or want to do away with all modern conveniences, just cut back, pare down, simplify. Interact with machines less and people more. Be inside less, outside more. Walk in the park or run at the beach, instead of stomping on the Stairmaster or trekking on the treadmill.

After re-evaluating my life, I concluded that I don't need all the products and services I think I do.

In fact, in the last few years, I read dozens of books on simplicity, spirituality, and wellness. Now, I just want to stop. I want to get off the merry-go-round of self-improvement and just be. I don't want a book on how to do it—I just want to do it.

I know, here I am a writer, suggesting that you, a reader, read less. But you know what? If my book sells fewer and fewer copies each year, because more and more people are out there *living* their bliss, that would delight me to no end.

51

Today's Action | Close the book, turn the TV off, and go outside for a change!

The Inner Light

For some reason I needed the wake-up call of cancer. My mother didn't need to wait for cancer to transform her life.

The daughter of an alcoholic father and an absentee mother, my mother was raised mostly by her grandmother, Gammy. Lost and unhappy, she left home at sixteen and married my father. By the time she was twenty-one, she had three children and two divorces under her belt. After struggling on her own for six years, she met and married my infamous stepfather. After a twelve-year relationship to an, at times funny, but mostly unfaithful, pill-head, my mother finally divorced my stepfather. With no marketable skills or money, she found herself starting over at forty. To make ends meet, she tended bar, waited tables, and sold health-club memberships.

Within a few years, she found her way into the carpet business. In time, she developed enough of a client base to start her own business. At first, she worked out of her home, filling it from floor to ceiling with carpet samples. People grimaced when they saw her tiny five-foot frame lugging carpet samples into their showrooms, "Oh no, here comes that carpet lady again!" Persistence was her middle name.

Eight years after leaving my stepfather, my mother opened a carpet showroom, aptly named *The Carpet Lady*. Today, more than twenty years later, her business is thriving, but more importantly, so is she.

Ten years ago my mother read Shakti Gawain's *Living in the Light*, which she refers to as a major turning point in her life. Up until then, she dated or married addicted or unavailable men, smoked pot every day to unwind, and didn't believe in power outside of herself. That one simple book marks the beginning of her spiritual journey back to herself.

Today, she has been happily alone for years and is no longer dependent on drugs or unhealthy men. My mother has become a strong, independent, spiritually centered woman.

I used to hate being compared to my mother. Now, it is one of the best compliments I can receive. Without a doubt, I know my strength and resilience comes from her. What a gift, to watch a woman transform her life, overcome obstacles, and become the light she was meant to be.

Today's Action | Think of a family member or friend who has turned their life around. Who is awe-inspiring? Write about their transformation and celebrate the limitless possibilities we all are!

The Wind Beneath My Wings

My younger brother, Brent, looks like a cross between Phil Collins and John Cusak, with his round face, receding hairline, and soft puppy-brown eyes. When you hear his story, you will understand why he is an inspiration to me of one who is truly living his heart's desire, taking risks, and believing in himself even in the face of great obstacles.

Brent got the worst of it when we were kids. If my mom was the "lost child," Brent was the "invisible one," except when it came to, "Who did this?" Blamed for everything, whether he did it or not, Brent soon started doing everything. Craving attention, he was always in trouble: running away, burning his bed, stealing, or skipping school.

He was such a handful that he was passed back and forth between our mom, his dad, his dad's second wife's parents, and back to us. Stability was not his middle name. Drugs and trouble followed Brent into his teen years. He was even nicknamed "The Quaalude Kid" back in the late seventies. Wrecking cars and motorcycles went with the territory. In school, Brent never earned more than a "C" and looked destined to be a delinquent forever.

Then, something happened. Brent was given an opportunity and a choice.

Fed up with his escapades, Brent's father said to him, "You can't live with me anymore, but if you want to get serious and go to college, I'll pay for half." The astounding thing is that Brent agreed. Out of nowhere, he decided to reach for that brass ring and make something of himself.

Brent's father owned a family-style restaurant that Brent was pretty much raised in. Now, with this offer, he decided to go all the way and become a chef. He studied restaurant management and was the first person of our generation in the family to earn a college degree. After graduation, Brent went to the Culinary Institute of America in Hyde Park, NY, and became president of their Saucier Club.

From there, he went on to work and study in Switzerland and France for a year, and even spent time under the tutelage of the world-renowned French chef, Paul Bocuse. During the next sixteen years Brent honed his skills by working at The Willard Hotel in Washington, D.C., The Fairmont in New Orleans, The Mark Hopkins in San Francisco, The Pier House in Key West, and Guidos in Aspen. Receiving rave reviews in every city's newspaper, Brent became the "star" of our family.

As successful as he was, it was not until he left his cushy job as executive chef of Guidos, took out a huge loan, and opened his own restaurant in Steamboat Springs that Brent truly began letting his heart sing.

For years, I have been in awe of this man's courage and vision. I am not sure I have the confidence to go into as much debt as he did to make his dream come true.

He is not my hero only because of his material success but because of his heart. The same year his plans were in the works to open the restaurant, I was diagnosed with cancer. Brent dropped everything to fly to Miami for a few weeks and take me to my chemotherapy treatments. What more could a sister ask?

When it came time for me to really go after my dreams, even though fear still stood in the way, I thought of Brent and decided—if he can do it, so can I!

Today's Action | Who is the wind beneath your wings? Who has taken big risks to realize their dreams? Seek them out and ask them how they did it. Get details—how they walked through each fear, overcame each obstacle, and kept going when the going got rough. Those who have gone before us can guide us best: Apply their lessons.

Let It Be

The internal critic seizes the reins on a regular basis. I don't know why the critic is so unhappy when things are going well, but it is. For instance, right now, my writing coach has me writing this book on huge, white poster boards, instead of on 8-1/2-by-11-inch paper or on the computer. From his experience of working with hundreds of writers, he found writing on poster boards overrides the internal critic, expanding and deepening one's writing. It has certainly been true in my case.

Dividing the poster board into four vertical rows, three about the width of a regular piece of paper, with the fourth column two to three inches wide, I write as fast as I can for two hours a day on the first three columns without editing or re-reading. In the fourth column, I record any thoughts that come up unrelated to what I am writing. For instance, if I remember I have to get bananas at the grocery store, it goes in that last narrow column. If I get an idea for a future project or need to check a fact in my current project, that's where it goes. Once I'm on a roll, not much interrupts me, and the last column stays empty. This method allows me to go full throttle on those first three columns.

The hardest part of writing this way is not editing as I go. Usually, if I make a mistake, it's my nature to fix it right away. However, every time I let the critic back in the game, it gains more control, and the quality of my writing suffers. Intellectually this makes sense to me, but practicing it is difficult. In fact, right now my logical left-brain wants to chuck the boards and go straight to the computer. It's faster, more efficient, and I can edit as I go. Plus, there is this side of me that is just dying to organize everything—dot all my i's and cross all my t's.

My ego wants to re-establish order and make things perfect. My right-brain creative side, on the other hand, is willing to go wide open and write whatever comes. As my ego-self battles my God-self to regain the control it once had, I resist. Writing as fast as I can, I access my Higher Self. From this holy place, my heart can speak to yours.

| Get out of the way. Let go and trust the process. Just . . . let it be.

Get On Your Feet

What makes *your* heart sing? Are you doing it? Do you go deep within and allow your Higher Self to run the show?

It's hard to let go of control and just *be*, as I am right now: no one to impress, no fancy sentences—just one heart, speaking to another.

What does your soul long to do?

A woman I work with, Dianne, makes delightful handmade gifts; she dreams of own-ing her own business someday. Both the Home Shopping Network and J.C. Penney's have expressed interest in her wares, yet she hesitates. When I asked why, Dianne had a million reasons why she couldn't follow her dream *right now.*

I know it's scary. I've been there. Still, it's important to move beyond the excuses and *just do it.*

I asked Dianne, "If a millionaire came through that door right now and said, 'I'm looking for someone to back financially. I'd like to make their dreams come true. Anything at all they want to do or be, all they have to do is say so and they've got it.' Would you pursue your dreams then?" Her eyes lit up as she looked into the future and saw the possibilities.

We must become our own benefactors. It's up to us to quit being practical and *make* things happen! If not us, who? If not now, when?

That afternoon Dianne e-mailed me that she was going to replace "but" with an affir-mation. Instead of "I'd like to follow my dreams but . . . ," she now affirms, "I *am* following my dreams."

Dianne's new anthem is Gloria Estefan's "Get on Your Feet and Make It Happen," and she is starting a *Bliss Luncheon* where co-workers meet once a month to discuss their dreams (personal or professional), set goals, and receive encouragement and support from each other.

It's amazing what a little brainstorming can do.

☀ Today's Action | If a millionaire wanted to back you at anything at all, what would it be? Take Dianne's lead and be your own benefactor. *"Get on your feet and make it happen. Stand up and take some action!"*

Dream On

Me, I love writing. Yet, if I could be anything at all—let's say I could have five lives—what would I be? Okay, one would be a writer—definitely! Two would be a mother, a stay-at-home mom. Three would be a singer like Tina, Celine, Barbra, or the band Heart. Four would be a photographer/writer for a travel magazine. My niche would be waterfalls, lakes, rivers, and oceans: capturing liquid beauty on film and in words. I would travel the world visiting majestic places from Hawaii to the Grand Canyon to the Amazon.

And last . . . hmmm . . . what would I be?

If money didn't matter and I could be anything at all, I would be an artist and a lover.

I would paint and make love only—that's all. All day, everyday. Colors—shocking pink, deep purple, periwinkle blue, turquoise green, lemon yellow. Colors and sex! Passion swirling, mixing, merging—making love on canvas, covered with paint.

Okay, okay, so I went off a little. But wasn't it wild, just for a minute, to think of a life so free—no responsibilities—just fun?

Who cares what sells—nothing but beauty and sex.

Great sex. Multicolored, passionate, red-hot sex—scorching sex.

Paint swirling all over our bodies.

There I go again! Well, we can see which life is resonating with me today.

What about you?

If you didn't have to worry about money or make a living and could do anything at all, what would it be?

☀ Today's Action | Describe, in detail, five different lives you would lead if you could be or do anything at all. By now you are probably breaking out of the norm a little, so go all out on this one.

Body And Soul

I woke up this morning to the most amazing awareness: my jaw doesn't hurt. For years, fifteen to be exact, I have been grinding my teeth at night. For the last eight years, I have slept with a plastic mouthpiece to prevent me from grinding my teeth down to nothing. If I forget to wear it, I wake up with my jaw clamped tight, as if it were wired shut.

This clenching started during my first marriage, when I was drinking, snorting cocaine, and fighting with my now ex-husband all the time. Caught in the grip of addiction, our marriage quickly turned into a nightmare, which mercifully ended in divorce before we killed each other.

My dentist fitted me with a bite splint while I was still using drugs, explaining that teeth grinding was a common phenomenon in Miami. Thirty percent of his patients needed bite splints. I thought to myself: *I didn't know Miami had such a big drug problem.* I was positive the clenching and grinding would stop when I stopped partying, but it didn't.

Next, I thought working in a stress-free environment was the answer, but it wasn't. In time, I accepted I would probably always grind my teeth. However, there's always been this nagging feeling that this *dis*-eased condition was not part of God's plan. The fact that it happened only when I slept baffled me even more.

This morning when I woke up with no tightness or pain whatsoever, I had an epiphany: It wasn't until I got down to the serious business of living my bliss that this pain in my body went away. It wasn't enough to stop destroying myself with chemicals. It wasn't enough to have a good marriage and a satisfying career. There is a specific purpose and plan for each of us. Ignoring it creates *dis*-ease within our bodies.

On the other hand, when body and soul are in alignment, physical ailments dissolve, and spiritually we are at peace.

57

I shared this awareness with a woman who is also using the index cards and poster boards to follow her dreams, and she told me that within weeks of working with the cards, her sexual abuse issues surfaced. She said that after dealing with these issues while in a deep, right-brain state, the extra twenty pounds she had been carrying for years just melted away.

Hmmmm.

Today's Action | Is there any *dis*-ease in your body indicative of a deeper purpose for your life that is, as yet, unlived? Try an experiment: Follow your bliss all-out for the next two months. If that means getting up earlier, working at night or on weekends—do it. Designate time, daily or weekly, to follow your heart's desire. Notice the effect on your body and soul.

The Story In Your Eyes

I have mentioned my mom's mother, Jackie, earlier, but to really give you a feel for this woman, I must tell you more about her. Yes, she is the absentee mother who allowed her only daughter to be raised by her grandmother. As a stewardess, flying mostly out of Central and South America, Jackie was not at home much. However, as a single parent, she did her best to provide for my mother.

She also earned her pilot's license and flew planes as a hobby back in the 1940s. There were not too many women doing that back then, but Jackie has always been ahead of her time.

Before telex and fax machines were commonplace in offices, Jackie started a telex and fax business from her home, which she still runs today. She recently purchased a new computer and took computer lessons so she could expand her business to include e-mail and other Internet services. She also runs a lampshade delivery business from her home, to further supplement her Social Security income.

Jackie volunteers at Fairchild Gardens every week and walks or swims for an hour every day. Recently, she joined an investment club and now researches the companies the club is interested in on her computer, before advising which ones to invest in. A couple of years ago, Jackie took piano lessons for the very first time, because it was, "something she had always wanted to do."

Last night, we took Jackie out to dinner to celebrate her eightieth birthday. Can you imagine, learning to use a mouse for the first time at age seventy-nine? Without question, she is the woman I admire most (Mom, please do not take offense). In addition to all she does, she finds time to send friends and family thoughtful articles, cards, coupons, and knickknacks.

Is this a grandmother or what?

To top it all off she is as calm and serene as a morning lake.

However, this past Christmas Jackie was a bit down. She had to buy new tires for her car and struggled to come up with the eight hundred dollars. All of a sudden, Jackie wondered what her life had amounted to and confided in me that she had nothing to show for her life.

I told her, "You can't put a price on being a grandmother."

For her birthday, I found this wonderful plaque titled *Priorities*. It read:

A hundred years from now it will not matter what my bank account was, the sort of house I lived in, or the kind of car I drove . . . but the world may be different because I was important in the life of a child.

Jackie, I am that child.

59

Today's Action | If either of your grandparents is still alive, show them today how special they are with a phone call or letter. If they are no longer alive, visit the cemetery or write them a letter thanking them for the influence they had on your life.

Tall Cool One

One of the hardest and easiest stories to tell is that of my husband: my rock—my hero—my spiritual giant. It is hardest because there is so much to say and no words can possibly capture him, as I know him. It is easiest because it is closest to my heart. It may take a few pages, so settle in.

Gary, okay, we will start with the physical. He is 6'1" (I almost wrote 5'1" – and thought of describing him as the character George Castanza from *Seinfeld* or Dennis Franz from *NYPD Blue* for kicks). You see, Gary looks like a *GQ* model or Paul Newman in his forties. But he also has a tremendous sense of humor—so if you want to picture him as a short, fat, bald guy—I think it would be a riot (just not the ugly, naked guy from *Friends*).

So here we have this tall, handsome, blue-eyed, gray-haired, funny man—my Gary, whom you already know from "Dharma—My Little Angel." So it is obvious he is a sensitive, nineties guy who was so there for me during my breast cancer experience. Actually, it was Gary who made it quite an experience.

Shortly after my cancer diagnosis, I was reading *Dr. Susan Love's Breast Book*, recommended by my oncologist. I was lying on the couch (yes, I laid there a lot), and reading aloud to Gary some of the possible side effects of chemotherapy. "Gary, it says I could lose my hair, get sores, and suffer from edema—which means I might gain weight. Are you still going to want me?" I asked in anticipation of his undying profession of love.

Gary responded, "Let me get this straight—you are going to be fat, bald, and have sores all over—and you want to know if I want to be with you?" I looked up expectantly, only to hear Gary snap his fingers twice and say, "Sure, Uncle Fester—can't wait!"

I was horrified at his response—but could not stop laughing long enough to admonish him. That joke was just the tip of the iceberg. The one-liners streamed out of him for months.

60

When my hair fell out, Gary lathered up my head to shave off the remaining strands. Tears rolled down my cheeks, as I started to look as sick as I felt. Here we were in my bathroom, during this very touching moment and without missing a beat, Gary says, "You know, honey, the couple that shaves together, stays together."

By this time, I am giving him little arm punches every time he tells another cancer or chemo joke, and he is black and blue all over. Just kidding! He does, however, refer to himself as a battered husband, explaining, "Every morning my wife covers me in eggs and flour." Do you get the nonstop picture of it yet?

I know, I know, some people cope with difficulties with humor. However, sometimes I would think, "Enough, already! Can't you be serious? I have *cancer* for God's sake! But Gary is Gary, and as fed up as I pretended to be—I cannot imagine having gone through my illness without him.

Today's Action | Who is the funniest person you know? Who brightens your day? Write what you like most about this person—then tell them. Bring more humor into your own life by watching funny videos, telling or listening to jokes, and being around funny people. Life really is not as serious as we make it. Lighten up.

♡

Have You Ever Really Loved A Woman?

The day I was released from the hospital, after my mastectomy, Gary arrived at the hospital entrance to take me to my mother's house to recuperate. With flowers in hand, he opened the car door, helped me get situated, and then inserted a CD from the soundtrack of the movie *Don Juan Del Marco*. Then, Gary sat next to me and sang Bryan Adams's "Have You Ever Really Loved A Woman?"

> *"To really love a woman, to understand her*
>
> *You gotta know her deep inside*
>
> *Hear every thought, see every dream*
>
> *Give her wings when she wants to fly*
>
> *And when you find yourself lying helpless in her arms*
>
> *You know you really love a woman*

61

Chorus:

> *When you love a woman – tell her she's really wanted*
>
> (Gary sang that line, and then whispered to me, "You're really wanted.")
>
> *When you love a woman – tell her she's the one*
>
> (Again, he sang the line and whispered, "You're the one.")
>
> *She needs somebody to tell her it's gonna last forever"*
>
> (He sang that as well, reassuring me, "It's going to last forever.")

At that point, I broke down in tears. I can't tell you how much I needed to hear that last line—"*It's going to last forever.*" After just losing my breast and hearing the word cancer related to *me*, I really thought I had only a short time left. It meant so much to me to hear Gary say our love was going to last forever.

I clung tightly to those words—until I could let go. Then I did that, too.

Amazing Grace

Do you get a sense of Gary yet? I bet you think you do. Boy, have I got news for you. This tender, funny man was not always this way. At one time in his life, he had a heart of stone and had iced-out all emotion from his life.

Gary spent seven years homeless in the streets of Boston.

Yes, actually homeless: standing in soup lines, living in shelters and abandoned buildings, body lice, teeth rotting right out of his mouth, occasionally even sleeping with freshly fallen snow as his blanket.

This was all before I met him, and although I know many of the details, I still cannot fathom the man I know today, living like that. But Gary *was* one of those filthy, unshaven bums we avert our eyes from as we hurry down the street.

Addicted to heroin for over twenty years, Gary earned a three-page criminal record, robbed drugstores, stole from his girlfriends and their mothers, and caused tremendous heartache to his own mother and family, before making his way through eleven treatment centers and finally getting and staying off of drugs.

Knowing this brief bit about Gary's past, you can imagine my mother's dismay at the thought of her little girl marrying *this* man.

But Gary is the man I chose and all the riches in the world do not come close to the treasure of a man he is.

"Amazing grace, how sweet the sound

That saved a wretch like me

I once was lost

But now am found

Was blind

But now I see

'Twas grace that taught

My heart to feel

And grace my fears relieved

How precious did that grace appear

The hour I first believed."

Today's Action | Open your heart and your eyes and see the possibilities that lie dormant in all of us, especially the down and out. Next time you see a homeless person, remember they are someone's child, maybe someone's brother or father, possibly someone's future love.

Dance With Me

Okay, so now you know I love him, but I bet you're wondering how we met.

Well, we met at a Thanksgiving dance in 1988. Gary, off drugs for six months, was at the recovery function with a few friends, and I was there with a girlfriend.

Trying to develop a relationship with a Higher Power, Gary tested spiritual waters by praying for things. Driven by fear most of his life, Gary prayed for courage in areas that come naturally for most people. He didn't know how to dance, was afraid to ask anyone, and yet was anxious to rejoin the human race. In the back of the darkened room, a girl caught his eye. He sat on a table and prayed for the courage to ask this girl to dance. He counted to ten, got up, started to walk over to her, sat back down and counted to ten again, praying for more courage. This went on for twenty minutes.

Finally, he got up, went over to where the girl was standing. When there was a lull in the conversation she was having, he stepped in and asked if she would like to dance. Without so much as turning her head, she said, "No."

Then, as he was walking away, she asked how long he had been in recovery. Not only did he not know how to dance, he knew even less about conversing with the opposite sex. After an awkward moment, he went back to his table, looked up, and said, "That was funny."

Continuing his conversation with God, Gary said, "Okay, if you really exist, I want you to put that woman into my life."

He had never seen her before, didn't even know her name—yet that was his prayer.

Nine months later *we* were married.

Today's Action	Pray for courage. Then take the next right action.

She Believes In Me

Not only was my mother not thrilled about me marrying this man, but my best friend of fifteen years, my therapist, and my sponsor all told me I was crazy. My sponsor said I had taken my will back, that I was no longer letting God run the show. My best friend thought I was settling. She told me the partying I did in no way compared to the life of a junkie, "Six months clean is a drop in the bucket off a twenty-year heroin habit. Eleven treatment centers must tell you something."

"But he's turning his life around." I said.

"Junkies are con artists—they have to be to support their habit," she replied.

The line that takes the cake, however, is when my therapist said, "Would you go into a store and buy a half a coat?"

I know they all meant well and I heard them, but your heart leads where your heart leads. Besides, I had already been on the clinching date with him.

We had gone to a friend's house for spaghetti and to play cards. Our friends interrupted our game of Spades to serve the pasta. While they were in the kitchen, I leaned over to Gary and jokingly motioned for him to show me his cards. He took offense and said, "That's cheating!" I told him I was only joking, but the strength of his convictions over such a tiny matter showed me his character. I was hooked.

Now, the fact that it was love at first sight does not mean we haven't traveled a rough road together. We have. Any couple getting together early in recovery complicates things. But we managed to make it work by placing spiritual principles at the center of our lives and our marriage. We found that as long as your priorities are in order, everything works out fine.

| Today's Action | Do you listen to your own inner truth? Or do others, who want to play it safe, easily sway you? Ruminate on that next time you need to make a decision. Go inward and ask, "What is *my* truth?" |

The Lord's Prayer

Many people are curious how the dramatic change occurred in Gary to take him from the person he was to the person he is today.

As Gary tells it, there was one kind of person he never saw in a crack house, shooting gallery, or homeless shelter, and that was a good person.

Gary met bad people. He met people who *wanted* to be good people, but had just sold their child's bicycle for drugs. However, he never actually met a good person in any of these places. Gary knew the key to changing was to *become* a good person. So how does a person go from being a cheat, a liar, a thief, and a drug addict to a being a good person? Divine intervention based on a sincere plea from the heart.

On December 3, 1988, Gary was in the ballroom of the Deauville Hotel on Miami Beach attending a Gratitude Dinner Banquet. The purpose of this particular banquet was to celebrate the people who have turned their lives around as a result of hearing a message of recovery in a hospital, jail, treatment center, or other institution, and the people who bring those meetings into those institutions.

They kicked off the evening with dinner, followed by a raffle, a meeting, and a dance. I sold raffle tickets at the banquet, even sold one to Gary. What I didn't know was that it was the same guy who had asked me to dance a few weeks earlier at the Thanksgiving dance.

Gary had six months clean yet did not believe this recovery thing would work for very long. After all, he had tried unsuccessfully to quit drugs many times before. Gary believed he was a lost cause.

The meeting was closed in the manner they closed most meetings back then, with "The Lord's Prayer." Something happened to Gary during that prayer. As he looked around the room, he saw eight hundred people doing what he never could—staying clean. In that instant, hope came into his life.

Gary describes it is as a warm feeling coming over his entire body. His heart opened and became full. His eyes filled with tears that he could not hold back.

Feeling the presence of God, Gary believed for the very first time that whatever was working in the lives of all those people could work for him. He believed that if he surrendered to that recovery program—maybe, just maybe, those people could show him a new way to live. Maybe he would not have to die a cold, lonely death with a needle in his arm.

Ten years have passed since that miraculous evening when hope entered his life. As Gary likes to say, "Hope is the one spiritual principle that you can actually hand to another person. You can't make a person honest and you can't give them integrity, but you *can* give someone hope."

That is what was given to him on December 3, 1988, and it is what he has tried to give to others on a daily basis for the last twelve years.

Hope is what this book is all about.

Today's Action | In what areas have you experienced success? Do you know anyone struggling in those areas? Today, share your experience with others in a way that lifts them up to their highest potential. Today, pass on hope.

The Man In The Mirror

One day the miracle of God's grace touched my life—changing me forever.

During the first thirty years of my life, I did not believe in God or in any Universal Power. I went through the motions of living. I had boyfriends, apartments, jobs, and was even married for a while. I went to concerts, plays, movies, football games, and traveled a lot. I went to nightclubs, discos, and bars—drank and did cocaine. I was the ultimate party girl. From hanging out in Hugh Hefner's Playboy Mansion in California to rubbing shoulders with celebrities in local South Florida hot spots, I lived hedonistically, for the moment—a far cry from my current mindfully in the moment style.

As my use of substances increased, so did my soul sickness. Life was empty and meaningless. I wasn't as cynical as "Life's a bitch, and then you die." It was more like, "Life's a party, and then you die." By the time I was twenty-two, I saw no reason to go on living. I decided to check out of this life I didn't understand and took two hundred sleeping pills.

However, the God I didn't believe in had another plan.

Not knowing what was wrong with me, eight years passed before I addressed my addiction to cocaine and alcohol. By thirty years of age, I felt like an old hag. The outside still looked okay, but on the inside, I was dying. After being up all night partying, I called in sick to work. I was sure I was close to being fired; it was the fourth time I'd called in sick in as many weeks. I had left my husband a few months earlier, and since no one was on my case anymore about how much or how often I partied, I was out of control.

My new boyfriend told me about Twelve-Step recovery, but my denial was so deep that I had no idea why he told me about those meetings. I thought he was just making conversation. He mentioned that he came from a dysfunctional family, and I thought he meant they were retarded. Come to find out that's not that far off.

The day I stayed home from work, my boyfriend saw the condition I was in, and asked, "What's wrong?"

"I don't know. All I know is that I'm crazy, and if you know what's good for you you'll walk out that door as fast as you can and never come back," I yelled as I ran into the bedroom, slamming the door.

"Is it drugs?" he asked through the door.

"Yes," I replied, being honest for the first time in my life.

He told me about the meetings again, but I balked, "I haven't slept. I look like hell. Maybe some other time." He said, "If you don't go right now, you never will." I picked a fight with him and made him leave. I ate dinner, got a good night's sleep, and went to work the next day. To my surprise, they didn't fire me. Driving home from work, I thought, "I'm not that bad. I don't need those meetings." One more time, I had escaped serious consequences and therefore didn't realize I needed help.

Then, as I pulled up to my apartment complex, a song came on the radio that I had never heard before: "The Man in the Mirror" by Michael Jackson.

"I'm standing with the man in the mirror, I'm asking if you'll change his ways

No message could have been any clearer:

If you want to make the world a better place, start with yourself and make that change."

The song ends with a whisper, *"Make that change."*

I stared the radio. *How did they know?*

I can't explain what happened, but that song reached me when nothing else could. I turned around and drove to my first meeting.

Now, whenever I hear "The Man in the Mirror," I am reminded of God's grace in doing for me what I could not do for myself.

With grace, nothing is ever out of reach. With God's grace, you can *"make that change."*

Today's Action | How has grace touched your life, miraculously changing it forever?

Coming Out Of The Dark

At that meeting, it was suggested that I rely on a power greater than myself for strength and guidance. I resisted. My whole life I was raised to believe I could do anything I set my mind to. Hadn't I had quit smoking cigarettes on my own? Didn't I get myself out of those bad relationships? Now, here I was being asked to surrender, "Give up the battle, the war is over." I resisted—big time.

Insistent about the God stuff, every time I had a problem, the people at the meetings suggested I pray.

Now how in the world could that help? I'm a person of action; just tell me what to do and I'll do it.

"Pray" came the answer. "Pray to whatever you want—call it anything you like—so long as it is loving and greater than you."

You would think they'd give me more guidance or tell me about their beliefs. Instead, they just said, "Be open to the fact that *something* must have created life. *Something* must have created the Universe." They said there must be *something* greater than me. I said I had to see it to believe it. They pointed out that gravity works whether you believe in it or not, and you certainly can't see it.

"Try it. What have you got to lose?" It took a crow bar, but they finally opened my mind.

Hesitantly, I prayed. "Okay, whoever or whatever you are—if you exist—please help me today." As simple as that prayer was, the results were astonishing. Mini-miracles happened at every turn, coincidences that were too far-fetched to be just coincidences. *A person I needed to talk to would show up unexpectedly at a meeting. I would think about someone I hadn't seen in years and then run into them the next day. I would struggle with honesty, pray for help with it, and honesty would be the topic at my next meeting.*

Maybe there was something to this prayer stuff after all. Maybe somehow the Universe does respond to the energy of prayer. Maybe there is a Universal Mind or Creative Force.

To this day, eleven years later, I still don't know the truth about God. All I know is I've tried life for thirty years without God and don't want to go through another minute of that meaningless existence. And I've tried the last eleven years with what I refer to as God. It's infinitely richer, more fulfilling, and far more exciting than I could ever imagine, even with all I've been through.

On the surface, worse things have happened to me in the last eleven years than in the previous thirty, but I wouldn't trade these last eleven years for anything. Today, I am so grateful today for the gift of life, whatever its form.

I know I didn't create myself, so there must be some kind of power greater than me, if only the force of nature, but I tend to think it is far greater than that and all encompassing.

Although I usually refer to this power as "God" or "the Universe," my Aunt Bobbie refers to it as "Goddess," and another friend of mine refers to it as "The Force," as in *Star Wars*. I don't think it matters what we call it or even if we really understand it—so long as we use it.

Today's Action | Pray that this Power—whatever it is—reveal itself to you today. Then sit back and prepare to be amazed.

I Believe I Can Fly

When I write, it is with a child's heart and a child's enthusiasm. Enthusiasm stems from the Latin, *en theo*, or "with God." And that is how I feel when I write. I am filled with awe, wonder, and excitement. When I sit down to write, it is with quiet anticipation of the adventure ahead. I am open to all possibilities, and my heart is full. I am with God.

It is my heartfelt desire to write in a way that touches and inspires others. Yet there are days when I do not feel up to the task, days when doubt creeps in. The little voice, way in the back, asks: *How can you possibly do this? Who do you think you are?* Once it has grabbed my attention, it continues. *You are not talented enough, disciplined enough, courageous enough, or well-connected enough to succeed.* Listening to that voice gives it power. Given time, it would have me believe that I am not good enough at anything.

There were many days when I have felt unworthy of my own dreams and aspirations. Days when I said to myself: *I should not reach for the stars—they are too far away. Surely, I will fall if I try.*

Still, the stars hung in their midnight-blue blanket, beckoning me: *We are well within your grasp.* And I would try one more time.

Then voices would come again—paralyzing me for a time. But the dream would not die. And so the battle raged. Until one day, I made a decision. I decided to pick one project, one tiny part of the bigger idea, and see it all the way through—no matter what.

My first commitment was to see "Dharma—My Little Angel" through to publication.

Initially, I wrote it for a *Guideposts* writers' workshop contest and was crushed when I was not chosen.

It was two months before I wrote again.

Finally, I picked myself up, dusted myself off, and tried again. Six rejections later, I stopped trying to get Dharma's story published and began handing it out whenever I heard someone had cancer. Soon the circle widened to anyone scared of dying, anyone facing a loss, women who could not have children, and people with lost dreams.

The story took on a life of its own. Men and women alike were touched by Dharma's message. Then one day, out of the blue, the original magazine that had turned me down contacted me regarding publishing the story in their new sister magazine, *Angels on Earth*. Ten months later, they sent a photographer to our home. A few months after that an editor called, and we edited the story for publication.

It was a long road, two and a half years to be exact, but during the entire time, I never gave up. I did the footwork, put my story and my dreams out into the Universe. I also took writing classes, editing classes, and worked on other writing projects.

The stars were so pretty, dazzling in fact. I wanted so much to live the dream in my heart—to *be* all God intended me to be—that I never stopped reaching. I stumbled and fell, skinned my knees plenty, but I always got up and with an open, trusting heart, tried again.

Today, I know I am enough.

Gary calls me, "The little engine that could," as in the children's book by Watty Piper.

And I whisper to myself, *I think I can. I think I can.* Then my voice becomes a little louder and I say, *I think I can! I think I can!* Then louder still, *I can! I can!* Then I shout to all the heavens, *I will! I will!* Then, the voice settles back down into that still, quiet voice in the center of my being that affirms, *I am. I am.*

And so I am.

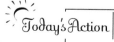 Today's Action | Affirm to yourself today that you are enough. Believe you can do or be anything at all! Reach out and pluck that shiny star from the sky. Believe you can fly!

What If God Were One Of Us?

The spiritual soil in Gary's garden, tilled with gratitude, is very rich, but it has not always been this way. One weekend, after Gary and I had been dating a few weeks, the realization hit him of how different we were. My bottom was champagne and cocaine and Gary's was shelters and soup lines.

Gary lived in a tiny efficiency that had a single, tacky velvet painting on the wall. He used plastic forks and knives, and was getting his very first driver's license at the age of thirty-four. I, on the other hand, lived in a nice apartment on Miami Beach, had oil paintings on the walls, used silverware passed down from my great-grandmother, and drove a sporty convertible.

My life looked good on the outside, and Gary did not know me well enough yet to know what gaping wounds those fixings covered up. Comparing his life to mine, Gary lost sight of how far he had come. Suddenly, he was not grateful for his first apartment in over ten years. He was not grateful to be off of drugs and turning his life around. He was not grateful for his job. In fact, he did not show up for work that Monday, Tuesday, or any day that week.

By Friday night, his night to feed the homeless in downtown Miami, Gary was angry at the world. Throwing baloney sandwiches at the men on the street, he snapped, "Get a job!"

Discouraged with his life, Gary sat down on a cardboard box where some homeless guys were hanging out.

He told them how useless he felt, how he had nothing to show for his life. As he spoke it all came pouring out, "Here I am trying to do the right thing, trying not to use drugs—but what's the use? I'll never amount to anything. In fact, I'm more at home with you guys than I am in that recovery program. Maybe I should just stay here."

A homeless man sitting a few feet behind Gary spoke up, "You know—you're all right. You keep doing what you've been doing and you'll be all right."

Gary welled up inside, much like he did the night he said "The Lord's Prayer" with a room full of strangers. But how could that be? How could a homeless man give Gary hope? How could this man who had nothing help Gary? Well, maybe that is just it—he had nothing.

All of a sudden, the efficiency did not seem as bad. Maybe he was on the right track. Maybe things would turn out all right.

The grateful heart Gary lost through comparing himself with someone who *seemed* to have more than he did was given back to him by someone who *seemed* to have less. Gary realized that there will always be people who have more than he does and people who have less. Comparing just separates people. Focusing on what you *do* have is what is important.

He went home to his cozy efficiency, with its tacky velvet painting, his heart filled with gratitude for all that was and all that was yet to be.

To this day, some ten years later, that sense of gratitude has never left Gary, not even for a moment.

Today's Action | Look around and count your blessings. List everything you are grateful for and save the list for a later date, in case the "poor me's" ever creep in.

I Can See Clearly Now

Speaking of gratitude, that reminds me of another story. One day, after Gary and I had been married a few years, we were driving home and got into an argument. Well, I count it as an argument, Gary doesn't. He's still sticking to the story that we've only had two fights the entire time we've been together. He says, "Debbie thinks we've had more, but I only count the ones I participated in." (Pretty full of himself, huh?)

Anyway, I was angry at how unavailable he was lately and went into my usual tirade, "You're always working! You never pay any attention to me! You . . ."

Gary interrupted me saying, "I think you need to get grateful."

Well! That incensed me to no end. I stormed into the house, headed straight for my bathroom, and slammed the door.

I had long been practicing a tool of journaling my anger. So I picked up my pen and reamed Gary out on paper, up one side and down the other, "Who does he think he is, that so and so! How *dare* he tell me to get grateful!"

Giving myself full permission to get it all out, I say whatever's on my mind. No holds barred. I call these my "F— You letters." I used to share them with Gary, wanting him to really *get* how mad I was. Today, although I occasionally still need to dump my anger, I no longer need to hurt him with it, so I don't share my ranting anymore.

Writing out my anger is an excellent tool for clearing it. Once the *charge* of the negative emotion is out of the way, I can deal with the situation in a more rational manner.

So, I'm sitting in my bathroom, going to town, "He's always been this way. He's always going to be this way. He'll never change and I can't take it anymore. We might as well get divorced now!"

When I'm done ranting, I try to always end these letters with something I'm grateful for about the person or situation. This keeps me from staying stuck in the negative energy. So I asked myself: *Okay, what are you grateful for?* I answer on paper, "Nothing!"

After a few minutes I wrote, "Okay, okay . . . at least he doesn't use drugs or beat me."

That was my gratitude list. At that moment, that was all the good I could see in Gary. However, at the time I was sponsoring a woman whose husband beat her and couldn't stay off drugs for the life of him. So I did have something to be grateful for.

After writing that, my perspective changed. My heart softened; I knew Gary was doing the best he could. Maybe my expectations *were* unreasonable. I began writing about all the good stuff between us. When I emerged from the bathroom, it was as a butterfly emerges from its cocoon: a completely different creature.

I hugged Gary and told him how sorry I was that I didn't notice how hard he worked at trying to please me. Then we kissed and made up—you know—the old gratitude saves the day stuff.

I think if you were to ask either of us what spiritual principle has been the key to our happiness, we would both say, "Gratitude."

Today's Action | Think of a person or situation you're angry about. Use this journaling tool to move through it. Dump your anger on paper—all of it—and leave it there. Finish by writing a gratitude list about the person or situation. Clearing your anger regularly leaves more room for joy and gratitude.

I Can't Get No Satisfaction

Ten years ago, Gary asked me to marry him. He says I asked him, but the truth is, he asked me.

In August of 1989, Gary told me he wanted to marry me, but was waiting for the right time to ask. A few weeks later, at a recovery convention, right after "The Lord's Prayer," I suggested, "Now's a good time," so he thinks I asked him. I just suggested the *when*—he did the asking.

Anyway, you would think we would be as happy as two recently engaged people could be, but we weren't. At least I wasn't.

A few weeks after our engagement, I complained about Gary to my sponsor at the time, Janie, "I don't know if I can marry him. He leaves stubble everywhere when he shaves and splashes so much water around that you'd swear you were in a birdbath. *And* he leaves the toilet seat up!" Janie listened as I went on, "Sometimes he even leaves the dishes in the sink with *food* on them, and we get *roaches*!" I was sure that would get her attention.

I was about to go on when Janie interrupted, "Debbie, I think you need to look at your history with men and ask yourself what your priorities are."

"What are you talking about?" I asked.

"Well, I've known you for quite a while now, and I've heard about your ex-husband and your old boyfriends. It seems there was always something wrong with them, never you," replied Janie.

"That's not true!" I replied, indignantly.

Janie went on, "Well, I happen to think Gary is a very special man. He is kind. He cares deeply about helping others, has a huge heart, and is handsome to boot. You are so blinded by the minutiae that you are about to let a really great guy get away!"

As she spoke of his good qualities, my heart softened and my eyes welled up with tears. "He really is a good guy, but I just can't live like this."

Janie suggested I draw a line down the center of a piece of paper. On one side I was to list all of Gary's negative traits and on the other side, list all of his positive qualities. She said that the number of qualities on either side didn't matter so much as how important I felt each was. Based on a comparison of his positive and negative traits, I was to make a decision about what was important to me. If the bad outweighed the good, I owed it to both of us to end the relationship. If, however, the good outweighed the bad, I owed it to both of us to *always* focus on his positive qualities, trusting that how Gary grew and changed was between him and God.

She reminded me that since I wasn't God and didn't know what Gary's lessons were, I needed to let go of trying to change him. Janie suggested I practice acceptance and gratitude. "Strive to accept Gary *exactly* as he is," she said. "Focus on what you are grateful for about him, rather than what you want to change."

What a concept! I had always focused on my partners' flaws. I tried to improve them—I thought for their own good. Now I realize I was selfishly trying to mold them into what I thought I wanted. If, by chance, they complied, I raised the bar and asked them to jump even higher.

In other words, I was *never* satisfied! Something was always amiss. I spent all my time and energy trying to change the other person, instead of trying to change my attitude. I'd had it wrong all those years! I thought it was *them*, and all the time it was *me*.

When you are never satisfied, bliss is elusive as a butterfly.

Well, I made the list. The good far outweighed the bad, so to the best of my ability, I have tried to practice acceptance and gratitude, always focusing on Gary's good qualities, trusting God with the rest. I fall short on a daily basis, but I keep at it.

This tool has worked in every area of my life. Whenever I need to make a decision, I draw a line down the middle of a piece of paper, weigh the pros and cons, and then make a decision. It helped me to not quit my job out of passing anger, it helped me to not buy a house that was financially way over our heads, and it has helped me in all of my personal relationships.

Satisfaction comes from adjusting myself to circumstances, not the other way around.

Today's Action | Is there any area in your life where you are dissatisfied or trying to make a decision? If so, use the inventory tool laid out above and see if it doesn't help you gain clarity.

Good Times Bad Times

Practicing gratitude came easy the first two or three years at my job. The salary was great. The yearly raises and bonuses were terrific. Twenty-five percent of my yearly income was matched into a pension plan. Insurance benefits were paid for employees and their families. Suffice to say they were very generous. Plus, I loved the work and the people I worked for.

Then things changed. The senior partner died of cancer, and one of the secretaries was suffering from a very rare form of cancer. This was the early 1990s, and many businesses were struggling with the high cost of health insurance. Our premiums increased sharply, and our firm began cutting costs. One by one, benefits declined, and salaries leveled off.

For the most part, I took it in stride, grateful to have a job and health insurance. The pension plan went from a 25 percent match to 13 percent and finally down to 2 percent. The medical reimbursement plan went south, along with our dental coverage. For a number of years that's the way it was. Two years passed with no raises. I practiced acceptance and gratitude. By the third year, it was getting a bit difficult because by now my bills were climbing noticeably higher than my salary.

At times, I felt resentful, but continued to focus on all I had instead of all I was losing. Many people left the firm for jobs with larger companies, but I stayed and by practicing acceptance and gratitude, remained quite happy.

By the fourth year, our firm recovered financially, and the future looked bright. When the partners took bonuses in the hundreds of thousands of dollars, yet neglected to give any raises to the support staff, I knew it was time for a change.

For years I had practiced "The serenity to accept the things I cannot change," but now it was necessary for my self-esteem to find "The courage to change the things I can," and ask for a raise. If they said no, it was probably time for me to move on. Although I hardly felt ready, I had practiced acceptance and gratitude long enough; it was time to bite the bullet and face my fears. I went to the senior partner and asked for the raise that I felt I deserved.

Believe it or not, I got exactly what I asked for!

Today's Action | Is there an area of your life that you need to practice acceptance in? How about an area you need to find the courage to speak up or take a stand in? Pray for the "wisdom to know the difference."

Third Month

Healing With God, Self, And Others

Instant Karma

*L*ooking back on my life, I see how the pieces fit together, how one thing had to happen exactly as it did so that something else could happen down the road. I see how each experience builds on the one before and prepares me for the next. That's how it was in the work arena.

In June 1995, not only was I faced with the possibility of losing my life, but everything else as well; I was losing my breast, my hair, my health, my savings, and sometimes my sanity. Financial fears cropped up, and I was afraid of losing my job.

When I told my law firm what I was up against, they asked what they could do. Without hesitation I said, "I need to know that my job is not in jeopardy. I have enough to deal with right now without having to worry about that." They assured me there was nothing to worry about.

I was told to take off whatever time I needed and focus on getting well. They hired someone to replace me while I was having my surgeries and chemotherapy. Salary-wise, they covered whatever disability insurance didn't, and my job was waiting for me when I returned to work seven months later.

My firm went above and beyond the call of duty, especially considering its size—four attorneys. If I had quit over my resentments the previous year, I would have missed the precious gift of time they gave me.

A friend of mine believes the way I was treated at work was a direct result of my straightening out my unfinished business with my previous employers. Over the years, I had sought out old employers whom I had stolen from, had a falling out with, or just simply been ungrateful for, and made amends to them. My friend calls it straightening out my *work karma*.

When you are right with the past, the future takes care of itself.

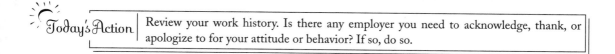

Today's Action | Review your work history. Is there any employer you need to acknowledge, thank, or apologize to for your attitude or behavior? If so, do so.

It's A Beautiful Morning

When I was so sick and didn't know how many mornings lay ahead, I listened to "Beautiful Morning" by the Rascals almost every day. I'd get into my car, put the top down, and blast the radio as I drove to the doctor's office, noticing how truly beautiful each morning was.

So many mornings, I drove to work without noticing my surroundings. Just one of millions stuck in rush-hour traffic, rolling to work. Sardines in a can. Stifled. Stuck. Then cancer struck—spinning me out of my rut.

Life is different now. I am awake. I can't take my mornings for granted anymore, thinking my life will really start when such and such happens. Life doesn't start when you retire, change jobs, find a man, or leave one. Life doesn't start when you win the lotto. Or when you get that degree, that new car, or house. It doesn't start when you have children or when they grow up and leave home. It starts right *now*!

They've already fired the starting gun. Wake up to life – *today*. *Today* is what's real. *Today* is all we have.

And oh, what a gift. Do you think Christopher Reeve would have enjoyed his last day walking more if he had known what the future held? You bet!

His accident happened the week before I was diagnosed with cancer. Watching his courage as he trudged his arduous path was all I needed to keep going. *Look what he's facing. If he can do it, so can I.* What's a little baldness in the face of breathing machines and wheelchairs?

And look at him now! Last week I saw Christopher Reeve walking on a treadmill, assisted by machines, but upright and using his leg muscles, preparing for the day when he will walk again. I believe he'll win his battle and so will I . . . so will I.

Oh, how almost losing it makes you treasure this precious gift of life. Damn the hair! To heck with the lopsided body! I'm alive. I can breathe and take in some clean fresh air!

It's a beautiful morning.

80

Today's Action | Look around as you go through your day. Look with fresh eyes. See everything as if you were seeing it for the very first time. Drive a different route. Take public transportation. Walk, savoring the sights, sounds, and treasures around you.

Carry On My Wayward Son

Letting your heart sing entails facing fears, such as those I walked through about my health, my mortality, standing up for myself at work, dealing with financial obstacles, and embracing my ever-changing body.

At times, life seems to be a never-ending series of challenges. But as long as we are restricted by our fears, we aren't living as our Creator intended.

It takes great courage to live authentically. Some of that courage comes from facing and healing our past. Any areas we are blocked in today are tied directly to our past. Everything is connected.

That's why I had issues with big powerful men. They are representative of my father and my inability to take a stand with him as a young woman. Every time I heal with a person similar to my father or circumstances similar to the ones I faced with him, I heal the original wound.

Each time a healing takes place, less holds me back from all I can be. Walking through my insecurities and fears about my writing is my biggest hurdle yet. Amounting to something my father said I couldn't feels like the final frontier. My entire life has been leading up to this point. When I'm done, I'll be at peace. Oh, how I long for that.

I'm tired of working on myself. I don't want any more "issues" to crop up. I want to be well in all areas. I don't know if I'll ever get there. In fact, the longer I am alive, the less I know. But I trust in the Divine Plan.

Divine Guidance is always with me, urging me to give a copy of "Dharma" to that person or to go to this meeting tonight. Read that book. Choose this teacher. I don't even worry about choosing the right agent or publisher. I trust the right answers will come. They always do.

How will I know if it's right answer? *Truth resonates with you when you hear it.*

Divine Guidance. I wish I understood it more. I don't know how it works; I just know that when I open myself up to it, it works.

Sometimes I'm in awe of how God or Universal Energy works.

Living can be *so* cool!

Take a moment to ponder the mysteries of life: the human body, the ocean, gravity, the Universe, intuition, birth, love, death, the earth, God. It's all so incredibly awesome! In quiet reflection, appreciate the miracle of life we all are by listing ten of your strengths.

I've Got A Feeling

About a year ago, on my way home from work, I heard an announcement for an upcoming Celine Dion concert. On a whim, I called and found out the concert started at 7:30 at the West Palm Beach Amphitheater—that same night.

Although I liked Celine Dion well enough, I only knew one or two of her songs and was not a huge fan. Nevertheless, for some inexplicable reason, I *had* to be there that night.

I told Gary I wanted to go and he said, "Are you crazy? It is 6:30 right now!"

"I really want to go. Will you go with me?" I asked.

"I am not about to drive over an hour to an outdoor theater on a night that looks like rain, to a concert that is probably sold out."

Well, like I said, something came over me, so off I went.

For the first hour, everything was fine, but as I approached the exit to the Amphitheater, traffic was backed up for miles. It was already 7:45 and I was beginning to feel rather foolish as dark clouds threatened overhead.

When I finally got to the fairgrounds, it was 9:15. I ran to the ticket booth, purchased one of the last remaining tickets, wondering how much of the concert I missed. To my amazement, the concert had not even started; it was delayed due to traffic. Because I was alone, I was able to sit among the first row of concertgoers in the open seating section.

Celine's family lives in Palm Beach, so this is her home turf. Chatting with the audience and singing with such exuberance, Celine obviously enjoyed being on stage. Watching her up there living her bliss was just what I needed to find my way again.

My heart had closed tighter with each rejection of "Dharma," and I didn't think I had it in me to keep going. My dream seemed out of reach.

Amazingly, when you are out there trying, the Universe responds in the most incredible ways. Celine began singing a song she sang at the 1996 Olympics—about believing in yourself, not giving up, about finding the strength and courage to reach for the stars and follow your dreams. I had never heard the song before and have not heard it since. Even as I write this I have yet to find out the name of that song, but boy did I need to hear it that night.

Sitting there, amidst the stars, with tears streaming down my face, I realized how very much God cared about me. He found a way to let me know, one more time, not to give up. Through Celine, God showed me the look and feel of someone living her bliss. And through that song, God spoke to me, letting me know my dreams were attainable too.

I cried when I first wrote this story, and I am crying now as I type it. It blows me away to think God loves me and believes in me this much.

Not spontaneous by nature, it is unusual that I would go to a show at the last minute like that, but the feeling that came over me was so strong, I had to follow it. The Universe speaks to me whenever I am willing to listen—how do I know this? Because—"I Got A Feeling."

One more time I picked up my pen and renewed my commitment to my soul.

Miracles Out Of Nowhere

One of the best ways I know to deepen your experience of life is to open yourself to Divine Guidance through meditation. I first began practicing meditation around ten years ago with a book called *A Course in Miracles*. For about a year, I had been trying to read the book, but it was way over my head. Then, one day I opened the workbook and began doing each day's lesson. From that, I found experiential learning works best for me.

The lessons in *A Course in Miracles* are designed to tear down your old beliefs and misconceptions, helping you to see things as though seeing them for the very first time. It is a very intense experience that requires tremendous discipline, but delivers astonishing results.

Lesson 153 from the workbook section of *A Course in Miracles* says, "In my defenselessness my safety lies."

Ten years ago, I attended a Twelve-Step meeting every day at lunchtime. The meeting was five blocks from the building I worked in and normally this would have been a nice afternoon walk were it not for the lecherous men who accosted me as I hurried to my meeting, "Hey, baby, what's happening! Hey mama, where you going?" followed by the usual kiss-kiss noises or leering smirks. Because of this, the walk became a dreaded minefield through which I had to pass to get to the meeting that would bring midday peace.

Many spiritual books, including *The Course*, spoke of attracting certain negative experiences and people because they contained lessons you needed to learn. Since I was now in recovery and dressing appropriately, I couldn't understand why I attracted this kind of negative attention. Wasn't I dressed in a nice dress or business suit? Didn't I look like I had important things to attend to?

As I reflected upon the defenselessness lesson, I realized I was attracting this attention by my *manner*, not my outward appearance. I *expected* to be accosted, based on all the years I had been accosted in the past. I put on airs and defended against attacks I *knew* would be coming. I walked down Flagler Street with disdain for men, *before* they even looked at me or said a word. And I got exactly the reactions that I expected I would.

When I finally understood that *my peace lies in my defenselessness*, an internal shift occurred. Instead of prejudging men, I softened inside and smiled at them. Instead of daring them to just try and deserve my attention, I looked at them as I would my brothers. The response was astounding.

Men no longer leer at me.

Now, we smile at each other, nod, and continue about our business.

Today's Action | With what people do you defend against an expected attack, *before* it occurs? Your mother? Your boss? A co-worker? A stranger?

Next time this happens, remember *your peace lies in your defenselessness* and comes from a place of trust and love. Expect everyone you interact with to come from this high place as well and behold: you will receive nothing less.

Just Dropped In

Around seven years ago I joined a thirty-two-week workshop that was also experiential in the most rigorous sense of the word. One of the assignments was to practice meditation for twenty minutes a day. The instructions were explicit: Sit in an upright chair, arms and legs uncrossed, eyes closed and breathe in the word *peace* and breathe out the word *calm* for twenty minutes. If you open your eyes before the time is up, just notice the clock and return to your meditation for the remaining time. When other thoughts arise, just observe them with an open heart. Then, with no judgment of yourself or your thoughts, let them go. Return to breathing in *peace* and breathing out *calm* as soon as you are aware that your thoughts have strayed.

After the first week of the assignment, many people complained they were too restless to meditate. Most said they couldn't sit still for twenty minutes and that out of the entire twenty minutes maybe one minute was spent focused on peace and calm. Everyone experienced some discomfort, whether physical, mental, or emotional. No one experienced oneness with God or a great sense of connection with the Universe.

The teacher explained that the purpose of meditation is to quiet the chatter in our minds. This is not accomplished overnight. The reason we needed to *practice* meditation is because we were not proficient at it. A successful meditation is one where you commit to a certain amount of time on a regular basis and stick to it, even when your life is hectic.

The days when our mind and bodies are racing are the days we need to meditate most.

Today's Action | Begin a meditation practice if you haven't already. Focus on your breath. Connect to the Universal breath. Breathe the breath of life. Gently bring yourself back to point once you notice you've drifted.

Discontinue the cards when you feel resolved and replace them with some form of meditation. Try one of the methods I've mentioned or buy a meditation tape. Any method you choose will open you up to Divine Inspiration and Divine Guidance. Your awareness of synchronicity in the form of *Godincidences* will increase proportionally.

Peaceful, Easy Feeling

For years I meditated, twenty minutes a day, breathing in *peace*, breathing out *calm*. Rarely did anything mystical or magical happen during the actual meditation. Instead mystical and magical things began happening throughout the day, or maybe I just started noticing them.

Occasionally, I would reach complete and perfect peace during meditation and stay there a few fleeting moments. But, mostly what happened was that my overall experience of life improved. If I found myself in a stressful situation, peace and calm would kick in. If I had difficulty sleeping, I'd be lulled to sleep with thoughts of peace and calm. When my mind would gnaw on something troublesome, peace and calm would take over, smoothing out the wrinkles of my worried mind.

As much of a struggle as it was in the beginning, meditation became as much a habit as brushing my teeth, and I've never been too busy to brush my teeth. When I was too sick or tired to wanted to meditate, I did it anyway.

My health was great, little bothered me, and if something did bother me, the answers came before I knew it. I tuned in to my inner wisdom. The more I practiced meditation, the smoother things flowed. Then guess what happened? I stopped. Not all at once, but little by little.

At first, I skipped meditation only if it couldn't be helped. Then, on vacation I got completely out of my routine. Soon I took my calm and connectedness for granted. Things continued going well, and I forgot certain things were necessary for the maintenance of my spiritual condition. Without question, I became spiritually complacent. Eventually, I stopped meditating altogether.

Meditation, much like exercise, can be very difficult to get back to once you are out of the shape. Cancer, however, has a way of bringing you back to center. Within a week of diagnosis I began meditating again. I'm not as consistent as I was, and I still need to remind myself that the benefit of meditation is in the practice of it, not in the perfecting of it, but at least I have a regular practice once again.

Today's Action | Commit to meditate for a specific length of time for a specific period. For those wishing a complete change in nature and outlook, meditate for twenty minutes a day for the next sixty days. Those happy with more subtle changes, make up your own routine. Whatever method you chose, find time on a regular basis to go inward and reconnect with the Spirit.

Because You Loved Me

During the concert, Celine introduced this song by telling how her manager believed in her so much that he mortgaged his home to help launch her career and how they later fell in love and married.

As she told the story, I noticed how no one was standing by my side that night. Now, I know I was supposed to be there by myself, but at the time I could not help but think, "Gary is not supportive like Celine's husband is. He is just a bump on a log who would rather watch TV than be spontaneous and come with me to a concert at the last minute."

Not only was I down about my writing that night, but it carried over to the state of my marriage. All I could do—while Celine praised her husband—was notice how wonderful mine was not. I wanted what they had and was envious of their love.

Then as Celine began singing, a feeling came over me. Looking up at the sky, I noticed the clouds had parted, and it was a beautiful star-filled night. A breeze caressed my face, and I felt kissed. My heart welled up with emotion and my eyes filled with tears as I realized for perhaps the very first time that "I'm Everything I Am Because *God* Loved Me."

I silently sang the words to God.

"For all those times you stood by me

For all the truth that you made me see

For all the joy you brought to my life

For all the wrongs that you made right

For every dream you made come true

For all the love I found in you

I'll be forever thankful

You're the one who held me up

Never let me fall

You're the one who saw me through

Through it all

You were my strength when I was weak

You were my voice when I couldn't speak

You were my eyes when I couldn't see

You saw the best there was in me

Lifted me up when I couldn't reach

You gave me faith cause you believed

I'm everything I am because you loved me"

From that night on, my relationship with God changed. I began to see God's hand in everything. My envy of Celine and her husband's love disappeared. Gary and I have our own brand of love that nothing can diminish.

Through that song, I realized where my true strength lies—in God.

Today's Action | Listen to "Because You Loved Me." Hasn't there always been an unseen Presence guiding and supporting you? That is Love in its truest form. Trust in the power of Love. Bask in it today.

Breathe . . . Breathe In The Air

Something so simple, yet so necessary: breathing. It's as necessary to life as life itself, yet we take it for granted until we see Christopher Reeve, who needs machines to help him breathe.

I am a very shallow breather by nature. This is not a good thing. It takes great awareness to remember to breathe deeply. I practice breathing from the belly, allowing my belly to expand ever so gently as I take in my next breath. Then I exhale, allowing my belly to flatten as the breath is released.

Air. We need it to breathe, and yet we never give it a second thought. Asthma suffers don't take their breaths for granted. I guess until something is threatened, we just assume it will always be there.

A woman in my cancer support group temporarily wore a bag outside of her body for waste removal. She sure appreciates the simple internal bodily functions most of us rarely notice.

Paying attention. Buddhists call it being mindful or practicing mindfulness.

Follow the breath all the way in and all the way out. See how it nourishes our organs, blood, and lungs. All the cells in our body are dependent on air for nourishment.

Breathe the breath until you are one with the breath. Then it is the breath taking the breath, not you. You are no longer. Only breath and breathing. Breathing in. Breathing out.

Just as shallow breathing is a sign of constriction, deep breathing is a sign of ease.

Many physical and emotional ailments disappear with proper breathing, but we are too rushed, too distracted. Some of us even have trouble "wasting" our time reading a page about breathing. Trust this page is here for a reason.

Follow the breath. Appreciate the wonder of air, our lungs, the gift of life. Appreciate the combination of oxygen and other elements on earth that are the exact mixture we need in order to live. The gift of breath—the gift of life—inexplicably tied together.

The saying on my refrigerator sums up this gift of life:

I asked God for all things that I might enjoy life—God gave me *life* that I might enjoy all things.

Be aware of your breath today. Notice: is your breathing shallow or deep? Are you inhaling or exhaling? Do you hold your breath when you are tense? Practice kind awareness of the *breath of life* today.

This Magic Moment

Buddhism's practice of mindfulness, kind attention to and appreciation of the moment, strengthens our connection with God and the world around us, allowing us to be more present in our own lives. Buddhists practice mindfulness as a way to deepen their experience of life. I do it for the same reason.

This morning I drank a glass of fresh-squeezed orange juice. Yesterday, Gary and I bought dozens of plump, juicy oranges. Today, he sliced while I juiced.

I thought of all the things that contributed to making the glass of juice I was enjoying. The people, trucks, planes, and materials that went into making the knife, the juicer, the cutting board, the plastic container we put the juice in, and the glass I drank from. I thought about the family-owned market that sold us the oranges, the farmer who grew them, the workers who picked them, trucks that distributed them, the mechanics who work on the trucks, and the sunlight and rain that nourished the orange tree.

So many people and processes went into making that single glass of pulpy, orange juice.

It takes a world to make a single glass of juice.

Drinking my first beverage of the day, I noticed, really noticed, what I was drinking, instead of mindlessly consuming as I usually did.

This mindful noticing is living blissfully at its purest: Aware and appreciative of the moment and all that went into making it possible.

In an instant, my heart expanded.

Today's Action
As you drink your tea, juice, or coffee, be aware of all that went into making that cup of liquid possible. Savor the aroma, the hot or cold sensations. Enjoy the taste as you roll it around in your mouth before swallowing. Notice everything. Be in the moment: fully present, mindfully appreciative.

Cheeseburger In Paradise

One of the first things that attracted Gary to me was the way I eat.

The movie *Accidental Tourist* was our first date, back in January of 1989. Gary bought buttered popcorn and then excused himself to the restroom. Waiting in the lobby, I began eating the popcorn. Not used to eating buttered popcorn, I licked my fingers after each piece. I stood waiting for Gary, popping and licking, licking and popping. Oblivious to my surroundings, I didn't notice Gary watching me. It was just the popcorn and me. I think he was hooked then and there.

Eating or doing anything with such complete abandon that you lose track of everything is another way of being fully in the moment. It is a practice of mindfulness that we rarely even notice because we are so lost in the moment. My husband teases me about the way I eat. I tell him, "There's nothing wrong with the way I eat. I eat with relish." And he says, "No, mustard."

I must admit I love eating. I love food; the taste, the texture, the sensation, the color, the aroma, everything! Food is a central theme in my family's life. "Where are we going for Mother's Day brunch?" Who's cooking Thanksgiving dinner this year?" "What restaurant do you want to go to for your birthday?"

My whole family is into food. None of us are particularly fat, although Gary kids me that he can tell my butt a mile a way. (If the truth be told, that's another thing that attracted him to me that first night.) I happen to think our society is too obsessed with thinness. I mean really, what difference is a few extra pounds going to make in the grand scheme of things? If attaining the perfect body were important to me, I wouldn't have much time to devote to this book, or any other spiritual endeavors for that matter. So I strive for good health instead of perfection.

I try to eat healthfully, but to me, enjoying what I eat is as important as what I eat. God wouldn't have made everything taste so good if we weren't supposed to enjoy it. So the next time you indulge yourself, savor the experience.

Recently I was preening in front of my husband, fishing for compliments and asked, "Don't I have a great body for a forty-year-old?" Catching my well-rounded behind as I pirouetted in my new jeans, he replied emphatically, "Yes!" Then, of course, I had to push it and ask, "And for a twenty-year-old?" Then came the silence. So I said, "Well, maybe not *great* for a twenty-year-old, but *good,* right? And he agreed. So I told Gary, "The beauty of it is that I am forty, not twenty—so I have a *great* body!"

Please allow me my denial. It wasn't that long ago, in fact it was right after my mastectomy, but before I had reconstructive surgery, that I asked Gary, "Can you tell I lost weight?" I was primping in front of the mirror wearing only a little tank top on and shorts and he looked up and replied, "Only on one side." Smart aleck. As usual—Gary won't let me get too full of myself.

Today, I know I am a healthy weight, and that's all that matters. That and what's for dinner?

Today's Action | Embrace your body today—it's the only one you have. Whatever you eat today, enjoy it! Eat with relish—or mustard. Live it up and eat well.

I Am . . . I Said

I'm 5'3", have blonde, curly hair, and a curvy figure. For years, I put a great deal of energy in to hiding these facts. I wore five-inch heels all the time. I mean all the time—on boats, at the beach, even when I got out of bed to go to the kitchen. People would say, "Get comfortable. Take your shoes off." I'd tell them I was fine, thank you very much.

From the time I was a little girl, I have always thought I was prettier when my hair was straight. My mom would take me to the beauty shop, and they would wrap my hair or I would sit under the hair dryer with my hair wrapped around huge cans. Thank God for blow dryers. Life is so much easier.

Part of the reason I always wore such high heels was because I thought they made me look slimmer. The same goes for the tight jeans I squeezed into. Christie Brinkley was my idea of perfection, and I was pretty far off the mark.

Then, one little book changed my entire view of myself. Around ten years ago, I picked up a book called *How to Raise Your Self-Esteem* by Nathaniel Branden. One of the first exercises in the book was to get naked in front of a mirror and study your body. With kind acceptance, look over every inch of your body and learn to love *all* of you.

The book's premise is that you can't change what you can't accept. Staying in denial or disgust of your body keeps you from embracing or changing it.

So off went the clothes and naked I stood: short, chunky thighs, curly hair, and breasts not as high as I would have liked. On the other hand, I found I liked my blue green eyes, my little waist, my well-rounded breasts, and my shapely butt.

92

The message of the book was to accept the things you can't change about yourself and find the courage to change the things you can. Obviously, my height was something I had to accept and so was my hair. So I bought some sneakers and began wearing them until I felt comfortable in them. I also stopped blowing my hair straight except on special occasions just for fun. Within days, I began practicing *the irreducible minimum* in the exercise department, changing the things I could.

Today, my body is pretty much the same as it was back then—okay, so I have *one* well-rounded breast and one man-made breast, but my height and weight are about the same. You'll usually find me running around in comfortable jeans and sneakers, with my hair au natural—I am much more content with myself these days.

By accepting myself as I am, I have more time and energy to channel into more important things, such as letting my heart sing.

| Today's Action | Get naked in front of a mirror and make peace with your body—the good, the bad, and the ugly. Embrace all of you. With kind attention, accept what you cannot change; change what you can. |

Brand New Key

During the first two years of my addiction recovery, I was a bit compulsive about recovery. I went to between ten and fifteen meetings a week, read only recovery books, and listened only to speaker tapes while driving. My life became pretty one-dimensional.

My sponsor told me to "get a life." She cared deeply about me and was concerned because she saw me switching one addiction for another, albeit something healthier, but unbalanced just the same. I was given an assignment to stop reading all spiritual, personal growth, and recovery literature, to stop listening to anything but music in the car, and to go to no more than five meetings a week.

I freaked out. There was no way I could stay off drugs and booze without doing everything I was doing! I was scared out of my wits at the very thought of not going to a meeting a day. I had no idea of what to do with all that extra time. Finally, I decided it was a perfect time to get back in shape physically. I would exercise night and day until I got my old body back.

Racing to the sporting goods store, I purchased a pair of roller skates. (This was before inline skates.) I laced up my new skates and took off down the block. I did not have the roller skates on ten minutes before a tiny pebble changed the course of my life. It presented itself as insurmountable to my new skates. Agreeing, they went flying out from under me. The sidewalk obliged by serving as a nice hard surface on which to break my arm.

So much for getting in shape! Ah, the best-laid plans . . . they say if you want to make God laugh—tell him your plans. Obviously, there was another plan for me than the one I chose.

Three things came out of this experience. First, I began getting comfortable in my own skin. I slowed down and began enjoying music again. It had been two years since I had even turned on the radio in my car; if I couldn't learn from it, I wasn't interested. Now, with this change of pace, I realized there is so much more to personal growth than cramming knowledge into my brain.

Second, for lack of something better to do, I went back to school and finished my degree. I had quit college years earlier after earning many F's and incompletes as a teenager. After a fourteen-year hiatus, I signed up for night courses at the local junior college. This did amazing things for my self-esteem. *And* it renewed my love of writing.

94

Lastly, I learned about balance. First you need it to skate. But more importantly, you need it to live a well-rounded life. Whether your main endeavor is your career, your education, a recovery program, your church, or your family—there needs to be some kind of balance between the emotional, the physical, and the spiritual. It doesn't serve to excel in one area to the exclusion of all others. I learned this the hard way. All it took was one little pebble. The ripple effect was incredible, and there wasn't a lake in sight!

Today's Action | Which areas of your life are out of balance? Take your brand new key and realign any areas the need balancing.

Help Yourself

After squandering so many years, it became extremely important to me to use my time wisely and be productive. For years, I tried to do the right thing, be a good person, and help others. Busy making up for lost time, I had no time left for simple pleasures such as gardening, taking a bubble bath, or walking on the beach. People needed me; I didn't have time for selfish things.

Cancer sure put things in perspective. I can't swear I got cancer due to self-neglect, but I had definitely been caring for others at my own expense.

A barren well has no water to give, and my well had run dry long ago.

The instructions that they give on airlines in case of emergency apply perfectly, "Should the oxygen mask drop down, place it securely over your own face *before* assisting others."

I can't help anyone if I don't take care of myself first.

I began saying, "No."

Cancer was the valid excuse I seemed to need. All demands on my time and energy stopped when I said, "I'm sorry, I can't . . . I have cancer."

It took a while, and I felt very guilty at first, but I finally got to the point where I could honor myself and say "no" without explanation. I guess until my life was threatened, I didn't feel worthy of putting myself first.

Through simplifying my life, I created the time and energy necessary to pursue my dreams. Just because they are *my* dreams does not make them selfish.

Today's Action | This page is your permission slip. You needn't wait any longer. You now have permission to put yourself first. It will be one of the most selfless and spiritual things you will ever do.

Heaven Is In Your Mind

There is a principle known as the magnifying effect, which states that anything you focus your attention on gets magnified.

Until ten years ago, I never stayed in a relationship, job, house, or apartment more than a few years. Once the initial bliss wore off—it was time to move on.

Now, the key to my happiness lies in focusing on what's right about something, rather than on what's wrong with it. It's my nature to want to improve myself and help others. Usually that's a good thing, but sometimes that magnifying mind of mine gravitates to what's wrong so often that I am rarely happy or satisfied. I've retrained myself for the sake of my peace of mind and happiness.

Today, I affirm, "Everything is perfect *exactly* the way it is."

My mind automatically focused on each husband, boyfriend, car, job, or apartment's glaring defects as soon as the novelty wore off. The more I focused on what was wrong, the larger the problems became.

One of two things was happening: either my picker was broken or my attitude was the saboteur.

I suffered from the "grass is always greener" syndrome. It was my *vision* that was off, not reality. If I focus on all the reasons why my job sucks, soon I'll be convinced that there is no alternative but to be miserable or quit. The same goes for relationships. Every man I was ever in a relationship with was fine, until I held him up to my wonderful magnifying mind.

By the time I was thirty, the patterns were repetitive enough even for me to see. So I started with that job and that man over ten years ago and began focusing on what was right with them instead of what still needed changing.

Today, I think I have the best husband in the world and a terrific job. Nothing is perfect, but if I do my part and focus on the positive, things seem to get better on their own accord.

I don't know about you, but I happen to enjoy looking at the world through rose-colored glasses.

| Make a list of the positive qualities about a person in your life that you would like to change. Then, make a decision to focus on those good qualities. Do the same for any person, place, thing, or situation that you wish were different than it is.
Change the tint of your glasses by focusing on the positive.

Before You Accuse Me . . . Take A Look At Yourself

Often, I'm so busy focusing on where others need to change that I can't see where *I* might need to change. In fact, any time I am overly focused on changing another person or wishing they were different, it's a sure sign that I need look within myself. Usually, the very thing that bothers me about another person is the exact area I need to address myself. This principle is known as the mirror effect.

A few years ago, I was complaining to my Aunt Bobbie about Gary. She asked what specifically I was upset about. I was only too happy to tell a willing listener, "First, I don't think Gary works his recovery program the way he should. At this pace he'll never change. Second, he doesn't help me around the house like he should. I'm always picking up after him. And last, he's not as affectionate as I would like him to be."

My aunt asked if I was where I wanted to be spiritually or did I still have room to grow? As soon as the question left her lips, I knew the answer. I wasn't meditating or praying as much as I would have liked, and I certainly still had control issues. Then she asked if I was happy with the way I kept house. In all honesty, it's both our belongings I pick up, not just Gary's.

By now I could see where my aunt was heading with all this, so I jumped in and said, "*I'm* very affectionate with Gary, so that's an area only *he* has to work on!"

My very wise aunt said, "Showing affection is obviously a way Gary can show love to you, in a way that means love to you, but do you show love to Gary, in a way than means love to *him*? Maybe there is another way he would like you to demonstrate your love for him."

Busted! Gary often complained that I didn't cook for him as much as I used to. Cooking was one of the things that went out the window when I went back to school. We were both leading such busy lives that we usually fended for ourselves for dinner.

Explaining the mirror effect further, my aunt said that any person or situation that upset me was a gift—a mirror held up to me of an area *I* needed to work on.

Then, she asked, "Do you sometimes see a person's faults and they don't bother you?"

"Of course," I responded.

"When your side of the street is taken care of, what other people do, or don't do, won't bother you. It's only when you need to take a deeper look at yourself that other people's behavior will annoy you," my aunt finished.

"Ah ha . . . I get it. *You spot it, you got it!*" I exclaimed.

Today's Action | Pick three characteristics or behaviors about other people that annoy you. Take a second look. See if, in fact, you could use some work in those same areas. The circumstances may be different, but the underlying issue will probably be the same. By looking at others in this light, you will gain the insight you need to get back on track with the focus on yourself.

In Your Eyes

After that conversation with my aunt, I focused on myself more and saw what needed changing in me, instead of where Gary was falling short. Praying and meditating regularly helped me feel good about my own recovery program. I picked up after myself a few minutes every day instead of letting the dishes and clothes pile up. Gary followed suit without my saying a word.

Next, I started fixing dinner a couple of nights a week. Gary did not become Romeo over night, but he was very appreciative and it showed.

Taking a long hard look at his past, I saw just how far he had come. Maybe he didn't do everything exactly as I would, but he was doing just fine. After all, he's not supposed to be a carbon copy of me.

Besides, I have enough work to do on myself to last a lifetime. I sure don't need to be worrying about whether someone else is growing as quickly as I think they should. They have their own lessons and their own Higher Power to guide them. In fact, God's plan for them might be to be a mirror in my life until I see my defects reflected and get busy with my own work.

For years, I only thought of the mirror effect as a negative reflection, until one day a woman came up to me and said how much she admired my courage. She went on to say how much she liked the way I spoke and how she felt a little intimidated by me and wished she could be more like me. I was taken back by her honesty and replied, "Everything you see in me is in you. If not, you wouldn't recognize it." It never dawned on her that she possessed the very qualities she admired in me. Her face lit up as she saw the beauty of the mirror effect. Then she gave me a big hug and we parted with our hearts filled.

As you read these pages, know that anything that resonates strongly with you, one way or the other, is a result of the mirror effect. We are all simply here to reflect light and clarity for one another.

Today's Action | Pick three characteristics you admire in other people and see how you embody those same wonderful qualities.

Right Or Wrong

Lack of forgiveness is the single greatest block to living blissfully. Whether asking for forgiveness, forgiving another person, or forgiving myself—forgiveness is a cool aloe on fresh wounds, healing ever so gently. The older the wound, the longer the healing takes. However, to truly live authentically, we must find the courage to say I'm sorry, right our wrongs, and finish any unfinished business.

My aunt, Bobbie, the one I think is so wise and wonderful, and I had a falling out over money a few years ago. I made a suggestion regarding a family trust fund that my aunt took offense to, and we said some hurtful things to each other. The bond of love and trust was broken by the incident. Our relationship was quite strained for a number of months.

We had never had a falling out before, and pride kept either of us from giving way. My sponsor suggested I write a letter to myself as if it were from my aunt. She said, "Start with, 'Dear Debbie,' and try to see the situation through your aunt's eyes, feel from *her* heart, and think from *her* mind."

This was a difficult suggestion to take. It meant I would have to give up being right. One of my less noble qualities is self-righteousness. When I think I'm right, I can be very stubborn. My favorite saying when I don't want to give in is, "It's the principle!"

As much as I did not want to do this, I have learned from previous conflicts, "It's not *who's right*, but *what's right*." And what's right is that a healing take place. It doesn't matter who initiates the healing as long as someone does.

After days of dumping my anger, hurt, and self-righteousness in my journal, I began my letter to myself. I meditated first to open my heart to hers. What happened next was incredible. I was able to rise above my own thoughts and feelings and see into her heart. By the close of the letter, my entire view of the situation had shifted. I could see how *my* words had hurt *her*. And I could see what her fears and concerns were. Through pen and paper my aunt's heart spoke to mine. My walls crumbled and my heart opened. It was enlightening, to say the least.

The next time my aunt and I saw each other, I was able to come from love instead of righteous indignation. I was able to extend an olive branch, and today we have a loving relationship once again.

Today's Action | Have you had a falling out with someone recently? Who came to mind as you read this page? Search your heart and you will know who your letter needs to be from. Open your heart to this forgiveness exercise and allow its healing balm into your life.

From This Moment On

A number of years ago, I heard a man share that he took his grandmother for granted. It was her birthday, and all she wanted to do was spend a little time with him, but he was too busy. In fact, he rarely even remembered when her birthday was. I immediately thought, "I know exactly when my grandmother's birthday is—February 18." Then I realized I didn't have a clue as to when my grandfather's *second* wife Betty's birthday was, and she had been my grandmother for over thirty years!

To make matters worse, my brothers and I are Betty's only grandchildren. I felt horrible about being so neglectful and wanted to make it up to her very much. I vowed to find out when her birthday was and to always remember it.

For her upcoming birthday, I painted an ocean scene using Betty's favorite colors of peach and aqua. It was the first painting I created with someone specific in mind and love in my heart. I had it nicely framed and it now hangs in my grandparents' living room. Then my mother and I took Betty and my grandfather, Hewitt, out to dinner for Betty's birthday. It was the first time we celebrated her birthday as a family. I'm sure she was delighted with all the attention, and it felt wonderful to be a part of making her feel so special.

Ten years have passed and I have never forgotten Betty's birthday—May 15. More recently I gave Betty a coffee-table book of Dan Marino and my mother and I gave her a watercolor painting of him—because she loves her Miami Dolphins—Dan in particular. Four years ago, Betty's family came from all over the country and had a huge eightieth birthday celebration for her, which I know she just loved.

Another way I tried to be a better granddaughter was when my grandfather died. For months after Hewitt's death, I spent Monday evenings with Betty, keeping her company. Initially, we talked a lot, but after a few months we settled into a quieter routine with Betty doing her needlepoint and me reading magazines. It may not have been much, but I hold those visits dear to me and I think Betty does too.

It took a while for me to understand how my lack of action could harm another person, but now when we celebrate Betty's birthdays, I see not only the joy it brings her, but I think of all the lost moments we could have had.

Reflecting on this makes me realize how important it is to treasure our loved ones while they are still alive.

101

 **Today's Action** | Is there someone you care about who you've been a bit neglectful of? Think of meaningful ways you could show them you love them, then do so.

Thank You

In my haste to straighten out my past, I neglected looking at anything but the most blatant harms. The more subtle harms, such as not knowing my grandmother's birthday, took a while. One such harm became apparent one day as I was walking down Flagler Street in downtown Miami and ran into one of my old bosses.

He was heading to the courthouse with another attorney from my old firm when we ran smack-dab into each other. I said, "Hello," to both, but only the associate partner replied. Ed, the senior partner, stood off to the side waiting for us to finish talking. I had worked for this man for over four years, and it had only been a couple of years since he had last seen me, so he certainly knew who I was.

When we parted company, it felt as if I had been slapped. My hurt and embarrassment quickly turned into righteous indignation, until I realized how hurt or angry he must have been to ignore me that way.

A few weeks later, I got up the nerve to call Ed. I asked if we could get to together to talk. He's a busy man, and I assumed we'd make an appointment for sometime in the distant future—like next year.

"Come on over now," he barked into the phone.

Ed has always reminded me of my father. Both were very large, powerful men who loved hunting and fishing and had a nasty flair for sarcasm. Of course all my scared little girl stuff kicked up, but I knew the sooner I faced him the better, so off I went.

My intentions were to apologize for the kind of employee I had been, give him a check for the money and office supplies I had pilfered or stolen over the years, and be done with it.

As I drove up to the building, I realized he probably didn't know or care about the things I had taken. So what was upsetting him? I had no idea. Shaking in my boots, I prayed for guidance. I desperately needed more power and courage than I possessed at that moment.

Entering Ed's office, I sat down, pushed a check face-down across his desk. I explained how I had taken things that weren't mine and was there to make restitution. Without looking at the check, Ed sat in stony silence, arms folded across his chest.

All of a sudden, it came to me. When I hit my bottom on cocaine and alcohol, Ed offered to pay for my treatment if insurance wouldn't cover it. I declined, explaining that I couldn't pay my bills if I went into a twenty-eight-day treatment program.

This big, gruff man, sitting across from me, had not only offered to pay for my treatment, but all of my personal bills as well. I declined his offer and never said so much as, "Thank you." Out of shame and embarrassment, I left the job soon afterward.

In an instant my wrong became clear. Tears welled up in my eyes and I thanked him from the bottom of my heart for being there for me in my time of need. As I expressed my gratitude for his magnanimous gesture, he softened.

Then this huge, grizzly bear of a man stood up and with outstretched arms accepted my apology, hugging me as I haven't been hugged since my father died.

Now, I can walk down the street with my head held high, knowing I no longer need to hang my head in shame. Not only do we say, "Hello," when we run into each other, but I leave with a smile in my heart and a warm feeling all over.

I learned it is not so much the outward harm we do to others that injures so much as the kindness and openhearted gestures we take for granted.

☀ Today's Action | Is there anyone you have neglected to acknowledge or thank? Who have you taken for granted? Seek them out—pick up the pen, the phone, or get in the car—and express what has long been left unsaid.

I Say A Little Prayer

The receptionist I worked with, after I left Ed's office, hated my guts. She slammed the phone in my ear when transferring calls, threw the mail into my inbox, and ignored me whenever I said hello or goodbye. At first I thought it was me, then I saw that she acted this way toward most everyone in the office. However, it did seem to escalate where I was concerned. I tried to turn the other cheek, but her actions were so outwardly hostile that it was very hard to do. Our conversations and interactions went round and round in my head, long after they were over.

My sponsor told me I was letting her live rent-free in my head and suggested I write how we were alike. Insulted, I replied, "I am nothing like her!" After obsessing on this woman's behavior for another three days, I became willing to write.

Grumbling about the suggestion and the person who gave it to me, I angrily listed the receptionist's faults, "She's materialistic, she gossips, she's oversensitive, she's self-centered, and she ignores me even though she has to sign me in and out every day." Halfway through my ranting, my vision shifted, and I began to see how, at times, *I* was materialistic, how *I* spoke about others behind their backs, and how *I* could be easily hurt, too. And there were definitely times *I* thought the world revolved around me or, at least, should. And *I* certainly ignored people I didn't want anything to do with. One more time the mirror effect rang true.

After getting all the "energy" of my negative emotions out through writing, I prayed for the willingness to take the next step in the healing process. Sometimes I thought:

She's the bitch, why do I have to do all of the work? But the bottom line was that I liked my job and didn't like having an uncomfortable work environment, so it was my responsibility to change it.

The deciding moment came when my co-workers were going to lunch one day and invited me to join them. The receptionist put her purse down on the table, motioned at me, and said, "If she goes, I'm not going." That statement showed me unequivocally that this was not in my head. After that I tried to see things from her perspective. I went back to when it all began and asked myself, "What part did I play in this?" It became apparent that it started when I stopped going to happy hour with her because I was trying to quit drinking.

Obviously she was hurt and took it personally. When I saw the hurt, my heart softened and I began praying for her. This was the next step in the healing process, which at times seemed like inaction; I wanted to *do* something to fix things. But I was told an internal change had to take place in me *before* I could take any outward action. It was suggested that I pray for her to receive double of everything that I wanted in my own life. And no, I couldn't wish to be blind in one eye.

I prayed for abundance, prosperity, loving relationships, personal and spiritual growth, happiness, and peace of mind to come into her life. I prayed that all her wishes come true. I did this daily for weeks, and then specifically whenever I felt tensions rise between us.

Accepting that she was the way she was, I began looking at her with kind eyes and an open heart. It took time. Our difficulties began in June, only weeks after I started working there. Every morning I said, "Hello," and every night I said, "Goodnight," regardless of her lack of response.

For six months, I treated her as I would like to be treated. Many times, I wanted to say, "To heck with this. She's just too pissed off to ever reach," but I kept at it.

On Thanksgiving weekend, she wished me "Happy Thanksgiving" as I was leaving the office. I almost had a heart attack. It was the first civil thing she had said to me five months. I knew at this moment, she was a gift in my life, teaching me to rise above and work through conflict no matter how difficult. She taught me that even when people come from fear and anger, I can respond with love and kindness.

We developed a relationship that lasted for years after she left our firm. One day we even talked about our early difficulties and she confided in me that she had felt rejected when I stopped going to lunch with her so that I could go to my meetings. She also couldn't understand why I couldn't go to happy hour with her and just have a soda. I apologized for inadvertently hurting her and tried to explain why I needed to do what I did. I don't know if she ever really understood, but she did accept my apology.

Me, I still work at the same firm, and a few years later I had another opportunity to practice spiritual principles with a woman who was even angrier than the receptionist was. Kindness and open-heartedness won out again, and I was able to be a light in her life and she a gift in mine.

Across The Universe

With cancer came the desire to reconnect with people from my past, partly for nostalgic reasons and partly to finish unfinished business.

Repairing broken relationships was something I had been working on for the previous six years. However, I had been unable to locate three people I had harmed.

The first, Pixie, was my best friend from the time I was three until I was in my late teens. Then there was, Lynn, who I was friends with briefly when I was nineteen and living in California. And the last person was Joanie, a friend I played backgammon with for a number of years. Finding them was not easy. I didn't even remember Lynn or Joanie's last names, and Pixie (Teri is her real name) wasn't listed under her maiden or married name, leaving me with no idea of how to find any of them.

It's funny how a life-threatening illness can bring a sense of urgency to resolving conflicts. Once I began brainstorming ways to find them, the Universe responded in astounding ways. While driving on the expressway one day, I heard the name "Boyd." Then I remembered that was the last name of the couple who ran the backgammon tournaments some twenty years ago where Joanie and I met. On a whim I checked on the Internet, found a local number, called it, left my name and who I was looking for on their answering machine. Later, the man who led the backgammon tournaments so many years ago called me with Joanie's mother's phone number. He also gave me the phone number of an old boyfriend of mine who had been friends with Lynn's old boyfriend.

After speaking to her mother, I called Joanie the next day. The last time we had spoken was over eighteen years before when I drove with her to her new apartment in New Jersey. At the last minute I refused to stay with her through New Year's Eve as I had promised. We got into a huge fight over it, but I was insistent about getting back to Miami. I didn't seem to care that I would be leaving my friend all alone in a new state on New Year's Eve. I left her apartment in a huff, took a taxi to the airport, and never saw her again.

I recognized her voice as soon as she answered the phone. With a trembling voice, I said my name and asked if she remembered me. After a long pause, she said, "Yes."

I swallowed hard and proceeded to tell her that I was calling because I still felt bad about the way things ended between us. She listened without saying much as I apologized for being such a lousy friend. As the conversation continued, she softened a little and not only accepted my apology, but filled me in on some unpleasant details I had forgotten. One night, when we were partying at Turnberry Isle with Rod Stewart, a waitress accidentally banged into Joanie with a tray full of drinks. Joanie thought she broke her nose and asked me to take her to the hospital. I refused, telling her it was probably nothing (I wasn't about to leave *Rod Stewart*). She drove herself to the hospital and, as it turns out, she *had* broken her nose.

We reminisced a bit more and by the time we got off the phone, Joanie thanked me profusely for calling her. She said she had been having one of the worst days of her life when I called. But after talking to me, her perspective changed. Now, she was filled with gratitude.

We made plans to see each other later that year when she visited her family in Florida. We had such a wonderful time catching up on each other's lives. I can't tell you how much it warms my heart to mend this fence and have my old friend back in my life.

Today's Action | Who comes to mind as you read this story? Is there anyone from long ago that you had a falling out with and need to make amends to? Pray about it. Then put it out into the Universe, setting a Divine Energy into motion. Be open to what your next step is to be.

I Gotta Try

The next amends didn't go as well. When I was nineteen I went to Los Angeles. After burning out from my stay at the Playboy Mansion, I ran into Lynn, whom I had known through our boyfriends back in South Florida. We decided to get an apartment together and when it was time to decide on a one or two bedroom and give a deposit, Lynn asked if I was staying in California for sure. I told her yes and at the time meant it, but changed my mind a few days later and went back to Miami. She probably got stuck for the rent on the larger apartment or lost her deposit altogether. As much as I hate to admit it, after leaving town, I never spoke with her again.

Facing my mortality brought back haunting memories of behavior such as this that I would just as soon have forgotten. But when the memories came up, I trusted it was for a reason. So after finding Joanie through mutual friends, I thought maybe I could find Lynn through our old boyfriends. I called my old boyfriend, and he gave me Lynn's old boyfriend's last name and suggested that maybe they had kept in touch or that at least he would know her last name.

I went back to my trusty resources on the Internet and found her old boyfriend. I called him and told him why I wanted to find Lynn, and asked if he knew her last name. He laughingly said, "Yes, I know her last name," and repeated his own. As it turns out, she had come back to Florida, gotten back together with him, and they have been married ever since. He gave me his wife's work phone number, which I promptly called, but she had stepped out. She returned my call that afternoon, but I was out and missed her call. I called a few more times that week, but she didn't return any more of my calls. I guess after talking to her husband and finding out why I was calling, she decided she didn't want to speak to me.

At some point I had to accept that Lynn did not want to speak to me. I wrote her a letter of apology and offered to repay any money she was out as a result of my taking off as I did and sent it to her husband's office. I never heard back from her. Obviously, not all things can be righted. However, my willingness to make every effort to amend the situation was all that was necessary for my release. And released I was—from my own guilt and shame.

Today's Action | Did anyone come to mind with this story—anyone you need to straighten things out with? Or is there someone you have tried to reach and been unable to get through to? As with all healings, remember: do the footwork and trust the outcome to God.

My Second Home

Each time I make peace with someone, a weight is lifted, increasing my sense of completion. The amount of joy in my life is proportionate to this ever-increasing sense of peace in my life.

The next amends story is my favorite, even though it is not yet complete.

I met the first member of the Rhoades family, Butchie, when I was three years old. My older brother and I were trying out my new tricycle and literally bumped into Butchie as we turned the corner. He told me he had a new little sister, named Pixie, and we could come back to his house to see her if we wanted. We did and I remember feeling very welcomed in their home. As Pixie and I grew up we became fast friends even though we were a few years apart. (I also had a crush on Butchie from the day I met him.)

Pixie collected glass cats and cat figurines. Tiny cat families of all colors and sizes were arranged on her shelves. I followed in her footsteps, collecting many of the same ones. One day she bought a family of little glass calico cats and when I went to the store to buy a set like hers, they were sold out. I spent the night at her house soon afterward and took the calico cat family. She came to my house a few weeks later, saw her glass cats on my shelf, and accused me of stealing them. Indignant, I said, "I did not!" We got into a huge fight over them—kicking, screaming, biting, and pulling hair—that ended with me throwing the cats at her saying, "You can have them if you want them that bad!" acting as if I were the one betrayed.

Lying and stealing from my best friend was the first real harm I ever inflicted on anyone, but my hurting Pixie didn't end there. As a teenager I spent many a night at Pixie's house, as much as I could, really: partly to get away from my stepfather and partly because I loved being at her house. Pixie's mom, Joanne, was like a second mom to me. She didn't work, so she was always around, and she seemed to really enjoy having me there. I spent more time at their house than in my own during my teen years.

Butchie grew up and insisted we call him by his real name, Ronnie. My feelings for him increased and he became my first love. I would spend the night with Pixie and sneak downstairs to be with him. When she got wind of this, she accused me of wanting to be with him more than her and of using her to get to him. She and I had another fight and drifted apart. We saw each other a few times over the years, but things were never the same. Then Pixie married and moved to Hawaii. I last saw her when she came back for a visit—she was in her late teens and I was in my early twenties. Soon afterward, her parents divorced and moved out of South Florida; Pixie and I lost touch completely.

My heart ached for my best friend and the family I had once felt more comfortable with than my own. The last time I saw any of them was in 1980. Over the years, I tried to locate Pixie through directory assistance, the Internet, and even had someone look for her in Hawaii, all to no avail. After this many years, I had all but given up hope. When the cancer came along, I redoubled my efforts and found Pixie's father on the Internet.

I was so nervous when I placed the call—just hearing his voice on his answering machine made my heart skip a beat. I sucked in my breath and left a message for him to please call me with Pixie's number. A week went by with no word. I knew I was a little hellion as a teenager, but hadn't thought he would hold it against me for this long.

It turns out he was out of town. As soon as he got back he called with Pixie's new married name and phone number in Maui. I took another deep breath and dialed her number before I lost my nerve. She answered right away, but I didn't recognize her voice. She is in her late thirties now and I hadn't heard her voice since she was eighteen. She told me she and her mom were just talking about me, wondering whatever happened to me.

We've been in touch for over a year now and my husband and I visited her mom and Ronnie for the first time in nearly twenty years last summer on our way to Kentucky. It was a homecoming of sorts. I recovered a piece of my soul when I rekindled my relationship with my childhood friend and her family; I feel whole again. It was well worth the risk and the fear.

One of my biggest regrets, when I thought I might not live much longer, was that I had never been to Hawaii or seen its magnificent waterfalls. Now I have another compelling reason to go.

Today's Action | Are there any friends you've lost touch with that you would like to rekindle your relationship with? Go into your heart and see what action can be taken to recover the pieces of your soul through reconnecting with your past.

Love Will Find A Way

Letting your heart sing is not only about one dream and finding the courage to live it. It is a whole way of life.

From the moment you wake up, you are ready for the day. There is a joyful expectancy and curious wonder about what the day might hold. A sense of adventure permeates your whole being. A childlike love of life guides your thoughts, feelings, and actions.

You have made peace with your past and are content with your present circumstances—not content as in settling for something, but deep contentment—where you know you have made the right choices. You are happy to be exactly where you are. Lastly, you are excited about the challenges and surprises that lie ahead.

Living from the heart means you leave this life with no regrets. When it is your turn to go, you know that you did not shrink in the face of fear or adversity. You lived up to your highest potential.

When cancer struck, my four biggest regrets were: my writing, that illusive Hawaiian vacation, broken relationships, and that I rarely found time for something I once loved—the ocean.

Today, for me to have a sense of peace and completeness about my life, I need to be walking through my fears, living my dreams, bringing more love into my heart, and more joy into my day-to-day life.

Today, I write daily and envision myself earning a living as a writer within three years, yet, I am okay with whatever God's will is for me. I show up and do the footwork; the results are out of my hands. I write, trusting this book will be published . . . if it is God's will.

Today, Gary and I have a "Hawaii" savings account and are each putting twenty-five dollars a week in it. We also put all of our living expenses on a frequent flyer credit card. Each trip to the grocery brings us closer to our trip to Hawaii. Our goal is to go to Hawaii within the next two years. I have wanted to go to Hawaii for at least twenty years; for some reason it has always seemed out of reach. Not anymore. I will do whatever it takes to make this dream a reality.

Today, I no longer take the ocean for granted. In fact, I walk on the beach at least once a week and absolutely love it.

All that is left is relationships.

Having located and made amends to three childhood friends: Joanie, Lynn, and Pixie, I cannot think of any relationships that still need repairing. Ah-ha, that is a lie—there is one more: my great aunt, whom we call Fi (pronounced Fee) or Aunt Fi. I have not seen my Aunt Fi or her son, Dean, in over three years. I guess it is time to seek them out.

Get Together

Personally, I don't have any beefs with my Aunt Fi, but she has not spoken with her sister, my grandmother, Jackie, or my mother in over twenty years. How sad. Both my mother and my grandmother have approached Fi and tried to discuss things in a civilized manner, but Fi rages at them and won't hear of it. She ignores my grandmother, *her own sister*, if they run into each other in a store or restaurant. I am not even allowed to mention my mother's or grandmother's name to my Aunt Fi.

I usually visit my aunt once a year during the holidays. We catch up on irrelevant details of each other's lives, while there's this huge hole in our family that we can't even discuss. Four years ago, on Christmas Day, my aunt said such nasty things about my mother and grandmother that I left and never returned.

The family feud had finally carried over to the third generation as both my brothers and I stopped talking to Aunt Fi and her son. First, it just seemed we were all too busy. Then, I realized that subconsciously I did not want contact with anyone who spoke so venomously about my mother and grandmother.

Thinking back, I can only remember good times at Aunt Fi's house. She had a huge barbecue pit in her back yard. Most weekends we grilled hamburgers and hot dogs and ate her famous baked beans in the backyard picnic area. Then the kids ate watermelon and took turns riding in my cousin's go-kart, while the adults played cards and listened to my uncle play the piano. They were fun times.

Then, when my great-grandmother, Gammy, retired from teaching, she moved in with my Aunt Fi. Things were fine for a few years, and then Gammy came down with colon cancer and needed more care. The family took turns at first. Then came the arguments about how to best care for Gammy and who should pay. No one could agree on anything, especially whether or not to put her in a nursing home. Eventually, the inevitable happened and Gammy was placed in a nursing home.

The last few birthdays and Christmases of her life were sad. All Gammy said was, "I don't want any presents. All I want is peace in the family." Try as I did, I could not grant her this last wish.

I was nineteen when Gammy died. The gap widened, as fighting over money—a lousy five or ten thousand dollars—severed all relationships between my great-aunt and my grandmother and mother.

As I write this, tremendous sadness sweeps over me; I feel powerless to do anything about this family riff. Don't people understand how important family is? Don't they realize that we won't live forever? Don't they know that what Lillian Hellman said was true, "The bitterest tears shed over graves are for words left unsaid and deeds left undone?"

I miss my family and want it whole again.

Butterfly Kisses

Man or woman alike, didn't you just cry when you first heard Bob Carlyle sing "Butterfly Kisses"? This father captured the love between a parent and a child so beautifully. In an instant you realize how much the little things mean, how quickly children grow, and how soon they leave home.

I don't even have children and I cried. I probably cried more because I don't have children. I'll never experience the goodnight prayers and kisses, or the tugs, "Come here. Do this with me," or "I'm too old for that now," and the heartache that comes when they leave the nest.

Please don't feel sad for me, just notice the gift you *do* have. The kids will be gone before you know it or perhaps they already are. Do you treasure them? I hope so.

My niece, Sarah Hope, is seven years old. I adore her, but she lives in Kentucky, so I only get to see her once or twice a year. We talk on the phone, though, and send cards and letters. We even e-mail each other; I gave them my old computer so we could. (Actually, e-mail brought me closer to my sister-in-law, and that's a relationship I truly treasure.)

My best friend, Janis, just adopted a baby girl from China, and I saw her daughter for the first time a few days ago. She is just precious. Now, I know, without a doubt that I would have bonded with an adopted child just fine. I guess I was just too fearful.

For the most part, I'm happy with the way things turned out. But there is so much I'll miss that I'm sure most parents take for granted. Don't.

Perfect

I never thought of myself as a perfectionist, but the longer I wanted to write and didn't, the more I realize that perfectionism was the reason behind my paralysis. Writer's block didn't seem like the right word because I was never at a loss for words, but something kept me from writing nonetheless.

Having a dream, believing it is from God, and then not acting upon it is as painful a place to be as I've ever experienced. But once I fleshed out *why* I wasn't following my heart, the *how* of it fell into place. What terrified me about writing was being locked into something *permanently*. My fear was that once something was committed to paper and actually published, I couldn't go back and improve it, perfect it, or change my mind. It was done and that was that. The finality of it scared me. The perfectionist in me was freaking out, and I hadn't even picked up a pen yet! Then I heard someone say, "Every book, painting, and song—every work of art—is a work in progress. At some point the artist just decided to stop."

Nothing is ever really complete. Life is always evolving, and our view of things is constantly changing. Now, everything I write is from the perspective I have at that moment, not the one I will have in five years. How freeing.

I recently talked with a man who has been working on the same book for twelve years and another who has been working on and off for twenty years on his book. Both are caught up in the editing of their work—making sure all of the punctuation, spelling, and grammar is *perfect*. The problem with that is that art is subjective. Sure, there are some rules, but a lot of things fly that are not necessarily perfect or the norm. I think the best creations are when someone dares to put their heart into it. When that occurs, it's so moving—no one even notices whether it's perfect or not.

I was always waiting for the perfect situation to arise in which to write. I thought I had to wait until I had enough money to retire or work part-time to be able to write. And I was sure I couldn't write for a living because I wasn't disciplined enough. Well, I've proven myself wrong—I've been writing along side my day job for years now. I guess I *can* do anything I set my mind to. The key is moving beyond my *own* mind and tapping into the Universal Mind.

I write first thing in the morning, right after meditating, when I am in a right-brain, creative state. I write as fast as I can to stay ahead of the perfectionist within. When I'm in this right-brain state, I don't worry about spelling, punctuation, or grammar—that comes later—I just open my heart and write. Most important, I keep moving.

Today's Action | Is perfectionism keeping you from starting, working on, or completing something you enjoy? If so, take some action toward your goal today. Any action will do. If nothing specific comes to mind, do something you've never done before, just for practice.

I'm Only Human

Last week at work, I made a couple of mistakes. I overstated the available cash to one of the partners, and we've had a tight cash-flow problem for some time now, so he wasn't too happy about that. The other mistake was not following the office manager's wishes regarding handing out payroll checks. Because of these mistakes, I have been a little fearful about losing my job. Now, I've been there over ten years, and I seriously doubt that they are going to let me go over a couple of minor mistakes!

Yet even after all these years, a little paranoia still comes out whenever I make a mistake. If they talk to the man I replaced ten years ago, I think my job is in jeopardy. Since he's the office manager's brother, chances are good that they will keep talking to him. The other day all three partners went to lunch together. So, of course I think they are discussing me. Some of my fears come from the fact that our firm is not doing well financially—the worst I have ever seen in my time there. But most of my fears stem from my own insecurities and my desire to be perfect. I guess I should strive for excellence, not perfection. That way, I can't lose.

I get down on myself because I thought I was beyond these unfounded fears, but the truth is, my self-doubts run deep. I never thought I could please my parents. My father had very low expectations of me, and my mother had very high ones. I seldom received the approval and validation I needed, hence my insecurities with authority figures.

Bonnie Raitt was on TV yesterday talking about her music and how wonderful it was to be acknowledged and validated for doing something you love. Well, at work, I don't get any compliments on how well I do their bookkeeping. I get nice raises and bonuses, but never any verbal validation. So I give it to myself in the form of affirmations. On the other hand, when I share from my heart through my writing, speaking, or leading a workshop, I get all the validation I'll ever need. Many people even take the time to drop me a note about how much "Dharma" touched them or how something else I wrote helped them.

Lately I've taken to saving the notes for when the internal critic says, *You can't write— what do you think you are doing?* I can say: *Thanks for sharing, but these people think differently.* No, I'm no Pulitzer Prize winner, but I *do* write from my heart, and that's what counts.

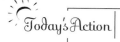

Today's Action | Save encouraging notes, letters, and e-mails, and jot down positive feedback others give you. Reflect on them whenever you need a little encouragement.

Hurting Each Other

Two couples I know are getting divorced. I hate hearing news like this. Why can't we be more loving, especially with the people we care about?

One husband poured his heart out to me about how critical his wife was; nothing he did was ever good enough. He felt like a failure. He said it was as if he were living with his mother again. As much as he hated leaving his son, he just couldn't take it anymore.

I had dinner with the wife of the other couple and she was in the same boat as the first man I spoke to. She felt she never measured up. Her husband wants a divorce because, as he puts it, "You're not the woman I married. You have too many issues." I know she struggles with food addiction, but for the most part, I think she is doing great. She told me he thinks she's fat. Now if she's fat, I'm a cow! And I'm certainly not a cow.

Bottom line in both relationships: unreasonable expectations. I know because I've been there. The hardest thing I ever had to do in my marriage was to accept Gary exactly as he is. Don't get me wrong, he's a great guy, but he could be better if . . . *if only he'd work less, manage money better, be more loving with me*, and on and on.

If only he did this or didn't do that. I constantly tried to control, tweak, or improve Gary, and it made both of us miserable. Finally, I stopped trying to make Gary different or even *wish* he were different and just gave him to God. My hands are full just working on me.

I heard someone say once "God doesn't make junk!" So, if I am complaining about Gary, basically I am saying to God, "You didn't get it quite right. I can do better."

Today, I believe my husband is perfect exactly as he is, flaws and all. This unconditional acceptance has been the key to our marital bliss.

116

Today's Action | Practice total acceptance, 100 percent acceptance, of the people you live with or love— your spouse, your children, your parents—everyone. As you go through your day, affirm that they are exactly the way God intended. See beyond their flaws to the God within. Repeat to yourself as you go through your day: *I lovingly allow others their own lessons.*

Hard To Say

Now that's not to say that if you are in an abusive relationship, you should stay. My first husband became verbally abusive when he drank. On occasion things turned nasty. Sometimes it was provoked, and other times it wasn't. We both abused drugs and alcohol and were clueless when it came to having a healthy relationship. As is usually the case, the verbal and physical abuse escalated.

It took months of planning, but eventually I saved enough money and summoned enough courage to leave. I will never forget our last fight as long as I live. He started in on me one night and wouldn't let up. It was our usual fight about money. I tried ignoring him. I asked if we could talk about it in the morning. Finally, I yelled at him to shut up already, but he just kept at it.

I tried to get to my purse or car keys so I could leave, but he wouldn't let me. I tried to get dressed, but he pulled my jeans off me. We struggled some more, and I tried calling the police, but he wouldn't let me near the phone.

Feeling trapped, I made a mad dash for it and fled, wearing only a long T-shirt and nothing else. I hid in a field of tall grass about a block away. I remember feeling like a hunted animal. When the coast was clear, I called a friend to come and get me.

We tried therapy after that, but I could never put that night behind me. Thankfully, our marriage didn't last much longer.

I cannot in good conscience put all the blame on him though; I was no picnic. In fact no one deserves to be treated the way we treated each other. The worst part was that we were both good people. We didn't plan to act the way we did, we just did.

There is a saying I hear at my Twelve-Step meetings that says, "There is no situation so bad it can't be bettered." Although I believe that's true, I am grateful my ex-husband and I split up. Today, we are both happily married to other people—so splitting up turned out to be best for both of us.

I saw my ex-husband last week for the first time in eight years. We talked for over an hour and as I was leaving, he said, "You know, I think the drinking was our downfall." How right he was. Within six months of leaving him, I got help for my substance-abuse problem, and things have been getting better ever since.

It's hard to say whether leaving is the right thing to do or not. The only thing I know for sure is that God intends for us to be happy. So we must be courageous enough to do whatever it takes, whether that means acceptance *or action*.

☼ Today's Action | Are you in a relationship in which you are not respected? Are you settling for less than you deserve? Are you in an abusive relationship or do you know someone who is? If so, get help or help your friend get help. By improving our self-esteem, we can gain enough courage to do the right thing, whatever the circumstances. Don't deny the truth. Don't enable.

Interfere. It's time we told the truth about what is going on in our homes—be it a neighbor, a co-worker, or ourselves. Lend a hand. Lend an ear. Let's stick together and support each other on this one. You can't reach for your dreams if you're dead.

Fourth Month

Discerning Your Divine Purpose

I Apologize

*J*ust as I straightened out my karma in the work environment, I also sought out my ex-boyfriends and my ex-husband to accept responsibility and apologize for my part in the demise of our relationships. Obviously it wouldn't be a good idea for me to maintain relationships with my ex-boyfriends and ex-husband, so I make amends by being the best wife I can be to Gary and by not repeating the same mistakes. I have worked hard on my attitude, on looking at the positive, on being grateful, and on remaining faithful—all things that were not my strong suit before.

Gary has done his part as well. His destructive behavior in relationships was rooted in his heroin addiction. You certainly can't keep a girlfriend long if you steal from her and her family all the time. In fact, Gary became homeless in 1981 because he stole his girlfriend's mother's silverware and was caught trying to pawn it. His girlfriend, Pam, and her family wanted nothing more to do with him. After he lost his apartment with Pam, he began sleeping in his sister's cellar near the furnace to keep warm during those cold New England nights. Eventually, he couldn't even keep it together enough to stay there and began living in abandoned buildings, sleeping in shelters, and even lived in the woods for a while.

His pattern with women was that they would rescue him, his addiction would take over, and he wouldn't be able to hold down a job. Next, came the arguing over his drug use, and the lying and stealing to support his habit. It was never too long before they would kick him out or he would split town—hardly the white-picket-fence-story of healthy relationships.

Just as I had to learn not to run home to my mother or into the arms of another man, Gary had to learn not to leave town when things got tough. We didn't have to worry too much about his stealing since he no longer had a heroin habit to support. But we both had pretty intense histories to recover from.

One of the most courageous things Gary did early on in our marriage was fly to Boston so he could make amends to Pam's mother, Lillian, for stealing her silverware. We both know that you can't go forward in good conscience until you've straightened out the past.

We went to Lillian's house, and after they reminisced a bit, I excused myself so Gary could tell her why he was there. It had been ten years since he had stolen the silver, and he had not seen her since. She was gracious enough to allow us into her home, but some things still needed repairing.

"I'm here to repay the silverware," Gary said.

"Don't worry about it. We haven't used it since you stole it," Lillian replied. They both laughed and then Gary said, "I'm here to try to make things the way they were before I did what I did. I would like to see the pattern, so I can replace the pieces I stole."

Lillian brought out the box of remaining silverware, and Gary took pictures of it. As he left her house that day, he walked just a little bit taller, for he gained back a piece of himself in the process: his self-respect.

Tracking down the pieces wasn't easy. They no longer made that particular pattern, but he searched diligently and found them downtown, in an antique store. Gary purchased the pieces, had them polished, and sent them back to Lillian. When he mailed those polished pieces of silver back to their rightful owner, he regained another piece of himself: his integrity. He was now a man of his word.

Every year when we go to Boston, we are welcome in Lillian's home. His old girlfriend Pam was not quite as open to seeing Gary; she wanted to leave the past where it was. But in time, she saw his consistency with her mother and her heart opened as well. Last year both Pam and her mother came to Gary's mother's funeral. I know it meant a lot to him.

It has been an awesome thing to witness—the healing of lives, the regaining of self-respect, the repairing of souls. As Gary and I continue to do the right thing, in the present and regarding the past, we both heal and bring healthier people into our relationship. I *know* the wonderful marriage we have today is because of the work we have done regarding our pasts.

Today's Action | In the relationship arena, do you have unfinished business that needs to be taken care of? Do you need to apologize and ask forgiveness of anyone? Do you need to forgive someone? Remember, whatever you hold against one man or woman, you hold against all men and women.

Please Forgive Me . . . I Know Not What I Do

The hardest amends Gary made was to another girlfriend's mother. After Gary had been clean two years, we were in our timeshare in St. Maarten. He was working steadily, had just gotten an American Express Gold card, and life was good. He was feeling proud about how far he had come in just two years. Then he found out his ex-girlfriend, Darlene, had just died of AIDS.

"Why am I alive and Darlene is dead?" Gary asked God, feeling responsible for Darlene's death. Although Darlene was already using drugs when she met Gary, she contracted the HIV virus as a direct result of the things she was doing to get drugs for her and Gary.

For a while, Darlene's family tried to help Gary and Darlene. Her mother, Mary, even put up bail for Gary once, to the tune of fifteen hundred dollars. He, in turn, stole a check from her that was to go to the care of Darlene's five-year-old daughter. Gary still felt the hot sting of Mary's last words to him ten years ago, "You bastard!"

Though Gary's heart was heavy with guilt and remorse at the news of Darlene's death, the only way he knew to help lift his burden was to try and make amends to her family. Most people he talked to said, "Gary, this is one of those situations where seeking out her mother would probably do more harm than good." (Mary was well aware of Gary's influence on her daughter.) When Gary asked his sponsor what he should do, his sponsor asked, "Have you talked to God about it?" Gary answered, "Yes." "Then you know what to do," his sponsor replied.

That Thanksgiving, much like every other Thanksgiving, Gary and I flew to Boston so he could visit his family and continue making amends to them. After visiting with his family, Gary drove up to Ipswich and knocked on the door of Darlene's parents' home. Three cars were in the driveway, but no one answered the door. Gary left thinking that they had seen who was at the front door and chose not to answer it.

The following year he decided that the least he could do was start paying back the bail Mary had posted and the money he had stolen from her. So, he drove up to their house again. This time Darlene's brother was outside hanging Christmas lights on the house. He did a double take as Gary drove up the driveway and got out of the car. As Gary approached, Darlene's brother reached out his hand to shake Gary's. Gary asked if Mary was home. She wasn't, so he left a note for her with two hundred and fifty dollars tucked inside and asked Darlene's brother to give it to her. Once again, Gary walked away feeling just that much taller.

Each November for the next three years, Gary drove up the New England coast and dropped a check off in Mary's mailbox. On the fourth year, Gary got lost for about ten minutes. When he finally drove up to the house, Mary was in the driveway getting into her car. He said to himself, "This is too perfect." He approached the car and knocked on the window. Mary's mouth dropped open as she rolled down the window. "We were just talking about you." She said. And then she said, "Darlene loved you so much." Gary's eyes welled up with tears, and he knew he was forgiven.

Mary invited him to come back the next day when she was off work. They talked for hours, and Mary held Gary and rubbed his back while he cried, giving him the comfort he so desperately needed. And Mary received the gift of knowing just how much her daughter had mattered to another human being.

As Gary got up to leave, Mary said, "You are welcome in our house as long as we're alive." An awesome healing took place that day. Had Gary not been lost for those ten minutes, who knows what would have happened? It just proves to me one more time that God is watching out for us.

Everything is in Divine Order. Everything.

Today's Action | Is there anyone who is no longer here who you have regrets about? Is there some way you could let their family know the impact they made on your life and receive the closure you need as well?

God Bless The Child

122

The next year, Gary went to Boston and visited Mary again. This time he asked to see Darlene's grave. Darlene's family was poor and couldn't afford a tombstone, so Darlene's daughter, who was then seventeen, took a large rock, painted it white, put Darlene's name on it, and placed a picture of herself in the corner. At first Gary thought, "For amends, I could buy Darlene a real headstone." But the one her daughter made was too perfect.

Then, Gary caught sight of another grave next to Darlene's, a smaller one that wasn't so perfect. It turns out Darlene had had a four-and-a-half-year-old son, who died of AIDS shortly after Darlene died. Gary stood there, with tears streaming down his face, as he realized how his actions of a long time ago affected another person who wasn't even born yet. This little boy died as a result of the actions he and Darlene had taken twelve years earlier.

Silence filled the already quiet cemetery, as Gary fully comprehended his effect on the world around him.

Then Gary realized that his actions *today* affect people who aren't even born yet. Every drug addict or homeless person whom Gary helps has the opportunity to become a better father, brother, or son. Every time Gary shares his story, someone may find the courage they need to turn their life around, make a difficult amends, or become the person

God always intended they become. Pregnant mothers, in treatment centers, just might stay off drugs and become good mothers to their children as a result of Gary's sharing.

Gary takes great solace in this since he knows he can't change the past. However, he *can* heal the past by taking courageous action today.

Last year, Gary went up north on Mother's Day to put flowers on his mother's grave. While there, he stopped by to visit Lillian and bring her flowers. Then, he drove up the coast for his yearly sojourn to Mary's house. When he knocked on the door and asked for Mary, a stranger answered the door and said, "Mary died a few months ago."

Gary stood at the door, flowers hanging at his side, shocked, but somehow okay. Darlene's brother invited Gary in, and they spoke for a while. As Gary got up to leave, the brother said, "Mary always spoke highly of you."

Gary drove away ever so grateful for the man he had become. That someone could go from saying, "You bastard!" to speaking "highly of him" baffled him. As he drove back down the coast, he thanked God for the opportunity to make his peace with Mary before she died. In doing so, *he* was at peace.

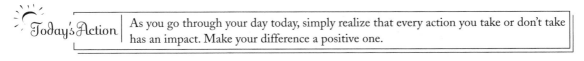

Today's Action | As you go through your day today, simply realize that every action you take or don't take has an impact. Make your difference a positive one.

How Is It We Are Here?

Three days before Dharma died, I spent the night in the hospital after my final reconstructive surgery. It was after midnight, but I was restless and unable to sleep. My mind kept drifting back to thoughts of whether I was going to make it or not. I had finished the chemotherapy and was supposed to go back to work in a few weeks, but life still seemed surreal to me. I couldn't quite grasp that I would pull out of this and my life would return to normal.

As my mind danced its tango with death, a nurse dressed in everyday clothing came in and asked if I wanted something to help me sleep. I hesitated in telling her my thoughts and fears, but for some reason it all came pouring out. I told her how scared I was and how I had been reading everything I could get my hands on about death—*Many Masters, Many*

Lives by Brian Weiss, *Embraced By The Light* by Betty J. Eadie, and *On Death and Dying* by Elisabeth Kübler-Ross, yet I could not tear my mind from death's grasp.

After listening patiently, she told me she had no doubts or fear about the afterlife—only faith. I asked where her faith came from. Speaking softly, she took her time, as if I was her only patient and told me she was a student of the Kabbalah, an ancient mystical book of wisdom from the Jewish religion. She went on to tell me that it felt like truth when she first began studying its teachings. But she also believed there were many paths to God. She said, "Have no fear, you will find your way."

It was as if time stood still while we talked into the wee hours of the morning. To this day, I think she was a messenger from God. It wasn't her particular beliefs that brought me comfort, just her simple message that there was nothing to fear. She had such a peace about her—how could I not trust her? She spoke about death as a transition, not an end. It felt as if she was speaking from a place of knowledge, not just belief.

I can't explain it, but it was if that night was preparing me for what lay ahead—with Dharma. Sometimes it feels as if God knows our every need: getting lost, while driving somewhere you've driven to dozens of times before—altering the course of your life; or a messenger appearing in your moment of need. These *Godincidences*, or miracles, constantly amaze me.

How can you tell when you are in the presence of a miracle? You will feel kissed by the sweetness of a perfect instant created just for you. It's a moment when you know how very much God cares about you. That's how Gary felt when he got lost driving to Mary's house. And that's how I felt the night in the hospital when a special messenger made that late-night call.

Today's Action | Ruminate a bit about your own beliefs about life and death. What does the center hold? Delve deeper, trusting that you will find the answers you need. Everything you need will be placed in your path. Open your eyes to the miracles occurring around you every single day.

Working Nine To Five

I was reading a book about Zen Buddhism and the eight gates of Zen. These eight gates address different areas of our lives, but the one that interested me the most was called the "work practice." It explores the spiritual essence of Buddhist teachings on *Right Livelihood*—work that does no harm and nourishes ourselves and others.

That really hit home. Certainly my work in a law firm does no harm, but does it nourish me or others? I have long made a practice of serving God at work by doing my job to the best of my ability and by trying to make my co-workers' loads a little lighter.

Knowing that God is my ultimate employer, and that my job is so much more than just crunching numbers, helps. Practicing spiritual principles, working through conflicts, facing fears, and seeing opportunities for growth in each experience, helps. Still, there is that nagging question, *Is this my Right Livelihood?*

No, although I practice honesty and integrity in the workplace and strive for personal excellence, the work itself does not nourish me or others. Doing financial accounting for a law firm, even a law firm with integrity, does *not* make the statement about my life that I want to make.

For whatever reason, I am not ready to move on, so in the meantime I am cheerful, helpful, and efficient.

However, when I look into my soul, I see a longing to make a much greater contribution than balancing books for a law firm. I believe I make a contribution in my personal life when I help others, but when I read about *Right Livelihood* I knew a new level of commitment would soon be necessary. One where my chosen career is who I am—where my work *is* my contribution.

When I think of *Right Livelihood*—work that does no harm and nourishes my soul and that of others—I think of serving others and making a difference in the world through my writing. The very thought brings my soul contentment.

Today's Action | What does the term *Right Livelihood* mean to you? Are you living up to your highest potential? If not, do some soul-searching and discern what would be more satisfying. Remember you do not have to quit your job today if you decide that it is not what you want to do forever. Just view your work as your spiritual practice while you flesh out a plan of action that will take you to your *Right Livelihood*, a.k.a. *your bliss.*

The Voice

Sometimes I am moved to give "Dharma—My Little Angel," to a complete stranger.

One such Tuesday evening I hadn't been to my breast cancer support group in months, but they were so supportive of my writing that on the day *Guidepost's* magazine sent a photographer to our house, I went that evening to share the exciting news of "Dharma's" imminent publication.

As usual they were happy to see me and let me know what an inspiration I was to all of them—that me living my bliss—gave them the courage to do the same. It was a typical night with lots of laughter and hope, as well as a few tears. One woman in her sixties was there for her first time. Diagnosed just one week before, it was a pretty emotional time for her, and she faced many difficult decisions. Luckily, she had her two daughters with her for support.

When it came my turn to speak, I shared on the importance of gathering all the facts, and then making a decision based on those facts, combined with what your gut tells you is best for you. And to not second-guess your decisions—no matter what! We all do the best we can, and then we have to let go of the results. Our sanity depends on this—and on trusting God. I finished by telling the group how much I missed them, but that my favorite Twelve-Step meditation meeting met on the same night and that I hated to miss it, but would come as often as I could.

After the meeting ended, one of the new woman's daughters, Mary Jo, came up to me and said, "I'm in recovery eleven years and would love to try your meditation meeting sometime." We got to talking and found that we both liked cats and that her mother was terrified of dying so I gave Mary Jo a copy of "Dharma," thinking it might comfort her mother.

A few days later I got a card in the mail thanking me for sharing my story and telling me how much it touched her and helped her mother.

The very next day I received an e-mail from a friend I hadn't heard from in seven years, but had been thinking about constantly and wanting to get in touch with. It turns out that an old friend of mine, Malerie, rents the cottage behind Mary Jo's house. Mary Jo shared my story with her and Malerie recognized my name right away and e-mailed me.

The synchronicity is astounding when you listen to your gut.

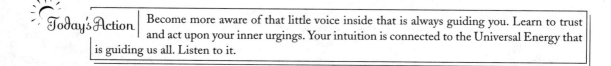

Today's Action | Become more aware of that little voice inside that is always guiding you. Learn to trust and act upon your inner urgings. Your intuition is connected to the Universal Energy that is guiding us all. Listen to it.

Miracles

Malerie and I met about ten years ago through a mutual friend who had told me about her Mother's Day meditation, which I went to with Gary and my mother. We became fast friends through our love of cats and our similar spiritual journeys. We found out we lived in the same North Miami apartment complex and soon began cat-sitting for each other. Malerie traveled quite a bit and asked if I would spend some time in her apartment and play with her cat so he wouldn't be so lonely. He was a six-month-old orange tabby named—guess what—Dharma! I guess the named resonated with me for more than one reason.

Malerie's books fascinated me, and I spent hours perusing them. One in particular stood out, maybe because it was always on her night table: the *Bhagavad-Gita*. I was overcome by the profound nature of the book, although I must admit most of what I read was over my head.

Eventually, Malerie moved out of our apartment building. We kept in touch for a while, but when Gary and I moved to Hollywood, we lost touch completely. When I became ill and was so scared of dying, my quest for answers about the afterlife led me to study many different religions and philosophies. Malerie came to mind frequently. I just knew she could help me. I even searched for her on the Internet, but since I couldn't remember her last name, Malerie B. didn't get me very far.

Then out of the blue, I received an e-mail, "I don't know if you remember me but..." from Malerie. She still had Dharma, who is now a fully grown orange tabby and was floored when Mary Jo handed her, "Dharma—My Little Angel" by Debbie Blais. She exclaimed to Mary Jo, "I know this girl! Her husband's name is Gary and we used to cat-sit for each other!"

All I had to do was put the thought out into the Universe that I wanted to find her, and there she was. One more time, I amazed by God's timing. Here I was in need of a spiritual teacher, and Malerie was leading meditation classes. And Malerie was struggling with a spiritual book she was working on and was in need of encouragement. Talk about meant to be!

Could all of this be a coincidence? I don't think so. There *must* be some cosmic, intelligent energy responding to our needs—something beyond our human comprehension causing miracles to happen.

Miracles—things beyond human explanation, seemingly improbable or impossible—occur around us all the time. We need but open our eyes.

Think back on some of the *Godincidences* in your own life. Reflect on the mysterious wonder of it all. Be open to the idea of the Universe responding to your every thought and request. Put something out there today and see what happens.

Om Gam Ganapataye Namaha

Tonight, I attended a Bhakti Yoga meditation, which my long-lost friend Malerie led. This particular form of yoga is devotional rather than physical. Bhakti is considered divine devotion to God—your *God*—however you define or understand God, so it is all-encompassing, rather than limited to any particular belief system.

For two hours Gary and I chanted *OM*, read from the *Bhagavad-Gita*, sang and meditated as our hearts filled with love. In Friday evening Bhakti class, we express love to God. We sing and chant love to God. We see God, experience God, merge and become one with God. It's an extraordinary experience. Your heart is so expanded that when you go back into the world, you are filled with compassion and love and better able to demonstrate that love in your life.

128

We chanted in Sanskrit, the second-oldest language in the world. It has kind of a singsong, Native American sound to it. My favorite chant is, "*Om Gam Ganapataye Namaha*," which is a prayer for the *removal of all obstacles and success in all noble endeavors.*

That chant resonates deeply with me because I believe this book is one of the most noble and humbling endeavors I have ever undertaken. I stand before you scared, uncertain, hopeful, shy, excited, joyful, and open. All of my thoughts, feelings, insecurities, flaws, and strengths exposed for all to see.

Yet, I show up as *me* every time I sit down to write—holding nothing back. And I *do* pray for the removal of all obstacles and success in this endeavor—because I only want God's will in my life. If it is meant to be, you will be holding a book in your hands as you read this. If it is not God's will, these words will remain words on paper for my eyes only.

Only God knows what is for my highest good and that of others. I show up and do the footwork—the outcome is none of my business. My heart is noble in this moment regarding this endeavor. My prayer is for God to remove any obstacles—if it is his will.

Om Gam Ganapataye Namaha.

Don't Forget To Remember

After meditation, Malerie spoke of attachment and how we are not our bodies. We are not our minds or our egos. One of the main blocks to divine union with God is that even though we want to melt into God, into Oneness, we hold on to and remain attached to our individual identities. We cling to our personal identity: our ego, our lower self and its base desires.

We want to experience Oneness, but we don't want to lose ourselves in the process.

As soon as she said this, I knew that was what I feared about death. Not nothingness as I had thought, but the merging, the Oneness—the total loss of self. I don't want to just go on; I want to go on and *know it.*

I am afraid that when I die, I'll lose my heart—my essence—what I think makes me me. I don't want to lose my memories, the love I've experienced, or the people I care about. I want to keep it all.

So even if we are reincarnated, we are born into forgetfulness. I am attached to non-forgetfulness. I don't want to lose the memory of this life or the people in it, even if we continue to reincarnate together and have that sense of having known each other before.

If there is a soul connection—I want the memory, not just the cellular or soul memory—but the *mind* memory. Ah! So that's it. I'm more attached to *my mind* than *my heart or soul.* Hmmm . . . food for thought.

All I Really Want

In Alanis Morissette's song "All I Really Want," she leaves a few seconds of silence right in the middle of the song. The abrupt silence makes a very powerful statement about how we use noise to run from ourselves and from God.

A few years ago when I broke my arm, it was suggested that I learn how to relax and have a little fun—to lighten up. I was at a loss as to what to do with myself. What I was most afraid of was the stillness, the quiet—the sound between my thoughts.

Meditation helps me to quiet my mind and be more conscious of the space and time between my thoughts. A quiet mind, a mind not full of its own chatter, can hear God. A quiet mind is teachable. A busy mind thinks it knows everything and is too full to take in anything new.

Getting and remaining quiet has been one of my most difficult challenges. Busyness is my nature. Although I have gotten to the point where I am content in my own company, there is almost always something else going on. Either the TV or stereo is on or I'm busy cleaning, reading, or I'm on the computer.

The summer of 1996 I made a decision to work fewer hours, turn off the TV, the radio, my computer, and to use the phone minimally. Taking a time-out from all means of mass communication was a vastly enriching experience. Most of my time was spent out-doors in nature, reading spiritual books, or in meditation.

I call it my magical summer because it was a summer like no other. At the onset, I thought it would be a very calm and peaceful summer, the summer where I would become one with God. What actually happened was that in the stillness, the feelings I was normally too busy or too distracted too feel, emerged. Fearful thoughts and feelings of death, my own and the deaths of others, rose to the surface. Feelings of loss—current and past and even losses I might experience in the future—all rose to the surface. I re-felt losing Dharma. I re-experienced the pain of not being a mother. I grieved friends and loved ones no longer in my life.

I felt very different and alone; few in my immediate circle understood what it felt like to be alive, one year after a cancer diagnosis, knowing a drastic change has occurred in your life, but uncertain of what comes next. Through meditation it came to me to let go of all the women I was sponsoring and to take some time just for myself. It was a scary decision, but necessary for my healing.

If nothing changes, the same person will get the same thing again, was a fear that went round and round in my head. Yet, since I didn't know what caused the cancer, I didn't know what I could change or even if it was in my power to change anything.

Helpless. Powerless. That's how I felt. There were no guarantees that even if I changed *everything*, the cancer wouldn't come back to its old familiar host. I had to accept, at a very deep level, that *I* was not in charge. I could do all the positive footwork in the world, yet the outcome was still not up to me.

In the quiet moments of meditation, I surrendered. I surrendered to that fact that either God was all or God was nothing. There either was a plan or there wasn't. I had to trust or live in fear.

I chose trust. And with that trust, came peace.

Today's Action | Create more space in your life for quiet reflection. What needs shifting? Where do you need to surrender? Let go and trust.

I Can't Make You Love Me

Most people who know us think that Gary and I have a perfect marriage. I would have to agree that it is a perfect vehicle for our individual transformation and growth, not always easy, but perfect nonetheless. You see, I married my father.

My mother and father divorced when I was an infant and even though he lived in the same city, I rarely saw him. When I was eight years old, I contracted scarlet fever and was hospitalized for almost a month. It was touch and go for a while, and my father came to see me every day—at breakfast time. Even at this age, the idea that my father could love me was so foreign to me that I was sure he came for the free food, not because he loved me.

These feelings of unworthiness continued in my subsequent relationships with men. Although I was much stronger and confident by the time I met Gary, I often overreacted and took things personally. One of our main recurring issues was how much he worked and served our community and how neglected I felt as a result.

I know it sounds noble to work six days a week and then spend four nights a week helping homeless drug addicts recover from addiction, but the reality of living with someone who stays this busy is a very lonely existence.

During the week, Gary got home after 10 P.M., so we rarely ate dinner together. By Sunday, he was so exhausted that he never did much except watch TV and sleep.

The first few years of our marriage, I wondered, "What's wrong with me. Why doesn't Gary want to spend time with me?"

Before we were married Gary drove across town in the middle of the night just to spend an hour or two with me. What had I done to push him away? Now, whenever I wanted to make love, Gary claimed he was tired and rolled away. Many a night I cried myself to sleep looking at those cold shoulders, wishing I could make Gary love me, like I loved him.

I volunteered my time at a nursing home, went back to school, and was active in my spiritual community, but nothing filled the void. The busier I got, the less Gary's absence bothered me, but whenever I slowed down long enough, there was that old familiar ache— *I am not worthy of your time.*

I did my best to turn to God with my pain and to look to God, myself, and my other friends for fulfillment, but the fact that Gary and I were living as roommates hurt.

We rarely fought, but there was no magic or passion either: just this dull, going-through-the-motions kind of marriage. I longed to feel treasured and adored—not just comfortable, like an old shoe. Two years of marriage felt like twenty. I did not think the spark was supposed to die this soon. Our sex life was already down to the perfunctory once a week, and the intimacy I craved eluded me.

When I got cancer everything changed.

Gary became devoted to me. For once, I was more important than work or a homeless drug addict. I have to admit I love how he loved me during this time.

One day in particular, a week after my mastectomy, I was getting ready for my first bath since the surgery. Taking the bandage off, I saw myself for the first time in our mirrored closet doors. On one side I had a breast and the other side—nothing—just a long scar across the center of my chest where my breast used to be. The full force of what happened hit me like a ton of bricks. It was not something I might have to do, or was going to do—it was done!

I lost it. I broke down sobbing. Gary came in from the other room and asked what happened. I could not tell him, and I did not want him to see me. He would not leave. He took me into his arms and would not let go. The unspoken loss hung in the empty air. No words could fill the void. Nothing could assuage the pain or bring back my breast. We just stood there, bonded together by our grief. Gary cried for me. I cried for my loss.

Finally, I was able to tell him how I felt when I saw myself in the mirror. Gary took me by the hand, walked me to the bathroom, and gently sat me down in the bathtub.

Embarrassed, I covered myself with the washcloth. Gary took it from me and ever so tenderly began washing me—all of me. I sat in the warm soapy water with tears streaming down my face. And this man I loved so very much, bathed me, wiping my tears away, showing me how truly worthy I was.

Today's Action | Reviewing your life history, do you see any connections between your current relationships and unresolved issues with your parents? Spend some time reflecting on those connections.

More Than Words

I couldn't have asked for a more perfect husband to help me through this very difficult time. In fact, Gary was wonderful the entire time I was out of work. Then, seven months later, I went back to work and everything was supposed to go back to normal. It didn't. It couldn't—I was irreversibly changed—inside and out.

A few months after I returned to work, I asked to work a pared-down workweek of four days instead of five. My firm agreed and I began my "magical summer" by embarking on *The Artist's Way* in order to recover my creative soul.

During this inward journey, something shifted. I became aware of how busy I had always kept myself and no longer wanted to live that way. I let go of commitments and began living moment to moment, spontaneously doing whatever I was moved to do. Exhausted from trying to save the world for so many years, I let go. Gary, on the other hand, took on even more commitments.

As the months wore on, we saw less and less of each other. Gary began working six days a week again and had nightly service commitments, Monday through Thursday. In August, he took on two more commitments, which meant even more committee meetings.

Well, I didn't go through all those surgeries, have all that chemo, and fight this hard for my life, only to spend it with someone who didn't have any time to spare for me! I was tired of trying to change or control Gary—tired of trying to make him love me. And I was not about to wait until I got cancer again to get his attention. At summer's end, I left Gary.

I knew how important it was for Gary to help the still-suffering addicts, not only for himself, but also to repay his debt to society and the fellowship he is recovering in. I applaud him for that. However, on more than one occasion, Gary had told me he was going to help the homeless for seven years—the number of years he was homeless. Well, I don't mean to be selfish, but it's been eight and a half!

With a very heavy heart, I wrote Gary a letter, letting him go. I told him I knew he believed he was doing God's will, and I didn't want to keep him from doing what he felt he was on this earth to do. And that although I thought it was possible to balance having a loving marriage with service to God and your fellow man, it wasn't working out that way. I let him know how much I loved him, but that I no longer wanted to stand in the way of what he felt was his path. And there didn't seem to be any room for me on that path.

Admitting that hurt like hell, but I just got my life back and not knowing how long I was going to live, I wanted to really live! I wanted to experience passionate love-making with someone who really wanted to be with me. I wanted to ride bicycles in the park, go to the beach, to art shows and concerts. I wanted a partner all the time, not only in times of crisis. And for once, I knew I deserved it.

I let go with love, not anger. I told him that if he felt the need to serve so strongly, to the extent that he did, then he probably shouldn't be married. A good marriage needs an investment of time and energy that he didn't seem willing or able to make. I told Gary that no matter how much this was breaking my heart, I couldn't live on the back burner forever. I asked him to think this over and not call me until he had reached a decision. There had been too many broken promises over the years, and I didn't want any more empty words. I told him I loved him enough to let him go, if that's what he needed, and would he please do the same for me.

Days passed and I heard nothing. Though my heart was filled with sadness, I was strangely at peace. I knew I deserved to be loved. I deserved to be special in someone's life and I was willing to claim it. I also trusted God implicitly. I knew he would lead us both where he wanted us to be.

Midday on the fourth day, Gary called. He told me he had stepped down from being chairperson of one of his most treasured committees—the one that is devoted to carrying a message of recovery to addicts in jails and in institutions like his homeless shelter. He said he didn't want to call me until after the committee met and he actually stepped down, because he knew he needed to *show* me how important I was to him.

Upon hearing that I broke down in tears. I couldn't believe Gary had said no to a committee that he felt needed him, because his wife needed him more. Of all the ways Gary has shown me love, nothing shouts: I LOVE YOU more than his stepping down from those commitments.

No, I can't make anyone love me, but I can love myself enough to ask, and then to let go.

☼ Today's Action | If this touched a chord in you, share it with the one you love, ask for what you need, then trust the outcome.

Tell Him

One of the more dramatic changes in our relationship came about recently.

Gary became more loving, affectionate, attentive, and even more romantic, since I began writing. He has actually been pursuing me and initiating sex, which for Gary is unheard of.

When I asked, "What's up?" Gary replied tentatively, "With all your writing, I'm afraid you'll outgrow me."

Now, I don't believe that's possible. We may grow differently as a result of the new path I'm on, but spiritually, Gary will always be the leader in our family. Still, his vulnerability was touching. It takes a very secure man to be that open with his fears and insecurities.

135

I certainly didn't set out to write to get Gary's attention, or keep him on his toes. But it's true, my focus is no longer on him and what he is or isn't doing. It's on my dreams and how I'm going to achieve them.

Gary says I'm different now. I'm less needy, so he wants to be with me more. He respects and admires me more because of my dedication to my writing. You won't hear any complaints from me because I *love* being pursued for a change.

When you live your bliss, the rest of your life falls into place.

☼ Today's Action | Is there something or someone that is taking more of your attention than is healthy? Try shifting your priorities and focusing to what's really important in bigger scheme of things. Follow your bliss and see if everything doesn't just fall into place.

Money

I just got off the phone with a friend of mine, Melissa, who, after being a legal secretary for almost twenty years, is now in law school. A friend of hers is getting married and Melissa asked, "Do you love him?" Her friend replied, "He's really good to me." (I don't know about you, but I take that as a no.)

Anyway, this friend is having the wedding of her dreams; Melissa is a single mom struggling to make it on her own. Melissa's friend and fiancé both just bought new cars; Melissa's car has seen better days. Her friend has a very prestigious job and is marrying a professional man; Melissa has no job right now, took out thousands of dollars worth of school loans, and her boyfriend is a blue-collar worker.

Up until this conversation with her friend, Melissa was fairly happy with her life. Now, she's comparing herself on all levels: professionally, financially, and in relationships, and is coming up short. She forgets she's a great mom, gets top grades, and was courageous enough to quit her job in order to follow her dreams.

I've learned from my own experience that comparing never works. There will always be someone who has more or less than you do in any given area. Whenever I compare myself to others, it is because I feel less than; I either want to wallow in self-pity or feel better about myself by putting others down. Temporarily, that may work. But, in general, comparing just separates us spiritually—from each other—and from God.

Hardly in competition with one another, we are brothers and sisters on the same path. We each have strengths and weaknesses. Material things are nice, but they can't "fix" us. They can't change how we really feel about ourselves—that's an inside job.

True prosperity, happiness, and contentment are by-products of right living. They are elusive if pursued. (Trust me, I know all about pursuing.)

If I set my sights on gathering and obtaining material possessions, material possessions would be all that I had. If, instead, I try to live up to my highest potential as a human being and try to do the right thing spiritually, I will attract all need and more.

Gary and I live modestly, but very happily. We don't focus on acquiring things, but they seem to come to us when the time is right. As a result of being grateful for what we do have, we are constantly blessed with more.

Gary used to buy lottery tickets until he realized that what he was saying with that action was, *God, I'm not happy with what you've given me so far, I want more.*

If you come from "lack" mentally, no matter how much you have, it will never be enough. I've spent too much of my life coming from "lack."

Now, I affirm abundance in my life by looking around me at the multitude of gifts from God, particularly in nature. The countless varieties of fish, flowers, trees, and birds prove God is an abundant God. The bounty that surrounds us is limitless.

Today's Action | Affirm that *you are on a spiritual, not material path.* Affirm that all of your needs are met, always have been, and always will be. Trust in the abundance of the Universe. Open your eyes today, and see, really see, the abundance in your own life. We are far richer than our limited vision can see.

I Feel The Earth Move

Whenever I need to get centered, I reconnect with nature. Walking barefoot in the cool grass or on hot sand at the beach grounds me. The first time I did this was two years ago when I got the urge to walk barefoot to the lake two blocks away. It had been so long since I had walked anywhere without my shoes that before the two blocks were up, the entire bottoms of both of my feet were covered with blisters. Take heed and step into this gradually.

Today, go for a walk outdoors, taking in all the sensations around you.

Take your shoes off.

Feel the earth beneath you. Is the ground warm or is it cool?

Smell the flowers. Is spring peeking its head out in the form of little blossoms everywhere?

Hear the birds and the wind all around you. What kinds of birds are there where you live? Magnificent, wild, green parrots fly through our neighborhood, squawking all the time. My favorite treat is when a bright yellow, orange, and black Baltimore oriole rests in the hot pink bougainvillea bush in our backyard.

See the multitude of colors everywhere. There are so many shades of green, just in leaves alone.

Drink it up. Soak up the beauty of your surroundings today. Reconnect with your spirit with a brisk walk around your neighborhood or in a nearby park.

Today's Action | Walk barefoot on the earth. Find a beach, a park, a yard—whatever. Take your shoes off and get grounded.

Everything Is Beautiful

I just took my own advice and got up out of my chair, left my computer in mid-sentence, and went outside for that barefoot walk.

I headed for that trusty lake two blocks away, the same lake where I found my Dharma three and a half years ago. I can't believe it's been that long. I'm so different than I was back then, so sick and so scared. Now, I'm healthy, free-spirited, and very much at peace.

The grass was still wet from yesterday's rain. It felt good beneath my feet. And I ran into my favorite hot pink bougainvillea bush, looking riotous, like Phyllis Diller's hair. I sang "It's A Beautiful Morning," "I Feel the Earth Move," and "Everything Is Beautiful" as I strolled to the lake.

138

It's a beautiful spring day, about 70 degrees outside and the sky is a crystal-clear, bountiful blue. As I sit on the bench by the lake, I am overwhelmed with a sense of gratitude for all that I have and how far I've come. Sometimes I get choked up when I think of the possibility of my not being here—of my not surviving the cancer.

Looking out over the water, a breeze caresses my face, and I feel blessed to live in South Florida. Then, thinking of my brother in Colorado, I realize he is no less blessed than I. He may be looking out over snow-covered mountains, but then, *Everything is beautiful in its own way.*

If you haven't already done so, kick off those shoes and take that walk with God.

Today's Action | Take a walk with God and count your blessings.

Reach Out And Touch Somebody's Hand

I stopped at the grocery store this evening just before closing time and grabbed a few quick items. As I put the divider between my groceries and those of the man behind me, I noticed he was debating between the corn chips in his cart and the newspaper in his hand.

He had a few other things in his cart and was counting them and counting his money. He picked up the chips and put them down on the conveyor belt. Then he hesitated with the newspaper in midair. Finally, he put the chips back in his cart and put the newspaper on the belt. Then I heard him say very quietly, "Man, I really want them chips."

Without thinking twice, I said to him, "If you like, put them with my groceries. I'll pay for them and then give them to you." Astonished, he said, "Really?" I said, "Sure. I'd be happy to. I know what it's like when you have a craving for something." He asked, "Are you sure? It's only 99 cents, but are you sure? I just paid my rent and this is all I have left." I assured him it would be my pleasure. I paid for the chips and handed them to him.

The cashier said, "Aw, that was nice." And the woman bagging the groceries said, "God bless you." I responded, "It really wasn't that big a deal. I could, so I did."

The man, still looking somewhat amazed, thanked me again, and we parted ways. He left with his newspaper *and* his chips and a big old grin on his face. And I left with the good feeling you get inside, knowing you did the right thing. Both the cashier and the lady bagging groceries were left with a little more faith in humanity.

I didn't even think about whether to do it or not—the words just came. I'm glad he wasn't embarrassed by my offer. That's the last thing I would have wanted. I think we all shared warm fuzzies. Remember them? That warm, fuzzy feeling of comfort and safety and happiness?

When I related the story to Gary, his eyes welled up with tears, and he said, "You just do this stuff so you have something to write about and to make me cry." It didn't even occur to me to write about it until well after the fact. But how can stories like this not go into a book about blissful living? It's all part of the plan.

The ripple effect of kindness is a wondrous thing.

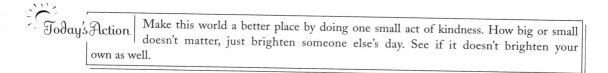

Today's Action | Make this world a better place by doing one small act of kindness. How big or small doesn't matter, just brighten someone else's day. See if it doesn't brighten your own as well.

This Is My Life

One of the most important things I did to do to prepare myself for living my bliss was to create some space for it in my busy schedule by not "people pleasing" so much. I found I spent so much time helping others live their dreams that I had little time or energy left over for my dreams.

Work, obligations, social engagements—things that I either enjoyed or felt I *should* do—filled my life. The first step was to stop volunteering for everything that pulled at my heartstrings and begin saying "No." One person I remember saying "No" to early on was a woman I was sponsoring who wanted to stay with me until she got on her feet again.

This woman had just been kicked out of her apartment because she couldn't find a job and could no longer pay her rent. She had no family or friends and was going to end up on the street if she couldn't find a place to stay. How could I say no?

My heart tugged at me. *You can't let this happen. You're the only one who can help.* As the debate within me built up steam, I found out she was also schizophrenic and not yet stable on her medication. My rational mind was saying: *You hardly know her. She could clean out your place, burn it down, or worse, she could harm you.* Still, I was torn. Most of me felt I should say no, but I also felt an obligation and a responsibility to help another person in need.

I spoke to a very spiritual friend of mine about my dilemma. I told her I was leaning toward saying no, but felt very guilty. She told me, "Do what you need to do to take care of yourself and trust that it will end up being best for all concerned."

Rescuing someone isn't always in their best interest. I ended up saying no and felt a little guilty anyway. By the end of the week this woman was admitted into a hospital in order to stabilize her medication. I realized this hospital was exactly where she need to be, *not* with me.

| Today's Action | The next time your intuition guides you to say "No," honor it, trusting that if you take care of yourself first, it will end up being best for all concerned. |

Think Twice

The second time it was hard to say "No" was when I was facilitating a Twelve-Step recovery meeting in a woman's work-release program. A work-release program is where inmates go when they get out of jail but are not quite ready for society. Anyway, one of the women in the work-release program told me the group had gotten permission to go to outside meetings. All they needed was someone to drive them. Would I?

I already felt overwhelmed by my schedule and had some practice at taking care of myself, so I said, "No."

"What do you mean *no*, you can't say *no*! You're always supposed to say *yes* when asked to do Twelve-Step service," was her response.

Very nicely, but firmly, I reiterated, "Yes, I *can* say no and I *am* saying no. I have enough on my plate. I'm sorry, but you will have to find someone else." This time I hardly felt guilty at all. I was beginning to *know* my truth and respond accordingly.

Setting boundaries and saying "no" gets easier with practice. But time and again, when I am not paying attention, my plate gets too full, and I have to let go of things. For the last year and a half, I have been doing pretty well in this area. I take on no more than one commitment a week. If occasionally there is something else I want to do, I skip the first commitment. I also limit the number of women I sponsor, so I don't get too drained and have nothing to offer. This seems to be working well for me and still leaves me plenty of time to spend with my husband, with nature, and for just plain kicking back and having fun.

I've found what my friend said is true: All I need do is go inward and listen. When I take care of myself, it *will* be best for all concerned.

Today, I know I am not God and therefore I am not the only one who can help.

Today's Action | How do you feel about your commitments and obligations? Are you able to say no *before* you are overwhelmed or stretched to the max? Do a little soul-searching and see if there is anything you need to let go of to create more time and energy in your life for letting your heart sing.

I Haven't Got Time For The Pain

My health is the first thing that is affected when I overextend myself. It starts with my feeling overwhelmed. Then I get resentful, as if I am carrying the weight of the whole world and no one else is doing his or her share. The longer I ignore these feelings, the greater the health issues I have to deal with.

These illnesses and accidents don't appear to be psychosomatic, and I am certainly not consciously bringing them on myself, but there have been too many over the years to ignore. And I can always trace any physical aliment or accident back to feeling overwhelmed and taking on too much right before they occurred.

In my first couple of years in recovery, I was addicted to my new way of life and was doing way too much. Then I broke my arm. A couple of years after that, I totaled a brandnew car and injured my upper back and chest. At the time I was working full time, going to school at night, still going to a good seven to ten recovery meetings a week, helping my husband at the homeless shelter, and volunteering for the Red Cross and Habitat for Humanity. It was weeks after Hurricane Andrew, and there was much to do. Possibly, I took on just a little too much?

A year later, I got painfully excruciating kidney stones. I was sponsoring nine women at the time and couldn't see straight. I tend to sponsor people "hands on," and maybe that means I can't sponsor as many people as others do. I always seem to have difficulty balancing, taking care of myself, with helping others.

After each of these incidents, I slowed down for a while, usually because I had no other choice. But I always felt a sigh of relief that finally I could take a break.

It was as if I needed permission to slow down.

By the time I contracted breast cancer, the pattern was well established. Now, I have no clue as to whether my lifestyle contributed to the cancer or not. The cancer could be strictly genetic. I honestly don't know the direct cause of any of these accidents and illnesses. All I know is that they gave me the permission I needed, but couldn't give myself, to slow down.

I'm happy to say the breast cancer lesson took. I have been able to focus on self-care, stay relaxed, and still make a positive contribution. Today, I pay more attention to my *inner* calendar, than my *outer* one.

When I am overdoing it, I am more susceptible to illness and accidents, so I keep my commitments to a minimum and take breaks between commitments.

If I want to be here for the long haul, I need to take better care of my physical body and trust that I will make a fine contribution by doing less for a longer period of time. It is certainly better than the "crash and burn" manner in which I had been serving. Less *is* ultimately more.

Today's Action | Is there a connection in your life between times of high stress, busyness, overcommitment, and colds, illnesses, and injuries? Next time you feel a bit stressed, use this page as permission to slow down and do less.

To Dream . . . The Impossible Dream

Talking with a friend last night, I realized that we all have fears and blocks—reasons we think we can't do what we really want to—right now. It's always someday in the future . . . *I'll begin living more authentically, as God intended . . . but for now I have to do such and such. I have to raise the kids, pay the bills, help these people, take care of this project, or work at this job.* Fear rules, and we convince ourselves we don't have enough time or money to do it now, whatever *it* is.

Our beliefs can be so limiting. Mine were. *I'm too busy helping others. I'll start writing when I retire. I'm too busy, too tired, don't have enough time, talent, money, or support from my family.* It wasn't until I got cancer that I realized they were excuses—not the truth—just excuses.

That's why cancer was such a blessing in my life. I consider it one of God's greatest gifts to me. It allowed me to prioritize my life—big time! I began living as if there was no tomorrow, because I truly believed there might not be. I was motivated not so much by fear as by a sense of urgency.

Cancer helped me get my affairs in order. And I'm not talking financial. I'm talking about getting right with God, myself, and others. I'm talking about finding my true purpose and finding the courage to live it. I'm talking about letting my heart *sing*.

Deepening my relationship with God brought greater clarity into my life and helped me see where I needed to heal with others. And I've been graced with the opportunity to spend many of these last years repairing damaged relationships and deepening healthy ones.

143

I learned to look at life as *I get to* instead of *I have to*. By living in this manner, I am no longer weighed down by my burdens but lifted up by my highest aspirations.

God planted in each of our hearts—a longing—something we want to do or be more than anything. This yearning is God's plan for our lives. We need simply to reach for it, and it is ours.

Today's Action | List the reasons you give yourself why you can't do all the things you want to. Twenty years ago, when I was selling health club memberships, I learned you can't overcome anyone's objections, unless you know what they are. Let's punch holes in these stories we tell ourselves and let the lies drain out.

No Time Left For Me

144   I don't know what your days are like, but if they are anything like mine, you probably think, "I hardly have time to read this book, much less follow my dreams."

Last night a friend told me she felt most connected when she was outdoors, but that she no longer had time to go outside. She prays while driving to work and maybe notices a sunset out of her rear-view mirror at a stoplight.

From where I sit, we don't have time *not* to do what fulfills us. We don't have time *not* to realize our dreams. We don't have time *not* to spend in communion with God and nature.

Most decisions I make today are about letting go of obligations, creating more time in my life for the things that matter. That committee will survive without me. If it's important, it will get done.

Life has become too precious to squander. I want each day to be a perfect day—one that I would live over again if I could. I'm not saying they all turn out that way. I still have computer-crash-days-from-hell. The point is, I now consciously choose how I spend my time, instead of just doing the next thing that seems to need doing.

A life-threatening illness increases our appreciation of time. For all I know, these might be my golden years. I am certainly living as if they were. The worst that could happen is that I get another forty or fifty years of bliss.

When I say to myself: *I don't have any time to pursue my dreams,* I'm really saying, *There's no time left for me.* I did that for too many years. Today, I can't afford *not* to make room in my life for me. Me and God. God and me. God in me. Me in God.

Time. Time is all I have. There is an abundance of time if I choose to look at it that way. There are more than enough hours in the day for me to live as God intended. Heck, God created the timetable of twenty-four hours, with the sun rising and setting each day. He must have known exactly how much time each of us needed in a given day.

Twenty-four hours is an abundance of time. What if there were only ten hours in a day? See, we already have more than we might have had.

Today's Action | To the best of your ability, live today as is it really mattered—as if God were with you every second of the day. Live each day as if it were your last day on earth.

Hot Fun In The Summertime

Since the summer of 1996, I have used summers to shift gears. As a child I always looked forward to the carefree days of summer. Now, I give myself permission to let go of all commitments and just have fun for the entire summer. The thirteen-year-old is in charge in the summertime and can do whatever she wants.

That first summer I went to the far end of the pendulum, cutting everyone out of my life and turning everything off, experiencing total peace and quiet. I believe I needed to go to this extreme before I could come back to center. I had been "other" focused for so long that I needed an extended period of time just for me. I needed to put myself first for a change—in a nonselfish way.

Not understanding what I had just been through, some people judged me. So be it. I honored my truth, and unless someone has walked in my shoes, he or she can't say what is right for me. Only God knows. And I believe God guided me to a simpler life, filled with fewer commitments and more fun.

This turned out to be a time of great internal change in my life, some of which was very painful, but all of which was healing. I had the support of a few women who knew what I needed and allowed me to just be. I played every day by ear, deciding at the last minute what I *felt* like doing.

This commitment to quiet and to self-nurturing has become an ongoing part of my life, and I now take breaks like this often, not only in the summer. Saturday morning, no one calls our house because they know this is *my* time, and I don't come out to play until around 2 or 3 P.M. Sunday, Gary and I enjoy a leisurely morning in bed and make it a point not to answer the phone. Our marriage is richer because of this special time we created.

How far we've come from being two ships passing in the night.

How far I've come from that first distressing, "Mayday! Mayday! Wake up. You've got your priorities all mixed up" message of cancer.

Today's Action | Let go of an obligation.
Create space in your life by saying "no" to most everything asked of you for the next three months. This will leave time for the things you really enjoy. Start using wonderful phrases like, "Let me get back to you on that," before committing to *anything*. Rarely does a decision need to be made on the spot—we just think it does.

Careless Whispers

Yesterday, I woke up early, got on my knees, and asked God to guide my day. Next, I meditated to get centered and then wrote for an hour. Then Gary and I hopped on his Harley for a ride to a recovery convention that was taking place in Ft. Lauderdale. I had been asked to share my experience, strength, and hope at one of the convention's workshops and was honored to do so.

I spoke on my early days in recovery, on coming to believe in a Higher Power, and on what I believe God's will is for me today. I told a few stories of marital struggles, financial fears, and the rich and rewarding life I now have as a result of working through conflicts and trusting God. I also shared my joy about the little orange tabby that changed my life. I felt blessed to be able to share a message of hope and possibility.

Gary and I ate lunch with friends and then hung out by the pool and enjoyed the day. In the afternoon, we went home for a little while, and I read a book while Gary napped. Next, it was off to another good meal and back to the convention on the Harley. The weather was gorgeous, and it was turning into a perfect day. We went to a meeting where I heard heartwarming stories of repaired relationships and reunited families.

We topped off the evening by spending some time with my friend Melissa and her boyfriend. I teased them about a recent tête-à-tête of theirs. He seemed embarrassed, and the two of them went up to their room shortly afterward.

Regretting what I said, I prayed to God to help me not obsess on it and to forgive me and help me to do better in the future. As I write this, I know I will seek them out tomorrow and apologize for my thoughtless teasing.

It is uncanny how the mind can take an almost flawless day and focus on the one instant in which you fell short. This day had all the elements of my ideal day: good food, time with friends, being outdoors, writing, solitary time with God, sharing hope with others, and quality time with my husband. Then I go and screw it up with my big mouth.

I know I won't rest until I ask Melissa and her boyfriend to forgive me. I do hope I didn't cause any trouble between them. I would rather have them both mad at me than at each other.

I guess even with this blemish, it was a perfectly imperfect day with many opportunities for growth. Obviously, I need to learn to be more discrete and hold confidences better.

Today's Action | Notice the perfection of your imperfect day. If you fall short in any way, quickly seek to repair the damage, if any, and tuck the lesson away for future reference.

Words

First thing this morning, I sought out Melissa and her boyfriend, admitted my error, apologized, and asked for their forgiveness. He was very magnanimous, gave me a big hug, and said it was no big deal. Melissa however, said jokingly, "No problem, I just won't share anything with you anymore," but there was an undeniable edge to her voice.

Apologizing again, I assured her I didn't mean to hurt her, but because she had told me about her romantic interlude in front of my husband yesterday afternoon, I didn't think of it as confidential. I told her I would use more discretion in the future. She hugged me and said all was forgiven and then pulled me aside to get my input on something else that was bothering her. It took a little time for the awkwardness to go away, but within minutes, everything seemed back to normal. I was so happy that no permanent harm had come to their relationship or ours as a result of my indiscretion.

Practicing *restraint of pen and tongue* in the future will leave less room for regret in my life. I'm human and will make mistakes, so it's nice to know I can apologize and straighten things out right away, instead of carrying guilt because my pride keeps me from admitting I'm wrong.

Anyone is capable of being oversensitive or insensitive at any given time. We are all capable of having our feelings hurt or having our trust breached at any given time. Forgiveness is a wonderful thing, though. The relief I felt after our conversation was immediate. To be able to talk it out, honestly repent, forgive one another, and move on, frees both people—the one who did the harm—and the one forgiving it.

| Today's Action | Have the courage to forgive and be forgiven. |

Step By Step

For years I have thought there's so much to change about myself, so many character flaws, when in fact I only have one: *knowing what the next step is to be and not taking it.*

Now doesn't that just about cover everything? It applies to living my dreams, righting wrongs, and just about any decision I need to make. It's all about faith and taking that leap into the great unknown.

Certainly there's a time for gathering information and a time for preparation. But nine times out of ten, we know what we are to be doing well before we do it. For instance, I've wanted to leave my job for some time now, but fear keeps me from taking that next step. So I write—praying I can write my way out of this job and into a writing career.

In the meantime, I seek out whatever tools I can to help me on my way. Whether the tools are books, motivational tapes, teachers, or seminars, I trust that I will be guided. I trust that truth will resonate with me when I hear it, whatever the source.

I'd been too busy to hear my inner guidance, so I took a personal day off work today to get quiet. I sense a change in the air. I just don't know what shape it will take yet.

While I am in this in-between state, I trust the process. I open myself to universal good, knowing I will take the next step when the time is right. For now, it's baby steps. I put one foot in front of the other and trust everything will fall into place.

Today's Action | What came to mind when you read our only flaw is *knowing what our next step is to be, but not taking it*? Apply the *irreducible minimum* to this area. Take one small step in the right direction today and trust the path will appear in front of you as you move forward. All you need do is take the next step, and the next, and the next.

I Believe In You

Warm winds caress my face. I'm lost in the roar of silence. Waves pound the shoreline, sand swirls in the ocean air as I try to keep my poster boards from flying out to sea.

Yes, I said poster boards—one of the tools my mentor taught me—designed to open me up, expand my heart, and my writing.

The index cards were designed to flesh out and remove blocks. The poster boards, terrifying to the average blocked writer, unbelievably freeing to an openhearted, trusting soul, are designed to *expand* vision. One month on index cards, writing one thought per card as fast as I can, prepares me for the next step of pushing the outer limits of who I am, of becoming the open, fearless, limitless person I was meant to be.

Over the next few months, we will push the envelope by stretching beyond our comfort zone.

Chances are your still, quiet voice has gotten louder by now. Quite possibly, it's shouting, jumping up and down with excitement and joy—open to new possibilities for the first time in a very long time.

However daunting or far-fetched your secret dreams are, just keep putting one foot in front of the other. It *will* happen.

By now you've probably noticed the Universe responding to your soul's longing in the most amazing ways, almost as if it's reading your every thought. It is.

It's exhilarating, isn't it? Haven't you been more excited about life in these last few months? Just wait. More is yet to come.

149

Today's Action
Think back over the last few months and count the miracles or coincidences that have occurred in your life since you picked up this book. That is the Universe responding to your heart's desire. Everything is working toward making all your dreams come true. Let that little spark of belief fly free. Believe that I believe.

Magnificent Madness

My favorite jazz tune is "Magnificent Madness" by saxophonist John Klemmer. Over the years I have tried unsuccessfully to replace an album I lost with this song on it, so I haven't actually heard the song in more than fifteen years, but isn't the title alone delicious?

Ten years ago, a therapist of mine noticed what a slave driver I was with myself and insisted I get a hobby.

"A hobby!" I cried, thinking, *What a waste of time. I have important things to do. I don't have time for frivolousness.* She persisted, and eventually I went to an art-supply store. Although I had always wanted to paint, I felt I had no talent, so I never tried.

That afternoon, I bought some oil paints and brushes, a book on painting, and a few canvases. I tried to follow the book and paint objects that were discernible, such as a bowl of fruit or a vase, but that didn't work very well; my paintings were as crude as those of a child in kindergarten. It was pretty frustrating.

Then, one day, I put an old sheet on the floor and said, *To heck with it! I'm going to paint what I want, the way I want!* Off came the gloves. Down went the paintbrushes and a multitude of colors splashed onto the canvas. Blues, greens, aquamarines, purples, and midnight blues, interspersed with dabs of white, yellow, and red covered the canvas. Looking closely, with blurry eyes, you could see a dolphin frolicking in the ocean. Another with more green, orange, red, and yellow became a parrot in the jungle. I just made it up as I went along. No one could really see anything, but it didn't matter, I was finally having some fun!

I broke out even further from the binds of the "shoulds," cranked up the music a notch, and splashed, zinged, dabbed, stroked, and flung paint everywhere. There was usually more paint on me than on any canvas, but a purple butt and blue legs were half the fun of it. A profusion of color appeared everywhere—wild—exuberant—passionate!

I framed my favorite in a wonderful black and red triple frame and proudly titled it "Magnificent Madness." It was the freest I've ever been *and* the closest to my true nature.

From these small canvases I graduated to bathroom, kitchen, and office walls. You name it. I painted it. Turn up the volume on some old-time rock and roll, put some paint in front of me, throw the brushes away, and let me loose. I did the entire kitchen wall of my mother's old house. When it came time to sell it, I offered to paint over my madness, but the buyer said no, he wanted it exactly the way it was. I guess there's a wild child in all of us.

We May Never Pass This Way Again

A woman came up to me this weekend and thanked me for sharing that *living your bliss* and *God's will* were one and the same. She said she needed to hear that God's will for us *was* our very own heart's desire, and that we will know what our bliss is because it's whatever makes our heart sing. For me, that's writing and sharing with others. Nothing, not even sex or chocolate, gives me as much lasting pleasure.

We fall asleep to this truth and need constant reminding to wake up—at least I did. We may or may not have another life, but we will never pass *this* way again.

We were each created with a special purpose in mind—our Creator's plan for us. Some of us don't know what it is and are seeking to find out. Some of us know, but fear still paralyzes us. Then there are those who are living in synch with God's plan for their lives. You know these people when you see them. There's a glow about them. They radiate joy and peace.

Writing daily for the last few months, I have never been more at peace. The ongoing inner struggle is over. I know I am doing that which I was meant to do. I know this down to my very core. I was born to write.

I love doing many things, but writing is my highest possibility for myself. I can tell, because I remember how it felt before I awakened to writing as my bliss. I remember how it felt when I knew writing was *it* for me, but I had yet to find the courage to do anything but dabble in it. And finally, I remember how it felt to put pen to paper and give God the floor. *My heart sang.*

Once you've awakened to your soul's purpose, you will always know where you are on the continuum of authenticity, based on your actions.

Today's Action | Knowing you will never pass this way again—what are you called to do or be? Are you living up to that? If not, why not? Get beyond the excuses. The truth *will* set you free.

I Saw The Light

Some time ago, I participated in an eight-month workshop designed to stretch you beyond your comfort zone and give you practice at going to any lengths to effect change in your life. Everyone in the workshop had the opportunity to experience his or her willingness to change, or lack of thereof.

Up until this workshop I thought of myself as very willing. During the course of the workshop I went on vacation for a week with my mother and asked the man leading the workshop if I could have the next week's assignment ahead of time to do while I was on vacation. He said no. Stunned, I replied, "Why not?" He then told me to make arrangements to call one of the other members of the workshop the following Monday to get the assignment. I explained that I would be in another country and that not only would it be a very expensive call, but it was not always easy getting through at an appointed time. I asked if he could give me the assignment now, if I promised not to look at it until next Monday. He said no—that it was nonnegotiable. I left feeling resentful—big time!

I complained to Gary, "He could have done this if he wanted to. Who does he think he is anyway—God? He's just a control freak—who has to have his way. I'll be damned if I'm going to make an unnecessary twenty-dollar phone call. Screw him and his stupid assignments."

Well, I went on my trip, got over my anger, made the phone call at the appointed time and paid the eighteen-dollar phone bill. I also received a very memorable lesson in willingness. I found that yes, I was very willing to do the things I already wanted to do, but not willing at all to do the things I deemed unreasonable or didn't understand. In the past, I plopped down twenty dollars in the blink of an eye for drinks or cocaine, but here I was unwilling to spend the same on my personal growth.

It's been over seven years since that workshop and the lesson remains—How willing am I?

To be perfectly honest, I usually pay my credit cards in full, but at the moment I've charged a new computer, a four-hundred-dollar computer program, and my ongoing two-hundred-dollar-a-month sessions with my tutor to my credit cards. It's scary to see my debt rise and my bank balance drop, but I ask myself, "What lengths am I willing to go to? Am I willing to do whatever it takes to get where I want?" Heck, I'd spend fifty dollars a week for therapy, why not the same towards living my bliss?

My dreams deserve my financial backing, and today I am willing to back my dreams with action.

153

Fifth Month

Expanding Love

Take It To The Limit

*I*n that eight-month workshop, which I went on to lead, we asked ourselves four questions each day.

1. What did I notice that had nothing to do with me?

2. What did I do today that I respect myself for?

3. What did I do to help another person today (anonymously if possible)?

4. What bothered me today, if anything?

The assignment was to consciously seek out something to notice every day—not to just record something in retrospect—but to stretch beyond who you normally are. Anything you do without thinking about it is something you would normally do and doesn't count. The same goes with respecting yourself and helping someone. First, connect the thought to the action, *then* take the action. Record what you have done afterwards.

155

Noticing things around me that had nothing to do with me vastly enriched my life. I began by reconnecting with the earth. Whether noticing a magnificent magenta and purple sunset or the faint pink veins in a hibiscus flower, I was awestruck by nature's beauty.

As for respecting myself, this was during the time when I had difficulty saying no. I was overcommitted, overwhelmed, and exhausted all the time. I enjoyed many of the things I was doing, but hadn't learned when to stop. To respect myself, I would take a night off, turn the phone off, and soak in a nice hot bubble bath. I stopped being so stingy with myself and treated myself to a few small luxuries such as fresh raspberries, even when they cost $4.99 for a half-pint.

One day, while driving back from a day in the Florida Keys, I began obsessing about having a hot fudge sundae at the mile marker 98 Dairy Queen. Then the thought occurred to me that I could respect myself by not giving into the craving; I could drive right past the Dairy Queen. I wish I'd never thought that thought. For miles I wanted it, tasted it, and salivated just thinking about it. Rarely am I able to pass up chocolate once I start thinking about it.

Torn, I finally made my mind up *not* to stop at the Dairy Queen. Instead, I would treat myself to something healthier later. However, I wasn't sure I could really make it by the Dairy Queen without stopping. As I approached, I had to laugh out loud at God's sense of humor. The Dairy Queen was closed due to construction. I got to respect myself in spite of myself.

Helping another person was much easier because I had been working on getting out of myself and doing nice things for others for years now. For me, the stretch part was to do *small* things and not tell anyone. The ideas were endless: put a quarter in someone's expired parking meter, throw someone's newspaper closer to their front door, slip some money into someone's purse without them knowing, anonymously send flowers to someone, sharpen a co-worker's pencils at work. Anonymity was important, but I didn't lie if I was caught. Being a good fairy out in the world gave me a wonderful feeling about myself that carried into every area of my life.

As for what bothered me—many days I answered "nothing." Other times, it would be my attitude in traffic. (My behavior had already changed, but what went on in my head was another story.) I wrote when I talked about someone behind their back, under the guise of not understanding how they could be that way. It was still damaging to their character and their spirit even if I meant no harm. I recorded when I neglected to hold the elevator door for someone because I was in a hurry and they were far enough away that I could pretend that I didn't see them. I wrote when I teased someone and hurt their feelings.

The subtle things I don't like about myself ended up in this section. At the same time I had to remember that it was "progress not perfection," and not to be too hard on myself when I fell short.

That workshop taught me to live more consciously but also to be more compassionate with myself. It was most definitely a transformational experience.

Today's Action | Practice the four questions daily for the next month. Use them as a guide, an ideal, not something to get down on yourself for not doing perfectly. Stretching and disciplining ourselves builds character and courage and gives us the fortitude we need to make our dreams come true.

Changes

Another thing we worked on in the workshop was change. Whatever is comfortable—shake it up.

For instance, if you are normally talkative, say as little as possible during the next week. If you are normally shy or introverted, make it a point to speak to at least one new person each day, even if all you say is "hello." If you are in a support group and normally share at meetings, don't. If you normally pass, raise your hand and share this week.

If you usually drive to work, take public transportation, and vice versa. If you take the expressway, allow extra time and take the scenic route for a change.

If the kids usually hang out at your house after school, send them elsewhere and enjoy a few hours of quiet time. If they usually go to a friend's house, invite them over to bake cookies, finger paint, or play an old-fashioned board game. Remember board games from the pre-computer days?

If you've never been comfortable around computers, take a beginner's course or get a tutor. If you feel less than whole when not plugged in, stay off the computer for a week. I know, I know—what about your e-mail! Remember, it's only a week. You'll survive and cyberspace will manage without you for a week. Trust me, it's worth it.

It's so easy to get stuck in a rut, confined to our comfortable routines. Transformation requires that we stretch beyond our comfort zones. This builds the courage and self-esteem necessary for living our bliss.

Go for it! Make that change!

 **Today's Action** | For the next week, do things differently. Be as contrary to your nature as possible. Throw the routine out. Make it up as you go. Experience liberation!

Masquerade

Assertiveness was another lesson from that trusty old workshop. At first, we practiced with strangers. Later, we brought our assertiveness closer to home.

The assignment was to "Tell someone something they don't want to hear, in a kind and loving way." Some examples were: "Excuse me, my food is not cooked the way I specified. Could you please take it back and ask the cook to redo it?" instead of, "This meat is raw! Do you call that well done? What kind of a place is this?" or pushing the food around on the plate, not wanting to be a bother.

In the parking garage of the building where I work, people often don't want to drive up an extra level so they will be facing the correct way when they park. Instead, they ignore directional arrows, cut across, race around the corner in the wrong direction, and then go through all kinds of maneuvers to park their car, since they are now facing against the angle of the parking spaces.

Many a morning I've come within a foot of being hit by someone cutting through to a space they spotted. A few close calls rattled me to the point where I was shaking. I was so angry afterward that I really want to give them a piece of my mind. Instead, I just muttered to myself, and ignored or glaring at them when we got to the elevator.

On the week of this assertiveness assignment, I had another narrow escape from a man barreling around that corner. However, this time when I ran into him at the elevator, I said very nicely, "I don't know if you realize it, but you were going the wrong way and almost hit me." He looked away. I spoke up again firmly, but not angry, "It's very danger-ous to do that and it really shook me up. Please don't do it again."

When you approach someone in this manner, you're much more likely to be listened to than when you are screaming at them. Attacking someone puts them on the defensive. Speaking up in a kind and loving manner—stating how you feel and asking for what you would like in the future—often produces unexpected results.

158   Believe it or not, this big, gruff, harried man turned to me and said, "I'm sorry." I accepted his apology and we parted ways, having had an authentic encounter that neither of us will soon forget.

Later, I brought this practice of speaking up for myself in a kind and loving way closer to home by practicing it with my mother and my husband. It is very empowering.

Today's Action | Keep your eyes open and when an opportunity presents itself, say something to someone else that they probably won't want to hear, in a kind and loving way. Note how you feel about yourself afterwards.

You Can't Always Get What You Want

A week before I was scheduled to start chemotherapy, I was advised by my oncology nurse that it would be less awkward to buy a wig while I still had hair. A few weeks earlier, my mother, my husband, and I had a conference with the doctor about whether chemotherapy was necessary, and if so, what to expect. The doctor told us his recommendations and that if I chose the clinical trial he was suggesting, there was a 100 percent chance I would lose my hair.

Once the decision was made, I went to a wig store in search of new locks. I must admit I was more than a little excited about my new purchase. I had already cut my long blonde curls to just above my shoulders in preparation for D-Day. I was told this would be less of a shock and make losing my hair easier.

Initially, I tried on wigs similar to my own hair, but they all looked like big, floppy mops. Then, the owner of the shop suggested a new look altogether. As we talked, she confided in me that she opened this wig store fifteen years ago after she had lost all of her hair due to chemotherapy; another little *Godincidence*.

The wig I finally picked out was a dramatic Cleopatra style wig. I looked like Barbara Feldman from *Get Smart* or Uma Thurman in *Pulp Fiction*. I felt exotic in my sexy, swingy, new hair. Who would have thought you could actually look pretty while fighting cancer? Yet the contrast of the sleek, dark hair against my light eyes was striking, and I felt beautiful.

When I excitedly told my mother about my new wig, her response was not what I had expected, "Well honey, if you think you're going to lose your hair, you will," as if I had some kind of mental control over my hair loss! And I suppose I willed cancer on myself, too! I could feel my anger welling up. Then, I remembered "kind and loving." I stopped, took a deep breath, and replied calmly, "Mom, the doctor said there were no if, ands, or buts about my losing my hair. It's a scientific fact due to the chemical changes that will be going on in my body, not a psychosomatic reaction to them. I'm preparing for that reality in the best way I know how, and I could really use your help right now."

Although my mother is a breast cancer survivor, she doesn't believe in traditional medicine. In fact, she calls chemotherapy *poison* and tells me she would never put it in *her* body. Lovingly, but firmly, I asked my mother for her support; I was having a hard enough time dealing with the cancer and subsequent decisions about treatment, I didn't need the added friction of my mother's judgments.

It was hard for me to ask for what I needed and I assume hard for her to hear. But I spoke up for myself at every crossroad and for each decision. I know my mother loves me and means well; she was probably filled with fear, but it came off as negating my own beliefs about what was best for me.

Financially, my mother made the alternative medicine approaches possible and for that I am very grateful. However, I chose a *combination* of traditional medicine and alternative therapies and would not have been comfortable with alternative medicine alone. My mother, on the other hand might be, and I would honor that. When it came to me though, I had to follow my own internal wisdom about what I believed would be best, and enlist those closest to me for support me.

Speaking up for myself with my mother was assertiveness on a much deeper level than with a stranger in a garage, and even more empowering.

Today's Action | Who do you need to take a stand with, speak up to, or in some way state your truth to? Do so in a kind and loving way.

Respect

The boundaries I set with my husband early set the tone for our entire relationship.

My husband, as I've mentioned, was an IV drug user for many years and had a long history of unemployment. Both of these issues surfaced during our first few months together and needed to be addressed. First, although we had been practicing safe sex, Gary had not been tested for the HIV virus and was certainly at high risk for it. Second, Gary was periodically unemployed during our first few months together, and I began picking up the tab for most of our movies and meals. I didn't want to be stingy, but I also didn't want to enable someone, or be taken advantage of.

I sought a friend's guidance because I was beginning to get a little resentful. I thought I was angry with Gary, but really I was angry with myself for crossing my own internal values. My friend assured me that it was okay to state my needs and ask for what I wanted—but that I had to be willing to let go completely if Gary could not hear me. It is my responsibility to take care of myself, but it's *not* healthy for me to try to control another person's behavior. Sitting around wishing someone would do the right thing or nagging endlessly, no longer cut it for me. I had to take action, then let go.

I called Gary and we went to a park to talk about what was on my mind. I assured him I cared very much for him and did not want to stop seeing him. However, there were a couple of things that were bothering me. It went something like this:

"Gary, I have been a caretaker all my life. Although it's none of my business whether you work or not, I need to be with someone who is fully self-supporting. I can't *tell* you to get a job, but I can let you know that I am no longer comfortable seeing someone who is not working, and I am not willing to pick up all the tabs any longer. Also, I can't tell you to get tested for the virus, but I value my life too much to bank on whether some prophylactic holds. I will no longer have even *protected* sex with you until I see a negative HIV test result."

Whew, it was done. I had said what I needed to say and didn't feel anxious anymore. In fact, it felt great to speak my truth. It was unbelievably self-affirming to take a stand for myself, not out of anger or control, but out of self-love and knowing my own worth.

Within a week, Gary had a job and a negative test result. No coercion was necessary, just simple truth. It turns out Gary was scared to take the test, so it was a big relief for both of us when it was over.

These simple actions on both our parts set the tone for our entire relationship. Self- and mutual respect for each other is, some ten years later, still the cornerstone of our marriage. To this day, I think respect is *as* important as love in any long-term relationship. In fact, the first thing I ask someone who's having relationship difficulties or trying to decide whether to stay in a relationship or not is, "Do you respect them?"

Their answer tells me all I need to know.

Today's Action | Is there any area of your life where you have been afraid to speak your truth? Take a risk and ask for what you need. Let go of control and anger, but claim the respect you deserve.

Leading With Your Heart

One day I considered changing sponsors from Patricia, my spiritual guide of the last seven years. I called a woman who spoke at a recent recovery convention. During our conversation, I sensed that, although this woman was a wonderful speaker, she was the ultimate taskmaster. By the end of our brief conversation she had given me three self-improvement assignments. This was not what I needed.

After years of working on myself and trying to please others, I am finally living as *I* choose. I write daily, but I also find time for play, spiritual growth, physical activity, and relaxation. I no longer compulsively work on myself. I honor my inner guide.

Today, I am gentle with myself. I live my bliss and am comfortable in the moment. If I am moved to take a particular action, I take it. If not, I let it sink in for possible future use. *Letting Your Heart Sing* guides you to *your* inner truth, not mine or anyone else's. Some actions take courage, some take discipline, and some simply reconnect you with Spirit, helping you enter that quiet space necessary to nurture your very soul. All exercises are designed to help you live the way you really want, the way God intended.

Ask your Higher Power or Higher Self to guide you. Then trust and let go.

Let everything quench your thirst, revitalize your spirit, nurture your inner child, and lift you up to the highest possibility for yourself.

| Today's Action | Enjoy the mix. Allow your heart to guide you. Trust the process. |

You Taught My Heart To Sing

A young woman approached me after a recent "Bliss Workshop" with tears in her eyes and said, "I really needed to hear what you said about knowing your bliss when you find it—because it will be whatever makes your heart sing. I don't know what mine is yet, but you gave me hope that I will know what it is when I'm singing on the inside." I was so touched. Thank you, God.

There is so much we are meant to do during our time on earth. We each have responsibilities and opportunities. We can choose to shirk or ignore them. Or we can step up to the plate and say, "I am ready." Even when we don't know what we are ready for, we can open our hearts and say, "I am ready." The lessons will come.

If you have not found your bliss or *Right Livelihood* yet—stay open, it will come. Stretch, risk, and listen, it will come. And you will recognize it when it comes. Trust that. Know that. Be that.

One way I open myself to my divine purpose is to attend weekly meditation meetings. The first ten minutes are for quiet meditation. During this time you can focus on your breath, listen to the music, pray, visualize, or simply be quiet. For me this is a very sacred time. It is a time to commune with my Higher Self, a time to experience my connection with others. It is a time of infinite power and peace . . . deep, perfect peace.

After the quiet time, a speaker shares his or her spiritual experiences. It is a time for identification, bonding, and enlightenment. Something miraculous happens when like-minded people gather—spirit expands and deepens.

Our lights burn brighter. We rejoin the world with our spirits restored.

Today's Action | Where do you experience a sense of community with others? Do you have regular spiritual practices? If not, be open to finding a spiritual home, a spiritual resting place.

You Encourage My Soul

Namaste.

Namaste means *the light in me honors the light in you. Namaste* is a traditional Indian soul greeting. When I say, "*Namaste,*" to someone, it is my highest self, my highest possibility, honoring the same in them.

163

A meditation tape I listen to called *Meditations with Gail,* ends with Gail saying, "*Namaste, my loved one.*" And that is exactly how I feel when I finish listening to the tape, like someone's loved one.

Guided meditation tapes are wonderful tools for spiritual growth. I have developed quite a collection over the years: Shirley MacLaine, Shakti Gawain, Louise L. Hay, and others. However, my absolute favorite is a homemade tape someone gave me of *Meditations with Gail.* I would advise you to buy it, but I have never seen it in a store. By writing about it here, I hope that someone reading this book will know Gail and e-mail me at LetYourHeartSing@aol.com. I would love to thank her. (By the way, I welcome all e-mail.)

You see, *Letting Your Heart Sing* is not only about breathing out, but breathing in as well. As I breathe out some of my knowledge, I breathe in knowledge from others. There have been so many synchronistic occurrences around this book that I half expect Gail to drop me a line.

But just in case that does not happen, I want to thank the Universe for Gail's soothing gift. Thank you, Gail. Thank you, God.

The Way We Were

"Memories . . . misty water-colored memories . . . "

This morning, in meditation, my great-grandmother Gammy's spirit guided me to bridge the gap in my family caused by long-held resentments. I saw the faces of my grandmother, Jackie, and her sister, my Aunt Fi, and felt their hearts' sorrow. Tears streamed down my face as I felt their pain and my own loss.

In the background, Gammy's voice quietly urged me, "Don't give up. Try once more."

164 As sad as I was, hearing her voice brought back wonderful memories. Gammy loved chocolate candy. On special occasions someone always gave her a box of chocolates. After Gammy took the first piece, the rest were fair game, so I poked the bottom of every piece to see what filling was inside. Gammy called me persnickety.

With Gammy you got more than just a grandmother, you got the English teacher in her, "*May* I have some chocolate? Not, '*Can* I.'" Fifty years of teaching English at an all-girls' school indelibly shaped her as a grandmother. I learned all my pleases and thank yous as Gammy tried to teach me to be a proper young lady—an impossible task to a sixties' child. However, Gammy wasn't all prim and proper; there was a mischievous side to her, too.

On Gammy's eightieth birthday, we had a huge family dinner in the back room of our favorite Italian restaurant, Valenti's, in downtown Miami. Mirrors covered the wall of the long, private room where twenty members of my family gathered in celebration. Dinner took forever to serve. Restless, my brothers, cousins, and I flicked garbanzo beans at each other from our salads to pass time.

When no one was looking, Gammy put a pat of butter on her napkin, pulled the napkin hard and fast and the butter flew to the ceiling, sticking there. It was a riot. Careful not to let any adults catch her teaching us that trick, she put her napkin back in her lap and pretended it never happened. The only tell-tale signs were the twinkle in her eye and the pat of butter on the ceiling. What a wonderful moment—young and old—bonding together forever through shared naughtiness.

More than twenty years have passed since Gammy died, and her daughters have not spoken a civil word to each other since before the funeral. No more big family dinners, no more barbecues. Hundreds of lost memories, memories that will never be, because they never were.

Today, I am not sure anyone even remembers why they stopped speaking, they simply don't.

"Memories may be beautiful and yet . . .

what's too painful to remember, we simply choose to forget."

For years I tried to heal the wounds and bring them together, but the resentments ran too deep. Eventually, the hatred carried over to my mother and then to her children. My mother and grandmother say they are willing to work it out; however, Aunt Fi is adamant and will have nothing to do with my mother or grandmother. Can anything be worth holding onto for all these years?

Ten years have passed since I last tried to get them to speak to each other. I guess Gammy thinks it is time again.

It is so sad to see families split over petty differences. We ought to be able to forgive the past and live in the present. But can we?

Time is short. My grandmother and her sister are in their eighties and will not live forever. I will try to bridge the gap again, for Gammy, for all of us.

God, I pray that a healing takes place in my family, that we might find peace, healing, and forgiveness while there is still breath in our bodies.

Today's Action | Are there rifts between any of your family members or friends? Have you tried to restore relations? Maybe it is time to try again—time to allow God's love in, time to heal the wounds.

Teach Me Tonight

When Gammy died at age eighty-seven, guilt overshadowed my sadness. I had not been the best granddaughter I could have been. I did not go to the nursing home as often as I should have.

Towards the end, she did not even know who I was, so I thought it did not matter. And I hated going to the nursing home; it smelled like old people. I probably visited more than I remember, but I felt it was not enough. I should have done more. I also carried the weight of not being able to give Gammy the one thing she wanted most: *peace in the family*. I had tried and failed. My heart was heavy with remorse.

I buried my pain as best I could with my ever-increasing consumption of alcohol and cocaine, but I felt shame whenever I thought about Gammy.

Fifteen years after Gammy died, I found some semblance of peace. I stopped partying and faced my past. Sitting still for perhaps the first time in my life, stone-cold sober, I grieved. I looked at old pictures, reminisced with family members, and wrote letters to Gammy. And I cried.

Over time my feelings of loss lessened, but the guilt and shame remained. It was not until I took action to spiritually atone for my wrongs, that I truly began to heal. I decided to make amends to Gammy by volunteering in a nursing home—the last place I wanted to spend my Saturday afternoons—but the exact place I needed to be in order to heal.

The stark odor filled my nostrils the moment I walked through the big, double doors of Villa Maria Nursing Home in North Miami. I wanted to turn and run, but I did not. I embraced my remorse, my guilt, and my shame and signed in at the front desk. Every Saturday afternoon for the next four months, I visited elderly people, took them outdoors for fresh air, and read to them.

My official duties: to attend to patients' spiritual needs. I noted who wanted to see the rabbi, attend Mass, or wanted members of their congregation to visit them. But mostly I listened. I listened to their complaints. I listened while they reminisced. I listened to their stories: everyone had a story. And I listened as they called me by their granddaughters' names, knowing these granddaughters probably didn't visit as often as they would have liked, either.

My eyes well up with tears every time I think of the healing I received that fall. I regained my integrity and experienced a deep sense of peace. I ministered to those in need in ways I was unable to for my own great-grandmother. Yet somehow, spiritually, they are all one and the same.

As I gave back to the Universe in memory of my great-grandmother, my heart opened to the truth: *Any harm you do to one—you do to all; any healing you bring to one—you bring to all.*

I have had many spiritual healings, but none more healing than the day I read scripture to a blind woman. Sitting in her dimly lighted hospital room, I read Bible verses, and she explained their meaning. Listening to that very frail woman lie in bed interpreting Bible stories was like being taught by my great-grandmother one more time. One last lesson. One final story.

I Am A Rock

I have not spoken to my cousin, Dean, or his mother, Fi, since she verbally trashed my mother, in my presence, three-and-a-half years ago. Until that moment, I knew Fi and mother didn't get along, but we just never talked about it. After the Christmas incident, though, I decided I could no longer be in a relationship with anyone who hated my mother that much. Then came the meditation and Gammy's words, "Let there be peace in the family." Nervous, I dialed Dean's number. He sounded so different; he is forty-six years old now, and a grandfather—amazing. I still remember him as the lanky teenager with a go-kart.

We caught up on each other's lives, and then I inquired about Aunt Fi. She still lives in the same house and as he says, "She hasn't changed a bit." I told Dean I felt it was time to mend fences. He said, "I've tried on and off for years, but gave up. My mother doesn't have it in her to forgive your mother and grandmother. When it comes to this she is like a mammoth granite cliff: immovable."

I expressed my disbelief and Dean continued, "There's not enough dynamite in the world to budge her. I love a challenge, that's why I tried so many times, but she is beyond challenge, she's impossible." I can't tell you how sad I was to hear that. The thought of these three women dying with no forgiveness in their hearts just broke mine.

When I see movies of healing broken relationships or read articles on forgiveness, I always think of my mother, Aunt Fi, and Jackie. I had hoped that someday, someway . . . now I wonder if it is even possible to heal resentment so deep that it is imbedded into your very being. My cousin suggested my energies could be put to better use elsewhere.

But the meditation, what did it mean if not to try again?

I have decided to pray to God for *his* will and the courage to carry it out—whatever it is.

> **Today's Action** Is there a seemingly impossible situation in your life? Try prayer. The energy released through prayer is powerful medicine. I will keep you posted as to how this prayer gets answered.

The Prayer

As we look back on our lives, we will find many pleasant and unpleasant memories both. The task is to embrace our fond and loving memories and to heal the unpleasant ones. Looking forward can be as difficult as looking back, for in looking ahead, we need to envision how we might forgive ourselves and others. This is a necessary part of the journey though, and freedom and peace await us on the other side. Knowing that, how can we not move ahead?

Looking ahead, I hold tightly to this prayer:

Lord, make me a channel of thy peace—

That where there is hatred, I may bring love—

That where there is wrong, I may bring the spirit of forgiveness—

That where there is discord, I may bring harmony—

That where there is error, I may bring truth—

That where there is doubt, I may bring faith—

That where there is despair, I may bring hope—

That where there are shadows, I may bring light—

That where there is sadness, I may bring joy.

Lord, grant that I may seek rather to comfort than to be comforted—

To understand, than to be understood—

To love, than to be loved.

For it is by self-forgetting that one finds—

It is by forgiving that one is forgiven—

And it is by dying that one awakens to eternal life.

169

Basically, the prayer says: *Where there is a problem, let me bring a solution.*

As we bring more love into each area of our lives, we change the world—one household at a time, one community at a time, one state at a time, one country at a time—until the entire planet is changed.

When we act out of love, shifts too profound to imagine occur all around us. The ongoing ripple effect of our tiny lives is beyond comprehension.

The one small act of my calling my cousin will affect his life and mine in ways we cannot even fathom. Merely writing about it will touch chords, provoke memories, and inspire actions that change the course of lives.

One never knows how God is going to use these acts, and we must always be open and ready to be that channel of light and love we are called to be.

Contemplate the St. Francis of Assisi prayer and bring its meaning into your heart. Watch its healing power as you take it into your life from this moment forward.

Me And You And A Dog Named Boo

Karma likes to play fetch; a bit unusual for an orange tabby, but whenever I crumple up a piece of paper, he comes a-running. I throw it, and off he barrels after it. Then pounce, pounce, pounce, comes the kitty, right up to my chest, dropping his makeshift ball for me to throw again. There must be some "dog" in him, although to my knowledge he has never been around a dog. Maybe in another life . . .

My other cat, Magic, loves to be brushed. He constantly rubs up against my legs, especially when I forget to shave; anything to get a good whisker rub. His idea of heaven is having his shiny coat brushed until it feels like velvet.

My brother's dog loves to romp in the fields and valleys of Colorado, chasing whatever moves. Rabbit, deer, or tennis ball—watch out when Cody is on the prowl.

Winky, another kitten I rescued, is content to curl up next to me in bed while I scratch her head.

Something happens when you play or spend time with animals. It reconnects you to your spirit and fills your heart with joy and love. Animals are so unabashed with their affection for us—whether it's the wag of a tail or a motor purring—you always know you are loved.

What I love most about animals is they are not shy about asking for what they want. I have recently taken to asking Gary to pet me. He thinks it's silly, but obliges. If I could come back as someone's adored cat I would. Except for the food (I hate fish), the life is great. You get to sleep and eat all day, and people are at your beck and call. Sounds grand.

The love exchanged between animals and their human caretakers is so unconditional. It is perfect to get us back in touch with our loving spirit.

Spend some time today, real quality time, with your pet. If you do not have a pet, volunteer to take a neighbor's dog for a walk or stop by a pet shop or the local Humane Society and find a new friend. It will expand your heart and increase your capacity for love.

Feeling Groovy

I must say, these poster boards are a bitch to write on at the beach. And of course, today is particularly windy. With boards flapping and flying around every which way, I write.

I write because I can't not write. I write because I breathe.

When you do that which you love, it takes on a life of its own. You become the supporting staff—the center. And the center is bliss. You become it. It becomes you.

It really does become you.

Haven't you noticed you are smiling more? Don't you look at others with more compassion? Isn't judgment slipping away?

There is no time for any of that now. You are living as you have always wanted. Each day you gain more courage to take another step. It feels good. It feels right.

You are not even sure where you are going. You don't care. You are just living and breathing bliss and loving every minute of it. Ain't life grand?

Today's Action	Engage in your bliss. Do what you love. Dive in and have a magnificent day.

From The Beginning

At birth, God placed in each of our hearts a desire, a plan for our lives. This plan is God's will for us here on earth. To live it is to fulfill our highest purpose. When we are in sync with this plan, everything feels right. Conflict disappears. Difficulties fade. Our step is lighter, our voices clearer. People are attracted to our light. They see the spark in our eyes and want what we have. We are beyond happy—we are joyful.

What is our unique contribution? It could be anything. How will we know? We just will. If there are any doubts, all we have to do is put it out into the Universe that we are looking for a sign. It will come. Just like in the movie, *Field of Dreams*, "*Build it and they will come.*" Trust and it will come.

If you are living from the heart, you know what I am talking about. If not, you know that, too. It is our dharma; that which we are meant to do. Our destiny. Each of us has an inner knowing, a connection to the Divine Plan. We may need to clear and heal the past in order to get to it. Or we may need to suffer a tragic event to awaken fully to it.

The John Walshes and Jim Bradys of the world know how great that loss may be that calls us forward. Christopher Reeve knows. Michael J. Fox knows. The woman who started Mothers Against Drunk Driving (MADD) knows just how angry we sometimes need to get before we can effect change in our lifetime.

There are thousands of organizations where we can make a contribution. Or maybe the contribution we are to make will come through our careers or, quite possibly, through parenting. We never know when or where our opportunities will come, so we must always be ready. With everyone we meet, in every circumstance, great or small—we have an opportunity to make a difference.

Today's Action | Awaken to your dharma today by asking, "What kind of contribution am I going to make today?" Pick flowers from your garden and give them to neighbor, take a home-cooked meal to a new mother, write a poem to cheer someone who is a bit down, or paint picture for a friend. Do what you love, then pass the love on.

You Make Loving Fun

Play and laughter are two things we don't do or hear nearly enough. When they tell us to come to God as little children, they are referring to our spirits—that our spirits be open, trusting, filled with awe and wonder, alive with excitement and anticipation of the adventure ahead. My heart and my spirit are childlike, though my years number forty.

I am often told I look younger than I am. Frankly, I do not care. My body is only a vehicle. Yes, I take care of it, but I have never been much on adornment or accessories. That is why I love the recent simplicity books. They speak to my soul: less *is* more. It is liberating to be in the downsizing mode as opposed to the accumulating mode. I love it. I embrace it. It keeps me in touch with my childlike spirit.

Instead of shopping or taking hours to get ready to go somewhere, my free time is spent singing, swimming, or building sandcastles at the beach. Riding my bicycle, reading, writing, golfing, going to the movies, or riding on the Harley with Gary is so much more fun than spending hours in front of a mirror.

Gary and I tease each other often. Sometimes we laugh so hard we literally fall right out of bed. I wish I could remember some examples. Well, actually I can, but this will not be for the prudish.

We read a flyer about a book called *The Tao of Love and Sex* and one of the concepts was "1,000 Loving Strokes." That is all the information we had, so we made up our own story and made it sort of a goal to reach in our sex life—you know actual strokes—or was it thrusts? Anyway, you can imagine some of the resulting jokes . . . er . . . uh . . . strokes.

The first time we made love after reading this flyer, we counted the . . . you know . . . uh . . . strokes. Laughing and a stroking, we got as high as sixty-four—and then Gary stopped. "What happened?" I asked. "You were laughing so hard . . . the contractions from your laughter felt so good . . . I couldn't help myself." And we both cracked up all over again.

Next time we tried this, we debated over who would keep count. We decided to take turns. When Gary counted, I asked, "How many was that?" and he answered, "One hundred sixty." Then a few strokes later he began counting out loud, "one hundred sixty-four, two hundred sixty-five, three hundred sixty-six," until we fell into a mass of giggles. Next time, I counted normally and we quadrupled our count, but one thousand was still so far away that Gary asked, "How many tries do I get? How many lifetimes?"

You can imagine how hysterical the last few weeks in bed have been. And of course I tell all my girlfriends. And of course they tease him about the sixty-four on the first attempt. Now the whole world will know. It is a good thing Gary has high self-esteem and loves a challenge. We both agree—progress, not perfection. I figure we can only go up from here.

Today's Action | Where can you bring more laughter into your life? Work, home, family, your love life—there are so many opportunities. Embrace your playful spirit and that of others; come to God as little children.

I Will Walk With You

The night I took my bandages off, I experienced a side of myself I had never seen: Helpless. Even after Gary bathed me, I was still crying. After he left the bedroom, I tightened the sash on my bathrobe and got down on my knees for the first time since my diagnosis.

I prayed as I have never prayed before. "God, I know you're there. I know you are walking with me, but I need to *really* know it. I can't handle this pain alone. I need help. I don't know what to do or how to cope. I have never prayed for a sign before, but I need one now. I need you to let me know, without a doubt, that you are walking with me. God, *please* help me."

While getting dressed, the title of Betty Rollins's book, *First You Cry*, came to me. Written in 1976, it was the first book about a woman's personal experience with breast cancer. The title alone comforted me.

Up until this point, I had been putting up a brave front. Now, my defenses were stripped away with the bandages. Everyone I knew was coping so well that I felt there was no one I could turn to. Besides, my pride did not want anyone to see me this vulnerable. I felt so scared and all alone. *The author of* First You Cry *will understand. I need to get that book.*

I asked Gary to take me to the bookstore. Then the phone rang. It was a woman named Pam whom I had met at a Twelve-Step meeting a couple of weeks earlier. I had shared about having cancer and being scared. We talked for a few minutes after the meeting, but I do not remember giving her my phone number.

"How are you doing?" she asked. Since I was still in the thick of it, everything came out: how scared I was of dying, the shame I felt about my disfigured body, how irreversible it all was—everything. Pam told me she had the same surgery and chemotherapy seven years ago and had been scared of dying, too. She said she cried a lot, too. Pam understood everything.

Pam assured me that I would be fine and that she would be there with me to celebrate my five-year milestone of being cancer-free (a big deal in cancer circles). We cried together and promised to meet the following week. As I hung up the phone, *hope* hung in the air that had previously held only *despair*.

I rushed to the living room, "Gary, Gary! I just finished praying. I asked God to give me a sign to let me know he was with me—hearing my pleas. I hadn't been off my knees two minutes when the phone rang. It was Pam, a woman I met a couple of weeks ago. I don't remember giving her my number. In fact, I barely remember meeting her—but there she was on the phone. Somehow she knew the exact moment to call. God isn't just listening, saying, 'Someday I'll get back to you.' He's *really* listening!"

I was ecstatic. I could not believe how quickly and perfectly my prayer was answered. I guess I should be used to it by now, but it never ceases to amaze me how closely God walks with us. The multitude of inexplicable, synchronistic occurrences cannot be explained away as simple coincidence.

This incident reminded me, one more time, that God is always there. Through the laughter and the tears, God is *always* there.

Today's Action | These *Godincidences* are the miraculous ways in which God reveals himself to us time and again. Today, with open eyes and open heart, notice the *Godincidences* in your life. If you have a particular need—put it out into the Universe in the form of a prayer. Then watch as the inexplicable happens. Allow God's perfect timing to reveal itself to you today.

Yes I'm Your Angel

Off we went to the bookstore to buy *First You Cry*. God had more surprises in store for me as Gary and I made our way to the ever-increasing section of cancer books. When we passed the audiotape section, my eyes were inexplicably drawn to a section of wellness tapes by Belleruth Naparstek. Two titles jumped out at me *Cancer* and *Chemotherapy* and I purchased them.

The next morning, I lay down on my trusty beige couch with my headphones and wondered what Belleruth and God had in store for me. It turns out the tapes were guided-imagery tapes designed to promote healing in the mind, body, and spirit.

The soothing voice on the tape brought me to a place of deep relaxation and then I was guided to look up and see someone familiar coming towards me. As clear as day, it was my great-grandmother, Gammy. She took my hands in hers and I was overcome with emotion. I had not seen her in almost twenty years.

At first, joy filled my being as I experienced Gammy's presence. Then it hit me. *Gammy died of cancer.* Without my even expressing my fear to her, she answered immediately, "No, I'm not here to come and get you. Yes, I died of cancer, but you are not going to. I am here to help you *through* it."

Tears of relief streamed down my face as my great-grandmother's spirit comforted me. I reflected on her words and began to believe I might actually make it.

I had no idea that a meditation tape could be so powerful.

Whether the healing took place in my mind, heart, or spirit does not matter—its impact was profound. And I just *know* it was Divine Intervention that had me in *that* bookstore, *that* night, buying *that* book, seeing *those* tapes on *that* shelf. It could be no other way. From Gary's bathing me so tenderly, then the thought of *First You Cry*, then my prayer, then Pam's phone call, and finally finding the tapes in the bookstore—it was all too perfect. God was finding many ways to let me know he was walking with me.

That night, only one week after my mastectomy, was the first of many harrowing nights to come, but my ever-increasing faith carried me through them. Whenever I lose my way, I remember how perfectly God answers prayers.

He knows our every need, sometimes even before we do.

Draw strength from the knowledge that our loved ones who have gone on ahead are always there to help us.

Today's Action | Reconnect with your loved ones in spirit. If you have any physical ailments, check out Belleruth Naparstek's audiotapes on heart disease, diabetes, depression, stress, and many other topics. They will bring great healing as they deepen your spiritual connection with the mysteries of life and possibly even the afterlife.

Reunited

The most exciting thing happened this weekend. I can't wait to tell you about it. Saturday, the day after I spoke with my cousin Dean, Gary called to say he would be working until midnight. Normally, this would upset me, but not this time. I made the best of it and went to the new Robert Redford movie, *The Horse Whisperer*. It was wonderful—all about healing the past, grieving wounds, and dealing with relationships.

The movie ended at 7:30 P.M. and I did not feel like going home yet, so I went to a Twelve-Step meeting near the theater. Arriving early, I said hi to a few people, and sat down. As I sat down, a feeling came over me. *I am not supposed to be here.*

Funny, I thought, *Why not?*

Next, came a sensation, not a thought, but an inner knowing, a feeling of being pulled. I got up, left my seat, and went to my car. As soon as I sat in my car, I knew where I was meant to be: my Aunt Fi's house.

Mind you, this is the immovable aunt, whom I have not seen in more than three years. But for some reason, I just knew I was supposed to be there. I thought of calling first, but the voice said, "*Just go.*" So off I drove.

I was not nervous at all, which was unusual considering the circumstances. There was a strange mix of peace and quiet anticipation. Time felt suspended in a surreal kind of way.

It was getting dark as I drove into the driveway, but I could still make out the old Poinciana tree that covers the entire front lawn. Heavy with its huge orange and crimson blossoms, you have to duck under the branches to reach the front door. A smile came across my face as I ducked in that old familiar way and approached the front porch with its expansive windows.

"Is anyone home?" I yelled. One of her boarders came to the door. (Aunt Fi rents out rooms to supplement her income.) I told him who I was and that I had not seen my aunt in a very long time. "This should be interesting," he said and called her to the front door. "Good luck," he whispered as he turned to leave.

177

My aunt opened the door, and I took in her features. Her dark eyes were set in a kinder, older face than I remembered. Her rich auburn hair was now a duller, bottled version. Watching her, I realized she was eighty years old.

She had just come in from having dinner with friends and seemed delighted to see me. She showed me around the house, pointing out items of interest: a yellowed copy of "The Lord's Prayer" on the wall, pictures of her son and his family, a frayed picture of my great-grandmother and me. As my aunt held the picture, I noticed she had Gammy's hands; the same hands her sister has and my mother is getting. Our family's hands: the same hands I will have someday. Weathered hands. Strong hands. Soft hands. Kind hands.

I had not thought of Aunt Fi as kind in a very long time. For years, I thought of her as crazy and incredibly hateful and scary, like Glenn Close in *Fatal Attraction.*

I realized that in all the years this feud has been going on, I never once asked Aunt Fi about it, only my mother and grandmother. Aunt Fi was always so unapproachable. But not now; somehow the years had made her less threatening.

We caught up on everyone we were allowed to talk about, and then I told her why I was there.

"Aunt Fi, this might be hard to talk about, but I want to know what happened to break up our family."

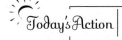

If I Could Turn Back Time

"You don't want to know, and *I* don't want to talk about it!" replied Aunt Fi, fury descending upon her face.

"My mother and Jackie haven't been much help and I'd really like to understand what happened," I replied calmly.

"I don't want to turn you against your mother or grandmother. And I don't want you to know how awful they were to me and to Gammy. You should never have to hear that!" she spat out viciously.

"It hurts that our family is broken apart and I don't even know why. No one will tell me," I responded evenly.

Before she could stop herself, everything poured out. "This is not about money, but your mother stole my mother's home and her money." (Now I know my mother never stole anything from anyone, but I was not there to defend, just to listen.) Aunt Fi went on to tell me every wrong ever committed against her. Every time she paused I opened my heart and extended love. For the very first time, I was able to hear beyond the anger to the pain.

I saw the hurt little girl inside this eighty-year-old woman's body.

As she ranted and raved about my mother and grandmother, I listened. I did not become defensive or try to change her point of view. I just listened. I learned long ago that one of the most powerful ways you can show someone you love them is to listen with all your heart.

My aunt gave twenty-five years of resentment a voice and was heard, unconditionally, for perhaps the very first time.

Finally, the charge of her anger subsided, and I asked if she thought it was possible to heal these wounds.

"Never!" replied my aunt, unequivocally.

"Aunt Fi, I know a healing would mean a lot to Gammy, because I remember Gammy once took my hands into hers and said, 'Debbie, if anyone can bring this family together, you can.' I know you feel my mother wronged you, but the woman I know today is warm and generous and would never knowingly hurt anyone. She loved you very much."

"And I loved her too, but I will never see or talk to her again. Debbie, you have your family and I have mine. Let's just leave it at that," my aunt replied.

We talked of other things, and I shared Dharma's story with her.

When I was ready to leave, I asked my aunt if she would do me a favor.

She nodded.

I took her hand and walked down the hall where the aging copy of "The Lord's Prayer" hung on the wall.

"Would you say this prayer with me?" I asked.

"Of course I will, honey. I would love to," Aunt Fi responded.

Today's Action | Take "The Lord's Prayer" into your heart and look at an old wound in new way.

In The Living Years

We knelt down together and I prayed out loud, "Dear God, thank you for placing my aunt back in my life. Thank you for this wonderful time together. Please, God, help us see what we need to see and heal what we need to heal."

Then we prayed "The Lord's Prayer" together, paying special attention to, ". . . *and forgive us our trespasses as we forgive those who trespassed against us.*"

She finished with a few words of her own and we headed back toward the front of the house. I could tell she did not want me to leave.

Lingering in the darkened hallway, she confessed, "Debbie, you know I have nightmares every week. It's always the same—your mother, Jackie, and I are fighting. Then, Gammy comes in and tells me to give them whatever they want so that there will be peace in the family. Then she pushes me down."

"Do you think your dream signifies that you won't find peace until you resolve this unfinished business?" I asked.

"I knew you were going to say that, but I just cannot see or talk to them. I can't take the yelling that would come back to me. I just can't." Fi responded, her eyes pleading with me to understand.

My heart filled with compassion and sadness.

"What do you want from me?" she asked.

"Do you really want to know?" I asked.

"Yes," she answered.

"I envision my mother coming here and listening to you as I have and making whatever amends or restitution that would make things right. I think she would do that," I said.

"No, no, no. I cannot see her!" she wailed.

"Okay. It's okay. You asked, so I told you how I would like things to be, but I accept that you are not able to see her yet. It's okay," I said.

We hugged goodnight, and my aunt said, "I'll think about it."

God placed me in the right place at the right time that a healing might take place. Something shifted in me that night, and I am sure the same is true for my aunt.

My last words to her were, "Sleep well tonight."

This story is a work in process. I do not yet know the ending. I *do* know God is leading and I am following. I do not believe, as my cousin does, that my aunt's position is immovable and that a healing is impossible.

I believe that *with God . . . all things are possible.*

No matter how great the wounds, God can heal all things—if you let him.

☼ Today's Action | Pray for guidance. Ask where you might be used, so that a healing could take place. Sometimes we do not owe the amends ourselves but are meant to facilitate them. Be open. Trust your intuition.

More Than A Feeling

Nancy's Rosanoff's *Intuition Workout* suggests a surprisingly effective exercise. With a certain situation in mind, ask, "How am I to proceed?" Then look around the room and jot down the first three objects that grab your attention.

This exercise seemed silly at first. Then, I tried it.

My question was, "How am I to proceed with my life?" Randomly, I chose a file folder, a high-rise apartment building, and a sailboat. The skeptic in me laughed: *Right. How can these three things have any intuitive meaning?*

Before you read on, ask, "How am I to proceed with . . . ?" then look around and pick three items.

According to Nancy, "The first object is symbolic of an action that you need to *start* taking in regards to the given situation. The second item represents what you need to *stop* doing. And the third, something you need to *continue* doing."

Brainstorming on the file folder, I realized it represented the need to start looking for a job. Now, I am fairly satisfied at my job, so this came as a complete surprise. Ten years is a long time at one job; fear rises up at the very thought of change.

Although I am not ready to actually look for a job, I can gather information and work on my résumé. In other words, I can build a personal file and *start* the process of leaving my job. Developing a file, fleshing out ideas, and gathering information are not nearly as threatening as going on an interview or quitting my job to write full time.

My intuition tells me there are steps I can take right now, steps I can handle.

The high-rise apartment addresses my material concerns. Intuitively, I know this means *stop* worrying about maintaining my lifestyle. I need to trust God more. God is, after all, my ultimate source and my true employer. And if God is my ultimate source and employer, then no fear is too great to conquer.

Lastly, the sailboat represents play and fun. I need to *continue* finding time for fun and relaxation—two things that tend to be last on my list.

Amazing little exercise.

The message is clear: *We intuitively know what our next step is to be.*

Put A Little Love In Your Heart

Speaking of God as our ultimate employer reminds me of a story told by a woman named June. Working as a waitress, she found the days were always too long and the tips never large enough. Disgruntled customers always needed more of *something*—coffee, cream, mustard—whatever. June felt unappreciated and couldn't wait to get out of there every day.

Then, June heard something that changed her life, "*If you work Monday through Friday, just to get a paycheck and have the weekends off, you are cheating yourself and everyone you come in contact with.*"

182

After that June no longer worked just for her paycheck and time off—*she worked for God.*

As her attitude about work changed, so did her experience of it. Showing up ready to be of service, June now took delight in meeting her customers' needs. She began thinking of her customers as God's kids, and if a little extra mustard would make their day a little easier, then they were in the right place, because that was her job.

The more June went to work with her new employer in mind, the quicker the days flew by. She no longer watched the clock anticipating when her life would begin. In fact, sometimes when she glanced at the clock, it was ten minutes past quitting time.

Abundance and prosperity were natural by products of living life looking for what you can give, instead of what you can get. And June's tips increased proportionally.

When we look to make a contribution, the Universe jumps up and down, blessing us in return.

June's lessons as a waitress served her well. She put herself through law school and has a flourishing law practice in California where she continues to practice that same principle: "What can I do to make one of God's kids' day a little easier?"

| See what you can give rather than what you can get. Be of service *as* you move toward your dreams. Life does not begin someday after you achieve your goals. It is happening right now. Today, ask, "Are any of God's kids in need of some mustard?" Then take the next right action.

Love Can Move Mountains

June's story had a huge impact on my life. I never viewed myself as a taker, but at work I stayed in my own little world. I did what was asked of me, but knew my real life began at five o'clock. And boy, did I look forward to Friday! When I heard June talk about working for God, my perceptions changed.

Implementing the attitude of serving God's kids in the law firm where I worked, I began asking my co-workers about their weekends, their families, and even their pets. Expressing a sincere interest in their lives took conscious effort, but in time I became more involved with the world around me, not only at work, but everywhere.

When attorneys were demanding, I remembered I was there to serve and gave them whatever they needed. One attorney in particular was always on deadline, and nothing was ever quite right. I practiced these principles with him and helped his secretary to do the same. We both had plenty of opportunities to practice patience and tolerance, because if he wasn't an alcoholic, he certainly drank and acted like one. His secretary left in tears on more than one occasion.

When I heard his marriage was in trouble, I had only compassion. When he barged into my office demanding, "I need this yesterday!" I smiled and got the document to him faster than he thought possible. My job title may be controller, but my real job is being of service to God's kids, no matter how difficult. The angrier they are, the more miserable their lives must be, therefore the more in need they are of love and compassion.

Any time someone acts in an unloving manner, I realize they are coming from fear and view their actions as a plea for love. It is surprising how many people melt when their unpleasant behavior is continually met with love and kindness.

I try to see the child within, no matter what the person's age or circumstances. With God as my ultimate employer, it is never too hard.

183

Think of the angriest or most difficult person you know or work with, and from this day forward, extend love to this person. No matter what their behavior is, open your heart and extend love. Remember, the nastier they seem, the more desperate their plea.

God Is In Control

I guess it is obvious by now that I was raised in a dysfunctional family. They say 94 percent of American families are, so I am hardly unique.

Being raised in a family where you never knew what to expect molds you into a person who likes to control their circumstances. For me, this is connected to the powerlessness I felt as a child when my stepfather came on to me sexually. I could not exactly live on my own at thirteen just because things were not right at home.

Today this reaction to the past takes shape by my going into "control mode" whenever things feel out of control. It is my way of coping.

184

"Control mode" can be a double-edged sword. It is great when someone can step in and say, "This will solve the problem." The world needs take-charge people, but that is not the kind of control I am talking about. I am talking about the insidious kind that shows up when people are not doing what you think they should or being as efficient as they could. This is when I go into "control mode" and give unsolicited advice or assistance.

This shows up most with my husband and when I feel out of control myself. For instance, if I feel unmanageable financially because I have overspent or believe there's not enough money to go around, I tend to switch the focus to my husband's financial affairs, *Gary spends too much, is in debt, and is way too generous.* Next thing you know, I am running around the house after him turning off light switches or admonishing him for leaving the air conditioner on when no one is home.

Gary responds to my controlling behavior as a child would to a critical parent, with rebellion and withdrawal.

Even though I know my "control mode" pushes people away, when I am in it, I cannot see it until the other person snaps at me or pulls away.

A number of things help me address this deeply entrenched habit, such as the mirror effect: *If you spot it, you got it.* If I am focused on Gary's financial affairs, it is a sure sign I need to look at my own—is there anywhere *I* could improve? Books and codependency support groups also help, but the single most effective tool that alleviates my controlling tendencies is to simply *live my bliss*.

When Gary had to work late the other night, instead of getting angry, I went to a movie and ended up visiting my aunt. A couple of days later, Gary worked until after 10 P.M.; instead of bitching, I got in another writing session. Last night Gary worked late again, and I was delighted to have extra time with my new voice recognition program.

The more I live as God intended, the less my life revolves around others. Today, as a result of letting go of control, I am more flexible, less needy, and happier than ever before.

Let go and trust—God *is* in control.

> **Today's Action** | When overly focused on or imposing your will on someone, use one of the above listed tools: Take your own inventory, attend a support group, or read a good book on codependency.
> And last, or maybe first, ask, "What action am I taking toward my dreams?"

Enough Is Enough

Speaking of control issues, Leah, Gary's niece, came to live with us a few years ago and boy, did that kick up my control issues. Bright, but willful, Leah was what they call *wicked* in her hometown of Salem, Massachusetts. Her own mother and grandmother could not control her.

When Leah asked if she could stay with us, Gary and I said, "Sure," thinking we could pass on the spiritual principles we were learning about.

Married only six months, our marriage was fraught with problems. Gary was battling frequent unemployment, and we were seeing a marriage counselor to improve our communication skills (and if the truth be known, our sex life).

We picked up Leah at the airport, against the better judgment of our therapist; we thought were up to the challenge. Little did we know this would be the ultimate test of our marriage.

Leah is a good kid, but the teen years can be rough, particularly if you did not get the love you needed as a child.

Leah's plan was to get a job and enroll in summer school to make up for some of the classes she flunked earlier in the school year. Instead, she watched TV all day, cleaned out the fridge, and left us phone bills larger than our car payments.

I woke up to sticky, kitchen countertops and sugar-coated floors. At night I came home to crumbs and clothes everywhere. Typical stuff for a fifteen-year-old, but because I was not a parent, I was unprepared for the way a teenager takes over the house, or in our case, our tiny two-bedroom apartment. If I said anything, Leah sneered, "You're not my mother."

Other than a few briefs visits, Gary had not seen his niece much during the past ten years due to his drug addiction (the homeless shelters didn't have visiting hours). In fact, when Leah was five years old, she saw her Uncle Gary injecting "medicine" into his arm and told her mother. That was the last time Leah was ever alone with Gary.

So here we have this troubled teen who hopes her cool, handsome uncle will rescue her from her horrible life up north and the remorseful uncle wanting to make up for not having been there all those years.

That is the background. Now enter me—kind, loving, spiritual, supportive wife—with tendencies toward control and martyrdom.

Gary, who already found it difficult to spend time with me because of his low self-esteem, was now spending all his free time with Leah. On an intellectual level, I understood their need to make up for lost time, but the little girl in me felt rejected: *Gary never gives up commitments for me. He never talks to me about his day.*

I felt the same as when I was ten years old, and my father remarried and adopted his new wife's daughter, Debbie. We already shared the same first name, now she had my last name *and* my father.

Watching Leah get the attention I craved sparked jealousy and competition in me, not in a sexual sense, but my fears and insecurities rose to the surface just the same.

To top it off, our marriage had no foundation, no united front on which to stand. Leah, like most kids, intuitively knew the score and played on our guilt and fear, pitting us against each other. She didn't mean any harm; she just did anything to get what she wanted.

Gary and I were no better. Partying or running for our entire lives, we never grew up emotionally. It was as if three teenagers shared the house—all doing the best they could, but none succeeding very well.

Within weeks, our marriage was headed for trouble, but we stayed the course, trying to give Leah guidance and a stable environment. After two months, I was at my wit's end.

Leah had not gone to school, was not working, and came home whenever she felt like it. I wasn't allowed to discipline her and Gary wouldn't. Finally, I had enough.

"You are going back to Boston. You need to work things out up there," I said.

"I'm not going back up north and you can't make me. I'll run away!" Leah threatened.

"It's not that we don't want you, but we just aren't able to take on raising a teenager. It's time for you to go back to your family," I explained.

"You're not my mother and you can't tell me what to do." Leah slammed the bedroom door in my face and began packing her things.

When I stopped her from running away by blocking her path, she taunted, "Go ahead, hit me. I know you want to." She had no idea how true that was. Somehow I restrained myself, but I did go into "control mode" long enough to make sure she got on that New England-bound plane. Then the real fun began.

187

Communication Breakdown

I often refer to the first year of our marriage as the marriage from hell. Things got worse, not better, after Leah left—not what we had planned at all.

In our fantasy, we were a positive influence on Leah and everyone lived happily ever after.

In reality, Leah was miserable and Gary and I argued constantly. Emotionally, he was so distant that I was sure he was leaving me. Paranoia grew as Gary closed himself off in another room every time he got a call or letter from Massachusetts. He did not have five minutes to spare for me, yet spent hours on the phone with Leah. I just knew she was saying horrible things about me to Gary.

Somehow, by trying to do the right thing, I ended up the bad guy. My marriage was ending, and I was furious. *Leah had torn my marriage apart.*

My friends tried to help me deal with my anger. One woman said, "Bang pillows and scream to release your anger." At this point it was no longer just anger, but full-blown *Rage* with a capital R. But beat pillows I did.

Someone else said running helped her get her anger out. So I pounded the pavement. There were not enough miles on the planet to get all of my anger out, but I ran my little heart out. A third woman said, "Rip up a picture of Leah, say a prayer for forgiveness, and burn the picture. Let your resentment dissipate with the smoke."

Willing to try anything, I tore up a picture of Leah, went onto the balcony, lit a match, set the picture on fire, and prayed for my anger to be carried away with the wisps of smoke. I must say I rather enjoyed ripping and burning Leah's picture, but the anger remained.

When Gary saw that I had destroyed his only picture of Leah, he was livid, "I can't believe the level you've sunk to."

"Well, she destroyed the carpet and walls in our spare bedroom, ripped up my old pictures, and left us with a huge phone bill," I retorted. This tit-for-tat mentality brought me, a supposedly sane and spiritual woman, down to the level of an angry teenager.

My next fearful act was the blow that threatened to end our marriage. A few days after the picture incident, a letter came from Leah addressed to Gary. I steamed it open, read it, and sealed it shut again.

Later, my conscience bothered me so much that I ripped the letter open so Gary would know I had opened it. When he saw his mail opened after having asked me not to touch it, he flipped out.

"And to think I once had you on a pedestal. Well, you have certainly fallen off it. You are not the woman I married. I don't even know who you are anymore," he said.

Talk about pain. My heart was ripped out and thrown in my face. I was crushed. Our marriage was over, and we both knew it.

We stopped talking to each other and slept in separate bedrooms, with me sleeping in, of all places, Leah's old room. Crying myself to sleep, I desperately prayed to a God I wasn't sure was listening anymore.

Not wanting anyone to know how bad things were and how unspiritual I was, I isolated myself. My sponsor insisted I go to a meeting and share what was going on. I usually recount my difficulties *after* I resolve them, not while in the middle of them.

Hard as it was, I went to the meeting and got honest. I let a roomful of women know the real state of my marriage and that I blamed my husband's niece for everything, "If she hadn't come down, this never would have happened." Then, I admitted to the group the one thing I was most ashamed of: I was wishing this fifteen-year-old dead!

What a horrible space to be in, much less have to admit. Yet, that night I experienced true freedom. The women held me, cried with me, and accepted my humanness. My behavior, my feelings, even my thoughts were okay. They assured me I would survive, even if my marriage didn't.

Letting those women in was like letting in pure sunlight: My soul was cleansed.

Today's Action | Let someone in completely. Reveal your dark side, your secrets. When we risk and let others in, we rid ourselves of shame and spiritual isolation. When one heart shares with another, we all heal.

From The Heart

A few months before the Leah incident, our therapist told us, "Marriage is like a camping trip. When the family sets out, they have high expectations. There is this vision of your family happily hiking, canoeing, and pitching tent. Everything is perfect.

"However, when you actually go camping, someone invariably sprains an ankle, gets poison ivy, or the canoe flips, soaking all your belongings. By the end of the trip you are fighting with one another, swearing off camping forever! A few weeks pass, perspectives shift, and the catastrophe becomes a wonderful anecdote."

"Great story, but what does that have to do with us?" I asked.

"Marriage, like camping, is rarely how you picture it. Often you end up at each other's throats over inconsequential things, but in time you can look back and laugh. Life's tragedies bond people together," she responded.

Then, one day, about two months after Leah left, Gary broke the silence, "Some camping trip."

Those three words spoke volumes.

In a moment, hope replaced despair. I *knew* we would get through this. That life experience became our camping story, as did cancer, and Gary's turning himself in to the Boston Police.

We learned how to work *through* conflict, how to rise above adversity instead of running at the first sign of difficulty. Perspective is a wonderful thing; too bad you can't have it when you're *in* the problem.

In hindsight I learned that anger usually crops up when we feel threatened. I am afraid I will lose something I have or not get something I want. Fear is channeled into anger, causing me to act irrationally, bringing on the very thing I fear.

Faith, the opposite of fear, dissolves anger. If I let go and let God, everything works out fine.

The situation with Leah was one of my biggest growth experiences. If there were no lessons or gifts as the result of our trials and tribulations, I, for one, would not want to face some of the things I have faced.

But the other side has *always* been worth it. These life experiences are our *necessary losses*.

In times of adversity, God is polishing us to better let others see the true treasure that resides within each of us: Our ability to love, to forgive, and to heal.

Today's Action | What are the "camping trips" of your life? Are you on one now? Where would you be if some of the trying situations you experienced had never occurred? Use this analogy to put things in perspective. Begin to view things *from the heart*.

Hopelessly Human

Things were not magically perfect the instant Gary said, "Some camping trip," but it was a start. After our marriage started to heal, it was time for me to heal with Leah.

I was still pounding out my anger on the pavement when part of "The Lord's Prayer" hit me square in the face, "Forgive us our trespasses *as* we forgive those who trespass against us."

Who was *I* to hold such judgment and contempt for Leah? Had I never done wrong? Was I not in need of forgiveness myself? Would I *never* be in need of forgiveness? Who was I to judge? I certainly was not perfect. I, too, had acted out of fear and harmed others. I was once a teenager desperate for love myself.

My heart opened as I realized I wouldn't want my wrongs held against me. With this clarity came understanding and compassion. I am held in bondage by whatever I hold against you. We truly are all *one*.

For the next seven years, Leah lived with her other uncle, David, and his wife, Alicia. They were much more stable than Gary and I, and able to give Leah the family, love, and discipline she needed. Leah finished high school, went to college, and is now doing quite well as a graphic artist. God obviously had a plan.

The license plate number on my car happens to be LMK 590, which I translate to be loving, mindful, and kind and to never forget May 1990, when Leah brought the gift of herself to us.

I am who I am today, in great part, because of the rich, learning experiences that occurred that summer when a little girl almost destroyed my marriage—or so I thought.

I will always remember my first camping trip. Thank you, Leah. Thank you, God.

Today's Action | Is there anyone you blame for something, perhaps unfairly? Anyone you harbor resentment towards? If so, now is the time to let it go. That person was a gift in your life, there to teach you lessons you could learn no other way. Resentment is like a steel cable, forever binding you to the person you resent.

Let go and heal. The two of you are one and the same. Open your heart and let forgiveness wash away all the pain, anger, and hurt. Let it all go. Let the healing rain of your tears wash away all remaining hurt.

Can't Buy Me Love

To be free to live our bliss we must be free of resentment. Forgiveness leads the way. Expanding our hearts to forgive, even unforgivable acts, frees us from our past, and enables us to embrace our future.

Betrayal; physical, sexual, or verbal abuse; and theft of money or material possessions are all hard to forgive—money often being the hardest.

The only disagreement I've ever had with my paternal aunt, Bobbie, was about money. She said it was about trust. For me it was about money and what each of us thought was "just." I often said to my husband when dealing with less-than-reputable businessmen, insurance companies, or government agencies, "It's not the money, *it's the principle!*"

Bottom line though, if they did what I thought was fair, *monetarily*, I would easily let go of my self-righteous indignation about the principle.

One of my main problems with Leah was the hundreds of dollars she rang up in long-distance calls. Yes, there were other issues, but most of our fights were about the money.

When I finally let go and trusted Gary to handle the situation, I accepted that we would probably never see a dime. I looked at the bigger picture and asked myself: *How important is it?*

I use that catch phrase whenever Gary, or anyone else for that matter, isn't doing things the way I think they should, especially when it comes to money. I ask: *How important will this be ten years from now, or a hundred years from now?*

If money is involved, I remind myself that God is my ultimate provider and that all of my needs have always been met. Whenever I expend my energy trying to get my way, get someone to do right by me financially, or act as *I* think they should, I remind myself that *peace of mind is the goal.* How people act, what their lessons are, and determining what is best and fair is God's job, not mine.

When I let go of the reins, I am at peace. When I am at peace, I am happy. So, do I want to be right or happy? When put to me that way, I usually choose happiness. Soon after I let go, Leah repaid us for her long-distance calls.

Letting go of money worries, along with letting go of control and turning outcomes over to my Higher Power, brings me complete and perfect peace. I would rather be serene and happy than right, rich, and miserable, any day.

Today's Action | When trying to control the uncontrollable, ask yourself, "How important is it?" Then, let go and let God handle it.

All You Need Is Love

Healing our marriage was a process—not an event.

Gary and I struggled with intimacy for years before we found that every time we worked on our marriage, it got worse. Finally, we decided to just work on ourselves and trust that as we grew emotionally and spiritually, we would each bring healthier people to the relationship, and it would improve naturally.

As simple as it sounds, that is exactly what happened. Whenever I get angry with Gary, I do something loving for him. When I bring him breakfast, he knows something is definitely up (just in case he didn't get my hints). Gary, in turn, gives me huge bear hug when I am upset with him or he with me. We extend love to each other, whether we feel like it or not. Instead of yelling or fighting, we wait until our emotions calm down and then discuss things rationally.

We were given our most powerful tool, "My Commitment to You," at *A Course in Miracles* workshop nine years ago. We were told to personalize it according to our needs and say it to each other regularly. We read it to each other nightly to remind us of how we wanted to be in our relationship. We laughed when it was clear we were falling short, recommitting to do better next time.

I have also read this commitment to my mother and to a good friend when we were having difficulties. Any time Gary or I feel we are getting off track, we both read it out loud, reminding us of our intentions.

My Commitment To You

I promise to trust you enough to treat you lovingly, gently, and with respect, in my thoughts, words, and actions, whether in your presence or not.

In every interaction I will surrender to LOVE, our true nature. Being connected to God and my relationship with you, will always be more important than any issue that may come up.

If anything unlike LOVE comes up, I will do my best to work *my* program and take my *own* inventory. I will hold us in my heart as we each experience, speak, and are responsible for our own realities. I will be there for and with you, keep communication lines open, and keep LOVE conscious, active, and present as we heal.

Today's Action | Use this commitment in any relationship where you feel you are not living up to your highest potential. In problematic relationships say it out loud for thirty days, then use as needed.

Sixth Month

Empowerment

Question Of Balance

*a*fter Leah left, I realized my abandonment issues arose because my father left when I was so young and was unavailable during my formative years. As part of my healing process I read books, attended meetings, and went to therapy.

Without realizing it, I had made Gary the center of my life and was devastated at the thought of his leaving. As I grew, I became less fearful of Gary leaving and less needful of his approval. I became more God-reliant and less Gary-reliant. I learned I would be fine whether Gary stayed or not. And Gary learned to not leave town at the first sign of conflict.

I let Gary be part of my life instead of my whole life. My life became well rounded, consisting of relationships with God, myself, and others. I returned to college, volunteered in the community, and explored different hobbies and interests.

For months I focused on my studies and recovery program while Gary focused on his job and serving others. We didn't see each other very much during this time. We both needed to regroup and grow as individuals. When we came back to center, we were once more a part of each other's life, but not the center.

Our relationship went from an unhealthy, codependent relationship to a rich and thriving relationship, one that everyone admires. Sometimes even we can't believe how happy we are.

Transforming a relationship is hard work, but it can be done. It starts with *self*-transformation. Some excellent starting places are *Struggle for Intimacy* and *Adult Children of Alcoholics* (even if your parents weren't alcoholic) by Janet G. Woititz and *Stage II Recovery: Life Beyond Addiction* and *Stage II Relationships: Love Beyond Addiction* by Earnie Larsen.

Today's Action | If you have any unresolved childhood issues or unhealthy intimate relationships, decide to do what it takes to get them resolved and get happy. There's no reason that these issues need interfere with your bliss any longer.

That Was Then, This Is Now

Healing relationships is such a vital part of living blissfully that no matter how much personal success we achieve, we are never fully satisfied until we are right with God, ourselves, and others.

My sponsor, Patricia, traveled a rough road during the past few years regarding her parents. Shortly after her mother died of cancer, her father married a much younger woman and contested Patricia's mother's irrevocable trust, which had left everything to Patricia and her sister.

Devastated by the loss of her mother and her father's sudden remarriage, Patricia felt this lawsuit was the final betrayal. It was as if she lost her mother *and* her father.

Now legal adversaries, Patricia and her father spoke only through their attorneys. Negotiations got nasty and dragged on for months, until finally, Patricia and her sister gave in and agreed to give up their inheritance. After the legal matters were settled, her father and his new wife moved to another state and broke all contact with his daughters.

In the ensuing years, a cloud hung over Patricia's every achievement. Not only could she no longer share her successes with her mother, she couldn't share them with her father either, although he was very much alive. The wounds ran deep. For years, all Patricia could do was pray for her father.

Last week, after not speaking to her father in more than three years, Patricia called her father and asked if she could come for a visit. Gruff and hesitant at first, he finally agreed.

Two days ago, Patricia boarded a South Carolina-bound plane in an attempt toward radical forgiveness: "My father greeted my at the airport alone, as if testing the waters. We hugged awkwardly. Then he suggested we get a bite to eat before going back to his house, where his wife was waiting.

"The first thing he asked about was my health. I guess he thought I had to be dying if I wanted to see him. When I assured him I was fine, he asked in his stern, businesslike manner, 'What brought on this desire to see me?'

" 'I miss you,' the little girl in me answered. With that, he softened, and we began rebuilding our relationship.

"If his 'executive' self asked questions about what my husband or sister thought of my visit, I kept the focus on us, 'Daddy, I just want to talk about you and me.'

"If he tried to rehash the past, I reminded him, 'That was then, this is now,' again keeping the focus on us and on today.

"Back at his house, I assured his wife that I held nothing against her. I admitted it was hard accepting her initially, but that was then and this is now. Now, I only want happiness for my father, and she obviously makes him happy.

"I held back my tears as best I could, but I was so overjoyed that we were speaking that it was difficult. When it was time to leave, my father and his wife drove me to the airport and we said our goodbyes. Safely in my plane seat, I allowed the tears of gratitude to flow. With each tear I knew my heart was being renewed."

Patricia then added, "Forgiveness is hard work, but I now have my father back in my life. The best part is that we didn't have to wait until one of us was ill, or dying. Or worse, living with the regret of not acting in time."

Today's Action | Is there anyone you need to straighten things out with? It doesn't matter who is to blame, or who is right or wrong. What matters is that a healing take place, that broken hearts mend, and that damaged relationships are repaired.
    Facing cancer at thirty-seven showed me none of us truly know how long we have. Now is the time to make amends, before it's too late.

Colour Everywhere

Inherent in living blissfully is the expansion of our hearts, not only toward others, but toward God. Often in our busy lives we forget about God—our Higher Power—the Force that created us.

The first thirty years of my life were spent with no belief whatsoever in God, which led to a dull, self-centered, meaningless existence. It was suggested I develop a personal relationship with the Creative Force or Energy of the Universe. I was told that my life would improve if I tapped into this Power for guidance.

"Draw strength and courage from this Power. Call it whatever you choose, so long as you use it," I was told.

Prayer is the most universal way of connecting with and tapping into this Power, but God can come into our lives in many ways. One way is to acknowledge God's presence with a simple, "Hi God," or "Thank you for the gift of life" every time you see your favorite color.

Before I came to believe in any Higher Being, I felt either lucky or unlucky, depending on whether things went my way or not. Everything was left to chance. Developing a conscious, interactive relationship with a Supreme Being increased my ability to experience gratitude. There *was* some rhyme and reason to life, Something, or Someone to thank!

Life has been far richer since I opened to the possibility of a God who cares about me personally. Some people are raised with spiritual beliefs, and this is as natural to them as breathing. Others, like myself, have to cultivate this belief and relationship.

Today's Action | Say "Hi, God," or "thank you," every time you see your favorite color. Expand your awareness and your heart by developing or renewing a personal relationship with a God of *your* understanding.

Down On My Knees

To have a relationship with and reliance upon God, we need to communicate with this Higher Power.

My spiritual journey began in 1988, when it was first suggested that I pray in the morning for help and say thank you at night to whatever Power helped me abstain from drugs and alcohol that day. I was told I did not have to understand or believe in it, just try it and if it works, keep using it. For a few weeks I sat in my bed, looked at a certain spot on the ceiling, asked for help and said thank you every day.

Then it was suggested that I pray on my knees. I resisted. "Be open minded," I was told. I tried it and hated it. The bed cut into my chest, my knees hurt, and the connection I got when I sat in bed and chatted with "God" was not there when I was on my knees. "Write about your resistance," I was told.

What surfaced was that although I did not believe in a punishing God, being on my knees felt like a punishing position. When I was six years old, my mother's live-in boyfriend spanked me a lot. Before we could be excused from the table, my brothers and I had to eat all our food. As a child I was a very picky eater. I hated vegetables, eggs, and fish, and my mom's boyfriend made sure there was something I hated at every meal. Consequently, I was punished a lot. Hairbrushes, sticks, switches, belts, and a big wooden paddle with the words "The Paddle" painted in big red letters were his weapons of choice. And I was always spanked while *down on my knees*, bent over my bed.

No wonder I hated that position! Funny though, once I wrote about it, my discomfort disappeared. The Higher Power I was beginning to believe in was *not* this punishing power from my past. With that realization came freedom. I was now free to choose how I wanted to pray. Initially, praying on my knees was important because it demonstrated humility and acknowledged that this power was *greater* than me. Today, I am comfortable praying in any position, though my most heartfelt prayers are often said *down on my knees*. Either way, the Higher Power I believe in listens to *all* my prayers.

Twelve years later, I still have no real understanding of God. My mind cannot fully comprehend a Creative Force large enough to create the entire Universe, yet small enough to help me with my day-to-day problems. Although I cannot grasp *how* God works, I know without a doubt *that* God works.

Today, I pray for anything I need help with, and the help always comes.

For instance, I'm taking Gary rock climbing for an anniversary present. I'm not particularly interested in rock climbing, but Gary is dying to try it, and I love a challenge.

I can't imagine undertaking a climb such as the one we are attempting today. Losing thirty-one of my lymph nodes affected the flow of fluids in my left arm and often causes swelling and loss of strength. I pray God will give me the strength to rise to the challenge and complete at least one climb.

199

Today's Action | Ask for specific guidance or assistance in any area with which you think you might need help. If you already have a routine of prayer, bring more energy and aliveness to it by praying for specific help.

Falling Into You

Rock climbing perfectly symbolizes the journey of *living from the heart*.

Sometimes the next rock is just beyond our reach, and it takes all we have to go for it. We pray we will grasp it, or that our partner will catch us if we fall. Other times, we lose our way and need to call out for guidance.

In indoor rock climbing, two people are involved, the climber and the person handling the belay. Belay is a system of ropes, knots, and stops a person uses to assist the climber. The belayer takes up slack, prevents falls, and helps the climber down at the end of a climb.

The belayer is the safety net for the climber. Should the climber lose their footing and fall, it is the belayer's job to catch the climber by stopping the rope from flying up as the person's weight brings them down. Proper braking can mean the difference between life and death. Even on twenty-foot climbs, people can fall to their deaths or be seriously injured on the unforgiving, cement floor.

After admitting in writing that we knew we could die, we took the required forty-five-minute belay class to learn how to assist each other effectively. There are four basic signals of readiness before starting a climb, "On belay?" the climber asks their partner. "Belay on," is the response if the belay partner is ready. Then the climber says, "Climbing," as he or she gets into position. Finally, the belayer gives the go-ahead, "Climb on."

The belay signals remind me of checking in with God. In the morning I ask, "Are you there?" and God answers, "I'm here." Then as I walk out the door, I let God know, "I'm heading out," and God reassures me he is on standby should I need him, "I'm ready."

In rock climbing, you do not start a climb without first checking in with your partner. It could result in disaster. This is a good reminder for me to always check in with God, before heading out. God being my belayer—my safety net—that additional strength I need to avoid disaster.

Today's Action	Check in this morning. Allow God to be your belayer—your safety net.

Up Where We Belong

Feeling adventurous, I went first. Heading up the first set of notches in the wall, I found it was not much harder than climbing a giant ladder. Even so, I could feel Gary not picking up the slack quickly enough, and I did not feel secure. The second climb, designed for an Amazon, was a true test of my strength and abilities. The third and final climb was even more difficult as my muscles were already tired, and I was sweating profusely, making the rocks slippery and hard to grasp.

I chalked up and checked in, "On Belay?" "Belay on," Gary responded. I got into position with two hands on one rock, both feet on notches, and my body plastered against the curved wall. "Climbing," I said. And Gary responded with the final command, "Climb on."

The path was arduous, to say the least. Halfway through the climb I faltered, "I can't do it!" I exclaimed. Footholds disintegrated beneath my feet, and my left arm swelled as I pushed its limits.

The next rock was more than a foot beyond my reach. I would have to leap to make it. I would also have to trust my belay partner, my safety net, if I did not make it. Otherwise I would be kissing some pretty cold cement.

I yelled down to Gary, "Take up the slack quickly and be ready to brake!" I went for it and missed, dangling in midair as Gary braked hard. I regained my footing and tried again. Taking direction from down below this time, I made it.

Not able to see any notches beyond the next curve, I yelled down, "Is that it? Am I done?" "Not yet. There's one more notch just over the hump," Gary called back.

I leaned back and realized there was no way I was going to make it. I rested against the wall to catch my breath. 201

While there, I remembered praying that morning for strength and courage. Plastered against the wall, eighteen feet above ground, seemed like a fitting place to continue my prayer, "Okay God, I cannot make this without you. I *really* want to complete the climb, but you are going to have to be my strength."

I crouched down, sprang up, and grabbed the highest rock on the wall. I made it! Shaking all over from exertion, I called down to Gary, and he gently brought me back down to earth.

Looking up to where I had just come from, I knew that last jump was totally God. In fact, it was almost easy once I prayed. It reminded me of a poem, called "The Difference," about not having time to pray and the day not going very well. Then the person realized they didn't have time *not* to pray—because prayer made all the difference.

I don't always remember to pray, but rock climbing was a vivid reminder of how much easier things are with the "Belay on," and God on standby.

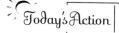 Today's Action | Do something adventurous, such as rock climbing.

Where You Lead, I Will Follow

Yesterday I spoke with one of the first homeless men Gary helped get off drugs ten years ago. Mike, known as Filthy McNasty on the street, calls us regularly from North Carolina just to keep in touch.

We met Mike in a small Twelve-Step meeting on Miami Beach. He was the only black person in the room, and he spoke so softly that you had to get right up next to him to hear what he was saying. Mike asked Gary to sponsor him and from there, a friendship developed.

After a couple of years in Miami, Mike moved back to his home state to marry Stephanie, the woman who had gone to hell and back with him during his drug addiction, and to help raise her teenage son. One day Mike is eating out of Dumpsters, and the next he is a responsible husband and father.

Things were tough at first, but Mike worked hard to make up for how irresponsible he had been in the past. He often worked two or more jobs to provide for his family, a far cry from the man who used to steal from others to get high.

Mike called to tell us he was coming to Miami. Their son just graduated college, signed on with the Washington Redskins, and gave his parents tickets to the Super Bowl. Mike is so excited. And Gary and I haven't seen Mike and Stephanie since we visited them in Raleigh more than six years ago.

Then Mike told me Stephanie was out of work. The job, where she worked for years helping low-income women lose weight and decrease their health risks, just folded. Not wanting to abandon the women merely because big business said there was no profit in helping inner-city women lose weight, Stephanie decided to address their needs directly. Mike quit his job. Then he and Stephanie mortgaged their house and went into business together.

Today's Action | Trust that God has a plan for each of us. It's our job to follow our hearts—wherever they lead us.

Note: It's been a year since I wrote this story. Mike and Stephanie's business is a huge success, showing what happens when you let your heart be the guide.

Voices In The Sky

Someone asked me recently if I have always followed my intuition.

For years I was not even aware of my intuition. Then when I stopped drinking and drugging, my mind cleared, and I began to get little internal urgings. Most seemed silly, so I ignored them.

Then one day, at a gas station, I got a funny feeling that made me go back to my car and take my keys out of the ignition before paying the cashier. Normally, I would brush off the feeling as ridiculous and keep walking toward the cashier. However, when I returned I found my purse had been stolen from underneath my car seat. Had I not gone back for my keys, my car would have been stolen, too.

Now, when I get these inner urgings or gut feelings, I listen. Sometimes nothing comes of it. Other times something as monumental as visiting my long-lost aunt occurs.

These days, I take it for granted that I am being guided by God, angels, or a Higher Being of some kind.

 Today's Action | Tune into your divinely inspired internal wisdom. It is there for a reason.

Sweet Dreams

Another way I honor myself is by tuning into my body's wisdom about food. If I crave something, I try to find as natural a source as possible. For instance, eating fruit after meals nips my craving for sweets in the bud. If I crave something salty, pickles, olives, popcorn, or a salad with feta cheese does the trick. If I desire comfort food, good old-fashioned mashed potatoes or ice cream hits the spot. Depriving myself tends to backfire, and I end up overindulging. Instead, giving in to my cravings, in reasonable amounts, keeps my weight constant.

I honor my body's natural cycles by slowing down and doing nothing during certain times of the month. Our cycles are our bodies' signals that it is time to draw inward and replenish our strength. I gave up trying to keep up the pace regardless of how I felt. Now, I have no qualms about canceling plans if I am tired.

Since going into menopause at thirty-seven, I try to avoid stress because it increases the intensity of my hot flashes. And I found keeping active reduces almost all symptoms related to hormonal cycles.

Our bodies contain internal wisdom about when to rest, what and how much to eat, and what kind of movement our bodies need. Sometimes I feel like walking, other times only a good run will do. Other times, rhythmic bicycling or wave jumping is what the child inside needs. I strive for mindful movement instead of mindless exercising. Viewing my body as a vehicle and food as the energy source has helped me treat myself more lovingly, so I can be here for the long haul.

Today's Action | Turn off autopilot and go back on manual control. Check in with your body. Ask, "What do I need right now?" and "What do I truly want to do?"

Feel and sense what your body longs for. If you get a craving, fill it. If you are tired, rest. If your body yearns for movement, ask, "What kind?" Skip gym class and dance to oldies if the spirit moves you. Ask and listen. Clarity will come.

Love Changes Everything

Listening is one of the most profound ways that I can demonstrate love, whether it is through listening to my inner voice, listening to my body's natural rhythms, listening to God, or listening to people. That which I give my time and attention to, I love.

The greatest gift I gave my aunt last week was openhearted listening. When I work with others, I ask what *they* want. By listening intently, I can then guide them back to their truth.

What children want, more than toys or money, is their parents' undivided attention. Since I did not get this as a child, it is very important that I have my partner's full attention.

I used to talk to Gary in between TV shows or during commercials and only got part of his attention. It left me feeling unimportant. Now, I no longer compete with the television, I wait until the show is over or ask to turn the television off for a minute. By doing this I honor myself and acknowledge my importance.

When listening to someone I am sponsoring, I focus all of my attention on what they are saying, to show them they are worthy of my time.

If I am at a meeting, I always listen intently whether I have heard the speaker before or not. This honors the person speaking and respects the people around me. Plus, I never know when I might hear something I need to hear.

For years I developed this habit of active listening with others, but only recently have I begun paying attention to myself. At first it seemed like a waste of time. But I could sense the child within me longing to be heard, *really heard.* She desperately needed her desires and wishes to be first for a change.

I remember when I decided to take some time off and let go of all the women I was sponsoring. I had been tuning in and giving my inner child a voice when suddenly I changed my mind and decided to just sponsor fewer women instead of taking a complete break.

The teenager within threw a tantrum, *Why can't it be just me for once! Why do I always have to share you with others? If cancer didn't get your attention that we need to lighten up, play, relax, and go to the beach more—what will? No! I want you all to myself. It's been eight years. I'm tired of sharing.*

Boy, was she angry, but oh so right. Thank God I listened. For nine months, I did not sponsor anyone. For the first time in my life, I gave myself the time and attention I had always needed as a child. I let my kid be in charge. The first thing we did was go away for the weekend, just me, myself, and I. It was wonderful.

Today's Action | How well do you love? How well do you listen? Today, begin listening, I mean *really listening.* You will intuitively know whom you need to tune into. Listen and allow yourself to be guided.

Sometimes I Wonder Why

Letters to God can be a form of prayer. It also helps me gain clarity. Here is an excerpt from my journal shortly after I was diagnosed with cancer.

6/22/95

Dear God,

I was diagnosed with breast cancer 20 days ago and it has consumed my life. Surgery is scheduled for June 24. I still have a hard time believing that I have to have a mastectomy at my age. Sometimes I wonder if I bring things like cancer and infertility on myself. Or maybe I just had premonitions, because the thoughts and fears were there long before they were facts.

I also wonder if things just happen or am I singled out to go through difficult times to make me stronger or bring me closer to you. Or maybe I am supposed to help others as a result of these experiences. Since the diagnosis—I certainly am closer to you—sometimes out of necessity to relieve the fear, sometimes for comfort, and sometimes to give thanks for all the blessings that *are* in my life: health insurance, support from my office, friends, family, support groups, and that my spouse is so loving and supportive.

I guess I picked good there. From that rough piece of coal came this beautiful gem called Gary. I am truly amazed that I saw in him what others couldn't. Here we are years later— truly blessed to have each other.

Well, I'm going to close for now. Thanks for keeping my spirits up and helping me trust you, my medical team, and my own fighting spirit. I love you and am so glad you are in my life.

Love, Debbie

God is such a good listener.

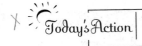 **Today's Action** | Write a letter to your Higher Power or the God of your understanding.

Hello It's Me

Every morning before writing, I use the belay signals to check in with God.

I sit at my desk and ask, "On Belay?"

When I am centered the internal reply comes, "Belay on."

Then, when I feel ready to write I say, "Climbing," signaling that I'm up to the task.

The final reply of, "Climb on," tells me I have God's blessing.

Checking in with God daily feels great. I used to, but got out of the habit. My morning routine usually consists of reading some spiritual literature, journaling, and meditating. Now I take a few minutes to pray before beginning my day.

Some days are hectic, and I don't have time for my routine. It's not as if my world falls apart or anything, but I *do* notice that I am a bit more impatient.

My little check-in with God, "On Belay?" "Belay on," "Climbing," "Climb on," definitely makes a difference.

Today's Action | Check in with the spirit or power that guides you. Ask and get confirmation that you are, in fact, plugged in. Then "Climb on."

207

It's My Turn

I have always equated summer with change. As a child, when school let out, I was free. When I was older, reruns on TV stepped in, and I had more time for other things. As an adult, summer signals time for vacations and weekend getaways.

In 1996, a year after my summer of surgeries and chemotherapy, I found I longed for the summers of my childhood, which were spent at summer camp or hanging out with friends. Thirsty for more play time and quiet time, I decided to create the summer of my dreams and do anything I wanted. Just making the decision felt liberating. It had been years since I listened to the earth's seasonal cycles, much less my own.

I declared the summer of 1996 as my time. A year had passed since my cancer diagnosis, and it was time to rejoin the living, this time without the obligations or constant busyness that my life usually entailed. The thirteen-year-old was in charge, so look out. The entire summer was like the movie, *Ferris Bueller's Day Off.* If the adult wanted to do anything, she had to get permission from the thirteen-year-old.

When I finally turned the reins over to the thirteen-year-old, it was as if she had been waiting her whole life. Her favorite word was "No," and she used it frequently. If laundry beckoned me, she said, "Nope, we're riding our bike to the beach!" If I wanted to take a class or seminar I'd get, "Not until September. This is *my* time!"

After a while, the adult in me learned to kick back and stop being so darn responsible. Sometimes I didn't answer the phone or return a call for days at a time. My favorite line was, "Let me get back to you on that" if asked to do anything, since I tend to overbook myself even with things I enjoy.

Practicing restraint was difficult at first, but after a while, the flyers, invitations, and phone calls settled down, and I didn't have as many decisions to make. Life became simple. Ahhhh . . . .

I had been so busy for so long that I didn't even notice how frantic my pace had been until I shifted gears. There were always so many things to do—recovery conventions, seminars, spiritual retreats, or volunteer opportunities.

At some point though, enough is enough.

I don't need to keep working on myself. I don't need constant fixing. I'm fine just as I am.

In fact, this book is designed for people to take what they like and leave the rest. You don't have to *do* everything to reap the benefits. Do what you are drawn to, but most importantly, learn how to just *be*.

Today's Action | Say "No," or at least, "Let me get back to you." Clear as much space in your life as you can, then go beyond your comfort zone and clear more.
At first it may feel disconcerting, but trust that all will be well. The world won't go away. It will all be waiting for you when and *if* you want to return to your old way of living. Or you may find you enjoy the space you've created for yourself and want to keep some of the boundaries in place even after summer's end.
It's your turn—enjoy!

Recover Your Soul

"Release, relax, let go, and recover your soul."

Ah, yes, doesn't that sound wonderful? Just let go. Release, release all you've been holding onto, all you've been doing, and let go. Let go and trust. Things will get done in their own good time. You can relax now—finally—and recover your soul.

Creating space for yourself and freeing up your time may feel strange at first, but that will pass. You may want to run from feelings that arise, but eventually you will settle down and learn to just *be*. In time, you will get to your natural state—a calm, relaxed, peaceful X state.

To be honest, this is the first year I have felt relaxed in a long time. It has taken months, but the stress is leaving my body. I can feel it slip away. No more tension in my neck and shoulders. I don't *need* a massage. I can enjoy one instead of needing one.

When you finally let go of all that seemed important, you begin to recover your soul, your true nature.

Trust. Trust and allow the healing energy in. Step back. Get out of the way. Go *with* 209 the flow. Let someone else be in charge. — God / my inner spirit.

Doesn't it feel good just reading that?

Take a deep breath and let the weight of the world slip off your shoulders. Shrug and it's gone. It's okay. You have permission to *release, relax, and let go.*

Today's Action | Settle into a peaceful state and see what arises naturally for you to do or *not* do today. Just relax and be.

Sunny Came Home

Housework and yard work were two things I had a hard time letting go of. Saturday was usually spent doing laundry, cleaning, and straightening up. Then, when the inside was done, I moved outside and pruned bushes or began the never-ending task of pulling weeds. I was constantly busy, constantly improving things, myself included. Nothing was ever okay.

No *more*. Shortly after I hired my wonderful housekeeper, Blanche, I hired a yardman who doesn't do things as well as I would do them, but at least my time is my own. I'll redo the yard when I finish this book.

For years the care of the house and yard dominated my time. No wonder I never had the time, energy, or inclination to write. Between the laundry, the weeds, my recovery program, and helping others, I taskmastered myself to death.

I have learned to live with imperfection. Bushes may not be pruned to my exact specifications, towels may never get folded, my defects of character may need tending, but hey—I'm sitting here writing my little heart out—living the life I've always wanted, having a ball!

So what if the laundry doesn't get done until I have absolutely nothing, and I do mean *nothing*, to wear. I have enough underclothes to last three weeks, and that's how often I do laundry now. Gary does his own laundry now, and you would be amazed at how capable he is.

Yes, I have less money than I used to because I pay people to help me, but as a result of reclaiming my time, I'm beginning to really *love* my life.

Today's Action | Clear, delegate, and let go of whatever you need to so that you have time for what really matters. Trust me, having the perfect house and yard just is not that important when there's a dream in you that's dying—dying to be expressed.

I Am Woman

It doesn't matter if you are a man or a woman—only that you've found your voice.

Having freed up some of my time, I can now address my fears. Far from being a thrill-seeker or enjoying living on the edge—I seek out life's challenges *only* to gain strength, confidence, and to increase my faith. I am not, by nature, a courageous person.

Obviously, life threw me obstacles that I did not seek out, and I think I've done quite well. Yes, I am a survivor, but I want to do more than just survive. I want to thrive.

Whether it's addiction, abuse, infertility, or cancer—I don't want to just get through it—I want to ROAR at it!

I challenge myself at every turn to expose my fears what for they truly are—things my mind invented.

Whether it's parasailing, rock climbing, diving with sharks, public speaking, or writing, the driving force behind the risks I take is to push myself farther than I think I can go, to do the uncomfortable, to stretch beyond my comfort zone, beyond my self-imposed limits. It's why I scuba dive, why I water ski, and why I bought a little ski boat with a girlfriend. Because either I told myself I wouldn't, someone else said I couldn't, or society said I shouldn't.

I am a warrior, a pioneer, a lioness! I *do* that which I think I cannot. And I *know* I will be stronger on the other side. Space isn't the final frontier—fear is.

I was afraid I wouldn't want to live if I couldn't be a mom, and here I am having the time of my life. I was afraid of cancer and death, and here I am healthier, more radiant, and more vibrant than ever before.

Some of the challenges ahead are: singing in front of people, taking a public-speaking course, sticking with this book until it's published, going up in a hot-air balloon, and sky-diving.

I hesitated in writing that last one because I have no desire to skydive and am terrified of the thought of jumping out of a plane. There was recently a skydiving accident in Miami where people died. I want to *live*, not taunt death. But I also believe as I walk through my fears, I experience freedom on the other side. I imagine, by the time I get to skydiving, I will have lost my fear of it or the need to continually challenge myself. If not, I'll go ahead and do it.

My mother thinks I'm crazy, but I know how fearful I used to be and I know how courageous I am now. Each time I tackle a new fear, I gain more courage. With every step forward, I loosen the chains that bind me and experience new freedom.

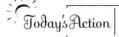

Spiders And Snakes

Some people are afraid of snakes or spiders. I am afraid of sharks. Living near the ocean my entire life, I purposely have not seen *Jaws I, II,* or *XX* because I didn't want to ruin the ocean for myself by feeding my fear.

Mostly I ignored my fear, but fleeting thoughts of shark attacks had me swimming closer and closer to the shore with each passing year. Day by day, my fear created a smaller world for me.

Eight years ago, I went to Bonaire on vacation with my mother. This small, arid, cactus-filled island off the coast of South America is known for one thing and one thing only: Diving. On the spur of the moment I decided to get certified—to dive, that is.

212

On the first day of class, the instructor said that for some inexplicable reason, there were no sharks in the ocean surrounding Bonaire, and that is why it's such a popular dive spot. Boy, was I glad to hear that!

I aced the four-day course, and my teacher said I was a natural. The coral reefs off the coast of Bonaire are some of the most beautiful in the world, and I thoroughly enjoyed myself, diving all day every day. By the end of the week, however, I wondered why the sharks stayed away from this part of the ocean and asked my instructor. He about fell overboard laughing, " 'Twas a joke, Mon!"

I look back now and wonder, "Could I *be* any more stupid!"

As much as I loved scuba diving, it was three years before I got the courage to dive again, mostly because of my fear of sharks.

As you step out of your comfort zones and begin living your long-buried dreams, fear *will* crop up. The secret to combating your fearful nature is to develop more courage. However, the only way to develop more courage is to walk *through* your fears.

Catch 22—huh? You cannot walk through your fears unless you have courage, and you cannot build courage unless you walk through your fears.

Today's Action | Since the only way through is *through*—what if you knew, without a doubt, that everything would be okay on the other side? What if you had a guarantee that your fears would not come true? Wouldn't it be easier to walk through your fears?

Visualize yourself doing what you are afraid of. Start with one fear and picture yourself walking through your fear. Visualize every detail.

The more you envision yourself doing something new, the more your brain accepts the possibility, and eventually, the reality of it.

Crazy

Walking through our lesser fears strengthens us and builds courage that enables us to walk through our greater fears more easily.

I stumbled upon this revelation when I was battling cancer and terrified of dying. Suddenly, writing didn't seem so scary, especially if I wasn't going to live much longer.

As I have mentioned before, I rediscovered my dream of writing as a way to boost my immune system. Secretly, I did not think I would live long enough to face finding an agent, editing the manuscript, or actually being published. I was inauthentically trying to live authentically. I was so scared of dying that I *pretended* I was going to be a writer. This worked for a while but *I* knew I was faking it—that I would not really go all the way.

In time, I closed up and stopped writing. And that's how I came to walk through, or in this case, swim through, my fear of sharks. So much fear had built up around my writing that diving with sharks seemed less frightening than writing.

While many of my friends go on "shark dives" all the time, I have always thought they were slightly insane. *Why would anyone of sound mind look for trouble like that?* I guess they like living on the edge; they actually seek out sharks to dive with—just for the thrill of it!

Even as my husband and I flew to the Bahamas, I had no idea I would soon be one of those nut cases.

It was a bright, sunny day as we headed out on a dive boat for our first dive of the day. Since Gary is not certified to dive, he usually snorkels while I buddy up with someone on the dive boat. On this day, there were no single divers, so I dove with the dive master.

Reaching to tie my hair back and put my mask on, I grasped air—it was exactly one year since I finished my last chemotherapy treatment and I still had the battle scar of extremely short hair to remind me how precarious life can be.

213

On the ride back to the dock, a number of divers asked questions about the "shark dives" that Stuart Coves is known for. I listened with keen interest as the dive master told of feeding chunks of meat to the sharks as they circled the divers—many times bumping right into them—still thinking, *These people have lost their minds. I've just spent the last year and a half fighting for my life. I'll be damned if I am going to volunteer to be some shark's finest meal!*

I cannot explain what happened an hour later when I got off the boat, but I signed up for the "shark dive." Somewhere deep inside, I knew I could not embrace my bigger fear of writing if I was not willing to feel the fear and do it anyway!

Sometimes you have to go crazy before you get sane.

Today's Action	Look back over your list of fears. Is there one you are willing to walk through now? Circle it.

Theme From Jaws

I did it!

I dove with SHARKS!

It was exhilarating!

When you arrive at the dive site, they "chum" the water. For you landlubbers, that means they put fish parts into the water to attract fish, or in this case, sharks. Now, my father and ex-husband were fishermen, so I've been on a lot of fishing boats. No sane person *ever* gets into the water after it has been chummed! But that is exactly what we did.

At first, we swam along a coral reef ledge about sixty feet below the surface. Sharks swam all around us, at first just a couple, and then more and more appeared out of nowhere. They kept their distance, swimming some twenty to fifty feet away from the divers. The dive master told us that this first dive was to get us used to being in the ocean near these awesome creatures without panicking.

As we trailed after the instructor, so did the sharks; his pockets were filled with chum. Actually, once you got used to being in the water with the sharks, it was like any other dive—deep, blue water, beautiful coral reefs—only this time, sharks circled in the distance. You definitely dove with a heightened sense of awareness.

After about an hour, we took a break and got our instructions for the next dive, which was the "real deal"—*the feeding of sharks—in open water!*

It is a bit disconcerting to slip into the water with dozens of dorsal fins circling the boat when your whole life you have been taught that if you see a fin break surface, get out of the water. Now, here I was doing the one thing I was always warned *not* to do. I guess I will do just about anything to avoid picking up the pen!

In we went, settling on the ocean floor about fifty feet below the boat. The dive master had two milk crates filled with huge chunks of fish and a spear with which to feed the sharks. And the sharks, they came a-feeding!

About thirty sharks, ranging from five to eight feet long swam around us attacking the spear as it came out of the crate with their dinner. And bump into me they did. After all I was standing, or rather kneeling, between the sharks and their food. And yes, I was in the open ocean with "wild" sharks—as if there is any other kind! And yes, yes, yes, I was scared to death. But after the third time a shark brushed up against me, my heart stopped jumping out of my throat, and, believe it or not, *I got used to it.*

Obviously, I lived to tell the story, and the experience accomplished exactly what it was supposed to. I can be absolutely terrified of something and do it anyway!

Now, I am not saying, "Suit up, we are going on a shark dive," but I *am* saying, "Begin walking (or swimming) through some of your fears."

Today's Action | Go over your list again and take *some action—any action*, that you are scared to take. It might mean picking up that 1000-pound phone and making that call you have been putting off. Or maybe it is picking up your own pen or paintbrush to let *your* heart sing. If I can do it, you can do it.

Don't You Forget About Me

Three years ago I took a couple of experiential workshops to further my personal growth. Unlike the eight-month Twelve-Step workshop I was in eight years ago, which had no charge, these were quite expensive.

The first one, "The Beginners," lasted three days and cost $400.00. It was a wonderful learning experience, affording me the opportunity to work through many issues.

"The Advanced" lasted five days, and I didn't take it right away, mostly because it cost $1,000.00. After three months, I was still drawn to it because others who took it said it would help me overcome my fears and limiting beliefs about myself. I needed a breakthrough and hoped this five-day transformational workshop would provide it.

Biting the bullet, I charged the workshop to my credit card. This was difficult for me, as I like to pay for things in full, and this would take many months to pay off. The decision challenged me on many levels—one of which was self-worth. Finally, I believed I was worth whatever it took—time, money, or energy—I was willing to give it my all, trusting I would come out the other side stronger and wiser.

Over the five days we did many games and exercises, most of which we didn't know what the object or point was until it was over. On the third day, we were told that we were on a sinking ship, and out of the sixty of us only four would live. It was up to us to determine a method for deciding which four would live and which fifty-six people would die. Whatever method we chose had to be unanimous. For now, we were just choosing the method—the actual deciding happened later.

Almost immediately, the majority decided that the four people who would carry on for the rest of us should be the mothers. The men would do the noble thing and let women with children live because "children are our future." They wanted to put all the women with children in a group and then decide which four of them would live to carry on for everyone else.

Now, I don't usually speak up, especially when it's an overwhelming majority, but I didn't go through all those surgeries and all that chemotherapy to be tossed aside, just because I didn't have children! What about *my* worth? Maybe *I* was that child that would make a difference!

Over the noise and excitement, I spoke up. No one heard. I continued raising my voice until the group heard. In a quiet but firm voice I said, "I am not a mother and cannot have children, but that doesn't mean I don't have value and can't make a worthwhile contribution. I am someone's child. Maybe *I* am your future. Maybe I am that one who is going to make that awesome contribution. I'm writing a book that is changing lives as we speak. Don't discount me. At least let me state why I should live. I will not vote for *any* method of choosing that does not give *everyone* a fair chance."

I got through, and finally they saw that no one group has more value than another. As the evening progressed, everyone was heard, and then a vote was taken: I was picked as one of the four to carry on.

I am worthy today. I matter. I will make a difference in the world. I *am* making a difference. I choose life.

We *all* get to live—but we must choose it for ourselves. No one else can say we are worthy. We must stand up and declare our worth!

𝒯oday's 𝒜ction	Would you speak up for yourself? Why? What contribution are you committed to making? It may well be that the awesome contribution you make *will* be your children. Who they become may be of utmost importance to the planet. But it also may be who your *parents* raised who has the extraordinary contribution to make.

Hero

On the fourth night of this experiential weekend, ten people surround you and slowly lift you high above their heads while a song, chosen just for you, plays in the background.

The song picked for me was "Hero" by Mariah Carey. The words drifted up and surrounded me:

"And then a hero comes along,

With the strength to carry on

And you cast your fears aside

And you know you can survive

So when you feel like hope is gone

Look inside you and be strong

And you'll finally see the truth

That a hero lies in you"

217

The group gently swayed, singing "Hero" to me. Tears streamed down my face. Even though I found my voice the night before and declared my worth, I still didn't feel worthy of being called a hero.

"Hero" was the final song of the evening. As it played, I sank into it, allowing everyone's belief in me to wash over me. My heart opened, and I was able to see what they saw.

Today, I cannot listen to that song without crying. Something touched me deep inside and let me know that I don't have to be afraid of my gifts. I *do* have the strength I need. I *can* survive. Not just cancer, but my internal doubts and fears.

The lyrics remind me of who I really am, that the truth and strength I need lie *within* me. I don't have to face the world alone. People who have gone down the path before are there to guide me. And there is "One" who knows me inside out and loves me, exactly as I am.

Going inward, I find the peace and courage I need.

Yes, the road is rocky and hard to follow, but no one can take away my Inner Light. I will find a way. Even when all hope seems lost, I will find a way.

Today's Action | Seek out and listen to this song today. Let the words reach your very heart and soul and give you the encouragement you need.

Anyone who has gotten this far, in a book that stretches and challenges you to the degree that this one does, is already a hero. Regardless of how many suggested actions you have or haven't taken, the stories alone trigger subtle, internal shifts and effect great change.

You are a true hero with immense courage. I *know* this. Allow yourself to see this truth.

I Like Dreaming

More excerpts from my journal as I journeyed toward my bliss:

7/13/95

I saw the cancer psychotherapist and feel optimistic about our work together: Getting rid of blocks to embracing life and my purpose. I'm reading *Cancer as a Turning Point* and its premise is if you really *love* living, your immune system will be stronger and your body will get the message that you want to live.

7/14/95

I'm doing better with the pain and the book is helping me to see what my life's purpose and goals are, by asking what my unique way of relating, creating, and being is and what my likes and loves are.

Obviously, sponsorship is something I love, as is writing. I love waterfalls and traveling. If I had a year to live, I would definitely go to Hawaii. I also love small quaint towns and farms. Someday I might want to retire to a small town in mid-Florida—but not any time soon. I'd feel stifled and would hate leaving my friends and family.

I love all types of water—beaches, bubbling brooks, rivers, oceans, lakes, and of course, waterfalls. I love fighting for justice and worthy causes, but get mad when things don't work out like I think they should. I love networking and helping people find the help they need, "So and so has been through that too, call them." I like painting. I love singing but have no ear for it.

I like dancing, but only do it once or twice a year. I love sharing about recovery and what the Twelve Steps have done for me. I like inspiring people. I love having sex and making love and playing in bed. I wanted to have a family.

I love learning and using new computer programs. I like working with numbers. I love reading. Working in a library has always fascinated me—networking, helping others, reading, writing, and now computers—all of it. But I really like my job, and I *love* being married to Gary.

Today's Action | Write a page of things you absolutely love. Cover all areas—career, family, fun, pleasure, hobbies, day-to-day living—everything.

Part Of The Plan

And still more excerpts:

7/15/95

I feel writing is my purpose and my gift. I believe its part of God's plan for me. But I feel if I don't write or don't get something published, then I haven't succeeded. At least that's what I tell myself.

Where am I at today? I fear that my defects of sloth and fear will prevent me from seeing my dream of writing a book through to fruition. I am so scared of the unknown. I don't think I can do this. Sometimes death looks like a better alternative than facing my fears.

I don't want to beat myself up for not writing, but can I be satisfied with writing just for me, in this journal? Or do I need to go to the computer and really *work* on a book? At least by journaling I'm getting into the discipline of writing regularly.

Maybe going to bed earlier and getting up at four or five in the morning to write is what I need to do. I know that I have a lot of vision and clarity in the middle of the night and during meditation. Like the short story I wrote—the best scene was written in the middle of the night when I couldn't sleep. I guess my left brain is still sleepy then.

8/4/95

It's nine days after my first round of chemotherapy. I feel very resistant to writing today. I don't want to *have* to do this to cure my cancer. I beat myself up when I don't write, thinking I am hindering my healing process. I love writing once I am doing it—sort of like exercising—but it's so hard to start *doing* it. Like right now, I really like putting pen to paper—*once I am doing it.*

What in me is so resistant to writing? I tried riding my stationary bicycle today, and my heart beat so fast it scared me. I stopped after two minutes. My esophagus seems swollen and irritated and I'm running a slight fever, so maybe I just have to chalk it up to having a down day.

Lighten up already! It's okay not to do everything on my list, probably healthy in fact! ✕

Well, I did it. I wrote. Even if just a little and only in my journal, I did it!

Looking back, I realize I was so hard on myself. Instead of accepting that growth is a *process*, I pushed myself mercilessly.

Today, I have much more compassion for myself as a writer. The beginning writer was in the throes of cancer recovery, desperately trying to save her life. My experience of writing is so different today. It's such an effortless pleasure. Now, I write because I love writing. It is easier to write than to *not* write. In fact, my mentor has to tell me to take a day or two off each week, otherwise, I wouldn't.

Today's Action | Use your journal to sort through any resistance you might be feeling. Regular journaling helps you gain clarity and perspective. And don't forget the wee hours of the morning are often full of insights that can help you achieve your dreams and goals. Most importantly, be gentle with yourself.

For Once In My Life

Reading back over yesterday's excerpt gave me a lot of hope. It was written almost four years ago when I was "trying" to live my bliss and was still so filled with fear. Obviously, the cancer weighed heavily on me, which made writing difficult—I thought I *had* to write to save my life. There's no room for enjoyment if something is a "have to."

Fear consumed me: Not only about cancer and dying, but about writing, writing well, getting published, the doing it—the idea of doing it—the responsibility of it, the following through with it, and the self-hatred when I didn't. Weeks would go by when I didn't write much at all. The inner struggle was overwhelming: Knowing what your bliss is, but *not* living it, is pure agony.

And sloth. Sloth is really just another form of fear, but it kept me too tired to write. I was, after all, busy doing more important things like returning phone calls and replying to e-mail, watching TV, cleaning house, pulling weeds, you know the deal.

The thought of living authentically was so terrifying that I would do absolutely *anything* but the very thing I longed to do. Busyness and TV numbed my mind. What was I so afraid of? I'm not sure—the unknown, maybe. Now that I think of it, when I finally committed to my writing, I *did* have to pull down those walls and face my demons.

It was painful revisiting my past. But harder still was facing my present—feeling unappreciated in my job of ten years and feeling abandoned and undesired by my husband and inauthentic as a person. It's funny how once you take the greater action, everything else falls into place. Now that I am committed to living my bliss—my writing—work is no big deal. I will work until I don't.

Moreover, my relationship with Gary has completely shifted. The more I write, the more attentive and affectionate he is. It's great. I don't think I'll ever quit writing now.

Yet, how was I to know it would take three long years of continually pushing through my fears before getting to the point where I hardly notice them?

However, here I am in a place of perfect peace and contentment. For months, nothing has bothered me. For once, I'm living by my own lights. I am doing that which I was created to do—that which makes my heart sing—and I *love* it.

222

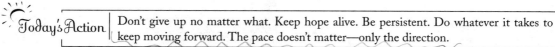

Today's Action | Don't give up no matter what. Keep hope alive. Be persistent. Do whatever it takes to keep moving forward. The pace doesn't matter—only the direction.

Lessons To Be Learned

Three affirmations from Belleruth Naparstek's cancer and chemotherapy tapes were essential to my empowerment.

"I tell the cancer these things:

Thank you for teaching me to stop and listen. Thank you for reminding me of what is truly important. You can go now."

These affirmations helped me embrace the cancer and the lessons it brought me. They also empowered me to tell the cancer that it was no longer needed. Accepting, thanking, and releasing brought me full circle with cancer. I've found these affirmations can be applied to most difficult situations.

"I know that I have things to do, gifts to give, purposes to accomplish. I require a healthy body for this."

By stating this truth I take back the reins—I remember my vision and know I need to be alive and healthy to accomplish my goals.

"More and more, I know that I am held in the hands of God. And that I am perfectly, utterly safe."

How can you go wrong with an affirmation like that? Whenever you are truly tested, there can be no greater reminder than that *you are not alone.*

Often, I pictured two great big hands holding me within them. I basked in the warmth and protection of those loving hands, letting love and light in, until I *believed* I was perfectly and utterly safe.

What a wonderful gift to have right in my own heart and soul: God's perfect peace and comfort.

Today's Action | Only you know what you need. Today, create three statements that empower you to overcome the obstacles in your life. Use the above affirmations or your own whenever you need a shift in consciousness.

Always Something There To Remind Me

The news program *Dateline NBC* recently profiled three women with advanced breast cancer. The cancer had spread to their bones, liver, or brain and their prognoses were poor. The women were trying a new drug, Herceptin, which attacks only cancer cells instead of both cancerous and healthy cells like traditional chemotherapy.

Dateline followed each woman's progress. The families' emotional roller coaster as hope came and went with each new MRI and bone scan, was heart-wrenching to watch.

In the last two years, I haven't dealt with anything more volatile than a raging hot flash or a swollen arm. Now my lingering side effects don't seem like such a big deal. After three years of cancer-free checkups, I guess I've started taking my health for granted again.

People no longer ask, "So how are you *really*?" fearing the worst. They do however, comment on how great I look, since I'm no longer that skinny, hairless girl with the gray pallor; I am back to my robust, golden-haired self.

The show reminded me how fortunate I am to have something as basic as good health. I don't ever want to get so far away from cancer that I forget its lessons and blessings.

Thank you, God, for my life. Thank you, God, for my health and bless those three courageous women and their families.

Today's Action	Today is a gratitude day. Be aware today of all that you have to be grateful for. Nothing is a given. Everything is a gift.

A little side note: When I was typing this page, I didn't know how to spell Herceptin, so I put a little question mark in parentheses next to the wrong spelling of it, reminding me to look up the correct spelling later.

Two hours later, a newsletter from the Florida Breast Cancer Coalition came in the mail with an article on Herceptin in it. Isn't God great?

Manic Monday

Some days are do-nothing days . . . fun days . . . whatever-you-want days.

Not much to read days.

Throw out the "to do" list days.

Skipping—dancing—laughing—singing days.

Crawl-back-into-bed, trade-exercise-for-sleep days.

Sip-a-cup-of-tea, go-outdoors, and listen-to-the-morning-wake-up days.

Today is your Sunday.

 Today's Action | Do whatever suits your fancy. Relax and have fun today.

Through The Noise

Discipline.

What a horrible word. It's sounds menacing, punishing, brutal.

Lack of it was one of the main reasons my dreams fell by the wayside. Granted, my lack of discipline was based in fear; I was too afraid to get down to the business of living my bliss.

After two tortuous years, I found you can't think or wish your way into right living, you have to live your way into right thinking.

The way through is *through*. You gain courage by *doing*. You gain expertise by *practicing*.

I didn't believe I could become a better, less fearful writer by writing regularly. And I didn't believe my doubts would disappear once I committed to a regular routine of writing. But that is exactly what happened.

I learned to write *through* my fears and excuses.

226   Sure, I feel tired sometimes. At times, I feel uninspired. And sometimes I even feel downright lazy.

Now, I write regardless of my thinking or feeling.

My writing has definitely improved as a result of writing day in and day out. I used to think I had to read more, study more, and take more classes to become a better writer. Instead, I found, as with a physical sport, the best way to build the muscle or improve the game is through practice. In fact, I don't know of any golf championships, tennis tournaments, or Super Bowls that were won as a result of taking classes or reading *about* the sport.

Daily workouts changed my life.

 Today's Action | Practice doing what you love. Build your muscles by using them daily. Prepare yourself for what dreams may come by *acting your way into right thinking*.

You Gotta Be Bad, You Gotta Be Bold

Whatever your dream or bliss is, you get there by doing what it takes to get there. Whether it's having a beautiful vegetable garden, writing, or becoming a lawyer like my friend Melissa, the dream won't materialize until you act.

If you want home-grown vegetables in your salad, you have to till the soil, plant the seeds, and water the garden. In my case, I want to write for a living, so I put pen to paper.

For years, my friend Melissa dropped her daughter off at her ex-mother-in-law's house after work so that she could complete her college degree in the evenings.

Since returning to school at age thirty-three, Melissa has earned straight As, in addition to working full time. She also trusted that as an African American, single mother, with good grades, there would be numerous grant and scholarship opportunities available to help her with her law school tuition. So, after earning her B.A., Melissa took a leap of faith and quit her secretarial job. No scholarships or loans had come through yet, but she had been accepted into at least one law school, and that was enough.

While her actions looked bold on the surface, inside Melissa was quaking in her boots. Shortly after Melissa quit her job, the rejections started coming in. First, the law school she wanted to attend most turned her down because her grades weren't as good as was required. She was crushed. It turns out that even though she earned straight As during the last two years she had been back to school, her grades from her reckless teen years were also taken into account, and the overall picture wasn't great.

A month before the start of school, scholarships and grants Melissa thought she would qualify for fell through, leaving her with no idea of how to pay for law school. Suffering disappointment after disappointment, Melissa realized her only options were loans, and even if she were approved, repaying them would take the bulk of her salary for years to come.

Plagued with doubts—*What if I can't cut it? I'll still owe all that money!* Melissa wanted to throw in the towel. But she didn't. She picked herself up, dusted herself off, and trudged forward.

It was a difficult summer.

Finally, Melissa was accepted to a law school convenient to where she lives. Then, three days before school started, a scholarship came through that covered most of her tuition. And to top it all off, Melissa's mother offered to move in with her and take care of her daughter, Brittany, for the next three years while she went to school.

Tough as it has been, Melissa excelled in law school and graduated this past May near the top of her class.

Melissa's determination, perseverance, and commitment to her dreams continually inspire me to follow my own. Her courage shows me that we *all* have within us what it takes to reach for our dreams.

Today's Action | Be Bold. Be Bad. Don't give up—no matter what!
When fear, doubt, disappointment, or rejection plagues you—seek out someone who is following their dream. Allow them to be your beacon in the night.

Soul Serenade

One of the things I did early in my cancer recovery to keep me going was to make a tape of uplifting songs. My first tape consisted of "I Just Want To Celebrate Another Day of Living" by Rare Earth, "I Will Survive" by Gloria Gaynor, "Coming Out of the Dark" by Gloria Estefan, "I'm Gonna Run the Race" by Kathleen Brown, "It's A Beautiful Morning" by the Rascals, and others. I listened to songs of hope, joy, and inspiration endlessly. Now I give musical compilations to anyone going through a rough time.

The healing power of music is awesome. I move to it, sing along, and let music take me wherever it wants to go. Music speaks to my very soul. Merging with it, I become one with the music.

Intuitively I know when it's time to relax with classical or jazz music or when it's time to deepen spiritually with Enya or chanting tapes. And there's always a time for reconnecting with the past through oldies, or letting the teenager have her way with Led Zeppelin or Alanis Morissette.

Music takes me where I need to go. My quiet, inward journey is enhanced by the music playing softly in the background. My outward energy is sparked by rising tempos.

Whatever comes up for you, see how music can deepen your experience, assisting you on your way.

Today's Action | This book's section titles are a compilation of songs that resonate deeply with me. Make a tape of your own favorites. Compile a collection of gospel or country—rock or love songs—whatever you need—make it up.

Try a different radio station and allow new words and music to revitalize your spirit. Today, let music serenade your soul.

Seventh Month

To Thine Own Self Be True

Free Spirit

*O*ne area I have trouble with is being too goal-oriented, mercilessly driving myself towards the finish line. Stillness and quiet are not natural states for me. I always look ahead, telling myself: *I can rest when I finish this . . . live my bliss when . . . change my job when . . . take time for me when . . .* The trouble with this thinking is that the finish line continually moves out of reach, making peace elusive.

Like a dog with a bone, my mind must always have something to chew on. Something always needs tweaking or improving. I move so quickly to the next item on my never-ending to-do list that I don't even stop to enjoy my accomplishments.

Even with this book, there is already a strong desire to finish. Knowing me, I'll probably be working on my next project before this one is even completed. It takes great effort for me to slow down and enjoy the moment.

When you really love something, you want to savor the experience, not rush through it. Living blissfully means slowing down and living each moment fully, not regretting the past nor wishing for some elusive future moment. It's living *now*. Straighten out the past, move toward things you like, but more important, enjoy today!

It's not about achieving. It's about *being*.

The taskmaster must die.

She's melting. She's melting.

When she melts, I live!

Today's Action | Throw out your lists, not only your written list, but also the one in your head. If it's important, it will get done. Free up your mind and energy by living today accomplishment-free.

At The Same Time

Do you pat yourself on the back for a job well done? Me, I tend to struggle with rewarding myself. Instead, I usually move immediately onto the next challenge.

For instance, today is my ten-year anniversary of being drug- and alcohol-free, and inside I want to brush it off as if it's nothing.

I guess I feel *I* didn't do it. I had help from other recovering people and a Higher Power. At the same time, ten years ago, I made a decision that I no longer wanted to be self-destructive or live unconsciously. I stuck by that decision through marriage and job difficulties, self-esteem issues, abuse memories, infertility, and even cancer.

Looking back on my decision and the major shift my life took as a result, I am amazed. So many people died as a result of their drinking and drugging, or are still numbing themselves and blotting out the world as I used to. I am ever so grateful that I chose *life*!

I feel the same way about my marriage and the ten years I've been at the same company. Usually I don't even notice these accomplishments. Lately, however, I experience a healthy sense of pride when I think of the things I've stuck with. And a smile spreads over my face when I think about the degree I earned a few years ago, even though I was one of the oldest graduates.

Yin and Yang—positive and negative emotions—coexisting. Today I'll focus on the positive. I am delighted to be alive: It's been four years since the doctor said, "It's cancer."

Gratefully, I thank everyone who passed this way before me, for their courage, strength, and grace. I am here *only* because others were there to light the way.

232

Today's Action | Take time to notice your own accomplishments and give thanks to all who contributed to your success.

Changes In Latitudes, Changes In Attitudes

As wonderful as yesterday started out, it ended up being a very frustrating day.

My grandmother's computer was on the fritz, and I spent the afternoon troubleshooting the problems. Two things I ordered through the mail were backordered for weeks. I'm bored out of my mind at work. And to top it all off, the main entertainment at a recovery convention I am going to is sold out. We are traveling across country to go to this convention, and I'm not even going to get to go to the main event. I *really* wanted to see Eric Clapton, but between getting the airline tickets and making the hotel arrangements, we didn't register in time, and the concert sold out.

Gary can't understand why I am so upset. When I told him how disappointed I was, he said, "I think there's a Mother Teresa special on TV tonight." Sometimes I just hate his self-righteousness.

I know, compared to losing a loved one, having cancer, or living in poverty, my problems are nothing. But that doesn't help how I feel.

I know it will pass. In the meantime, I put my concerns about the concert in my "God Box" to be taken care of one way or another by God. I'll trust and let go. At least that's what I tell myself every time my mind wanders back to, *I should have taken the money from my savings account and registered earlier instead of waiting. I can't believe scalpers want $200.00 a ticket. How dare they!*

I turn it over to God and trust that we will be where we are supposed to be on that night. Everything is in Divine Order. No one is happy twenty-four/seven. We all wrestle with sadness or disappointment occasionally.

In the scheme of things, it's no big deal. Besides, I saw Eric Clapton a few years ago in the Royal Albert Hall in London. I mean *really*, how much does one person want? I feel stupid complaining about my insignificant problems when people are facing real-life challenges like addiction, illness, homelessness, loss of loved ones, and war.

My problem isn't even a blip on the radar screen.

I need an attitude adjustment.

| Today's Action | List the blessings in your life. Fill a page with things you are grateful for and see if that doesn't shift your perception of reality. |

The Finer Things

I am grateful for . . .

My life

My health

My loving husband

The wonderful card he gave me for my ten-year-clean anniversary

The etched mirror of the St. Francis of Assisi Prayer that Gary also gave me

Six weeks of paid vacation

The Twelve Steps

The fact that I love recovery

God in my life

God's grace

Life *not* being fair and me *not* getting what I deserve

Music and colors

Flowers and waterfalls

My upcoming trip to Hawaii in the fall

My mom and family

My sponsees and sponsor

Living my heart's desire through my writing

Where I live—my city—my home—the ocean

Dharma and my other kitties: Karma, Winky, and Magic

Reconnecting with old friends

That all my needs are met

My beautiful, purple car

My arms, legs, and my eyesight

That my hair grew back

A job that pays the bills while I work towards my dream

God not forsaking me, even when I'm self-centered and pissy

My heart

My friends

My mind

Most of all, I am grateful for the ability to feel, to work through things, to change my perspective, and adjust my attitude. All of this is a direct result of God in my life. I am a walking, talking, breathing miracle.

Today's Action | Share your gratitude list with a friend and ask them to share their gratitude list with you.

Against The Wind

A baby dove found his way into our backyard a few days ago. At first, I thought he was dead, because he was so still and had hardly any feathers. Then his mother came and sat by him. While she watched over the little brown bird, I was careful not to let my cats outside.

Last night I realized in horror that our yardman cut the grass earlier that afternoon. Frantically, I looked for the little bird. No sign of him anywhere, no sign of feathers either—but it was dark. First thing this morning I continued my search for the baby dove. Finding no sign of him, I let the cats out.

Normally, after I let my cats outside, I come in and write. For some reason, this morning I hesitated. After a few minutes, I looked out the back door and saw Karma intently trying to dig under some pieces of wood on the ground. I shooed him away and there was the baby bird, still scared and featherless, but looking a bit stronger than before.

I dug up some worms and left them near him. I don't know if he ate them or not. I'm also not sure, since his mother is still around, whether I should take him to an animal hospital or just let nature take its course.

I'm amazed he managed to get under those pieces of wood at the edge of the lawn some ten feet from where he was yesterday. I guess he's seeking shelter from life's storms with its noisy lawn mowers, big cats, and big worm-bearing people.

God bless this little bird and help me help him, whether it's leaving him where he is or taking him to a veterinarian.

And thank you, God, for placing him in my life to remind me of what's truly important: life—a small bird's life—not some coveted concert tickets. You *always* find a way to reach me.

Higher Ground

Intention, that's what's important, whether it be caring for an injured bird or making plans for some future event. No matter what the outcome is, intention matters.

Today I called the Wildlife Care Center to find out how to care for an injured bird, this being my first. I provided him with food and water, was careful not to touch him, but was not sure whether to take him to a veterinarian or not. I was told since his feathers weren't fully developed I should place him back in his nest if I could find it or make a nest of dry twigs and grass. If his parents were nearby, they would care for the baby bird, and I should not force-feed him. I made a nest on the ground near where the bird was and then left him alone.

The center said handling the bird would not prevent his parents from caring for him, but forcing food and water on him could harm the bird. I was glad I called because although my intentions were good, I lacked proper information. Had I not sought guidance, the outcome could have been disastrous.

In the case of the convention entertainment, my desire to see the concert was greater than my desire to attend the convention. In other words, my intentions were not pure. I wanted to be in the "in crowd," the informed few who had inside information about *who* the entertainment was.

Yet, since I come from "material lack" (I don't believe there is enough to go around or that my needs will always be met), I don't trust the flow of money. I was unwilling to dip into my savings and register for the convention early, ensuring my place at the concert.

I learned my lesson—big time. First, my intentions should be of the highest nature in all I do. If my motives are impure, it's likely things will backfire. Second, the necessary action or footwork *must* be taken for the desired outcome to even be possible.

I've been told that God must really want me at that convention, or this lesson must be important.

Either way, I know everything is happening according to my highest good, and I am open to the lesson.

Today's Action | Be aware of your intentions. Are they pure? Before taking any action ask, "What are my motives?" Purify your motives and intentions, then follow through with right action. | 237

What Is And What Should Never Be

Desire is the cause of suffering. If I am attached to a specific outcome, I am sure to be disappointed.

That's a tough lesson I'm learning about as I study Buddhism. Yes, I was attached to going to the concert, but not trusting enough to let go of "money energy" and take the necessary actions.

In the case of the dove, I took many caring actions but was not attached to the outcome, so I feel good about myself regardless of the outcome. My intentions are pure—to care for the injured bird and keep him safe from harm.

This morning the bird ran about four or five feet on the ground. Later when I went to check on him again, I could tell one of his injured wings was on the mend because he flew very close to the ground for about a yard. As I turned off the sprinkler, I noticed two doves frolicking in the spray about twenty feet from the baby bird—the parents I presume. I am glad he is being watched over, much as God watches over me: neither too near nor too far.

Watching this little bird's story unfold, there is no suffering—only joy and peace. Glad to do what I can, I trust things will work out the way they are supposed to. Now, if I can just do that regarding the Eric Clapton concert.

I am unable to let go of it. I keep dwelling on what I could have done differently. The past is behind me, and I can't change it. I know that by letting go of attachment and desire, my suffering will be lifted. Peace lies in going *with* the flow, pain comes from the struggle—from resisting what is.

Go with the flow.

Hard to practice when you really want something.

☼ Today's Action
Looking back, can you see where attachment and desire have caused you pain? Live in the moment and practice nonattachment. Go with the flow. Find contentment with what is.

Remember, absolutely nothing happens in God's world by mistake. Everything is in Divine Order, according to our souls' lessons.

238

How Can You Mend A Broken Heart

This talk of intention and nonattachment to outcomes brings me back to the situation with my Aunt Fi. I believe my intentions are pure—I would like a healing to take place in my family. I am willing to trust my intuition and do what's necessary. Although there is a specific outcome I want, I don't feel attached to it. I want it only if it is God's will and if it is for everyone's highest good. I believe it is, but I do not see the whole picture, so I allow it the space and time it needs to unfold naturally.

I have not told my grandmother that I have seen and spoken with her sister. This is so *not* my nature. My life is usually an open book, and I tell everyone anything that I think might interest them.

But this situation is different.

I talk to my grandmother once or twice a week, but the subject of my renewing relations with her sister hasn't come up. I didn't set out to avoid it. We've just been busy getting her computer running and teaching her how to use it.

I have not called my aunt or spoken with my mother since telling her about our initial visit. Normally, I would try to force the issue. Nevertheless, here we are, weeks later, and I am not trying to control anything.

A small part of me wants to rush the process, but the greater part knows to *trust* the process.

This wound has festered in the morass of long-held resentment for many years. I have to remember a twenty-five-year rift won't heal in an instant. Yet, when it does, it will seem as if only an instant has passed.

I trust *God* can mend these broken hearts.

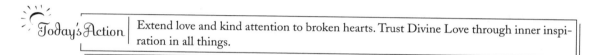

Today's Action | Extend love and kind attention to broken hearts. Trust Divine Love through inner inspiration in all things.

Dreamboat Annie

"Warm winds caress her . . . her lover it seems."

I am at the beach leaning against a palm tree. A breeze blows my hair across my face as I write. Suddenly, I realize this is bliss. Right here. Right now. This moment. Nothing could be more perfect.

I knew writing was my bliss when I asked myself, *If I died today, what would be my biggest regret?* Having such a strong desire to help others through my writing, I knew I was living inauthentically every day I chose to ignore that calling and not pick up the pen.

Eventually, I worked through the fears and blocks that prevented me from living my bliss, until finally, I arrived *at this moment* . . . this *one* moment.

I have yet to publish a book, but still could not be any more content than I am in this moment.

If I died today, I would have no regrets.

I am finally living according to my inner wisdom. Using the gifts God gave me, I am finally following the desire He placed in my heart. Nothing could be more perfect.

Gary is working today and as much as I love and adore him, I feel complete, whole, and perfect without him. I *know* I can be joyful and at peace, with or without him.

My dreams are my guide. My inner yearnings are the voice I follow.

Blue skies all around, ships passing in the distance, ants crawling on the page, crawling on me. I gently blow them off, desiring to harm no sentient being. Life is good. I am happy.

It *is* the journey that matters, not the destination. I finally get that for myself. I am experiencing it in this moment, this one perfect moment.

Goals and desires are nice, but in this moment, it doesn't matter whether my writing ever goes anywhere. I am experiencing bliss right here, right now.

I am doing something I thoroughly enjoy with no thought of reward. I will still do the footwork necessary for publication, but that is secondary now. And I will do the footwork with an open heart and no attachment to the outcome. I desire only peace and happiness for myself through right living and fulfillment of God's will for me.

240

Today's Action | Trust yourself. Trust your dreams. Trust that God placed that desire in your heart for a reason. Believe that and take the next step. Move forward.
Go to a special place today, outside if possible, and ask what it means to truly live your heart's desire. Give no thought to the impracticality of your dreams or any fears and doubts you might still have. Just journey inward and let your heart be your guide.

Your Song

Finding your voice is equivalent to finding your power.

In romantic love, couples have songs that are symbolic of their love. A special song becomes "their song." This month, spend some time listening to music. Listen particularly for a song that represents you and you alone, a song that embodies who you are, or best expresses what's in your heart. This is your anthem.

In your happiest moment, what song would you want to hear? In your saddest moment? What about on your deathbed—what medley of songs would you chose to represent your life? Many ancient religions believe that we should have a chant or song on our lips and in our hearts at the moment of death. What would yours be?

It may already have come to mind. It may take further exploration. Whatever the case, once you find it, sing your song aloud every day for a month.

Verbalize through song who you are and what is in your heart. Declare it to the world. Watch in amazement as you voice gets stronger and clearer as the month passes. This may seem silly or embarrassing, but do it anyway.

This one seemingly simple act will open you up to who you really are and deepen your connection with your Higher Self.

Trust and sing.

Today's Action | Find and sing *your song.*

Sing . . . Sing a Song

When I was thirteen I declared myself to the world with "Born to be Wild" by Steppenwolf. For the next seventeen years, I lived that song. It was my anthem. Sex, drugs, and rock 'n' roll were my wildness. That song gave me permission to live with complete abandon. But because mind-altering chemicals also alter your behavior, I acted in ways I am not very proud of.

When I turned thirty, another song became my song. "Man in the Mirror" by Michael Jackson was the catalyst that motivated me to seek help. It urged me, *"If you want to make the world a better place, start with yourself, and make that change."* It spoke to my lost soul, the part that was born with morals, values, and high ideals, the part of me that wanted to make a difference in the world. Within an hour of hearing that song, I went to my first Twelve-Step meeting. I began changing my ways.

To this day, that song has the power to move me to tears every time I hear it.

"Man in the Mirror" remained "my song" for the next eight years. Then, Celine Dion's "Because You Loved Me" entered my heart at her concert and let me know how much God loved me. To most people this song is a romantic love song, to me, it's a God song—and my current anthem.

Today's Action | Think back and pick three songs that best represent the different stages of your life. Listen to them. Sing them aloud and know they are your anthems.

Dazed And Confused

Journal entry:

8/13/95

God, why is it that I would rather write in my journal than work on my book, on the computer? I feel jumbled, confused, and not sure of what I want to write or how it's going.

I'm sleeping poorly again. But I've been doing well overall—getting most things on "my list" done.

So does this writing count? I know journaling is good for me, but it's not the same as working on the book. It doesn't seem important.

Why can't I be more like my cat, Magic—sleeping most of the day without a care in the world—only "When is my next meal coming so I can go back to sleep?"

Well, maybe this will clear me some, so I can write the more important stuff.

I look back with kind eyes on the woman I was. I was so hard on myself. August 13, 1995, was three weeks after my first chemotherapy treatment. What in the world did I expect of myself?

The reason I felt so bad when I didn't write was that I was convinced writing would boost my immune system and save my life. Therefore, if I wasn't writing, I was killing myself. How merciless I was with myself.

Now, I understand a little more. First, I am not that powerful. Yes, my actions can either be life-enhancing or self-destructive—but sometimes I have to trust the process. I can't always make myself do something by sheer will alone. I must allow things to unfold, according to the Divine Plan.

I think it's perfectly okay, even normal and healthy, to experience a period of being "dazed and confused" after just finding out you have a life-threatening illness. Dealing with any major change justifies a certain amount of confusion.

Today, I am able to embrace *all* of my emotions. I've learned to be where I am. Wherever I am is okay.

Today's Action | If you feel stuck or confused, just relax into it. Know that you are right where you are supposed to be, and it's okay. Be gentle with yourself. Allow yourself to relax into the moment. The feelings and the confusion will pass. Clarity will come.
    If you think nothing is happening, don't be concerned: Calm oceans often hide the flurry of activity occurring just under the surface.

The Long And Winding Road

When I began this journey, I had no idea just how much emotional clearing would be necessary before I could truly face my fears and embrace my dreams. Yet, through clearing my past, I found my true voice.

A great deal of prewriting takes place before the real writing begins. I need to sift through who I was and where I've been to get to where I am going. The index cards are perfect for this stage of writing.

Naturally, I wanted to go straight to the computer and get down to business. However, I found I write more authentically on paper than on a computer. When I'm on the computer, I'm in a left-brain, critical, editing state of mind.

The physical act of putting pen to paper grounds me. The essence of what I want to say shows up. The original thought hits the paper. When I'm connected to my heart, creation spills onto the page.

When you write from a deep place and then expand your words to poster boards, creative juices explode. Stretching beyond the normal 8-1/2-by-11 boundaries creates amazing results.

When I think of the years I wasted struggling. However, you only get where you are by going where you went. Looking back, I see I needed the struggle. I had to clear the past to get to where I am today. None of it was wasted time. It's all part of the journey.

I found my authentic voice by taking the long and winding road.

Today's Action | Be willing to do things differently. Be open to change. Sometimes the short road is a dead end and the long road, the best and most direct road.
In a logical left-brain world, the shortest distance between two points is a straight line. In a creative, openhearted world, sometimes the *only* way to span the distance is by taking the scenic route.

I'm Leaving On A Jet Plane

Clouds race by. Trees and earth rush toward me. The plane smashes into the ground, and I awaken with a start.

I can't remember when they started, but once they did, the nightmares came with terrifying regularity.

I have been traveling since I was a child and have never been afraid of flying. In fact, I love going to new and exciting places. I love getting away from it all—always have.

As my thirst for liquor increased, I enjoyed flying even more. It was never too early to drink in an airport bar, no matter what time it was. And the miniatures served on planes always came in handy.

The nightmares started shortly after I quit drinking.

A couple of times a year at first. Then, after Hurricane Andrew tore through South Florida in 1992, the frequency increased. Soon, I was convinced it was a premonition: I was going to die in a plane crash. I had had thoughts about not being able to have children and that came to pass. Maybe I *could* see into the future, or maybe the intensity of my fear attracts the very things I fear (all that New Age stuff was getting to me).

Then I remembered I had always gotten smashed before flying. Maybe I've always been afraid of flying, and booze kept the fear at bay. Suddenly, even with many years of sobriety under my belt, alcohol looked enticing every time I got on an airplane.

My anxiety about flying grew with each passing year. I prayed during takeoffs and landings. Holding the arm rests with sweaty palms, I'd glance over at Gary and wonder if this would be our last moment together. I used books and tapes to distract me. I meditated to the hum of whirring engines. I prayed for pilots and passengers. I counted takeoffs and landings (T & Ls) and inquired about direct flights every time I booked a flight.

I weighed the importance of each trip against the possibility of dying. Rationally, I knew flying was safer than driving, but I was crazy with fear. When I was first diagnosed with cancer I thought, *Well, at least this will get me before the plane crash does.* During the six months I was on chemotherapy, I took three trips. The first was to see my brother and his family in Kentucky, requiring eight T & Ls. The second was a visit with my husband's family in Boston, requiring only four T & Ls. And the last trip, my mother took me to an ashram in California, requiring six T & Ls.

Imagine how terrifying flying became when added to the fear that accompanies cancer.

As the frequency of the nightmares increased, I dreaded going to sleep. It was suggested that I explore my dreams by journaling about them upon waking. Every fiber of my being resisted. Desperation, however, prevailed, and I began journaling.

Through this exploration of my thoughts and feelings, I was able to gain freedom from my fear of flying.

One more time, the way through is *through*.

245

Today's Action | Begin recording your dreams in your journal. Dreams have important messages for us and deserve our attention, especially any recurring dreams or nightmares.

These Dreams

By journaling I discovered that what I was really afraid of was *dying*, not *flying*.

Deeper than that, I didn't want to lose control. Flying represented my fear of losing control. The pilot was in charge, not me. That's why knowing that more people die in cars than planes never helped me with my fear. I'm usually the driver, therefore in charge. Ironically, I feared that which I could not control, not that which was more dangerous.

It's funny how life brings you perfect opportunities to work through your fears, whether you want to or not.

Right in the middle of my flying nightmares, in walks the big "C." Talk about not having control! I never felt so small and terrified in my life.

The nightmares revealed the weak areas of my faith. I found I didn't trust God with the big things. I turned little things over to God with relative ease. But look at what he'd done regarding my desire to have children! How could I trust God with important things, like my *life*?

Once I realized faith and control were the issues at hand, I released control of *everything* every chance I got.

I already knew I was capable of taking charge. Now I needed to find out if I was capable of letting go.

I started by letting others drive as much as possible. Next, I stopped having all the answers. When a sponsee asked for advice, I guided them back to their truth. I found I didn't need to be in charge of everything. Others are just as capable as I and become even more capable when given the opportunity. God is in charge, not me. For once, that feels good.

My nightmares changed. Instead of plowing into the ground, the planes crashed into the ocean. I was still trapped in the wreckage, struggling to free myself, but the surface was in sight.

Then, on what was to be my last nightmare, I am in a car on a very high bridge. I drive off the bridge. The car turns into a plane and glides for about a mile before going into the water a hundred yards from a dock. This time, I manage to swim free, climb up a ladder, and collapse on the dock where a rescue team is waiting.

The progression of my dreams reflects struggle decreasing in my own life. As I trust and *allow* others to help me, help is always there. In the end, I am rescued, my faith salvaged.

The nightmares disappeared when Dharma died, with that last one being a message of hope: I have the power to swim to shore, but only when I stop struggling.

What a powerful vision. Terrifying as they were at the time, the nightmares forced me to look at my fear and challenged me to let go of the illusion of control. I needed to trust that help would be there when I needed it. And it was.

Dreaming With My Eyes Open

I had a very enlightening dream a few years ago where I was in a huge hole in the ground about four feet around and six feet deep. I had all this baggage with me in the hole—suitcases, garment bags, duffel bags, shoulder bags, and a tray of food. Gary and I were off on vacation when I fell into this hole. He stood above me, empty-handed, trying to help. With every step he took, dirt and clumps of grass fell in on top of me.

I yelled up to him, "Stop it. You're not helping any!" and a struggle ensued.

I woke up and wrote the dream down, not understanding the symbolism of it at the time. The dream stayed with me, so I shared it with my friend Dorothy who helped me to interpret it.

I felt weighed down with responsibilities, and Gary wasn't helping any. Cramped in this dark hole, I was carrying the weight of the world, while Gary stood in the sunlight, free of burdens.

It represented our marriage at the time. I handled all the money, made all the plans, and took care of the house and yard. I was burnt out and resentful as hell.

Up until that dream, I hinted at my predicament by occasionally nagging or pleading for help, but Gary was wrapped up in work and helping others and was seldom home. I felt taken for granted.

Boy, were my eyes opened. I processed my feelings in my journal, so I wouldn't over-react when I talked to Gary. What came up was that I wanted to feel less burdened and more in partnership with Gary. Coming from a calm, clear space, I let Gary know how I felt about the inequities in our marriage and suggested some solutions. Then I asked if he had any ideas.

The manner in which I approached him was so different than my usual bitching that he was very receptive. He agreed to specific things he would do around the house to lighten my load and took over all the bills for a while.

The relief I felt was immediate, as was my appreciation of Gary's ability to hear me and respond. Now, we take turns paying the bills, and Gary continues to help around the house. Occasionally though, I still have to remind him not to work too much.

Dreams address exactly what needs to shift for peace to enter our lives. My dreams help me to see and speak my truth. They are my deepest source of wisdom.

Today's Action | Record your dreams for the next month or so, allow them to guide you to your truth. Share them with another for even greater clarity, but always go inward and listen.

Another *Godincidence* to report: I haven't seen or spoken with Dorothy in over three years. As I wrote about her valuable insight in this story, my heart longed to see her again. I thought to myself, "I really *must* call her."

Last night, after typing this story, I went out with my family and who did I run into but Dorothy! And on the very day I wrote this!

I Believe

When you take risks, you are bound to suffer disappointments. It's the nature of risking. If you knew the outcome, where's the risk?

Well, I just suffered my first, no, second, major disappointment regarding my writing. The first was two years ago when I wrote "Dharma—My Little Angel" for that writer's workshop and didn't win. I put my heart and soul into it and went into an emotional tailspin when I wasn't chosen. I knew hundreds, if not thousands of people sent in their stories and picking only ten people wouldn't be easy, but I was devastated nonetheless.

After receiving no word by the deadline, my heart closed up, and I vowed never to risk again. This is the state I was in before the "shark dive" jarred loose my fears. In fact, the day after the "shark dive" I started writing again.

Shortly afterwards, I wrote the editorial staff of the magazine and asked how I could improve my writing and get into a future workshop. They responded with a nice letter and their guidelines for publication. This little bit of direction helped me get over my disappointment.

A year later an editor from the magazine called to tell me they wanted to publish "Dharma" in their new publication, *Angels On Earth*. She said they would be in touch. Another year passed before yet another editor called to say it was slated for publication in the fall.

A photographer was sent to our house to take pictures of Gary and me by Dharma's grave. Then, the editor called from New York and interviewed me for over an hour. After that, there were many calls back and forth, and I was thoroughly impressed with the effort they were putting into my little story.

Up until two days ago, the entire process has been very exciting. I enjoyed their original magazine and was told the subscription base of their new magazine was over one million readers, so I had no doubt they would do a fabulous job of editing my story for publication.

Well, Monday night, the edited version arrived. I ripped open the Federal Express envelope and poured over the story. I didn't get beyond the first paragraph before I put the story down. *They had ruined it!*

In an effort to make the story more dramatic, they sensationalized the events by adding untrue statements and made-up conversations. In the process they turned me into a helpless victim and cut out the heart and soul of the story. I was crushed.

Gary said that it had a tabloid feel to it and that the whole meaning of the story and my fighting spirit were gone. "What are you going to do?" he asked, looking up at my tear-streaked face.

As much as I wanted "Dharma" to be published, and as excited as I was about the prospect of finally being paid for my writing, I could never let this be published. I would be ashamed to have my name on this version! There, I said it. I would rather remain unpublished and unpaid than to sell my soul.

I haven't responded yet, and I trust this will be a huge learning experience for me, so I will keep you posted. At this point the message is clear as captured in today's action, and each of us knows exactly where and how it needs to be applied.

Treat Me Right

Melissa, my friend in law school, just found out that her adoring boyfriend has been stepping out on her. She has had her doubts for some time now, but gave him the benefit of the doubt. Her gut told her one thing while her heart longed to believe another.

When confronted, her boyfriend flat out told her that whoever said he was cheating was lying.

Not knowing what to believe, Melissa called a mutual friend and insisted on the truth. Her friend confirmed what she had been told, "Yes, he's been seeing his ex."

After the truth came out, Melissa's friends said, "What's a little dishonesty. That's the way men in the hood are. He's a great guy, don't let this stand between you two. Forgive and forget."

Personally, I think cheating is unacceptable behavior, and I do not say that from some lofty place. I've been there. I was unfaithful most of my life, until I began living by spiritual principles some eleven years ago. I used to think that just because you weren't faithful didn't mean you weren't spiritual. Now, I realize that the dishonesty that goes hand in hand with cheating is inconsistent with spiritual principles.

I know Melissa believes this as well, but when she talks to her boyfriend, he swears that he loves her and doesn't want to lose her. She doesn't know what to do: Her trust in men is destroyed, yet her heart still longs for this one.

I'll support her either way. If she wants to try to work it out, I'll help her forgive and heal. If she wants to end it, I'll help her be strong.

My main concern is that this is not the first time this has happened. Melissa's last few boyfriends were all unfaithful. Spiritually, I know we attract what we need to heal. And if you continually attract the same thing over and over, either your picker is broken, or you still need to heal the original wound.

I suggested Melissa read, *Is It Love or Is It Addiction?* by Brenda Schaeffer. It's one of the best books I've ever read on love addiction.

I know it won't be easy, but my prayer is that Melissa will learn her worth, heal her wounds, and learn to trust again.

Today's Action | Know your worth, trust your intuition, and live accordingly. List ten things you respect about yourself and why you deserve the very best.

Anticipation

I sent my original "Dharma" story back to the editors with a note thanking them for their work on the story and circled some of the important ideas that were left out of their edited version. And I sent their version back with everything crossed out that wasn't true.

I told them that I trusted that they too wanted to capture my fighting spirit and Dharma's impact on my life while keeping the veracity of the story. I gave input on how I thought that could best be accomplished.

So now it's a waiting game.

Patience. Deep breathing.

Trust.

Trusting God. Trusting the process. Trusting myself enough to take a stand for what I believe in. And finally trusting that the outcome will be exactly as it is supposed to be.

Whether the story gets published or not, I am glad I spoke my truth and held out for what I thought was needed to maintain the integrity of the story.

At one point, I had even assumed I would like their edited version better than my original because of their editing skills. I have since found that you can edit the heart right out of a story.

For this reason, my teacher doesn't use the word edit. He only *enhances* his work and encourages his students to do the same. He says if you write from a deep place to begin with, you keep your authentic voice. He also said that my passion shows that I write from a very deep place and am very emotionally connected to what I write, which is a good thing, but that I need to detach enough to work with editors during the revision process.

However, our versions are so drastically different that I am not sure it is possible to achieve the magazine's goals and keep my story intact.

Anyway, I remained true to myself; now the lesson is patience.

So as I sit here waiting, waiting for them to restore, or possibly even cut the story from the magazine altogether, I trust. I trust God is in charge, and I let go into that trusting space.

| Today's Action | Sometimes, waiting is a necessary part of the process. Breathe into that waiting period, trusting that all is well in God's world. |

Meet Me In The Middle

Part of the benefit of writing about the moment is that it is constantly changing. Yesterday, I was upset about the rewrite of "Dharma," thinking maybe it was too close to my heart, that no one else could edit it. Today, everything changed.

The magazine's editor called me late yesterday, as they hadn't received my corrections yet. I thanked her again, and reminded her I was new to the editing process, so to please bear with me. Then, I asked if we could go through the story, as there were many factual errors, and I felt the essence of the story was missing.

She assured me that they didn't want to publish anything that didn't properly represent the truth. We went over each detail, and she explained why they took some things out and changed others. Once I saw their reasoning and their objectives more clearly, I was able to help them achieve them without distorting reality.

By the end of the conversation, she told me they definitely wanted to publish the story and would work with me until we were in agreement.

I am so grateful for this editing experience. If I had let them print the story as it was, not only would I have been betraying my heart, I would have missed a great learning opportunity.

I am also proud of myself for calmly stating my truth, instead of exploding with my first reaction: *I hate it!*

My mentor says I did great! I remained true to myself, yet was detached, and grounded enough to work with the editors.

I did not sell out and put my name on something that was sensationalized or fictionalized. We were able to come back to center, keeping in mind their style and space constraints, but also keeping the essence of the story intact.

When we ended the editing session, they assured me again that I would be very happy with the final version.

It was an emotional, yet wonderful, learning experience for me.

Today's Action | When emotional about anything close to your heart, be it a creative project, a relationship, anything—find and speak your truth. Allow others to help you gain a broader perspective. Then, consider the other person's point of view, speak your truth, and see if it can't be a win-win situation for all involved.

Do You Know Where You're Going To?

Gary and I grew apart the summer after I was diagnosed with cancer. My life had changed—dramatically—and I was no longer comfortable with the status quo. I felt stifled in a marriage to a workaholic and needed to get away. On the spur of the moment, I hopped into my convertible, and went on the first of what Julia Cameron calls *Artist Dates*.

With the top down, oldies blasting on the radio, and me singing at the top of my lungs, I headed up the coast of Florida. I ended up on the eastern coast about halfway up the state, in Melbourne Beach. It was a very emotional weekend, partly because of my problems with Gary, and partly because my life was changing rapidly, and the future was uncertain.

I searched for answers. Who am I? Where is my life going? Where is my relationship with Gary going? Where is God in all of this and what is His will for me?

Arriving in Melbourne, I found a little seaside motel with a room right on the ocean. And I do mean right on the ocean. From my bed, I could see the ocean's edge—a mere fifty feet away. I was in heaven. For the next few days, I did absolutely any and everything I wanted to.

On the first morning, before going to the beach, I went to Ron Jon's Surf Shop in Cocoa Beach. It's this gazillion-square-foot store filled with surf and beach goodies. Although finances were tight, I quit being a miser with myself and bought a hand-painted T-shirt, a pair of shorts, new sunglasses, and a Sebastian Inlet baseball cap. A few treats here and there can be great for the soul. I also splurged and bought an aqua body board and went body surfing for the rest of the day.

Two hundred miles from home, I found myself—my *true* self. I laughed and cried, sang and ate, swam and sunbathed. I hadn't been away by myself in years. I enjoyed myself so much that I even considered quitting my job, divorcing Gary, and moving up the coast, permanently.

Instead, I got exactly what I needed, time alone to renew my spirit and get a new perspective on my life. There hadn't been much fun or frills in my life for a long time. This weekend, I recaptured the wide-eyed, free-spirited child I once was.

With this trip, my life changed: my spirit was lifted, my path shifted, and I came home. I came home, *to me.*

254 Today's Action | Plan a weekend getaway—just you—no one else. Where do you want to go? When can you get away? Instead of thinking why you can't, brainstorm how you can. Then go. Go, and come home to yourself.

When You Believe

I found this written in the women's bathroom of a little restaurant in Cocoa Beach:

The Courage To Be Me

I have the courage to embrace my strengths—Get excited about life—Enjoy giving and receiving—Face and transform my fears—Ask for help and support when I need it—Spring free of the Superwoman trap—Trust myself—Make my own decisions and choices—Befriend myself—Complete unfinished business—Realize I have emotional and practical rights—Talk as nicely to myself as I do to my plants (pets)—Communicate lovingly with understanding as my goal—Honor my own needs—Give myself credit for my accomplishments—Love the little girl within me—

Overcome my addiction to approval—Grant myself permission to play—Quit being a responsibility sponge—Feel all my feelings and act on them appropriately—Nurture others because I want to, not because I have to—Choose what is right for me—Insist on being paid fairly for what I do—Set limits and boundaries and stick by them—Say "Yes" only when I really mean it—Have realistic expectations—Take risks and accept change—Grow through challenges—Be totally honest with myself—Correct erroneous beliefs and assumptions—Respect my vulnerabilities—Heal old and current wounds—Savor the mystery of the spirit—Wave goodbye to guilt—Plant "flower" not "weed" thoughts in my mind—Treat myself with respect and teach others to do the same—Fill up my own cup first, then nourish others from the overflow—Own my own excellence—Plan for the future but live in the present—Value my intuition and wisdom—Know that I am lovable—Celebrate the differences between men and women—Develop healthy, supportive relationships—Make forgiveness a priority—Accept myself just as I am now.

I added one more for me: *Embrace the writer within me.*

Today's Action | First, thank the woman who wrote this, whoever she is, and the universal spirit that inspired her. Next, copy the entire piece, by hand, highlighting the lines that speak to you. Lastly, add one personal statement, just for you. Declare your truth aloud as you write it. Read this frequently.

Celebration

Last night I pushed aside my feelings of unworthiness and joined twenty of my closest friends at my younger brother's father's restaurant to celebrate my ten-year anniversary. It's been ten years since I had a drink, smoked a joint, or did cocaine. I'm sure some people know the value of moderation in this area, but I'm not one of them.

Because of the wonderful place I am in—healthy, cancer-free, writing daily, enjoying nature, connected with God—I wanted to celebrate this milestone with those closest to me.

The food was delicious with Maine lobsters, steaks, salads, and pasta galore. Mouthwatering chocolate cake and key lime pie topped off the meal. Then the real fun began.

The band started and we danced all night to "Unforgettable," "Last Dance," "I Will Survive," and "Electric Slide." I think the women had the most fun—taking turns in the middle, dancing to the music as rest of us cheered. We had a blast!

We danced with each other. We danced alone. We danced with our partners. We danced as a group. Spinning, dipping, doing "the bump," showing off old disco moves, until finally melting into a mass of giggles.

Everyone said it was the best party, ever!

One of the girls (yes, I call us girls even though most of us are over forty) recently separated from her husband, another is planning to become a nun, and a few others were uncomfortable because they were alone. Everyone was able to forget their circumstances and just have fun.

We celebrated like there was no tomorrow.

It was truly a night to remember.

Today's Action | Next accomplishment or goal you achieve—throw yourself a party. If you neglected to celebrate a recent success—it's not too late. Let your hair down, celebrate your worth, and go for it!

Baby Did A Bad, Bad Thing

I was just stung by a jellyfish. Man, did it hurt! My hands, legs, and stomach are covered with big, red welts. The lifeguard gave me a little vinegar and that helped a little, but ouch, ouch, ouch! It was a bad, bad thing.

That reminds me of my favorite story from Dan Millman's *Way of The Peaceful Warrior* about good luck, bad luck:

An old man and his son worked a small farm, with only one horse to pull the plow. One day the horse ran away.

"How terrible," sympathized the neighbors, "What bad luck."

"Who knows whether it is bad luck or good luck," the farmer replied.

A week later, the horse returned from the mountains leading five wild mares into the barn.

"What wonderful luck!" said the neighbors.

"Good luck? Bad luck? Who knows?" answered the old man.

The next day, the son, trying to tame one of the horses, fell and broke his leg.

"How terrible. What bad luck!"

"Good luck? Bad luck?"

The army came to all the farms to take the young men to war. The farmer's son was of no use to them, so he was spared.

"Good? Bad?"

It's all perception.

Maybe the jellyfish prevented me from being pulled out to sea by a riptide while swimming later in the day. Who knows?

I no longer judge things as good or bad. Cancer, a seemingly bad thing, brought me to my bliss. I'm not sure it could have happened any other way.

It took a great deal for me to wake up and pay attention, not that I wasn't living consciously before, but I thought I had all the time in the world. Fear and doubt kept me from doing many things that would have enriched my life. So the cancer turned out to be a good thing.

Someone recently looked at me with pity when hearing of my cancer and I assured them, "I wouldn't take my breast back for anything, not if it meant giving up all I've experienced since losing it."

What an awesome thing to be able to say. My life is so rich, that I wouldn't undo one single thing that led up to this point!

Today's Action | The next time you are tempted to label something "good" or "bad," just remind yourself, "Everything unfolds perfectly, according to your highest good."

Turn, Turn, Turn

I'm at the beach—waves gently lapping against the shore, sea oats swaying in the breeze.

I rarely took time to enjoy the ocean before mt illness. Now, it is one of my greatest pleasures and where you'll find me whenever I need to refill the well.

I've spent most of this week on the phone with or faxing last-minute changes to the editors in New York before the magazine went to print. Additionally, a few addicts, writers, and cancer survivors asked me to help them with their personal or spiritual growth. Second only to my writing is my love of helping others. But by week's end I felt totally overwhelmed.

To be of maximum service to others, I simply must meet my own needs first. Normally, I spend at least one night a week and one day on the weekend unavailable to others. I also try to write or meditate daily. This week, I got off track and didn't make time for me, so here I am at the beach getting my priorities in order.

I've been here since 8 this morning. It's now 1:30. The weather is lovely and I am alone. Just me, and God, and the ocean. We are breathing in and breathing out, together. In and out. Tide in, tide out. God within, God without.

The softest of breezes blows my hair across my face. I gently push my hair from my eyes in order to write the next words. All in perfect harmony. With each breath, my spirit is renewed. My cup fills and I feel refreshed.

My inner voice tells me it is time to be alone. I allow myself to be guided.

Just as the earth needs a break each day from the heat and energy of the sun, I, too, need a period of rest and renewal—daily.

Just as God rested on the seventh day after six glorious days of Creation, I, too, need a day of complete rest each week.

258

Just as the moon has cycles and disappears from our sight each month, I, too, need monthly retreats from the world.

This is how I maintain my health, my spirit, and my energy—by reconnecting with God, nature, and myself—daily—weekly—monthly.

There is a time and a season for everything—an ebb and flow to life. Honoring that time brings perfect peace.

Today's Action | Tune in to your inner cycle. Refill your well. Replenish your supply. Allow God's great earth to recharge your batteries.

You're A Shining Star

Living from the heart is enjoying each day to the fullest with an open and trusting heart—It's healing childhood wounds, long-held resentments, and resolving current difficulties with compassion and grace—It's having a vibrant childlike spirit that is not afraid to be spontaneous and playful— It's laughter and smiles, tears and heartache—It's experiencing the wide range of emotions that come with being fully alive—It's seeing the rainbow of possibilities that is your life—It's taking risks and walking through fears, trusting wisdom and growth await us on the other side—It's having the courage to get to the other side—It's reaching for the highest and brightest of stars, knowing that you are capable and worthy—It's dancing in the moonlight—It's belting out your heart's sweetest song at the top of your lungs—It's settling gently back into God's embrace, savoring the moment—It's vulnerability at its essence: not being afraid of who you are and gladly sharing your light with others— It's falling and scraping your knees, only to rise again stronger than ever, ready to run that race—It's kind and loving acceptance of others, just as they are, and yourself as well—It's a deep spiritual connection with the Universe and every living thing—It's the courage to face the challenges presented to you, embracing the lessons—It's taking the deepest love you've ever known and living that love, being that love, expressing that love, sharing that love, immersing yourself in that love and allowing it to flow out to all you come in contact with—It's knowing you are a unique and special child of God— loved just because you are—nothing to do, be, or prove—you are worthy in and of yourself—It is seeing the truth about yourself and recognizing it in others.

Our essence is Love. It resides in our hearts and shines outward through our actions.

Desperado

Maggie, a woman I've had the privilege of sponsoring for a couple of years, recently wrote this note to me:

Dear Debbie,

I know you didn't want a gift, but this is just a gift of the heart. I put together this cassette tape, which expresses my thanks and the sentiments of my soul.

Each time I hear the first song on side one, "Thank You," my spirit is filled with gratitude and I begin to cry. I think of you each time, because I thank God that you gave of yourself to help me. I thank God for having put you in my life. You have healed me with your compassion, given me self-esteem with your affirmations, and helped me believe in myself as never before. Through you, I saw God for the first time. I saw his unconditional love and I saw my true self. You were my first experience of the Holy and Divine. I cannot help but feel overwhelmed with gratitude each time I think of you and all you mean to me.

It has taken a long time for me to let someone thank me and love me at this level, knowing I am worthy. Acknowledgment and validation are wonderful things, seldom received graciously. Thank you, Maggie.

Today's Action | Let somebody love you. Allow compliments and acknowledgments to lift your spirit. It's a blessing to give and equal blessing to receive.

Can You Hear Me Calling?

Maggie, who recently felt a calling to become a nun, went on to say:

I don't know where I'm going, but it's because of all you taught me and showed me that I can be open to God's guiding spirit. Sometimes, I ask God, "Why? Why me?" Why are You calling me away from Twelve-Step recovery when there is so much need for light there? Why, when I found a home are You calling me into exile again?

People think that I *want* to leave them or that I think I've outgrown them, but that's not it at all. Something stronger than me is pulling me. As pilgrims on a journey, our first inclination is to be settlers, but God desires us to keep moving. I can't explain it, but I've resisted God's call to growth before and ended up in darkness. I must follow where I feel God is calling . . . . At times I'm scared and want to resist . . . . My heart breaks because it hurts to leave my family and my friends who I love so much, but when I think of staying, my spirit feels imprisoned.

When guiding others, I try to remember that I am not God and do not know their lessons or their paths. Maggie will find her way, just as I have, by following her heart. *261*

 Today's Action | As difficult as it may be to watch others struggle or suffer, teach them to listen to and follow their own hearts. Give them wide berth.
Allow their path to unfold as *God* wills it.

Forever Young

A thirty-eight-year-old mother of two was struck and killed by lightning yesterday, without a drop of rain in sight.

A seven-year-old girl died of brain cancer. She was the niece of someone in my cancer support group, who is now facing cancer herself.

We all think we have plenty of time. The truth is none of us really knows how much time we have left on earth. With this in mind, we need to get our priorities in order.

It astonishes me, in this enlightened day and age, how obsessed people can be with hiding their age. I watch women I admire have their faces pulled tight—beyond recognition—in an effort to defy age and gravity, losing sight of who they really are in the process. I want to shake them and say, "Wake up! Your priorities are all mixed up."

My grandmother, on the other hand, has never had any work done on her face and has never looked more beautiful. I love every line on her face, every wrinkle in her neck, and every age spot on her hands. To me these are badges of honor, grace, and courage. It takes courage to be who we are—to accept who we are—to embrace who we are.

I'm forty years old and look at every single birthday as a joyous occasion. Just a few short years ago, I wasn't sure if I'd make forty. So to me each year is a gift; each wrinkle, cause for celebration. I look forward to earning my badges, and hope I'll be as delighted to turn fifty, sixty, seventy, and eighty as I am to turn forty.

Knowing so many people haven't lived as long as I have and won't live to reach those milestones makes me ever so grateful for each new day of life. I guess my early brush with death intensified my love of life, and made aging a joyous thing, instead of something to be dreaded.

A *thank you* is in my heart for each and every one of my birthdays. And I pray to God I never want to cut, pull, or burn one single laugh line from my face.

Today's Action | Don't erase your badges. Celebrate and love yourself just as you are. Remember, each day is a gift, not to be taken for granted. Don't get caught up in trying to make your face a blank slate. You've probably learned a lot, lived a lot, and loved a lot over the years. Let your face show it.

Embrace the special beauty that comes *only* with age and wisdom.

My Prayer

I speak of God so often that it probably seems as though I have always had faith. Nothing could be further from the truth. My journey toward faith started when I began attending Twelve-Step meetings for addiction recovery. I was told, "If you don't have a belief in a power greater than yourself, you better find one quickly, because you obviously weren't able to stay away from drugs and alcohol on your own." As desperate as I was, I resisted.

Well, that's putting it mildly. Although I didn't call myself an atheist, I fought tooth and nail against believing in anything I couldn't see or touch. I was positive there was no God, and refused to pretend otherwise. At the same time, I was scared. What if I couldn't stay off drugs without this Higher Power? I was between a rock and a hard place. Again, I was told, "Pray for help to stay way from a drink or a drug today." Not wanting to be a hypocrite, I decided to investigate.

I read every spiritual book I could get my hands on: *When Bad Things Happen To Good People* by Rabbi Harold S. Kushner, *The Road Less Traveled* by M. Scott Peck, M.D., *Sermon on the Mount* by Emmet Fox. These books, combined with recovery literature, helped me find my way.

After a relapse, I found I didn't know as much as I thought I did. Drinking did, in fact, take me back to my drug of choice—cocaine. Humbled, I became teachable.

Then, one day shortly after my relapse, the obsession to use hit me hard. I was sure I was going to end up getting high before the day was over.

I had a doctor's appointment near the house I used to get high in, and this kicked up major thoughts of drinking and using. As I drove to the doctor's office, my car wanted to turn down those old familiar roads. I could barely keep the steering wheel from turning.

Not knowing what else to do, I repeated a line from a prayer they closed meetings with back in 1988—*Lead me not into temptation and deliver me from evil. Lead me not into temptation and deliver me from evil.* Gripping the steering wheel, I repeated this over and over until I got to the doctor's office.

Then, by a series of divinely inspired coincidences, *Godincidences*, I ran into someone I knew from that same party house. He had six months clean. I asked how he did it, and he told me about his coming to believe in a Higher Power. We talked for the better part of an hour.

By the time I left him, the desire to use had passed.

That night, when I lay my head on my pillow, I realized repeating part of "The Lord's Prayer" was my first real plea for help, and it worked! I was led from temptation. There *was* something watching over me, helping me when I asked!

I couldn't call that power God right away, but it was a beginning. Once I opened myself up to the possibility of a Universal Power, coincidences and miracles occurred daily, or maybe I just started noticing them. The inexplicable happened so often that I stopped questioning the existence of this Power and just began using it.

Today, I look back on what happened as a miracle. From adamant disbelief came a faith so deep that I know God exists as surely as I am breathing.

Since coming to believe in this power, which I now call God (just because it's a universal word for the thing none of us can really explain), it has never failed me.

☀ Today's Action | If you don't have a belief or faith in a Power outside of yourself, read some of the books that helped me. If you do, rejoice in that fact, because not everyone does, and many take it for granted.

Every Road Leads Back To You

Mother Teresa once said, "Our work as Christians and non-Christians is to do works of love. And every work of love done with a full heart brings people closer to God."

The book about Mother Teresa's life, *A Simple Path*, warmed my heart. I had always assumed that as a Catholic, Mother Teresa's mission was not only to do good works, but also to convert people to her faith. I was quite surprised to read the following.

"Mother Teresa's mandate of mercy is to spread love by relieving the suffering of others, through a Catholic sisterhood and brotherhood, who serve a largely non-Christian Community and who do not compel those they help to convert to the Catholic faith."

One of the sisters went on to say that Mother Teresa's mission was to help a Hindu become a better Hindu, a Muslim become a better Muslim, and a Catholic become a better Catholic. She believed faith should be shown through actions and dedication and not just by preaching religion.

To me, this is the essence of spirituality and how Gary and I try to live our lives— doing works of love with open hearts.

Both of my brothers are born-again Christians. My mother is a disciple of Paramahansa Yogananda. Many of my friends are Jewish, Buddhist, Christians, or practitioners of *A Course in Miracles*. I consider myself nondenominational, taking from many religions and philosophies, integrating what works best into my own life.

I believe that God meets us where we are. Considering the multitude of religions and philosophies available, I assume we are to choose whichever path works best for us, with no path being better than another; maybe better for a particular person, but that is all.

Sometimes I feel looked down upon by people who believe their way is the right way or the only way, even though I have a personal relationship with God and try to live my life based on spiritual principles. This used to bother me; now, I just strive to honor differing beliefs and accept people as they are.

Today's Action | Practice loving acceptance of others' beliefs, trusting everyone is exactly where God wants them to be.

Eighth Month

Nurturing Your Soul

Who Will Save Your Soul?

*A*nother thing I found impressive about Mother Teresa was that she took time for herself every single day. "Without prayer, Mother Teresa could not work for even half an hour because she gets her strength from God through prayer," said one of the sisters in *A Simple Path.*

Throughout *A Simple Path* Mother Teresa speaks of our souls' longing for God, "People try to fill the emptiness they feel with food, radio, television, and keeping busy with outside activities. But this emptiness can only be filled by the spiritual, by God.

"From what I have found there is just too much noise in modern life and because of this people are afraid of silence. As God speaks only in silence, this is a big problem for those searching for God."

Through prayer, meditation, contemplation, and daily devotion, Mother Teresa spent no less than one hour a day receiving spiritual sustenance. All these years I thought she just gave and gave and gave. It never occurred to me that she, too, needed to refill the well.

I now understand how she *could* give so selflessly all those years. She understood the value and practice of daily spiritual renewal. If you are constantly refilling the well, it never runs dry.

Unfortunately, it took losing my health for me to understand and begin *practicing* this principle.

Today's Action | Begin a spiritual discipline. For five minutes, working up to that hour Mother Teresa spoke of, read spiritual literature, pray, meditate, chant, or just sit in silence. This will do wonders for your soul.

A Million Reasons Why . . . You've Got To Try

You must do the thing you think you cannot.—Eleanor Roosevelt

The first time I heard this—I knew.

Don't you?

We are born knowing what we are meant to do. It resonates with us when we read it, hear it, or see it. We know.

The one thing I thought I could not do was become a successful writer. There were a million reasons why I could not write for a living.

I don't have enough time. I have to pay the bills with a real job. Maybe when I retire I'll have the time. I'm not disciplined enough to work for myself. I need to go to an office or I'll never get anything done. I'm not talented enough, smart enough, or skilled enough. I don't have a good enough vocabulary. I don't know how to edit. I'm too scared to write seriously, for a living. Everything I want to say has already been said. How could what I have to say be important? Who do I think I am?

The list goes on and on, where it stops nobody knows.

Just as there are a million reasons why I think I can't, there are a million reasons why I've got to try.

I *need* to write this book. For me. For my self-esteem. Because I love writing. To see something all the way through. To inspire others—if I can do it with this much fear, so can you. To leave a legacy. To use the gift God gave me. To be at peace, with no regrets.

268

For me to be at peace—*I must do the one thing I think I cannot do.*

I've known what this was for a long time, but remained paralyzed by the fear. Then along came cancer saying: *You don't have time to waste on fear.*

The struggle didn't end with my acknowledging my dream, but as I admitted what that one thing was, the Universe heard. And once I put it out there, there was no turning back.

It's true what the Bible says: "The truth shall set you free," for I am finally living my truth and have never been more at peace. It feels so right. So perfect.

There are a million reasons why you've got to try, but the number one reason is *because* you think you cannot. That is why you *must.*

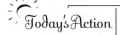 Today's Action | I know you know. And you know you know. Now—*right now*—put it out there. *Say it aloud.* Tell the Universe the one thing you think you cannot do.

All I Have To Do Is Dream

How does it feel to finally admit it? Relief? Doubt? Joy?

Whatever you feel is fine. Now feel the fear and do it anyway. Begin by visualizing a plan of action that will take you where you think you cannot go.

Seek the people, books, or workshops you need to help you on your way. The pace doesn't matter, so long as there is forward movement. Stretch. Challenge yourself.

Where do you see yourself in five years?

Flesh it out in your mind. Visualize a monthly, weekly, and even daily plan of action specifically tailored toward *your* bliss.

Get guidance. Very important. Seek out people who have succeeded at what you want to do and ask for help. Put together a resource list and use it. Employ whatever tools you need as you go. You'll need different tools at different times.

Whatever your dream is, don't lose sight of it. Believe in yourself. You *can* achieve it. You're further along than you think if you actually said, aloud, what it is that you want to do.

I want to be a writer! There, I said it—aloud.

I first said it two-and-a-half years ago, and I have just signed my first contract for publication.

It's not as hard as you might think. The Universe *wants* us to succeed. All we have to do is put it out there, be open, and trust. Everything we need will be placed in our path. We cannot miss it, if our eyes are open.

Just put it out there. Do the footwork. And trust.

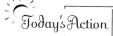 Today's Action | Mentally flesh out your plan of action. We'll fine-tune it later.

All I Need Is A Miracle

When I first heard of *treasure mapping,* I was skeptical to say the least, but seeing *is* believing.

Four years ago, I was upside-down in a long-term lease with a car I no longer wanted when Gary and I went to the Miami Beach Auto Show, and I fell in love with the new Toyota Celica convertible. Then I saw another Toyota in my favorite color—deep periwinkle purple-blue. I looked longingly at the Celica and asked if they had it in this mesmerizing color. They said yes, and told me the price. I almost fainted.

The price was way out of my reach, especially considering the loss I would have to take to get out of my lease early. I resigned myself to waiting a couple more years until the lease expired, then, maybe I could have the car of my dreams.

A week later, I saw a glossy magazine ad of the exact car I wanted, in the color I wanted, and remembered hearing about *treasure mapping.*

Treasure mapping is where you visualize your dream, in great detail, then collect pictures to represent it, make a collage, and affirm to the Universe that it is yours.

270

As I said, I thought *treasure mapping* was silly. But here was this picture of this gorgeous car I wanted—how could it hurt? I cut the picture out and put it on my wall at work where I could see it every day. Within four months, I asked for and received a raise, traded out of my lease with room to spare, and drove off the lot in my brand-new, purple convertible! I was amazed at how fast this dream came true. I didn't think I could afford that car for *at least* two years.

Recently, I did the same thing with a bigger dream. I collected pictures of Hawaii, waterfalls, beaches, and couples in love. I gathered photos of books, a girl typing at a computer, and even one of a girl writing under a palm tree. I pasted these pictures on to a poster board, and *treasure mapped* my way right into living my bliss.

Whatever your mind can conceive, you can achieve. Visual by nature, our minds are easily tantalized with *treasure mapping.* Miraculously, the Universe responds to our thoughts and dreams, the more concrete the better. So go ahead—make that *treasure map*—let it be your miracle.

 Today's Action | Collect pictures that represent your bliss. Then, create a *treasure map*. The Universe is waiting to respond.

Achieving Is Believing In Yourself

In five years I see myself earning a living as a writer.

After dabbling for years, on March 15, I got serious and asked a published author to help me achieve my goals.

Together we made of plan of action that started with me completing my first book within a year. This required certain action on my part and I committed, in writing, to take the necessary steps.

For the first month, I wrote on index cards, one thought per card, as fast as I could for an hour a day. I wrote faster and faster, building my writing muscles, removing emotional blocks. By month's end I was writing 3,000 words per day and had a pretty clear idea of what I wanted to write about.

Brainstorming on the index cards, I asked myself pertinent questions to flesh out the details. When things jelled, I switched to poster boards and fleshed out a chapter-by-chapter outline. On April 19, I began writing *Letting Your Heart Sing*. Within a few days, the outline changed from chapters to short stories, one for every day. Then the idea of tying the stories to song titles evolved. I wrote everything down as quickly as it came to me, as if taking dictation.

My teacher stressed "no editing." He insisted I write as fast as I could, not critiquing a thing. Instead, allow the words to come from deep within.

By June, I was writing twenty stories a week. By mid-summer, I had more than 215 stories roughed out. I was two-thirds of the way to my goal and flying high.

Letting your heart sing is so exciting! Here I am waking up and living each day exactly as I've always wanted. *Now, all I need to do is get rid of my day job and do this full time!*

By the end of the year, my rough draft will be completed and I'll have an agent. By February, the book will be ready for submission. I see myself achieving these goals.

The results are in God's hands. I just show up, live what's in my heart, and *do* the one thing I think I cannot. The rest will take care of itself.

Today's Action | Visualize your plan of action. Seeing *is* believing.

Silence Is Golden

The only way I find the energy to pursue my dreams, in the midst of my busy life, is by taking time to recharge my batteries. I start with small spiritual disciplines like daily prayer, meditation, quiet time, and work up to larger spiritual practices such as going on spiritual retreat or away for a weekend. This is how I renew my spirit and replenish my soul.

One of the hardest spiritual disciplines, but most rewarding, is to go on a *silent* retreat. Recently, I created space in my own home for silence.

I started with an hour and worked up to a whole day. During this time I turn everything off—no TV, no music, no reading, no phones, no computers, no communication with other people—no interruptions of any sort. I just sit quietly and be with myself. Sometimes this is easiest if I leave my house and go to the beach or to a park. However, frequently I let my family and friends know there are certain times when I will be completely unavailable.

At first, they thought I was off my rocker, but before long, they got used to my requests for quiet time. Now, my family and friends see the difference in me and respect the little pockets of space I create for myself. Many of my friends now take time for themselves.

Silence, Simplicity and Solitude by Rabbi David A. Cooper is an excellent resource for creating quiet space within your home. Carve out space in your life for silence and solitude. Enlist a friend or relative to help, or trade favors with another parent, if you have small children. This may feel uncomfortable at first, but it gets easier with practice. Our souls yearn for quiet in this fast-paced world. In fact, a great deal of *dis*-ease is caused by running ourselves ragged and not listening to the very bodies we inhabit.

Right now, even with all the resistance you feel and excuses you have—even with all that chatter—isn't part of you sighing at the very suggestion of quiet?

Today's Action | Listen to your inner yearnings and create space for yourself. Starting with five minutes and working up to an hour, a half-day, and then an entire day—spend time in silence. Some silent retreats last for months or years, so it is not as farfetched as it seems. Just begin where you are.

Deep Peace

Speaking of spiritual retreats, have you ever been on one?

Most states have retreat houses of some sort. Some are connected with religious or spiritual groups; others are available for a variety of purposes.

Consider going on retreat for an entire weekend. I have a reservation for September and am already looking forward to it. Prices start at as little as seventy dollars for a weekend retreat. Often you can arrange for a working retreat, where you can tithe your time and talent, in exchange for room and board.

There are Buddhist retreats, Christian retreats, Twelve-Step retreats, and Native American sweat lodges, just to name a few. The one I go to most often is at the Dominican Retreat House in South Miami. When I go, the focus is usually on the Eleventh Step of recovery: "We sought through prayer and meditation to improve our conscious contact with God, *as we understand him*, praying only for knowledge of his will for us, and the power to carry it out."

Although it's a Catholic retreat house, they keep it nondenominational during Twelve-Step weekends, and the more traditional religious rituals are optional.

Call around and find one that works for you.

Maybe you've been on retreat before, but it's been a while. Remember that feeling at the end of the retreat, usually on Sunday, when your batteries are recharged, and you feel at peace with the world? Life seems easy as you rest in the moment.

Well, it's calling again. The moment is calling.

273

Today's Action | Do the footwork and gather information on retreat houses. Then, pick one and go on a spiritual retreat. Your soul will thank you.

Angel Of Mine

When is the last time you went to a spa, not a gym to work out, but a spa to pamper yourself? When I travel I always try to take advantage of the hotel's facilities, but I haven't belonged to a gym with a spa for quite some time.

When I was younger, I worked in health clubs and took saunas, steam baths, and whirlpools all the time. Now, although I no longer work in the business, I do take spa days occasionally and treat myself to massages and facials regularly.

I just signed up for a complimentary pass at the Russian Spa on Miami Beach. It is supposed to be fabulous. I can't wait to pamper myself.

Usually, I'm too busy to take time out for myself like this. And if I'm not too busy, I think I can't afford it. Here comes that stinginess again.

Well, after the cancer, I began treating myself to a facial every three weeks. To be perfectly honest, I don't go for the facial per se, I go because Rita, the woman who gives it, massages my face and upper body for more than an hour and a half. Every time I see her, I feel spoiled rotten.

274   Rita is the gift I give myself at least once a month because I'm worth it. I also happen to think she's an angel, because every time I leave her, I'm in heaven. It is obvious she loves what she does and wants nothing more than to make sure you leave feeling wonderful. Everyone I've sent to her absolutely raves about her. What a treat, and she is only five minutes from where I live.

Today's Action | If you can, go to a spa for a manicure, pedicure, facial, massage—the works. Give yourself an entire day and use all the facilities, because you're worth it. If money is a consideration, get a complimentary pass and enjoy as much of their facilities as you can. If you're lucky, you'll find a real gem like Rita and pamper yourself regularly.

Jump Into The Fire

When I'm not pampering myself, I'm challenging myself. One of my biggest fears has always been public speaking. I am not alone. Public speaking and death are the two things people fear most.

Well, I've looked death square in the eye, so I guess it's time to stare down the other.

I signed up for a public-speaking course and went to my first class last Monday night. I'm not fearful in all speaking situations, just certain ones. I thought this class would be a perfect opportunity to build my speaking skills and self-esteem.

Over the next three weeks, I have to give three presentations. The first is an autobiographical speech, the second a book report, and the third a reading. The teacher will rate us and give pointers on how to improve our public-speaking ability.

Monday, he told me I have a nervous laugh, say "umm" and "you know" a lot, and play with my hair, not exactly the picture of a calm, professional, confident speaker. The teacher went on to say that *everyone* is nervous or fearful before speaking. For some people it's terrifying, for others it's just plain fear, and others only experience a little tension. The last category is the one we want to be in. The goal is to use the tension as "stimulation," so we experience *positive excitement*, instead of fear. Some people actually get to the point where they *want* to speak in front of others.

The way to get there is by practicing. My teacher practices with a nonprofit organization called "Toastmasters," which helps people become effective speakers. I speak in Twelve-Step recovery meetings, workshops, and conventions and have been doing so for more than ten years. I'm pretty comfortable in those situations even though I have all the undesirable mannerisms that my teacher said we should avoid.

Still, I love speaking at recovery meetings and never worry about how I look or sound. I just share from my heart, and it always turns out fine. Now, I want to take it to the next level and walk through my fear of speaking in front of nonrecovery groups, like this class.

Hopefully, by putting myself in uncomfortable situations like this, I'll gain the confidence I need to feel the fear and do it anyway.

Here goes nothing.

275

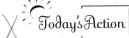 Is there something you're afraid of, that by actually doing, you could build your self-confidence? If so, do it. If you can't think of anything, sign up for a public-speaking course just for the heck of it. Or check out Toastmasters; it can't hurt, and it might just give you the confidence to take the next step in an area that really matters to you.

Reflections Of My Life

Today is a day of reflection.

The little bird that was in my protective care for a couple of weeks has flown the coop. I've yet to see hide nor hair—er—feather of him since last week. One day I went outside, and he was gone. I read an article on birds that said that's what happens; they get stronger and fly away. I know his parents were nearby, so I'm sure he's okay.

My job now is to let go. Just let it be. I guess we don't always know the outcome of those we help. Of the many addicts, cancer patients, and aspiring writers I try to help, sometimes I'm able to see how they fare, other times it's just a labor of love. Either way, I'm content just to be of service.

276

Humility is having the wisdom to do what you can and then let go, knowing there is a bigger Force guiding all.

I guess I must do that with my Aunt Fi. It's been three weeks since our extraordinary visit. And although I know that some things take time, I'm afraid that, one day, my mother, grandmother, or great-aunt, will die, and the other two will be left with regrets for steps they didn't take, calls they didn't make.

I think I'll call my aunt later, just to say hi and let her know I'm glad she's back in my life. Then I'll place the situation in God's care, trusting everything will work out for everyone's highest good.

Today's Action | Know that you are a pebble sinking forever deeper into love—not always able to see the ripple effect your life has in the great pond of life. Trust. Act. Then, let go.

The Water Is Wide/The River Is Deep

There's a scared child in all of us that occasionally peeks his or her head out when we are trying to live authentically and says, *No. I can't do this! I want to go back to the way it was. It was safer.*

It's important to allow that fragile child her voice.

This morning I gave her my undivided attention. We pulled out the spiral notebook, and I let her write everything she needed to say to me. This is very honoring and validating to the little girl in me. When she was done, I thanked her for trusting me enough to let me know she was afraid. I reassured her that it is okay to be afraid, but that things are different now. We are stronger than ever before. We *can* do this. God is protecting us. Yes, we may fall down and skin our knees, but doesn't it feel great to be living the way we've always wanted?

I am so excited to be living my dream that it overrides all fear. With each step forward I take in faith, fear lessens. I gain courage as I *do* that which I think I cannot.

I can no longer go back to living the shell of a life I use to live. I know my purpose is that which makes me feel *alive*. I know, because when I'm writing, there's nothing I'd rather be doing. Time stands still. It is irrelevant. I *am* the moment.

Amelia Earhart once said, "Courage is the price *life* exacts for granting peace."

I was restless, irritable, discontent prior to finding and living my bliss. Now, there is complete and perfect peace.

Today's Action | Give your inner child a voice. Reassure them it's safe, that you will be there if they fall. Let them know it's okay to *be* who they are.

You Oughta Know

There's one song I think every woman should have, and many men, too, but particularly the women—Alanis Morissette's "You Oughta Know," off her *Jagged Little Pill* CD.

It's a great "get your ya ya's out" song about the risk we take when we fall in love and the pain of betrayal. It explores hurt, pain, anger, hatred, and even vengeance. Most everyone has been burnt by love, at least once, and when I'm in that angry place I like to play this song really loud and sing it at the top of my lungs. This helps me process my anger.

The only way through is through. I wish there was another way, a way to avoid the pain, to wake up when the storm is over and skies are clear, but I've yet to find it. For now, I need to feel *all* of my emotions: the pain, the anger, the hurt, the rejection, the embarrassment, the abandonment, and even the rage!

The whole CD is about the very real and sometimes painful aspects of life. It's *in your face* honest. Many people are offended by Alanis's choice of words, particularly in "You Oughta Know," but the thirteen-year-old in me *loves* the energy and the anger.

After my friend Melissa caught her boyfriend cheating on her, she went through the gambit of emotions. First, there was denial, wanting it not to be true. Then, negotiating with God about whether to forgive or not. Then, there was shame and embarrassment, even though she'd done nothing wrong. After that, her walls went up, and Melissa swore she would *never* be taken for a fool again!

To help her through the anger, I suggested she take a *Jagged Little Pill.*

Melissa still wavers back and forth between anger and acceptance and is undecided about whether or not to give her boyfriend a second chance.

In the meantime, listening to songs like "You Oughta Know," writing F— You letters, reading codependency books, and just plain going through it, are the only ways I know to get to the other side.

And of course trusting God. Trusting that there is a plan—even when we can't see it.

Today's Action | If you are in the middle of a painful situation right now—trust that it will pass. It *is* passing. Move through it, knowing you will be stronger and wiser on the other side.

I'm Addicted To You

Speaking of love addiction, I happened to catch a recent Oprah Winfrey Show when she announced her latest book-of-the-month selection, *Here on Earth* by Alice Hoffman. It piqued my interest so I bought a copy. I identified so much with the story line that I was moved to write to *The Oprah Show*.

Here are excerpts from my letter:

My Hollis's name was Barrie and although by my best friend warned me about him—I couldn't help myself. I thought he was the love of my life. We were soul mates. When I touched his skin, it was as if I were touching my own. We both felt the same way. It was doomed from the start though. I was single at the time, but he was married, well not really though—you see, he was "separated."

In October 1982, we began a torrid, obsessive love affair that was to last for years, even after I married and he later divorced. He was always a mystery to me, his past filled with many secrets. My mother told me I only wanted him because I couldn't have him, that he was my "illusive butterfly." "You're wrong," I told her. "We are meant to be. It's destiny. It's only a matter of time." Then weeks turned into months, and months turned into years, and still he was married.

Eventually, I started seeing other people. At first, just to get him jealous, but he would say things like, "I love you, but have nothing to offer you and can't ask you not to see other people." In time, I got engaged to a "nice" man, who loved nature, had a dog, and wanted to have a family. Right before the wedding, I stopped by to see Barrie one last time. As I was leaving, he said, "Don't be surprised if when they ask, 'Does anyone object to this marriage? Speak now or forever hold your peace,' I jump out and say, 'Stop! She loves me!'"

On my wedding day, I got drunk and looked around for *him*—hoping against all hope . . . but he never showed. I tried to be good—I tried to be faithful—but couldn't help myself. I started fights with my husband, just so I could run to *him*. I won't go into all the gory details, but this went on for years. I tried to stop seeing him, but failed every time. There was a song out at the time by Chicago, *"I'm addicted to you . . . . You're a hard habit to break."* When I heard it, I thought that's me—I'm addicted.

Our affair ended when I stopped by his house one day before work. I hadn't seen him in a while—I had been trying to be good. Then I dreamed about him the night before and just had to see him. I told myself I just wanted to let him know that my husband and I were working things out and were much happier now. When I told him that, he said, "Then what are you doing here?" His stinging response was like a slap in the face. I gathered myself and answered, "I have no idea," and walked out.

For three years, I cried daily but refused to break down and go see him. I listened to Bonnie Tyler's "Total Eclipse of the Heart," over and over, thinking about his deep, deep—so deep you get lost in them—blue eyes. Finally, for my sanity, I turned off the radio. It was years before I could listen to a love song without my heart breaking.

Eventually, my marriage ended and my biggest fear was that I would run into Barrie. My second biggest fear was that I wouldn't. After I left my husband, I got help for alcohol and drug abuse. That helped me with my fears, but they never went away completely, that is, not until I saw him again.

Three years after not seeing Barrie, almost to the day, I was in my car, at a stoplight, with the man who is now my husband, and I saw a familiar elbow. There is nothing unique about this elbow—I just *knew* it. I pulled up next to the unfamiliar car and peered in. He had sunglasses on, so I wasn't sure. Then he took them off and those deep blue eyes pierced through me once more. I was drowning—I prayed for help, "Somebody, anybody, throw me a *life*-preserver."

It took all I had not to follow that car. When I got home I called my sponsor, Janie, who was helping me in my recovery. She suggested I do what's called "an inventory" on my relationship with him—it was time to face the truth. Painful as it was, I knew I could not go forward in the relationship I was in unless I let go of the past. I saw the self-centered, pot-smoking, partner-burning, past-hiding, dishonest, sneaky person Barrie really was, and the person I used to be—the same as him.

Denial can be so cunning. They say, "The truth will set you free," and luckily, I got out alive. Some women don't. Nicole Brown Simpson didn't. But I'm here to say, "Debbie made it!" Not only did I survive love addiction, I thrived.

Then, three years ago, I ran into Barrie in Coconut Grove, a place we used to go together a lot. I was with my husband, Janie, and her boyfriend. Barrie was sitting twenty feet away with his back to the band that was playing, staring at me. This went on for thirty minutes. Then my husband went to get refreshments, and I turned to Janie and said, "I don't know what I'll do if he comes over." She said, "Well, you're about to find out because . . . here he is."

Sure enough, I turned around to find myself within arm's length of Barrie. You could tell he still had it bad. He was nervous and his face was flushed. I kept my composure on the outside; acting cool, while on the inside there was still that spark of excitement. He wanted to know where I lived and what my new last name was, and even asked me to spell it. I started to and then caught myself and I said, "Oh, no you don't. Don't you dare look me up." I wasn't about to go down that road again. Before my husband came back, Barrie slunk away.

Occasionally, I go through stuff over him, but mostly I remember I'm not the person I was. I am a person who lives by her values now. And I also think of the wonderful man I'm married to—I've found my true soul mate, a man whose character isn't questionable and whom I adore kissing even after being married for more than ten years. Actually, it's something Gary said that really put things in perspective.

After seeing Barrie walk away that day in Coconut Grove, my husband asked, "Who was that?" I told him it was Barrie—I don't live lies anymore. Then, Gary asked, "Why did he wait until I left before coming over?" I didn't answer then, but I know the answer now: Character—some have it and some don't. Gary jokingly refers to Barrie as the "used car salesman," who's always trying to do some dirty deal on the side.

One thing I learned, though, is not to tempt fate by going to Coconut Grove anymore.

It's quite clear I know about love addiction, but thank God I also know about recovery from love addiction. If not, I would have settled for so much less than Gary. Who knew what awaited me just around the corner?

 **Today's Action** | If you are in an addictive relationship, take an honest look at that relationship on paper. You might find, as I did, that you deserve much more than you are settling for.

Back In The High Life Again

A week after I sent my letter to Oprah, my mother saw an advertisement for a writing workshop at a local university. Having attended many workshops in the past, my first inclination was not to go, but something drew me to this one. It was at this workshop that I met my mentor, Tom Bird.

There were four segments scheduled, and after attending the first one, I *knew* I was meant to be there. The workshop inspired me to take my writing to the next level. After enlisting Tom as my writing coach, I dove full force into my writing. On Tom's advice, I set aside the manuscript I had been working on for two-and-a-half years, and the book you are now reading emerged.

Waking up at 5 A.M. every morning, I wrote for two hours before going to work. It was as if I was in an altered state, high as a kite, immersed in my writing. I was in this space when the producer from *The Oprah Show* called and said, "I just read your letter and *had* to call." We talked for a few minutes, and he asked questions about the current book of the month. Although I had only read it two weeks ago, I was hard-pressed to remember much, and just fumbled through the answers. I was so into living my own bliss, everything else ceased to exist.

Afterwards, I mentioned the phone call to a few friends, and they were more thrilled about the possibility of me being on *Oprah* than I was. What I once saw as an exciting opportunity, now might distract me from living my own bliss. I was so elated to be working with my teacher, and writing every day, that nothing else mattered.

Don't get me wrong, the producer's call was a huge boost to my self-esteem as a writer; my letter stood out among thousands—*enough to warrant a phone call.* It was just the encouragement I needed to reassure me that I was heading in the right direction.

More importantly, writing that letter reminded me how much depth and beauty my marriage had, and I wouldn't exchange that for all the heart wrenching, flash-in-the-pan "love" in the world.

Today's Action | Re-assess what is really important to you. It might not be what you think.

Hold Your Head Up

Hilda, one of the most fearful people I know, used pills her whole life to help her cope. Pills took the fear away, but she had to take more and more, until they no longer worked. Six years ago, she stopped taking them and became filled with fear again.

Petrified of life, Hilda lived in the shadow of her man. Anxiety and panic attacks were a way of life and that she couldn't drive only increased her dependence on her boyfriend.

For years fear ruled her life. She was afraid her boyfriend would not marry her. She was afraid he would find other women more desirable. She was afraid he would cheat on her. She was afraid of driving; she had epilepsy—what if she had an attack? She was afraid of doctors, afraid of death, afraid of life, and the list went on.

Little by little, Hilda began making friends of her own. She began going places without her boyfriend. She joined groups and got involved on committees. Her self-confidence and courage grew in proportion to the actions she took. Her hair no longer covered her face, and her eyes no longer focused on the ground. This forty-year-old girl blossomed into a woman.

But life is life, and what fears you won't walk through, life will push you through. Hilda's life was getting better, but she was still very fearful.

Within six months of marrying her husband, she had to face her fear of infidelity. Without thinking it through, her husband kissed another woman. That's as far as it went. He felt horrible about it and told her the truth so there wouldn't be any secrets between them.

Hilda was devastated. Her worst fear was coming true. However, after a few days of ranting and raging, Hilda emerged a stronger, more confident woman. They decided to try and work things out.

Recently, Hilda suffered tremendous abdominal pain and her doctor recommended she have a hysterectomy. Filled with fear, she sought out other women who had been through this. She read books and gained information before deciding to have the surgery. Never having had major surgery before, Hilda had always equated hospitals with death, and battled her fear daily.

Then, from deep within, came a faith that surpasses all understanding. Last week, Hilda went through her surgery with the grace and calmness of a true champion.

Hilda now sees how one courageous act builds on another, each one making you stronger. This is one amazing woman, who is finally beginning to see her own worth.

During her addiction, Hilda's world became smaller and smaller, until eventually she stopped driving. We've talked about it a few times over the years and she has always said, "Never!"

After her surgery, Hilda asked me to help her walk through her fear of driving.

Think of your fears. Is there one you are ready to walk through? Choose one and visualize yourself doing it. For me it's singing. I love to sing, but am terrified of singing in front of people. But, I *will* do it before the year is out.

All About Soul

Yesterday someone asked me what my book is about. I told them it's about having the courage to find and follow your bliss, live authentically, and be who you really are. It's about having the courage to live the life you've always wanted, not the one you think you should, or the one you feel you have to. It's about stretching beyond our comfort zones, pushing the limits, then blowing the roof off them.

It's about being true to yourself, honoring your own internal guide above that of others. It's taking others' desires into consideration, but making a decision based on what you believe to be best for you, trusting it will be the best for all concerned.

284

It's about living simply, in the moment, trusting life's abundance. It's about being still long enough to hear that quiet voice within, trusting in your own highest wisdom.

It's about deepening your love of life through your connection with God and nature, and then outwardly expressing that love.

It's about using your gifts as God intended, making your life count for something; in your own small way, to make a difference in the lives of others.

Letting Your Heart Sing is about trusting yourself enough to pick healthy people to be in relationship with.

It's about healing relationships; making peace, bridging gaps, finishing unfinished business.

It's about living fully and loving deeply.

It's about helping others reach for their dreams, through the example of living your own.

It's about seeing God in every person you meet.

It's about balance and filling the well, through loving yourself enough to nurture and take time for yourself.

It's about never giving up on yourself—*no matter what.*

This book is about being more alive than you've ever imagined, by living each day exactly as you want to.

It's about being perfectly aligned with God's will.

It's about living in the light.

It's about having a deep appreciation for the miracle of life, and living accordingly.

Most of all, it's about finding the *courage* to do all of the above.

My personal mission is to share my stories in such a way as to inspire, encourage, and motivate others to follow their hearts' desires, so that they too can experience the indescribable joy that comes from *living their bliss.*

> *Today's Action* | Write your own mission statement. What are you here on earth to accomplish? What are your desires? What do you really want to do? What would like to be said about you at the end of your life?
>
> This statement can be a sentence, a paragraph, or a page. Begin by jotting down ideas and beliefs you value. Fine-tune it until it says exactly what you want to create in your life. Declare it to be true! Share it with another. Then live it.

Sunshine Of Your Love

Last night was the infamous Eric Clapton concert that I had wanted to go to so badly.

And I wasn't the only one; some twenty thousand people wanted to go, and the arena only seated five thousand. Ticket scalpers were asking five and ten times what they paid. There's no way Gary and I were paying that, so I resigned myself to the fact that we would not be attending the concert.

My friend Sari said a number of times before we left for California, "I don't know why, but I see you there." I said, "I don't see how, because we aren't going to pursue it." And we didn't. I did take a little consolation in the fact that someone said he would be playing his blues set, which I had already seen when we were in England, and I prefer his rock 'n' roll numbers anyway.

We arrived in San Jose Wednesday night, woke up early and drove to Carmel and Monterey. We had a wonderful time sight-seeing, then settled into convention mode—going to lots of meetings and workshops, and having a ball.

Every once and a while I felt bummed about not going to the concert on Saturday, but like most everything I put in my God Box, once I turn it over, I don't concern myself with it anymore—it's completely in God's hands. We didn't even ask anyone if they had extra tickets. We just went on our merry way, enjoying the convention.

Saturday night, at quarter of nine, we were walking through the convention center, heading back to our room after the main speaker meeting, when Gary saw a sign that said "One Eric Clapton ticket." When he pointed it out, my first thought was *Gary wouldn't mind if I go alone.* Instead, I shrugged figuring we couldn't afford it, and the concert had probably already started.

Gary turned around and asked, "How much?" The guy responded with some ridiculous amount, and we turned away. A guy manning a booth nearby overheard us and said, "I can't use my tickets—do you want them?"

"How much?" Gary asked.

The guy answered, "For cost. I don't feel right about making money on them."

Gary and I looked at each other incredulously, and I asked, "Why aren't you going?"

The guy hesitated and said, "I had hoped to go, but I made a commitment to man this booth, and wouldn't feel right about leaving."

"Are you sure?" I asked, not believing our luck.

"Yeah," the guy said.

I told him he had no idea how much I wanted to go—and that this was truly a God thing.

He gave us the tickets and told us to have a good time.

We raced down the street to the concert and they were just letting people in, so we hadn't missed a thing.

I called Sari from a pay phone as soon as I got in, exclaiming, "You'll never believe where we are! Never in a million years!"

I was astounded. How is it possible that you can end up somewhere you really want to be when you don't lift a finger to get there? All I did was put it out into the Universe, then let go completely.

There I was, standing in the sunshine of God's love.

For the next three hours I sang and danced less than thirty feet from the stage to "Layla," "My Father's Eyes," "Tears In Heaven," and all of Eric's greatest hits. Best of all, Eric gave us a real treat and played a song he usually doesn't play, "Cocaine." Although I'm not into it anymore, it was great to listen to for old time's sake.

Today's Action | Have you used your God Box lately? If there's anything you really want, put it on paper, tuck it in box, and turn it over to God, trusting it will happen in God's time, according to your highest good. *I'm still in shock. Talk about miracles! Wow!*

I've Got One Hand In My Pocket

287

Today, I have the courage to embrace my strengths.

I used to focus on my shortcomings. Now, I focus on my assets.

I am warm and caring, compassionate and courageous, and an impassioned writer and leader. I am honest, but can lie well enough to pull off a good joke or surprise party. I am spiritual, but funny; a good storyteller, but also a good listener; responsible, but spontaneous.

I am God-centered, yet free-spirited; smart, yet trusting; frugal, yet generous. I am happy alone or with others. I am full of paradoxes, but think they make me interesting and well rounded.

Today, I know who I am, believe I have much to offer, and am not afraid to take a stand.

I don't list my strengths out of pride, ego, or self-importance—but rather from a place of deep self-worth and self-love.

It has taken years, but I finally like who I am, and nothing can take that away from me.

"One Hand In My Pocket" suggests a sense of ease about oneself, not just the song, but also the phrase. Think of the stance—someone with one hand in their pocket looks relaxed, comfortable—*at ease*.

With one hand in your pocket, acknowledge and embrace *your* strengths.

did! it.

☀ Today's Action | List thirty of your strengths. On days when you are feeling less than wonderful, refer to this list as a reminder of who you really are.

I Just Want To Celebrate

Today, I have the courage to get excited about life.

Ten years ago, it was suggested that I tone down my enthusiasm; I could only get hurt looking at everything with such openness and optimism. For a while, I tried to rein in my spirit. Today, I see that excitement as my *life force*, the energy that makes me *me*.

It's why the very first song I played when I was diagnosed with cancer was, "I Just Want To Celebrate" by Rare Earth.

Instinctively, I knew my excitement and enthusiasm for life was the very thing that could *save* my life.

Over the years, I have watched many people accept a life-threatening illness with quiet resignation, slipping silently through death's door. They allow the diagnosis to drain their *life force*.

I may die tomorrow, but I'm going out happy, heels kicked high, doing what I love.

Regardless of the state of your health, *life is for celebrating*.

If you are not excited about life, make changes until you are.

What excites you? What, if you were doing it daily, would make you bound out of bed, excited about a new day?

What would cause such anticipation that you could hardly wait to begin the adventure?

Create that life, right now. Do whatever it takes. Just take the next step and the next one, trusting everything will unfold in Divine Order.

My journey toward my bliss began ten years ago, when I joined a Twelve-Step fellowship, which pointed me in the right direction. Then, my journey got a jump-start four years ago when I received the wake-up call of cancer. Then it took off a year ago, when I started writing every day. In truth, my spiritual journey began at birth, it just took a while for me to awaken from my slumber. Each day, I wake up a little more.

As I live more consciously, more authentically, my excitement grows. What a wonderful way to experience life, where nothing is bad, and all is working toward my highest good. Cancer—good or bad? Infertility—good or bad? Drug and alcohol addiction—good or bad? Marital difficulties—good or bad? All have been opportunities for growth, challenging me to open my heart; become more courageous and trusting. There's always deeper faith and greater reliance on God on the other side.

Today is the richest day I've ever lived. It's an awesome day, yet a very ordinary day. Today is a blank slate.

I have no idea what the day holds, but after two hours of writing, it's off to a good start.

So, here I go—whoosh, I'm gone.

Today's Action | Let the excitement within bubble up and spill over into the day, enriching and deepening your experience of life.

Blessed

Today, I enjoy giving and receiving love.

Last month, I received so much love from my friends and family while celebrating my anniversary. It was wonderful to just let their love wash over me. There was a time when I felt unworthy of people's time or love. I was comfortable only on the giving end. If someone gave me a present or insisted on treating me to lunch I'd say, "Oh, you didn't have to." Now, I say thank you.

As my sense of self-worth increases, so does my ability to receive. Why should I deny the person giving me a present that same pleasure I derive from giving?

And as my limiting beliefs leave, my ability to give increases. By acknowledging and allowing abundance in my life, I can let go of things I used to hold onto. Glancing at my Limoges collection, china boxes I have been collecting since I was a little girl, I see I am ready to give some of my treasures to women I treasure. The need to collect or possess is gone. I can pass things of beauty on to people who will appreciate them, with ease.

What a freeing place to be in, to experience joy equally giving or receiving. They are one and the same. Neither is more blessed, for there is joy and beauty in both.

In fact, when I go to Hawaii in November, my first amends with my childhood friend, Pixie, will be to give her one of my treasured Limoges boxes. The one with two kittens on it will be perfect.

Today's Action | Have the courage to receive, as well as give. Come from abundance and sink into it. List ten ways in which you are generous and ten ways you allow others to give to you.

I'm Gonna Keep On Walking

Today, I have the courage to face and transform my fears.

I have been run by fear in one form or another my entire life. It's why I drank and used drugs: I needed liquid (or solid) courage to face life. Whether dealing with my father's death or going to an office party, I always needed help, usually in the form of mind-altering substances.

Ten years ago, when I began living life without my previous crutches, everything was scary because I had never done anything straight before. I remember my first recovery dance. I was so petrified I couldn't even enter the building. I couldn't imagine dancing without drinking, so I stayed in the parking lot.

When someone tried to make me go inside, I left in tears, wondering *When am I ever going to be normal? Will I ever be able to do what others seem to do with ease?*

That night, instead of driving to a bar, I went to a recovery house and played cards with people, just like me. We laughed, cried, told jokes, and had a great time. I realized then, I had to start where I was. Although I wasn't comfortable in large groups, I could spend time with a small group of people, a little scary, but not terrifying. I learned to walk through my fears in baby steps.

I volunteered to answer phones, make coffee, clean up after meetings, and from there I went on to speak at meetings. First, in small groups, and then as time went on, I was comfortable in larger groups of people. Eventually, I became a group representative.

Next, I took meetings into hospitals, treatment centers, and women's work-release programs. Later, I went back to school and met people from all walks of life. This brought me to volunteering in nursing homes and with abused children. I even became a Big Sister. Each step took courage, but as I tried new things, my fear lessened.

Scuba diving, water-skiing, and owning a small ski boat were some of the fun things I tried, but even those were scary at first. Then came harder things like asking for a raise, asking my boss not to smoke cigars during working hours, and making amends to people I had hurt.

With each step I took, my self-esteem grew. In time, I "people pleased" less and honored myself more. I spoke out on things I felt passionately about, even when my opinion was in the minority.

Though my self-esteem is fairly high, I still experience fear. Which is why I signed up for the public-speaking course, where I'm learning to face, embrace, and walk through my fears, thereby transforming them. Every fear I face dissipates as soon as I walk through it.

Today's Action | List twenty more things you are afraid of doing. Pick another fear and walk through it. Start with the fear you are least afraid of and keep moving through them, building courage and character as you go.

Any Dream Will Do

Today, I have the courage to give myself credit for my accomplishments.

I am a success! A decade off drugs and alcohol, on the same job, and happily married to the same man are amazing accomplishments. So is earning a college degree. But the thing I am proudest of isn't anything tangible; it's who I *am*.

It's that I am finally willing to commit my time, energy, and resources to following my heart's desire. It's not if, or when, or that I've been published, it's that I get up everyday and write my little heart out, because I *love* doing it.

Something in me shifted while working with the editors on "Dharma." Until then, I believed achieving some outside goal: publication, money, recognition, would mean, "I've arrived." Instead, I found none of that mattered. What I believe on the inside is what matters.

Achieving the goal isn't the accomplishment. The accomplishment is setting goals and *reaching* for them. It's that I am willing to put myself out there. I am *willing* to live large. I am *willing* to stretch myself. I am *willing* to take risks, even if it means falling and skinning my knees. I have the courage to get up and try again.

My incredibly alive, joyous spirit is what I am most proud of, and what I have least to do with. All I did was have the courage to remove the blocks that were keeping me from being who God intended me to be, *who I truly am.*

I did not create myself. That wonderful, magical creative Force in the Universe we call God, did. It is the Debbie that God and I co-created, that I am most proud of, and oh so thankful for.

Today's Action | List your accomplishments, internal and external, for they are all wondrous things.

Get Off Of My Cloud

Today, I have the courage to set limits and boundaries and stick by them.

Do you ever have a day where you're just fed up with other people's dramas? Yesterday a woman I've been sponsoring for a couple years called to complain about her life. I had noticed her habit of always focusing on the negative a few months ago and suggested she tell me three areas she is happy about, making progress in, or is grateful for, *before* she tells me her problems. That worked for a little while, but now she rattles off three positive things as quickly as possible, so she can get to the garbage.

I feel drained when I get off the phone with her. She's always angry about something: her husband, boss, car, house, or money. I just can't take it anymore. It's toxic. I've tried to help her see the good in life and create a more positive reality for herself, but she seems insistent in staying stuck in the problem. A few times she took her anger out on me by yelling at me or hanging up on me.

A very spiritual man once suggested letting go of the deadwood in your life: the relationships or situations that are draining, abusive, or just no longer working. Initially, I was shocked at the thought. It seemed so cold. I had always been taught to work through conflict.

I guess there is a time for everything. A time to stay and a time to let go.

I've been patient and tolerant for as long as I can, now it's time to let go, for her sake and mine. She deserves to be with someone who can help her where she is. And I deserve to be treated with respect.

Today, I no longer need to stay in relationships that aren't working.

Life is too short.

☼ **Today's Action** | Do you have toxic people in your life? If so, re-assess those relationships. Pray for guidance and clarity. Then, honor yourself by doing what you need to do to free yourself from the bondage of other people's negativity.

It's now been almost a year since I stopped sponsoring this woman, and she has blossomed incredibly. Sometimes the best thing you can do for another person is *let go.*

Should I Stay Or Should I Go?

Last night I attended another wonderful Bhakti Yoga (divine devotion to God) meditation. One of the spiritual principles talked about during Satsang (truth gathering) was honoring each person's individual path.

We are each filled with divine wisdom. Spiritual teachers, guides, mentors, or sponsors are simply here to guide us back to our true nature.

I recently learned this at a deeper level while working with Melissa. After getting over the initial shock of her boyfriend's dishonesty, she had to decide whether to forgive and stay, or to let go and leave. As her inner battle raged, well-meaning friends had opinions, advice, and experience to share.

Ultimately, Melissa has to decide for herself what *her* truth is—what *her* lesson is. Although it's painful to watch someone struggle with addiction in any of its insidious forms, I needed the bottom I hit with love addiction, so I must allow everyone else the same freedom.

Even when I think I know what's best, it's not always my call to make. I don't know what their lessons are; only they do.

I've found the best way to guide others is by illuminating the broad path.

Today's Action | Honor your truth *and* that of others. We all have lessons to learn. We can best assist others by helping them find, and trust, their inner wisdom. Today, I lovingly let go of other's lessons. They will find their way.

Love Me Tender

Today, I have the courage to love the little girl within.

When we are chastising ourselves, we are not living in God's light. God judges neither our actions nor us. God placed us here to evolve and learn lessons. What we perceive as a negative experience may be just the catalyst we need to propel us forward.

So when I'm beating myself up for some mistake I made, or something I think I should have said or done differently, I am missing the divine moment—the perfect moment that is *this* moment. When I am living in the past, I am not experiencing God's unconditional love and am shut off from the sunlight of the spirit. I must embrace all of me—even my imperfections.

I have a stuffed koala bear that I bought years ago, while on a trip with my mother, which represents the little girl in me. Many a night during the first few rocky years of my marriage, I curled up with that little bear and cried myself to sleep, rubbing its velvet paws.

That little koala bear has more little girl tears on it than any pillow or blanket I ever had as a child. Tears don't bother me today. I think they are a sign of healing—a washing away of the old, making room for the new.

Tears are a sign of renewal—salty, wet renewal—like waves in the sea rising up and pounding the shoreline, merging back into oneness.

My little girl knows those salty tears all too well. But in the presence of the loving, nurturing mother within, she has healed old wounds and experienced joy, as well as tears. Now, she is free to have fun and live a worry-free life once more.

Over the years, I have been able to meet all of my little girl's needs. Whatever they are, she trusts me enough to tell me. Then, with my compassion and God's grace, all is healed.

Today, we dance, sing, and go to the beach together. Today, we treasure everyday pleasures like riding bikes and quiet walks to the lake. Today, we are one.

Today's Action | Give the child within the comfort he or she needs. If you don't already have a stuffed animal, buy one, and pay kind attention to the wondrous child within. And don't think you are too grown up for this. The very first thing a friend of mine in his fifties asked for, when he was diagnosed with cancer, was a teddy bear. No matter our age or circumstance—there will always be a vulnerable child within who needs our comfort and kind words.

True Friend

Today, I have the courage to overcome my addiction to approval.

Whether I am dealing with my mother, my husband, my boss, my friends, or my recovery circle, there will always be a part of me that wants them to like and approve of me. I relate to the honesty with which Sally Fields declared, "You like me! You *really* like me!" when she received her Oscar for *Norma Rae* in 1979. It's what we all want; she just had the courage to say it.

As much as I want approval, I may not get it, so it's important I give myself what I need and let my Higher Power's love heal all that I cannot.

For me, there is still an attraction to getting what I want from someone who cannot give it. From having conversations with my mother, where she gives advice or opinions when all I want is someone to listen, to wanting validation at work via some means other than money, from men that don't know any other way—all are fruitless endeavors. Hoping for an unsolicited compliment from Gary is another vain attempt at approval seeking. Trying to get others whose beliefs are different from mine to come over to my view is yet another lesson in futility.

Knowing all of this, why do I still seek outside approval?

It's the little girl in me, the one that didn't get validation as a child and is still so needy as an adult. The solution comes when I spend time nurturing, affirming, loving, and lifting up the child within.

When I am fully present for her, no one else need be.

From this space, whatever approval or encouragement I receive is a gift, not a necessity.

Today's Action | Give yourself the encouragement, validation, and support you need. As long as you are true to yourself, that's all the approval you'll ever need. Approve of your own thoughts, words, and deeds. Be your own best friend. Everything else is gravy.

Child In Time

Today, I have the courage to grant myself permission to play.

Do you remember flying kites, jumping rope, playing tag, or hopscotch? How about building sandcastles, body surfing, or flying down bridges on your bicycle? Do you remember the rich, warm aroma of Nestlé's Toll House® Chocolate Chip cookies filling the house?

Do you remember running until you were exhausted or swimming until your fingers were shriveled prunes? How about building a tree fort? Or did you have a favorite fruit tree or tend a vegetable garden?

What are your favorite childhood memories? Was playing a part of them, even a tiny part? Did you play with dolls or did you play cowboys and indians, or both?

My brothers and I had a Batman set, complete with boomerangs, secret rings, and Bat shields.

What do you like to do, but rarely find time for? Tennis? Golf? Bowling? Dancing?

Where is it written that once you leave home, or turn a certain age, you must stop playing? If you have children, you probably play more than the rest of us. Unless of course you are too busy cautioning, "Be careful. Don't get dirty. Don't break that. Don't get anything on your clothes. Get off the furniture." Next time you are with your kids, try being one of them. Play with them; don't monitor them.

In the book, *Feel the Fear and Do It Anyway*, Dr. Jeffers says fear became ingrained in us when well-meaning parents told us to "Be careful." She says rarely did any of us hear, "Go out and take lots of risks today, honey," from our parents.

If you don't have children of your own, play with your nieces and nephews or baby-sit for a friend. I had a blast doing cartwheels at the beach with Melissa's daughter, Brittany. Well, she did them. I just sort of sprawled about like a crab. Hanging out with Brittany is almost as much fun as visiting my seven-year-old niece in Louisville or Gary's niece in Boston. The only bad thing is that my nieces live so far away.

Today's Action | Go out and have fun today. Be sure to take lots of risks.

Turn Your Love Around

Today, I have the courage to nurture others because I want to, not because I have to.

This one took me a while. It wasn't until I began taking care of myself *first* that I could be there for others without anger or resentment simmering just under the surface, so far under the surface, that it took cancer for me to realize just how exhausted I was and how much I'd been neglecting myself.

There was a time when I dreaded answering the phone or returning calls. It seemed someone always needed me. I was the "fix-it" woman, and it wouldn't get done unless *I* did it. No one could make a decision without my help, at least that's what I thought.

My sponsor finally asked, "When did God put you in charge?"

I hadn't realized that I *did* think I was the only competent person around. When you act like that, it doesn't take long before others stop doing for themselves. I didn't realize I was creating dependency. I guess I needed to be needed.

Now, by leading others back to *their* truth, *their* inner wisdom, by lifting them up with messages like "I know you can handle it," they become more competent and *can* handle more.

With practice, we all get better. If I'm doing everything for everyone, how are they going to get better at anything? I thought being needed made me more valuable, more worthwhile, and made me look good. I found just the opposite was true. When I help others find their own internal wisdom, they don't need me, and *that's* when I've become an effective leader. The benefit is a surplus of energy, instead of feeling drained all the time.

It started with saying no to others, and taking care of me first. I trust they can and will handle it themselves.

Now, when the phone rings, it's a delight instead of a chore to answer it.

Today's Action | Look at your relationships. Are you creating dependency? Do you need to be needed? Is helping others keeping you from having time for yourself or your dreams?
If so, let go of control. Trust that others are competent. They may make mistakes in the beginning, but will gain valuable experience and knowledge as a result. So, let go of fixing or saving others and nurture yourself more. From that full space, you will *joyfully* nurture others.

Stairway To Heaven

Today, I have the courage to choose what is right for me.

I no longer need to get a million opinions before I making a decision. Intuitively, I know what is right for me. If by chance I make a decision I am not happy with, I can always course-correct and change it. If not, I can learn from it.

What I think of me is much more important than what anyone else thinks of me. It's infinitely more important that I be happy with my decisions than that anyone else to be happy with my choices. That doesn't mean I railroad people without taking their views into account, but ultimately I'm the one who has to live in my skin, so I must remain true to myself and God, above all others.

I've learned I can do this with love and respect by gently, but firmly, honoring my truth. As long as it's done with love, it's a win-win situation.

When I first decided to be a Big Sister, my old sponsor laughed at me. She thought I should just serve within my Twelve-Step fellowship. I felt I needed to spread my wings and fly farther. I also felt the need to heal the part of me that had wanted to be a mother. So, I thanked her for her input, but did what was in my heart.

When it came time for me to stop sponsoring for a while, people judged me, thinking you should never say "No" to helping others. They thought what I was doing was wrong, but I knew my heart and honored it.

Today's Action | Do you have trouble taking a stand? Do you bow to the wishes of others, all the while knowing it's not the right choice for you?

Whether it's ending a relationship, changing jobs, or saying no to a movie you don't want to see—big or small—have the courage to honor your truth. Listen to your inner voice, the one that knows what's right for you.

As Long As You Love Me

Today, I have the courage to have realistic expectations.

What's realistic, anyway?

I used to think it was realistic for my husband to take Saturdays off and to make love to me three times a week. Now, I want things exactly as they are. My best writing day is Saturday, so now I am delighted when Gary works on Saturday and I can write for hours undisturbed. Now that I'm in menopause, sex once a week is fine.

I think what I really wanted was to know that Gary loved me. I thought if he worked less and made love to me more, that was a sure sign he loved me. Well, I have news for you—some friends of ours who are getting divorced—the husband wanted to make love every night and rarely worked weekends. They are divorcing because he's cheating on her.

All I really want is an honest, loving husband, and I need to let go of the specifics as to how that shows up in our marriage. What if Gary tried to impose his will on me and didn't want me to write on Saturdays? I don't want him controlling my life, so I best let go of controlling his.

Having realistic expectations means I know what my bottom lines are, but am accepting of the small stuff. For me, it's unacceptable to be with anyone who uses drugs or drinks excessively, is physically or verbally abusive, or is unfaithful.

Those are my bottom lines regarding relationships. Everything else I must be realistic about. Everyone has character flaws and will fall short at one time or another. For instance, Gary isn't good with money and doesn't help around the house like I think he should. After living with him for over ten years, I can accept that Gary probably won't be changing anytime soon.

Weighing his flaws against his strengths, I would take Gary singing love songs to me, bathing me, and standing by my side, over nightly sex or financial wealth anytime. And I like sex a lot.

So, my bottom lines are more than met. When I let go of the rest, by practicing love, patience, acceptance, and gratitude, everything works out fine.

Yes, the bathroom has remained half painted for over a year, and the drainpipes remain unfinished, but I've learned to choose my battles wisely and not sweat the small stuff. Most, not all, but most of it, is small stuff.

I used to think it was all small stuff, until I got cancer. Then I realized some of us deal with some pretty big stuff. However, even the big stuff is easier to deal with if we don't sweat it.

Realistic expectations apply to all areas of life. And serenity and happiness are directly proportional to the height of our expectations.

Today's Action | Find out what your bottom lines are, then let go of the rest. Know that we all get better a day at a time, faster if we don't have to resist someone else's pushing.

Another Crazy Day

I have the courage to grow through challenges.

Life is full of challenges and growth opportunities. This week at work was a perfect example. A huge piece of property owned by our pension plan was sold, and the closing was this week. Crunching numbers like mad, I checked and rechecked payouts and percentages, handled last-minute calls from the attorneys, accountants, and brokers involved, and kept my own bosses pacified. It's been tough, but boy, have I grown.

In just one week, my affirmations paid off. Particularly, *I speak loudly and clearly*, and *I am a strong, confident, powerful woman*. I handled numerous conversations with more poise and confidence than I knew I possessed.

My voice was different—stronger, clearer, more confident.

I was truly an asset to the firm, gathering crucial information to back up this very intricate payout. It felt great to pursue loose ends until everything came together and everyone was satisfied. I was empowered with new confidence and strength; I gained courage by doing what I was afraid I couldn't do.

I could have turned the closing over to the accountants to handle, but I didn't. If I avoided the challenge, nothing would have been gained. Rising to meet it was an excellent growth opportunity.

Today's Action | Think of a decision you are contemplating. What would be the most courageous decision you could make? Make it, trusting you will grow through it.

Ninth Month

Building Strength And Courage

I Remember Who I Am

Today, I have the courage to befriend myself.

*W*henever I chastise, berate, or judge myself, I'm saying, in essence, "I didn't do it *right*," as if there is a single right or wrong way to do everything!

Befriending myself entails trusting God and being gentle with myself.

My inner critic used to be one of my dominant voices, always judging, condemning, or second-guessing me. Often, I fell short of my own expectations, always thinking I didn't do something quite as well as I could have.

If anything destroys my experience of life more than perfectionism, I don't know what it is. Although I knew perfection was impossible, I always wanted to be better than I was. This left me in a state of constant dissatisfaction.

My critic said:

You're not slim enough or firm enough. You're not tall enough. You don't exercise enough. You shouldn't have eaten that. You're not smart enough. You don't have enough education. You're not where you should be careerwise. Your giggle is embarrassing. You don't pray as often as you should. You don't meditate enough. You're not spiritual enough. You're too controlling. You're too judgmental. You can't even stop judging yourself.

Today, I know I *am* enough.

I *have* enough.

I *am* smart enough.

I *am* spiritual enough.

And I've learned to lighten up.

I am perfect in *God's* eyes.

Lately I've taken to borrowing God's glasses so I can see myself as God does—a perfect creation.

There will always be someone better if I compare our outsides. On the inside, our spirit—our hearts—look the same. We truly are one.

God sees beyond our outsides. In fact, sometimes he can't even recognize *who* we are, because he's so in tune with who we *are*.

Today's Action Let go of judgment. *Nothing* could make you any more perfect in God's eyes than you already are. Relax and breathe deeply. Sink into this truth: There is nothing to change— *You are a perfect child of God.*

Faith Of The Heart

Today, I have the courage to take risks and accept change.

304

The only way to become courageous is by *doing* courageous things. Whether venturing out into a new field: my writing; taking a scary course: public speaking; facing an intimidating person: asking my boss for a raise; or pushing through a fear just for the heck of it: diving with sharks—they all took courage. With each risk, I've become more confident and courageous.

Accepting change that is beyond my control is more difficult. I *chose* to take all of the above risks. I could have decided *not* to write, take a class, ask for a raise, or dive with sharks.

Life, however, often presents itself in ways I don't always have a choice about—cancer, for instance. I certainly didn't choose that experience, at least not consciously. But there it was.

I can't imagine anyone saying, "May I please have some cancer." We'd be crazy to choose it or to ask for a divorce, or to lose a loved one, or to be fired. We never ask for these changes, but they come nevertheless.

It boils down to choices. I can struggle against what is, making it even more difficult, or accept what is and be at peace.

"The Serenity Prayer" helps tremendously with whatever life brings:

God, grant me

The *Serenity* to accept the things I cannot change,

The *Courage* to change the things I can, and

The *Wisdom* to know the difference.

The one thing I can change is myself—my attitudes and my actions. Whereas whatever I resist, persists. Melting into all things I cannot change brings peace.

Three of my friends, Sari, Melissa, and Anita, are all dealing with tough situations. Sari, after finally getting pregnant through in vitro fertilization, lost the baby. Melissa, after finally trusting a man, was burnt. Anita's grown daughter keeps relapsing on drugs and is about to lose her husband and five-year-old daughter.

All three women face difficult circumstances. You can't bring a baby back, undo an infidelity, or reverse a drug addict's relapse. They all face the same dilemma; how are they going to *react* to life. What will their attitude be: acceptance or frustration? Faith or fear?

The sooner we move into acceptance, the sooner we experience serenity. With serenity comes clarity, which is needed for future decisions. Once clear, all we need is the courage to act upon our decisions.

Wisdom comes from knowing you can't change the past, or control the future, but that today is yours to do with as you wish. Let go of a relationship or try again, grieve and try to conceive again or not, accept someone's unacceptable behavior or try to change them, making yourself miserable in the process. Our reactions are our choice.

Today's Action | "The Serenity Prayer" gives options as to how to move into the solution. Use this prayer or design one of your own to remind you of the solutions at hand.

Honesty

Today, I have the courage to be totally honest with myself.

It's amazing how often we deceive ourselves. That's why they call it denial—we deny reality—but don't know that's what we're doing. Thank God, I can't think of anything I'm dishonest about today.

I'll look at my past if it will shed light on today. I'll review my relationships with others, and change if necessary.

I'm cash-register honest, no questions there. Not that I haven't been tempted. However, I found that any money gained through dishonesty, such as cheating on taxes, not declaring cash sales, or lying on insurance claims, is not worth the price paid in self-esteem. My motto used to be, "Everyone's doing it, where's the harm?" Now, I see that the harm is to my *personal integrity*. And chances are if I'm dishonest about money, it *is* affecting another human being.

A friend once said, "I look at all money as God's money, and if God needs to make a withdrawal from my account and deposit it into the U.S. Treasury's account, so be it."

I may be naïve, but I actually think it is a privilege to live in the United States, with its paved roads, public schools, police officers, fire departments, and disaster-relief funds. Paying taxes is a duty I gladly fulfill. I view my tax dollars as a form of charity, evening the playing field. Granted, Gary and I don't pay a huge percentage, but we are happy to pay what we do. Changing my attitude made all the difference.

Since cash-register honesty is not a problem for me, I need to look deeper. It's the subtler things like whether a certain relationship is healthy or not, whether I'm overcommitting myself again, or whether I'm being true to my Divine Purpose by staying at my job; this is the level of honesty I have trouble with.

I can only discern the truth about these issues when I'm taking time to get quiet and check in. Today, I *do* have the courage to be totally honest with myself, but must ask God and other people to reveal to me what I cannot readily see.

When you're in it, you're in it.

That's where higher wisdom and good friends come in: to hold the candle while we find our way in the dark.

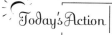
I Am Changing

Today, I have the courage to correct erroneous beliefs and assumptions.

One of the most effective ways to correct erroneous beliefs is to affirm the positive. X

Some of my limiting beliefs were: *No matter how much a person earns, they will always manage to spend right up to their means. I can't become a writer until I retire from my real job. I'm not a good speaker. Big, powerful men like my father will always intimidate me.*

Some of my affirmations are:

I am a strong, confident, powerful woman.

I am prosperous.

I *am* a writer.

I am whole, complete, and perfect.

I am a beautiful child of God, who is worthy of all of God's abundance.

I am loved.

I am loving.

I speak loudly and clearly.

Speaking from my heart is much more important than speaking perfectly.

I lovingly allow others their own lessons.

All of my relationships are healthy.

The first affirmation is my personal declaration. The rest are statements I affirm as the need arises.

Over the last few weeks, I've been saying affirmations about fear and public speaking. During this time, my confidence has grown, as has the strength of my voice and my clarity.

I find my voice as I declare who I am. My dealings with my boss went wonderfully this week. I was calm, confident, and spoke with great ease. The same happened at my public-speaking class. I can sense the fear leaving me as I grow through it.

Today's Action | Declare the truth about yourself today. Let go of old beliefs and assumptions that no longer work and embrace your *true* self.

List ten affirmations that combat your erroneous beliefs. Then, design one statement that embodies your essence.

Say these affirmations at least ten times a day, for a month. After that, use them as the need arises.

You may not believe these statements at first, but over time, your beliefs will shift to where you not only believe them to be true, you *know* them to be true.

We Have No Secrets

Today, I have the courage to respect my vulnerabilities.

When I first read that, I thought: *I don't have any vulnerabilities.* But, that's not true. Letting anyone know I'm embarrassed or fearful is very hard to do. In fact, most of what I write, I want to edit out, never letting anyone see my weak side. But one thing people know about me, if they know anything, is my willingness to share my flaws and shortcomings openly. It isn't easy, but I do it.

I'm forever busting myself and letting the truth out because I *really* believe it's the *secrets* that kill us, not what we think, feel, or do, but the part of us that wants to hide what we think, feel, or do. So, I show up and tell the truth, ridding myself of shame in the process.

Growing up with my particular family in the late sixties led me down a path of sex, drugs, and rock 'n' roll that took me until the late eighties to find my way out—though I must say not completely—I still love two out of three of those activities. As for the other one, drugs, I used up my allotment. Gary, however, still occasionally teases me about my past.

My "boyfriends" are too numerous to count, and having lived in South Florida all of my life, Gary and I are forever running into my old beaus. And wouldn't you know, not one of them is as gorgeous as when I was with them! Gary thinks this is hilarious and has great fun cracking jokes about my past. Sometimes I wish he never knew.

Another shortcoming is that I want everyone to like me, which frankly, isn't possible. I no longer compulsively try to get people to like me, but I *do* want them to. I think most people who know me like me, but I doubt everyone does.

The one thing, though, that could get me into the most trouble, is that not only am I open about my life, I'm pretty open with yours as well. The last thing I ever want to do is hurt someone, but not everyone's life is an open book. Most of my friends don't mind and even give me permission. It's just my nature. If I hear someone is going through something, I automatically think of someone else who has gone through the same thing and try to hook them up.

Just last week someone called me with money issues. She was coming from "lack," as opposed to "abundance," and was resisting being generous or trusting. I suggested she call another woman who is making great strides in that area through Debtors Anonymous.

Well, I guess if my honesty, my partying past, and my desire to be liked are my worst vulnerabilities, I can live with that.

There, I said them aloud . . . and I'm still here.

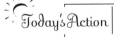 Today's Action | What are your vulnerabilities? Tell them to another person today; bring down the wall just a little more.

I Was Only Joking

Today, I have the courage to heal old and current wounds.

A certain friend of mine is hysterically funny. Occasionally, however, her sarcastic wit stings like the dickens. Though it's only happened a few times, we have both hurt each other accidentally. Usually, my honesty and her sense of humor were the offending parties.

Instead of pretending our feelings aren't hurt or holding a grudge, we clear the air right away by saying, "Ouch." Clearing current wounds immediately prevents them from ever becoming old wounds.

I have learned to address things with Gary, as well, when they come up, instead of letting them build. This keeps our marriage on an even keel.

If I was thoughtless in my choice of words or think I was misunderstood, I remedy it right away. A few months ago, a new sponsee of mine wanted to join a workshop I was leading. I was all for it, but wanted to check with the group. It turns out one of the women in the group was uncomfortable with anyone new joining at that point. I honored that and told my new sponsee that one member had reservations, so maybe next time.

What I said, in and of itself, was no problem, but I knew this sponsee's history. She was recently told she couldn't join a standing weekly dinner, when she had been previously told, "You're always welcome." As a result, she was insecure and had trouble with rejection. Knowing this, I realized, that she probably was hurt by our earlier conversation about the workshop.

It was much easier to call her and check things out than to worry if I was too abrupt or didn't explain that they didn't even know who the new person was. Once I explained, she completely understood and said, "It's just not the right time. Maybe next time." I felt so much better that I checked it out instead of beating myself up for being thoughtless.

Today, that sponsee is in that same workshop and loves it. The other woman worked through her issues with intimacy, and the group is doing great.

Today's Action | Clear up any recent situations that reverberate in your mind. I can't tell you how many people have told me when I call to straighten things out, "I'm so glad you called. I was feeling funny, too."

Questions Of My Childhood

Today, I have the courage to savor the mystery of the spirit.

Whatever you call it—God, the Universe, or your Higher Self—isn't it comforting to know that there is this awesome, mysterious power just waiting to be discovered and tapped into?

I don't necessarily understand it, but I know without a doubt that this power responds whenever I plug in. Even when I didn't believe in anything, there was always a Force guiding my life.

The more conscious I am of this power, the more it seems to work. By tapping in daily through prayer, meditation, and nature, I tune in to the miracle of life. The synchronicity that occurs around me all the time just blows me away.

Little things like a trail of ants, each carrying food ten times their size, to expansive things like the ocean's rising tide, rarely escape my notice. When you think about the moon's pull on bodies of water, it's no wonder people react strangely when there is a full moon, since we are mostly water ourselves.

I know there are scientific explanations for everything, but who can explain how everything works in such perfect harmony? I can't begin to fathom how big God must be, to be Creator of all. And how small He must be, to be personally involved in my life, responding to my every thought, desire, and prayer.

I read recently of a father and son meeting for the very first time in a small midwestern town. The son was conceived in Vietnam during the war, but never even knew what state his father was from, much less where he lived. Eventually, the son came to live in the United States. Then, through a series of miraculous coincidences, they happened to be in this gas station in the middle of nowhere, at the same time, only to find out they were father and son!

There is no logical explanation for things like this. And trust me, the skeptic in me is always looking for the loophole. There is none. It just is. God just is. Miracles *do* happen.

Life is an amazing adventure. Once you wake up.

There is so much more to life than our daily concerns of work, family, or health. Not that these things aren't important, but sometimes we need to look beyond our own little world. We need a fresh perspective. We need to see the world through the eyes of a newborn.

Today's Action | Go through your day as if experiencing everything for the very first time. Everything you eat, the words you say, the endless sky, the scent of a flower, the shadow cast by a tree, a puppy playing, a child questioning—see it all with fresh eyes.

So Long

Today, I have the courage to wave goodbye to guilt.

Guilt has but one purpose: To propel us to change. Other than that, it's useless. If I stole something, said an unkind word, or did an unsavory deed, then guilt could motivate me to amend the situation. To this end, guilt can be a good thing.

If, however, all I do is beat myself up over the situation and feel horrible, it's just wasted energy. And the present moment is wasted right along with it.

312   When feeling guilty about something, I apply "The Serenity Prayer" to the situation, asking for the courage to change what I can. I try to right the wrong—real or imagined, my fault or theirs—immediately. Then, I commit to do better by not repeating the same mistake. The last thing I do is say, "So long," and let it go, giving it to God.

I mean really, what's the point? It's a waste of time pissing and moaning about how bad I am. I am human; a perfectly imperfect human being. By nature, I am supposed to make mistakes. Therefore, nothing is a mistake! There are only learning experiences and growth opportunities.

Today's Action | Today, in this moment, straighten out what you can and let go of the rest. You have permission to live in the moment, blissfully in the present moment.

If you feel bad about something and can change it, do. If not, let it go. Just let it go. It's okay. It's *all* okay.

The Rose

Today, I have the courage to plant "flower" not "weed" thoughts in my mind.

Courage and discipline. That's what transformation takes. And courage and discipline come from doing what you think you cannot do, and from doing that which you don't want to do, but know is for your highest good.

My thoughts create my reality. Whatever I expend my energy on is what I create. Some people I work with start and end their day complaining about the special treatment certain employees receive. Frankly, I don't have time for that.

One employee at our firm does get special treatment—a preferred parking place, the opportunity to earn additional money, and shorter hours than other employees. It's rumored she's having an affair with the powers that be. Although I'm aware of the special treatment she receives, I also know there's probably a price being paid. Whenever we do anything unspiritual, unethical, or dishonest, we pay a price. It's our own personal price, and it carries its own lessons.

Whatever another person gets or doesn't get need not affect my experience of life. Therefore, when petty squabbles or jealousies break out, I give them no energy. It's none of my business. If an extra few hundred dollars is going to make someone else happy, God bless them.

My world is as abundant as I choose to see it. Do you know how many beautiful, coral roses are in bloom on my rose bushes today? So many I can't count them all. Do you know how expansive the ocean is near my house? It's so expansive that I can stand on the beach and look as far to the north, south, or east as I can and see nothing but the horizon. In all three directions there's just water, more water than the mind can fathom.

Some people focus on what they aren't getting. Others see what they are receiving and have the presence of mind to know it's all a gift. We're only here for a short while, too short to focus on lack, negativity, or "weeds" of any sort. There are thorns on every rose bush. I choose to focus on the rose, not the thorns.

Today's Action | Open your eyes. There is beauty and abundance all around, more than enough. Focus on what is, rather than what isn't. Wherever you choose to spend your thoughts, there you are. We create our own reality with our thoughts. Today, let's make it a splendid one!

Better Be Good To Me

Today, I have the courage to treat myself with respect and teach others to do the same.

People intuitively treat you exactly as you believe you deserve. It's amazing how that works. It wasn't until I started speaking up for myself at work that I gained my boss's respect. As long as I felt like a fraud, unworthy, and unsure of myself, that's how I was viewed.

Now, I see myself as so much more than my job title. As my view of myself expands, so does the respect I gain from others.

The time I asked for a well-deserved raise, the time I spoke up about smoking cigars during office hours, and the time I said to my boss, "As I recall, it didn't happen that way," all show me that I value myself. I am no longer afraid to speak up for myself or fight for something I believe in. Through respecting myself, I've taught others to respect me in the workplace.

At home, my husband couldn't be more respectful, but this respect has evolved over time. The first time I respected myself was when I would no longer have even safe sex with Gary until he tested negative for the HIV virus. He had also just lost a job, and I was picking up all the tabs and getting a bit resentful. I realized it wasn't my place to tell him to get a job, but I could tell him that I needed to be with someone who was fully self-supporting. With these two statements, I taught Gary who I was and how I expect to be treated.

Each time I set a boundary, honor myself, or state what is acceptable or unacceptable, I teach others how I expect to be treated. Previously, people trampled all over me. Then I'd complain I was a victim. As long as I was an adult, I was a willing participant, not a victim. Today, I am neither.

At the same time, I had to learn not to run at the first sign of conflict or imperfection, whether in my job, my marriage, or a troublesome relationship. Instead, I practice working through conflict and focusing on the positive. I give way on the less important things and save my energy for the things that matter.

All of my friends are nurturing, loving, spiritual lights. I don't attract negativity or whiners anymore. If I do, they either grow or go, rather quickly.

My time and energy are too valuable to waste trying to fix other people. I'm more than happy to share resources and personal experience, but they must do the footwork, or I lovingly let go.

☼ Today's Action | Re-assess your life. Are you treating yourself with respect in all areas? Do you take a stand for yourself when necessary? Are you teaching others to respect you by the example you set? Are there areas where you are not being true to yourself? If so, pray for the courage to take the next right action.

Kokomo

Today, I have the courage to fill up my own cup first, then nourish others from the overflow.

The last few weeks have been hectic, so I decided to take off and get away from it all.

My mother's house is forty minutes away from mine and is the perfect getaway: my Kokomo. Some people cringe at the very thought of going to their mother's for the weekend. But my mother is not your normal mother and I mean that in the best of ways.

As a disciple of Paramahansa Yogananda, she is into meditation, so her house is always quiet. The phone is never for me, and my mother doesn't approve of computers and rarely watches TV. I go to bed early and sleep late. Within days I am well rested.

315

We eat healthy foods, take long walks, work in her garden, and relax by the waterfall in her backyard. It's very peaceful. I need this. The stress slips away as my body sinks into itself.

My mom honors my quiet time in the morning and knows she won't see me until around ten, when I'm finished writing for the day. I have my own desk, on which the poster boards fit perfectly, and I write uninterrupted for two hours. It's a joy to leave my house if only for a day or two. Not that I dislike being at home, it's just that there's always something that needs doing. Here, at my mom's, there's nothing.

Turning the world off for a day or two is one of the ways I fill my cup. Mini-breaks and vacations nourish my soul. Honoring this need, I get away frequently and am the first to offer to house-sit if someone is going out of town. It's a real treat and costs nothing.

When I rejoin my life, I joyfully return phone calls and am delighted to see my cats, even if it means vacuuming kitty litter or cleaning up throw up. Gary and I are refreshed and happy to see each other. When I'm well rested, my family and friends get my better side. I'm rarely frazzled anymore, because I refill my cup regularly.

If I can't get away for the entire day or weekend, going to the beach tides me over until I can. These little respites remind me of a quieter, slower-paced life, one where there is complete peace.

> **Today's Action** | When can you get away from it all, even if only for a day or two? If you just told yourself you're too busy or you simply can't, all the more reason to. Maybe you can cancel your plans and refill your cup this coming weekend!
>
> Say, "I'm sorry, but something has come up," then take off. Doesn't that sound great—just *take off*. A motel, a friend's house, any quiet spot will do. Maybe even trade houses with a friend, with the stipulation that neither does the other's housework.

You Can Do Magic

Today, I have the courage to own my own excellence.

316

There was a time when if someone paid me a compliment, I'd discount it, or tell self-deprecating jokes. But those days are long gone.

I'm not arrogant or full of myself. At the same time, I know my worth.

You see, I *know* it took a great deal of hard work to get to where I am, but I also know I had help along the way. And then there's the unquantifiable grace of God; who knows where I'd be without that?

So yes, I think I'm excellent!

Yes, I'm courageous, awesome, and giving.

Yes, I have a big heart, and when I write or share, it shows.

Yes, I believe I'm worthy of an incredible man and a glorious life. Maybe it's because of my belief that I have both, I don't know, but I no longer question whether I'm worthy or not. I believe everyone is.

There's nothing unique about me, where I can attain peace and happiness, but others can't; where I can reach for my dreams and succeed, but others can't. What is possible for me is possible for anyone.

With the combined power of God, our inner strength, and the wisdom of those around us—anything is possible! Whether it's beating drug addiction or alcoholism, leaving a bad marriage, surviving childhood verbal, physical, and sexual abuse, surviving heartache and loss (Dharma), accepting lost dreams (not having children), dealing with marital difficulties, or surviving cancer—after all that—what *isn't* possible?

Seeing it all listed together looks daunting. Yet considering myself a victim never even occurs to me. Everything I've experienced has made me stronger, wiser, and more compassionate.

I believe the same is true for all of us. Survivor just doesn't cut it for me. I'm not just hanging in—surviving; I am victorious!

Today's Action | Write a paragraph summarizing the challenges you've faced thus far. Can you see that the most trying experiences made you who you are? Having had your mettle tested, haven't you emerged victorious? Today, own your own excellence!

This Is The Moment

Today, I have the courage to plan for the future but live in the present.

The first thing that comes to mind is four years ago when I began planning, in the fall of 1994, for a June 1995 trip to California. A friend and I were going to a recovery convention in San Diego and we wanted to drive up the coast afterwards staying in bed-and-breakfast inns along the way. Scouring the Internet, I burned phone and fax lines for three months gathering information for the trip. Then in January, I began planning where we'd stay, what we would do, comparing fares, and making all of our travel arrangements. I filled an entire box with travel brochures and other goodies I had gathered.

From September of 1994 until June 2, 1995, I was living in the future. My mind was always thinking about how wonderful that trip was going to be. I had every detail planned. It was going to be the best trip ever! Obsessive doesn't begin to cover it.

On June 2, when I woke up from my biopsy and heard the words, "It's cancer," everything changed.

Within days, my life turned upside down, and my plans for my wonderful trip went up in smoke—the convention that occurs only once every five years—gone. The quaint little bed and breakfasts—gone. The leisurely (planned to the minute) drive up the coast of California—gone. The doctors *strongly* advised against waiting until July to do the mastectomy.

My friend decided to go by herself. And me—well, I was in the hospital losing a breast. So much for the best-laid plans.

Although I knew every detail probably wouldn't go as planned, it never occurred to me there wouldn't even be a trip. Boy, did I learn a valuable lesson. Plan—but plan minimally, because ultimately God is in charge—not me.

Earlier this year, I spent a couple of hours trading in our frequent flyer miles and our timeshare, booking our hotel and transportation, and calling my friend Pixie, letting her know when we were coming to Hawaii and that's it. I haven't lifted another finger. Gary and I plan to show up and let God handle the rest.

Having let go of the planning trap—my todays are mine again. My mind still loves to plan, but I usually just jot the distracting thought down and return to living in the present moment. So much time is wasted on things that never come to be—I'd rather just be in what I know will come to pass—this moment. My life is far richer as a result.

Today's Action | Plan minimally, living fully in the moment instead.

Only You Know And I Know

Today, I have the courage to value my intuition and wisdom.

Without a doubt, the answers I need are within. I no longer second-guess myself. If I make a decision, I trust it. If I get a feeling about someone or something, I trust it. If I am guided, I follow. No questions asked.

Trusting my intuition set the stage for that magical night at my Aunt Fi's house a few months ago. This book is unfolding from that same place of wisdom.

I ask the women I guide, "Have you written about it? Have you prayed and meditated about it?" because that's how I gain clarity.

It is in that still quiet place inside that God speaks to us. This is where we find our highest good, no other place.

All seeking leads home, back to ourselves, back to what we already know deep inside. It's time we learn to trust that inner voice. It is *our* truth.

We all know which relationships are healthy and which aren't, whether we are living our *right livelihood* or not, whether our outer lives reflect our inner values or not. We know what makes our heart sing and whether we are being true to it or not.

We know what nourishes and what drains us. And whether we are spending time nurturing ourselves or exhausting ourselves. We know how we want to spend our time and if we are honoring ourselves or not. We know if we are treating ourselves lovingly, gently, and respectfully or not.

By now, we are either living authentically, or we are not. No one can say for us.

We know.

You know, just as I know.

 Today's Action | Trust your inner guidance. It is your one true voice. Trust it. Follow it. Live it. Relax into it and be it. *Namaste.*

My Eyes Adored You

Today, I have the courage to know that I am lovable.

Yesterday, I heard Bonnie Raitt's "I Can't Make You Love Me," and was reminded of when I used to try to win Gary's love. It wasn't until I stopped trying to make him love me that I was free to receive the gift of love he was capable of giving. As my acceptance grew, so did his capacity.

We've been married since 1988 and are one of the rare success stories of healthy relationships among addicts and alcoholics. The true story of our love began when I thought our marriage was over, and I knew I would be fine, whether Gary stayed or not. When I loved myself enough to let go, I received all I needed and more. When I looked to *myself* for love, instead of wishing someone else would make me feel loved, I realized I was loved all along. And because Gary and I are so content within ourselves, every encounter we share is loving, fun, funny, happy, intimate, and passionate.

God, self, and others are the key; when the love of your life becomes one of many, instead of the central focus of your life, that's healthy love. I am whole because I have not only Gary's love, but my love, God's love, and the love and respect of my family, friends, and co-workers. Gary has become part of my life, not the whole of it anymore. Now, I understand why they say "men are just desserts." Life is the meal—a full, well-balanced meal. Romantic love is just icing on the cake.

It's nice to know I no longer need to chase the unavailable, trying to capture my father's illusory love.

I am lovable. All I need do is stand still and allow the love that is already there to wash over me.

Today's Action | Stop trying to *get* love. Instead, *allow* it in. Just open your heart and receive all of God's abundance. You already *are* lovable. You needn't do anything to *get* love. You *are* love.

Hello, Goodbye

Today, I have the courage to celebrate the differences between men and women.

Thank God for John Gray and his Mars and Venus books! I finally "get it" that Gary gets his self-esteem from his work and accomplishments and I get mine from the quality of my interpersonal relationships, my marriage being just one of them. Now that that's settled, everything is as it should be.

Gary can go into his cave, click through his sports and news channels, work six days a week, mismanage money, and not ask for help. And I can know he is behaving exactly as he is supposed to. I no longer need spin my wheels trying to fix, improve, or change him. He is perfect exactly the way he is.

And Gary can love the part of me that wants to match everyone up with the right resources and people to help them deal with whatever they are going through. He can love the emotional woman who wears her heart on her sleeve and still bruises easily. He can laugh at the controlling, organizing woman who wants to make order out of chaos, especially when things feel out of control on the inside.

We can embrace each other's strengths and weaknesses, focus on what is good and right in each other, and give each other room to grow at our own pace.

We love each other's sense of humor. We share a love of good food, movies, and stories. We enjoy helping others, take pride in our work, and love hearing about people's spiritual awakenings.

Although our histories and personalities are as different as night and day, our hearts are one. We realize we have much to learn from each other, and accept our differences as just that—what makes us unique. We no longer try to change each other, or even want to. What a nice place to settle into.

Today's Action | If you've been struggling with your mate—let go. Let them be. They are perfect in God's eyes, just as you are—defects and all. Trust that they have a Higher Power working in their lives, that their lessons are their own, and that we aren't always privy to the bigger picture. Sink into acceptance today. Just relax and let go.

Don't Let Me Down

Today, I have the courage to develop healthy, supportive relationships.

Yesterday I spent time with a woman who was having trouble with a key relationship for those in recovery, her sponsor. Whenever she wanted to get together with her sponsor, her sponsor didn't have time. She felt her sponsor was abrupt and showed little compassion when she was in pain. In addition, her sponsor neglected to show up for her sponsee's important occasions.

As this woman relayed all this to me in tears, I felt it was crucial to get across to her that she was worthy of more. We all deserve to be in supportive relationships. Granted, no one person can meet all our needs, so it's important to have a support system—a handful of people who really care and can be there when it really matters. At the same time, it's reasonable to want compassion, a kind word, an occasional show of support, and our important occasions remembered.

We will be let down, no question. People will fall short or forget. Often, their lives are too full to keep up with things, as they would like. Therefore, forgiveness and understanding are important at our end.

We need to look at the patterns, though. Are you frequently stood up, forgotten, ignored, dumped on, or criticized? Are you repeatedly disrespected? If so, it's time to reassess your relationships.

Who puts a smile on your face? Who is always excited to see you? Who encourages and brings out the best in you? Who can you count on in a pinch? Who can be trusted with your innermost secrets and deepest fears? Are your peer relationships a give and take, or is one doing all the taking and the other all the giving?

Paramount to letting our hearts sing is that we be in healthy relationships, where our needs are met. Too many times, we stay in relationships that no longer work out of undeserved loyalty, familiarity, or fear.

Today, we can have the courage to develop healthy relationships and let go of ones we've outgrown.

Today's Action | Affirm that you are worthy of healthy, supportive relationships. Then, speak up in the ones that aren't working. Ask for what you need. Once the air is cleared, possibly the relationships can shift; if not, have the courage to move on.

I Feel Free

Today, I have the courage to make forgiveness a priority.

Whether it is long-held grudges, something that just happened, or whether we, ourselves, are the ones we need to forgive, now is the time to begin.

Forgiveness doesn't mean condoning unacceptable behavior, but it does mean we release our anger and self-righteousness and mentally move on. To forgive, we need to detach enough to understand why things happened the way they did, how we may have contributed to the conflict, and what our lessons are, so that we don't make the same mistakes again.

As forgiveness enters our heart, we heal and attract healthier people into our lives. However, this doesn't happen until we do our emotional work. We need to move out of denial, feel our pain, anger, and sadness, and then let go, making room for acceptance and understanding. Eventually, our hearts open, allowing compassion and forgiveness in.

The past is unchangeable. No matter how horrible the trespass—rape, incest, infidelity, physical or verbal abuse—you can move past it to a healthy, happy today. No matter how deep the pain, it doesn't have to hang over your life forever.

If you have trouble forgiving, saying the "St. Francis of Assisi Prayer" or "The Lord's Prayer" can help. If the resentment persists—try working with the index cards. Revisiting the cards at any time can assist you in moving through difficult emotions.

When I look over my own list of harms, I am amazed at the healings that have taken place over the last ten years. So many people accepted my amends and forgave me. I think most people, deep in their souls, want to be at peace with each other. Once the ego is out of the way, it doesn't matter who initiates the healing, so long as it takes place.

Although it took courage to seek out the people I harmed, own what I did, and repair the damage, it took even more courage to forgive myself. I used to be so hard on myself, always wishing I'd said or done things differently. I'm much better now, but occasionally my mind still wanders back into the unchangeable past. As soon as I notice this, I ask myself, "What can I do about it right now?" If some action will improve the situation, I take it. If not, I let it go.

I've found a sincere apology, followed by right action, can heal most any situation. I just need to remember we are human and will all let each other down at times. Today, I don't intentionally hurt anyone, and that is a huge change from who I was.

Healing the past left me free to pursue my dreams. With my relationships in order, I can devote myself to living my bliss, growing spiritually, and helping others do the same. It is so freeing.

Today's Action | Straighten out conflict as soon as it arises, leaving you free to live blissfully.

I Love You Just The Way You Are

And most importantly I have the courage to accept myself just as I am.

I no longer mind my curly hair, wish I were taller, or allow the scale to determine how I feel about myself. Even today, after having breakfast with a dozen women, most of whom have had their breasts and faces lifted, I am totally at ease with my less-than-perfect breasts and the ever-increasing number of lines on my face.

As to my nervous giggle when speaking—that's me. In fact, I disagree with my public-speaking teacher about my laughter being an undesirable mannerism—I think I'm just happy!

I am at peace with myself—finally. And I know God loves me just the way I am.

Whatever I think, say, or do is okay. I am getting better all the time. I am perfectly imperfect, and that's perfectly okay with me.

My past is my past and although I could never run for public office, it's who I am today that counts. Yesterday is gone, today is a clean slate, a fresh start. If I'm a little better each day, that's enough.

If, by chance, I have too much on my plate and snap at someone, or respond in an unkind manner, there's always tomorrow. Today, I have the courage to own my flaws and apologize.

Just for today, I'll keep my laughter. I'd rather be unpolished and real than sound phony.

Experts don't always know what's best. For instance, the magazine editor I worked with on "Dharma" may have *technically* improved my story, but they edited the heart and soul right out of it. So my intuition was right—my version was best.

I hope and pray that what you are reading right now isn't perfectly written, so much as honestly written, with an open, trusting heart. Through acknowledging my flaws as a writer and a speaker, I embrace myself as a person. It isn't about perfection; it's about authenticity.

I would rather imperfectly take a step forward, fall down, get up, and dust myself off, than to be so paralyzed by the fear of making a mistake that I don't take any step at all.

If I've truly turned my life over to God's care, there can be no mistakes, only lessons. Today, I welcome opportunities for growth because I know, "I can handle them!"

I am perfect just as I am. I accept myself exactly as I am.

Gary used to sing Billy Joel's "I Love You Just The Way You Are" to me whenever I said or did something less than loving. I'd be standing in the bathroom, with daggers in my eyes, pointing at the toilet seat Gary left up, and he'd take one look at my face and burst into song, "*I love you just the way you are* . . . . Yeah just like that," pointing at me. Then, we'd both crack up laughing.

Through his humor and reactions, Gary taught me about unconditional love. In time, I learned to love *him* exactly the way he is, because he already loves me exactly as I am. (If the truth be told, all our problems were resolved nine years ago when we splurged on a second bathroom.)

Having a sense of humor about your shortcomings and those of others is the quickest path to acceptance.

Today's Action | Learn to laugh at your perfect imperfections. You are perfect in God's eyes—*just the way you are.*

I'm Addicted To Love

If there is any reason to get out of an unhealthy relationship it is so that we can be more and give more to life.—Brenda Schaeffer

Melissa and her boyfriend resumed talking and he seemed very remorseful, so Melissa gave him another chance.

Yesterday, after another month of pain, it finally hit her: she wasn't in love—she was addicted! Three times last month, her boyfriend stood her up. At first, his stories seemed plausible, and she continued to forgive and trust. Then, she realized the real issue wasn't so much whether he was with another woman or not, but the lack of respect he demonstrated through these disappearing acts.

Melissa finally realized that she re-created the exact same situation she faced growing up. Her father had always been unfaithful and Melissa internalized, "That's just the way men are."

Now Melissa sees that *this* man is not *capable* of the kind of honesty and integrity she needs in a relationship. Not *all* men, just *this* one. Not willing to settle for less, Melissa ended the relationship.

The freedom she felt when making the decision contrasts greatly with how she feels carrying it out. Hurt, anger, and a tremendous sense of loss are consuming her, but she would rather go through the pain than sell herself short and settle for less than she knows she deserves.

I am honored to watch her grow. She has such strength and courage. It takes guts to face love addiction and even more courage to let it go. I told Melissa I'd bow when I see her because she is such an awesome woman.

It is so hard to see it when you are in it. *I wasn't addicted to Barrie—I was in love!* When you're addicted, you can't see straight, much less think rationally. In all of its forms: drugs, alcohol, gambling, sex, food, religion, or love, addiction keeps us so wrapped up in ourselves, that we totally lose sight of the bigger picture: our purpose here on earth.

Gary says, "Addiction is when you hurt yourself and/or another person to get what you want." The insidious thing about addiction is that the addicted person is unable to see the truth when they are actively engaging in addictive behavior, which is why the number-one symptom of addiction is *denial*.

Another telltale sign of addictive love is that as our self-esteem lessens, we lose interest in others, and fall backwards in our personal growth. Family and friends feel abandoned, important priorities are neglected, as the object of our obsession takes precedence over everything else.

For Melissa, the biggest price paid was how her love addiction affected her studies. She had given up her job to become a lawyer, but was so wrapped up in her relationship that she couldn't study effectively. Thank God, she was able to extract herself from the web of addiction before it completely derailed her dreams.

Because you can't see it when you are in it, the best way to tell if you are addicted is if anyone suggests you might be, assume addiction is in full force, and get help.

Today's Action | Seeking help when there is even the possibility of addiction never hurt anyone. So even if you're not sure, read a book, call someone, or go to a meeting. It is impossible to live blissfully while caught in the grips of addiction.

I've Never Been To Me

Whenever we think our happiness depends on another person, we are not taking responsibility for our own lives.

Hilda, my friend who wants to learn how to drive, is in a lot of pain right now. She's afraid her marriage might be over. She says her husband is not fulfilling her emotional needs and he says the passion is gone.

I've been down that road more times than I can count, although I was usually the one whose sexual needs weren't being met. It wasn't until I was with Gary that I learned each person is responsible for his or her own happiness. The person you are in a relationship with is not there for the sole purpose of meeting your needs. They are in your life to enhance it, not to be the source of anything.

When *A Course in Miracles* speaks of special relationships, it's speaking to the part of us that wants another person to be our savior or source of good feelings. If God is our true source, no person, place, or thing can ever take the place of spiritual fulfillment.

That ache or emptiness we feel when another person is not meeting our needs is really a sign that we are neglecting our own needs. We are not taking time to be with ourselves and our Higher Power. We are looking for the quick fix, that rush of good feelings when a person, behavior, or substance *temporarily* puts us in an altered state of bliss or brings relief. However, if the source is outside of us, the relief or bliss will not last.

Ideally, we want to get to the place in our lives where there is a healthy balance of God, self, and others, meeting our needs. But this only comes when we don't *need* another person to meet our needs. As long as we are needy or put the responsibility for our happiness elsewhere, we will find no lasting peace or joy.

Just as we can only give and serve from overflow, we can only receive from a fully primed pump. We have to already be in love—in love with ourselves, God, and humanity—before we can truly receive the gift of love another person has to offer.

Many times I thought Gary wasn't meeting my needs, only to find that if I but meet my own needs through self-love, nurturing, spiritual practices, giving to and receiving love from others, Gary more than meets my needs. When I am not attached to getting anything from Gary, he is able to give freely.

When I place demands or expectations on another, I may get what I want, but it was extracted not extended freely, and therefore has no lasting meaning.

When I am in a centered, loving place, unattached to *getting* anything, I am free to *receive* abundantly.

Make a list of all your wants and needs. Then, find ways to fulfill those wants and needs yourself.

If your mate is emotionally unavailable, don't project that *It's always been this way, so it's always going to be this way.* Instead, look for ways to meet your emotional needs yourself. Find friends that will give you a hug or lend an ear when you need it.

With gratitude, look at the good in your partner. Focus on that good. Let your feelings of love build. Soon, you'll find they are more willing and able to love you. And it will be love freely given—the best kind.

Baby, You Can Drive My Car

I told you earlier that Hilda was one of the most courageous women I know—probably because she's the most fearful.

Hilda was forty-three when she first told me she wanted to learn to drive again.

As a result of her drug addiction, Hilda's world had gotten smaller and smaller, until she could no longer get behind the steering wheel of a car. Over the past five years I suggested many times that she come out from under her husband's shadow and drive again, but she always had reasons why she couldn't. She had epilepsy. She suffered from panic attacks. Her license was suspended. She was too scared to take the driving test. And she couldn't drive in traffic.

Maybe years of watching me walk through my fears must have rubbed off on Hilda, because one day, instead of listing the usual reasons why she couldn't drive, Hilda said, "I think I'm ready."

I suggested she break down the steps it would take to accomplish her goal. First, she needed to find out if her medication controlled epilepsy enough to allow driving.

It took her a couple of months to see her doctor, but soon she had the permission she needed. Next, she had to pay a fine to lift her suspension. A few weeks later, that was done.

All that was left was to take the test. Weeks passed, and Hilda didn't take any action. I asked what the problem was. She said she was too scared to take the test. I reminded her of the *irreducible minimum* and suggested she get the manual and begin studying, not to even worry about the test.

She got the booklet.

Then, fear crept in again, and Hilda put off studying. She even lost the booklet and had to get another one. I suggested she put this one in her purse and read a page or two whenever she could. She did. Eventually, she made her way through the entire manual.

With much trepidation, Hilda made an appointment to take the test. When she arrived to take the written exam, something miraculous happened. An old friend of hers happened to be working at the Driver's License Bureau. When Hilda confided how scared she was about taking the test, the woman looked up her records. It turns out she didn't even have to take a test, all she had to do was pay twenty dollars, and her license would be reinstated.

Amazingly, this news terrified more than delighted her—*she was way too close to actually driving.*

| Today's Action | Break down the steps of something you are scared of doing into bite-size pieces. Keep in mind the *irreducible minimum* and take it one step at a time. |

The Greatest Love Of All

Walking, rather driving, through her fears, Hilda began driving short distances. At first only with her mother in the car, she felt safer somehow.

Then her marriage fell apart.

One day, her husband came home and told her he wasn't in love with her anymore.

Devastated, Hilda threw herself into making the marriage work.

They went to marriage counseling. Hilda gave him space, all the while wondering, "What's wrong with me? Why am I so unlovable? Why doesn't he want to be with me?"

She tried to be who she thought her husband wanted her to be. She tried to make herself more attractive. She tried to get along better with his son. Nothing worked.

Months passed. Hilda kept driving, but only with her mother and only a mile or two to nearby stores. She was so stressed trying to save her marriage that she couldn't handle more. I was amazed that she continued to drive as much as she did.

Her husband spent many nights away from home, and she was convinced he was having an affair. Within a few weeks her suspicions were confirmed; he was in love with someone else. She found something he had written that said he loved both of them and didn't want to choose. Her worst fears had come true.

Without hesitation, she packed his things.

He denied it, telling her, "You need therapy. You're insane with jealousy." She yelled back, "I'm not crazy. You are!"

She knew what she'd read, but started wondering if maybe she was crazy, maybe she *had* misinterpreted what she read. Not knowing what the truth was, she threw herself into working on herself.

Two weeks after her husband left, Hilda called exclaiming, "I did it! I did it! I drove to work all by myself!" Later, she admitted that on her way to work she had to pull off the road because she was crying so hard with tears of gratitude.

In the midst of gut-wrenching pain, Hilda stayed the course.

A few months later, she saw her husband out with his girlfriend. Her blood boiled, but she was able to act like a lady and hold her head high, exclaiming to her friends, "He can't take away my dignity." I guess she's been singing her anthem, "The Greatest Love of All," because she has grown beyond recognition in recent months.

Hilda finally realized her husband's behavior was no reflection on her or her desirability. In fact, she has had plenty of male attention since he left, but is working hard at becoming more God-reliant and less dependent on men for validation.

Although she hasn't forgiven her husband completely, Hilda is trusting of God's plan for her life, just for today.

Today's Action | Listen to this song, "The Greatest Love of All," and remember where your true strength lies. Trust that everything happens for a reason. No matter what is going on in your life, *don't ever lose sight of your dreams.*

Make That Move

If you truly want to live your bliss, courage will be your greatest asset. It takes courage to heal the past, accept yourself as you are, let go of things that are not working, and make things right with others. But most of all it takes courage to follow your dreams, courage to move beyond what's comfortable and really go for it.

In *Feel the Fear and Do It Anyway*, Dr. Susan Jeffers states that there are five truths about fear that if said ten times each, daily for a month, will greatly reduce our negative thinking about fear, enabling us to walk through our fear with greater ease.

The five truths are:

1. **"The fear will never go away, as long as you continue to grow."** A few years ago, when I was first recovering from cancer, I began walking through my fears in an attempt to rid myself of them. I thought if I walked through enough fears, I would eventually become fearless. Instead, I found that as long as I am growing, there will always be fear. I wasn't exactly thrilled to hear that, but I guess it's better than the alternative—*not growing at all.*

2. **"The only way to get rid of the fear of doing something, is to go out and do it!"** I found this to be true whether the fear is real or imagined. After I went on that shark dive, I was no longer terrified of running into sharks while diving. Being afraid of sharks is a healthy fear to have, but not when it keeps you from going in the ocean. This truth applied to my writing as well. Once I started writing, the fear of it left. So, I wholeheartedly agree: Just go out and do it!

3. **"The only way to feel better about yourself is to go out and do it!"** With my writing, I thought I had to improve my self-esteem as a writer by reading and taking more classes *before* I could begin writing. Instead, I found the reverse is true. As soon as I started writing regularly, my self-esteem *and* my skill improved.

4. **"Not only are you going to experience fear when you're on unfamiliar territory, but so is everyone else."** Everyone in my public-speaking course was nervous at first, but with practice, we all got more comfortable. And every writer I've ever spoken to suffers from doubts and insecurity at times, but writes *through* the feelings.

5.   "Pushing through fear is less frightening than living with the underlying fear that comes from a feeling of helplessness" (and I would add hopelessness). Living with a dream in my heart and a constant, overwhelming fear about taking action toward it was worse than actually picking up the pen.

Today's Action | Repeat each of the five truths ten times a day for a month, and watch your relationship with fear shift. Listen to Dr. Jeffers' book on tape if you really want to blow your fears out of the water.

Through The Eyes Of Love

Now that you are involved with like-minded people, people who are reaching for their dreams, and those who have already achieved some measure of success, you're going to need to expand your heart and your faith.

Trusting in the abundance of the Universe is especially important when you are stumbling on your own path, while watching others soar ahead. Emotions of jealousy and envy arise. You may want to pull away from others who *seem* to be ahead of you. This is a normal reaction to the success of others.

A perfect example is my friend Lisa. When we met at a workshop our mentor taught, I was squeezing in an hour of writing here and there, whenever I could. Lisa, supported by her husband, had just quit her nursing job in order to devote herself to her writing, full time. Having more time to devote to it, Lisa's writing took off immediately. Ideas flew onto the cards and her spirit soared. After only two weeks, she had a strong sense of purpose and direction. I, on the other hand, was stuck in the muck and mire of the past. As I waded through the debris, I was flooded with an array of memories and feelings, none of which I welcomed.

Here, I'd been writing for years, felt frustrated at having to chuck my first manuscript, while Lisa was in sync with her Higher Self and flying high. We talked often. One day, I let on how jealous I was feeling. Lisa responded, "Me too! Just last week when your short story was published, I was jealous, too."

After a good laugh, we realized there would always be highs and lows, successes and failures. Lisa and I have learned to rise and fall with the ebb and flow of ever-changing creative tides. We've both doubted our talent, our worth, and the feasibility of our endeavors.

We've also experienced the highest of highs when it feels as if God is talking directly to us on the cards.

Now, we trust each person's success makes for *more* abundance and possibility in the Universe, not less.

Today's Action | Support and encourage someone in your circle you feel envious of.

Believe In You

Although my body aches, my heart soars. Every day that I wake up and write is a victory. Every day I take a step toward my dreams—I am living my bliss. The destination is not important—*living the dream is.*

When I am actively engaged in the footwork, letting go of the results is easy. This is especially true with my writing. I just show up, live my bliss, and let God handle the results. What's supposed to come of it, will. I trust this completely.

I *believe* this work will become a book.

The fact that you are reading these pages right now, taking this incredible journey with me, is proof that dreams really *do* come true. If mine can, yours can.

I'm sure you can tell by now that my writing is nothing fancy. I just let my heart flow onto the pages and invite like-minded people to live their bliss.

From one heart to another—listen to your *heart* and its longings, not your mind and its fears. Follow your heart's longing and you'll find the peace you've been searching for. In time, you'll know without a doubt that you are living as God intended. You'll know because it feels so right.

Truth resonates when you hear it. When you feel it, you know. When you see it, you know. And when you live it, you know.

Don't ever give up on yourself. Don't ever give up on your dreams. Just start today, with baby steps, and walk toward your vision.

If you've already started and faltered, just start anew.

Take a deep breath and outline a plan of action that will take you to your goal. Break down the plan into bite-size, reachable commitments. Give yourself lots of leg room. Then, break the plan down into even smaller goals. Finally, you'll reach an action you are willing and able to take *right now*. Then do it! Begin with the *irreducible minimum*.

Today's Action | Make a list of the actions necessary to reach your goals. Add in a reasonable time for taking each step, large or small.
Today, reach for the stars and begin letting *your* heart sing.

Dream Weaver

In the first few months of dreaming, scheming, uncovering, excavating, and clearing, we open to our hearts' desire. Next, we create space in our lives for dreaming once again. Then, exposing our fears, we remove blocks and open up to possibility, regaining a sense of hope about the future. Finally, breaking through our fears, we seek out people we need to heal with and go forward with a clean slate. By continually taking courageous steps in the direction we want to go, we build enough self-esteem to get down to the nitty-gritty and actually see ourselves reaching our goals.

Visualizing can apply to any dream or goal: career or *right livelihood*, romance and relationships, health and fitness, home and family, or spiritual and personal growth.

Pick one area and visualize where you would like to be in ten years. Be specific. Next, determine what actions you need to take to realize your dreams. What action could you take today to move in the direction you desire?

For instance, say you want to get fit and lose weight, but you engage in no physical activity and eat a bagel with cream cheese every morning on the way to work. Maybe today you could do five, not more, just five sit-ups and eat half a bagel. Whenever I go to extremes, my plan is usually short-lived, because I end up sabotaging myself. Whereas, if I take baby steps, and break things down into manageable, doable goals, I am much more likely to achieve what I set out to do.

Say I want more peace in my life. Instead of running off to an ashram and meditating all day, I might begin by including five minutes of meditation in my morning routine.

334

In my case, my dream is to be a writer. I awakened to my heart's desire in the fall of 1995 when my cancer psychotherapist asked me to flesh out my dreams. I realized I wanted to write for a living. Meanwhile, I was earning a living as a controller in a law firm, writing a few articles here and there, yet was not earning any money as a writer. Still, I had a dream. My first goal was to be earning a living as a writer in ten years.

Ten years seemed so far off and the dream was so huge in my mind that the goal did not seem the least bit impossible or threatening. Then, I was asked to bring the time frame closer to home and visualize myself as a writer, *now*.

I could not even call myself a writer out loud. I certainly could not visualize myself as one. My therapist said, "If writing is the one thing that makes you feel most alive, then it is imperative that you begin writing at once to send your body the message that you want to live." What began as a fight for my life became my life.

Today's Action	Pick one area of your life and visualize the specifics of your dream manifesting in your life ten years from now.

After All

Somewhere, in a galaxy far, far away, I saw myself as a writer. Now, it was time to bring it closer to home. How about five years? What would that dream look like in my life five years from now? In five years, I wanted to have my first book completed and published. That seemed reasonable. And for someone who didn't even know if they would be alive in five years, it was no big deal. Pipe dreams—that's all they were.

In 1995, that was my dream and that's as far as I could take it. For the next two-and-a-half years, I dabbled as a writer. Although there were many stops and starts, *the dream never died.*

In March 1998, I found the teacher who was to become my mentor. In addition to helping me write for a minimum of an hour a day, five days a week, he got me working with the index cards, the poster boards, and meditating before each writing session. These actions, plus calling him for our weekly appointment, gave me the discipline needed to make real progress toward my goals.

One of the first things my mentor had me do was visualize myself achieving the things I said I wanted—for there is power in thought—power in what you put out to the Universe.

I visualized the specifics of my dreams. My five-year goal was the same, but now I was less fearful. I now knew I was a writer. Not because anyone called me a writer, not because I earned money as a writer, and not because I've been published. I am a writer because I write. It's as simple as that.

Now that I declared who and what I was, what was I going to do about it? Back to the goals. Initially, I wanted my first book completed and published within five years, but more than two have already passed, so that means three years from now.

Ah! Relief—fear—both. Yet, this is what I wanted for myself. Now, I need to visualize it and declare it for myself.

How about one year? I visualized myself finished with my first book, having an agent, in the process of getting my book published, and working on my second book, all within a year. It looks like I really do want a writing career. I also envisioned "Dharma," published within a year. Shortly after I visualized that, the editor from *Angels on Earth* called, and we began editing "Dharma."

Now, with my dreams beginning to come true, things got scary. I didn't want to commit to these goals on paper. *What if I chickened out? What if circumstances beyond my control circumvented my dreams?* All my fears came rushing to the surface as I declared my one-year goals.

Raising the bar, by visualizing my goals in three-month increments, intensified my emotions even more. I saw myself writing at least five days a week, working with my mentor weekly, and working on getting an agent. My heart beat faster with each commitment. *Could I really stick with this? What if I fail? What if I'm no good?* Yet, I continued.

My one-month goals: I see myself diligently working on the index cards as laid out by my mentor. I am committed to removing any blocks that stand between me and my highest potential.

Wow! Scary stuff. Declaring my goals was an anxiety-producing experience because I like to think of myself as a person with integrity; if I commit to something, I'm going to do my best to make it happen. Otherwise my word has no value.

I had two goals set for my first week. One was to get up early and write for at least one hour each day before work. The other was to commit *on paper* to my one-year goals and send it to two people who support me in my endeavors and to one person I don't want to fail in front of.

Talk about putting yourself out there! I bet as soon as I wrote that sentence, you knew exactly who the person was that you didn't want to fail in front of. Right now, you are probably thinking of an alternative person, instead of the first person that came to mind. That's how it was with me. But I sent it to that first person, and even though I am behind schedule as of this moment, I am still *totally* committed to my goals, long and short range.

Today's Action | Bring the dream closer. Visualize your five-year, three-year, and one-year goals. Where do you see yourself in five years? Where would you like to be three years? How does your life look in one year?

Don't Stop Thinking About Tomorrow

After getting an overview of where you would like to be by a given date, it's important to get specific. If you don't have a vision and a desired direction, you could end up anywhere.

337

My instructions were to visualize exactly where I want to be in five years. Then to write every detail really fast without thinking, in order to get as close to my heart's desire as possible.

Okay, in five years I see myself with my first book published, a second one finished and ready for publication, and a third in the works. I see myself with an agent, an editor, and a publishing house that believe in me, encourage me, and are excited about working with me. I see myself writing five or six days a week. I see myself earning a living as a writer. I see a check for $60,000.00 as an advance and royalties coming in from my first book already. I see my book selling hundreds of thousands of copies, helping thousands of people live their dreams.

I see myself corresponding with hundreds of readers who wrote to me about how *Letting Your Heart Sing* changed their lives. I see myself with greater vision and clarity. I see myself meditating and exercising regularly to keep balanced and healthy. I see myself going to the beach regularly to fill the well. I see myself with an assistant to help with the input, editing, and mail.

I see myself traveling to book signings and visiting national parks along the way. I see *Oprah* raving about *Letting Your Heart Sing*. I see myself *not* letting any of this get to my head. I still live in the same house, am happily married to Gary, sponsor women, go to meetings, and live a normal life.

Copies of *Letting Your Heart Sing* are donated to women who need inspiration but can't afford the book. I see women passing the book on to others when they are finished with it. As I share my heart and touch theirs, they are moved to share with others.

I see *Bliss Groups* starting up all over the country as men and women support each other and hold each other up to their highest potential. I see people living simpler, happier, more spiritual lives.

I see my boss, the big intimidating one, bowled over by my success, as my life is more prosperous than even I imagined. I see myself doing good works with the money I earn, mostly for those who need a jump start to begin living their own dreams—like a *Bliss Foundation*—cool!

I see my confidence growing as a writer and a speaker. I see myself as a guest on *Oprah* and my book getting great reviews. People can see the very heart and soul of *Letting Your Heart Sing* and *it is changing lives.*

Most of all, I see myself happy and healthy, joyfully living my bliss.

338

Today's Action | Get quiet. Take a few deep breaths. Exhale slowly. With your eyes closed, visualize where you see yourself in five years. When your vision is complete, write the details down as fast as you can.

Fly, Robin, Fly

Where do I see myself in three years?

Letting Your Heart Sing is published and doing well, and I've just finished my second book. I quit my job, now that I have an agent, an editor, a publisher, a contract, and an advance. Pretty much everything else is the same as the five-year vision, except I am just beginning to go to book signings and give talks on living blissfully. I am becoming a powerful speaker. My self-esteem is rising as I walk through my fears and accomplish my goals.

It's a little scary to have left the safety net of the law firm I have called home for the last thirteen years, but I am ready and it feels right. My bosses can't believe my success. All of my friends and family are happy for me and inspired by me. I spend lots of time helping others achieve their goals.

It's a very exciting time because everything is just beginning to take off. It's been a long road with many challenges, but I've been up for them all.

I see myself happy, content, excited, and awed by God's love and power in my life, and very, very grateful.

I write five to six days a week and enjoy not commuting two hours a day to my old office job. I am committed to my writing, and words just fly out of me. I've never had so much fun in all my life.

I make sure my books get donated to women's shelters, hospitals, and to other groups of people who want to turn their lives around. I remain true to myself, and am just as happy to be on *Oprah* as to speak at the YMCA. However the message gets out is fine with me.

People can read excerpts from *Letting Your Heart Sing* on my web page to help motivate them each day. They can also e-mail me, chat with others, and purchase the book online. There is now a collection of *Letting Your Heart Sing* CDs inspiring people through the same music that inspired me. *Bliss Groups* are starting up all over the country.

I am content with the ripple my little pebble made in the pond of life.

Today's Action | Adjust the lens and zoom in. Visualize what your life looks like in three years regarding your bliss. Record as much detail as possible. Write as fast as you can, so as not to let the doubter in. Just go for it. See it. Write it. Believe it.

Tenth Month

Deepening Your Vision And Connection With Spirit

In Your Wildest Dreams

*W*here do I see myself in one year?

It's terrifying to look so close.

I'm still at my law firm—for sure. I'm definitely not ready to leave there yet. *Letting Your Heart Sing* is in the hands of my agent, who is very excited about it. I'm still fine-tuning the manuscript, but the overall response is fabulous.

The literary agency is thrilled to have me aboard, and we all agree that a big publishing house would be wonderful, but a smaller one might be better, so *Letting Your Heart Sing* can get the attention it deserves. The specifics don't matter here, so long as we envision the same future for *Letting Your Heart Sing* with its accompanying CD collection, workbook, journal, and calendar.

Faxes, phone calls, and e-mails fly back and forth between my agent and me, as we burn the midnight oil on the finishing touches. The agency couldn't *be* more excited. We work well together as a team. And they love the title, *Letting Your Heart Sing*, and its subtitle, *A Daily Journal for the Soul.*

This is *the* most exciting time of my life. I can hardly contain myself. Which reminds me of my favorite bumper sticker: I tried to contain myself, but I escaped!

There are a couple of publishers interested, and we are deciding which one is the best for *Heart*.

I can actually *see* publication in sight, as my agent, my editor, and publisher all work as a team to make it happen. The best part is that they all really *get* me and want to keep the simplicity of the book. They actually find my voice refreshing. Not at all like my first experience publishing "Dharma—My Little Angel."

I am balanced, relaxed, excited, grateful, and amazed at my life. There's even talk of a movie about Gary's life. And to think, at one time I was scared to take a risk and follow my dreams. Thank you, God.

Today's Action | Where do you see yourself in one year? Visualize it, then flesh it out on paper. Be specific. Live large. See it all. Unless you put your innermost desires out there, the Universe can't respond to them.

Bring It On Home

Where will I be nine months from now? Let's see, that will be April 20th. I'll be finished with this book, including the input, enhancing, and editing of it—at least the pre-agent, pre-publishing editing. I'll be well into my next book project. I'll still be writing five to six days a week, my query letters will be out, getting lots of positive responses from interested agents. I'll still be working with my mentor, but possibly winding down to every other week.

I'll have been on my dream vacation to Hawaii, writing by waterfalls, experiencing the beauty and magic of them. I'll have made amends with Pixie while in Maui.

I'll have offers of representation by then. I'll have spoken at a number of places I was scared to speak, but felt the fear and did it anyway! I will have sung in front of people by then.

Bringing it this much closer to home is scary. It's so close. So real. But I can do this, I just know I can. I've come too far to give up now. Actually, the part of me that usually gives up when things get rough doesn't seem to be here anymore. Fear is *coexisting* with the excitement, creating exhilaration.

I'm so far into living my dream that the chicken in me is gone! Wow, life without my doubter. I can't imagine it. But here I am, pushing forward every week, believing that I can and *will* finish this book. I *will* get an agent. *Letting Your Heart Sing will* be published.

It was nice that "Dharma" was accepted for publication and even nicer to know I liked my own version best. It's nice to know that even though someone else may be technically correct, I like my own style, my own voice better. How affirming.

Today's Action | Bring the vision even closer. Where do you see yourself nine months, to the day, from today? When you get specific about the day, month, and year by which you intend to achieve your goals, you empower yourself to succeed. Stand on what you've already accomplished to give you the courage and stamina you need to succeed. How do you feel about what you've accomplished so far, compared to where you were a year ago?

One Belief Away

Six months from now, where will I be?

That will be January 20th. I'll be in the final stretch of input, editing, and enhancing. My query letters were mailed months ago, and I'm now getting responses to them. Much interest, a few offers.

By the end of the year, I'll have an agent. The phone is ringing off the hook: lots of excitement about my project.

"Dharma" has been published, and I was happier with the final version than the initial edited one sent to me.

Tom and I still have our weekly appointments.

I'm fleshing out where I want to go next: Cancer, Relationships, Practicing Spiritual Principles, Stories of Healing, Conversion Experiences, Stories about people who are letting their heart sing as a result of reading this book.

My actual deadline for finishing the book is exactly one year from when I went to my mentor's seminar on *How to complete your first book in 52 weeks or less*. Considering I'm working around the clock, I guess it's no surprise that I'm finishing ahead of schedule.

343

I sure bust my butt for this. Although it hardly seems like work since I love it so. I've never been happier in my life—doing what I love—and sticking to it, no matter what! To be walking through my fears, never giving up on myself. It is so exhilarating!

And to think it all started with a cancer diagnosis. Isn't life strange?

 Today's Action | Where do you see yourself six months from now? Visualize it. Write it out. Be specific. Write in the present tense as if it is actually happening.

Paperback Writer

Where will I be three months from now?

Three months from now, October 20th, I'll have received my check for the publication of "Dharma." It is at newsstands as we speak. It's official—I am a writer. I say that jokingly because I used to think publication would make me feel authentic. Now I know I am a writer, because I write.

The same goes with anything. You are not a mother because you've received acknowledgment or validation. Nor are you a mother because you've received payment. You are a mother because of your act of mothering. The same is true for a painter, a gardener, a birdwatcher, an actor, or a swimmer. Engaging in the activity makes you what you are. I put so much mystery around *being* a writer that it seemed it was something I could never achieve, never arrive at. Well, here I am!

Being a writer is a state of being, not a destination.

So, it's October 20th, and I've finished the rough draft and am about halfway through the revision of the manuscript. I still work with my teacher weekly and write five to six days a week.

The query letters were just mailed. While I wait for responses, I'll prepare for my trip to Hawaii. We leave November 14th.

I remember when I first got cancer, the one thing I really wanted to do if I didn't have much time left was go to Hawaii. Now, here it is three years later and I'm going, *I'm really going*!

I guess I need to find more dreams, since all my dreams are coming true, and it's obvious I've lived longer than I originally thought I would.

Today's Action | Where will you be in three months? Continue visualizing and fleshing ideas out on paper until they crystallize. Each time we bump it up a notch by shortening the time frame, we break down the steps necessary to reach our goals. Your written visualization becomes your plan of action—the steps you need to follow for your dreams to come true.

By continually visualizing and writing down your dreams, your vision becomes so real that your mind stops doubting itself and begins to follow the plan.

♡

Believe

Where will I be in a month?

Whoaaaaaa. It's getting *really* scary bringing it this close. Okay. Okay. Breathe.

I can do this.

By this day next month, August 20th, my rough draft will be completed. All 366 stories will be done. Granted, they may change form over the next few months, but they will be completed. The entire rough draft will be done!

Wow! That's amazing to even think about, much less write and do. But that's my goal, my commitment. And I *will* achieve it. Only my teacher changing the plan or an act of God will stop me from achieving this one feat.

It feels awesome to say it. But I *know* I can do it. I *will* do it. I *am* doing it.

God, please guide me in all noble endeavors, especially this one. ✗

Today's Action | Where will you be in a month? Set a specific goal, make a commitment to yourself, and do it. Write it down. Put it where you will see it every day. Believe and achieve.

I'm So Excited

I did it! I did it! I did it!

I sang karaoke last night!

After our favorite Monday night meeting, Gary and I went out for ice cream. On the way there, Gary saw a sign that said, "Karaoke on Monday Nights." He hesitated in telling me because he knew I would want to walk through my fear of singing in front of people *right then and there*, and he had to get up early for work.

When I wrote that I wanted to sing in front of people by the end of the year, I thought I had at least a few months to develop the courage. I had no intention of doing it anytime soon! But here it is, *one day after I wrote about it.* So when Gary said, "They have karaoke tonight at that place we just passed." My jaw dropped open, "You're kidding!"

The next words out of my mouth were, "Can we?" I *had* to do this. It was just too much of a coincidence.

We went inside and sat down. I looked around the packed little restaurant. Every table was full; at least forty to fifty people were jammed into the room.

Nervously, I picked up the book and chose "I've Got You Babe" by Sonny and Cher. The DJ told me it was a duet, so Gary said he'd sing it with me. While waiting for our turn, Gary leaned over and said, "Debbie, if you really want to walk through your fear, you should do it alone the first time." Swallowing hard, I went back to the DJ and picked another song, an old rock song from the seventies, "It's Alright Now" by Free.

The DJ introduced me to the crowd, "We have a first timer . . . a VIRGIN! We have a karaoke VIRGIN!" Next thing you know, the whole crowd starts yelling, "POP, POP . . . POP that cherry!"

Two tables filled with college students roared with laughter, "POP, POP . . . POP that cherry!" blasting the "Karaoke Virgin."

Could my face have *been* any redder? I don't think so. But sing I did!

I didn't follow the words very well, and I'm sure I was way off key, but I did it! I sang in front of people! To be honest, it wasn't nearly as scary as I thought it would be.

When I think of how many fears I've walked through and continue to walk through, I'm amazed. I really *am* becoming less fearful with each fear I walk through.

I never thought I could become confident, courageous, and spontaneous, but I am. Who would have thought that the girl who couldn't even walk into a dance ten years ago can now sing in front of strangers! Life is so awesome!

Today's Action | Walk through a fear today. Choose anything you are afraid of and just do it! Whether it's speaking in front of people, calling someone you've been meaning to, calling a stranger, or singing and dancing in front of strangers, do something out of the ordinary today. Stretch yourself. Move beyond your comfort zone. With each stretch you increase the size of your comfort zone, leaving you more room within which to be comfortable.

Bridge Over Troubled Water

My Aunt Fi sent me some old photos of my maternal great-great grandparents last week. In her letter, she mentioned how much my mother and I look like my great-great grandmother. Further on in the letter, she reminisced about a trip she took with my mother to West Virginia when my mother was a little girl.

I was delighted she wrote me, and that she mentioned my mother, *twice*. I just know a softening is taking place in her heart.

This woman, who has been filled with venomous hatred for my mother for more than twenty years, can now write conversationally about her in a letter! I just know it's going to work out. One of them will come to her senses before it's too late.

I really believe a healing will take place in my family. I just have to be patient. I just hope they don't wait too long. My mom is sixty and my great aunt and grandmother are in their eighties. From where I sit, they are alive twenty and forty years longer than I thought I would be.

My aunt's letter starts:

"Dear Debbie, Your sweet visit to me meant more than words can tell. Thank you for your genuine sincerity."

My eyes well up with tears even as I rewrite that line. I just love the heart God put in me and the willingness I have to go to any lengths to bring more love and healing into this world.

Thank you, God, for my life and my heart.

Today's Action | Follow up on any healings that are beginning to take form in your heart and in your life. Take the next step toward forgiving, bringing others together, or mending fences. Finish any unfinished business.

Nick Of Time

As soon as you trust yourself, you will know how to live. —Wolfgang von Goethe

This takes me back to a decision I made almost two-and-a-half years ago to simplify my life. Creating more space in my life was necessary for me to find the energy to *truly* live my bliss.

Although many people did not understand when I asked them not call or told them I'd be unavailable for the next few months, that I was taking some time off to refill the well, I trusted my inner yearnings and did it anyway.

If there is a part of you right now that says, "I wish I could do what Debbie did. I wish I could shut the world off and renew my spirit," rethink it. What if it meant life or death?

Seriously, what if you were told that unless you made drastic changes in your life, you would die an untimely death? Would you turn the phone off then? Would you set boundaries then?

For me, it seemed like a life-or-death decision. I could either go on as I had, living a stressful, fairly happy, but inauthentic life. Or I could begin a new way of life, a way that stretches and challenges me. I could begin living a life that I *love* waking up to every morning, a life where there is time for simple pleasures like morning walks on the beach.

A life where it's not unheard of to take an evening off just for me, to soak in the tub or curl up with a good book, a life where my body is not rebelling against my lifestyle. Can I live a life where I give to others from an overflowing cup, not a parched, empty cup, a life where my cup runneth over because I'm *selfish* enough to fill it first?

Can you imagine a life filled with peace, bliss, and joy beyond measure?

348

Today's Action | Take a close look at your life. Go inward and ask, "What changes do I need to make to begin living more authentically, the way God intended?" Flesh out the areas of your life that are still unsettling. Have the courage to make the necessary changes. Trust yourself.

Abraham, Martin, And John

Everyone can be great because anyone can serve.—Martin Luther King, Jr.

I write because I *love* to write, and because I want to help others. I once thought I wanted to write because of the easy hours, the money, the recognition, and the immortality of having my words in print. As it turns out, I put in longer hours writing than I ever did on any job.

When I could have signed off on "Dharma" and didn't, I learned what was truly important to me: writing from the heart. It wasn't about the money or having my fifteen minutes of fame.

If one story, one page in this book, helps one person walk through a fear, follow a dream, heal a wound, or make peace with an enemy, my job is done. If these stories bring one person closer to God—or instill the courage necessary to trust their intuition and follow their heart, I will be at peace.

This is my intention and it's more important than earning a living as a writer or having my name recognized any day. I don't say these things so you can say, "How noble." I say them because it's what's in my heart.

We are on this planet to learn lessons, grow spiritually, and help others do the same. Any one of us can make a difference.

It may show up in the form of peanut butter and jelly sandwiches, or a painting that moves someone to tears, or finding a cure for cancer, or smiling at a stranger who has lost faith in human kindness. The specifics don't matter, so long as we live joyfully and make a contribution in our little corner of the world.

Today's Action | Be that smile, hug, kiss, or sustenance for another soul today. Place your thoughts, words, and actions in God's hands. Allow God to use you. Open . . . Receive . . . Then give back.

Take It Easy

Backsliding.

I must fill the well *before* I can give to others.

Between the public-speaking course, the workshop I lead, sponsoring women, and helping others that call me—I am overextended, one more time.

I love working with others, whether it's relationship addiction, alcohol or drug addiction, cancer, self-esteem, or writing—if someone needs help—I'm there.

I love my open, giving spirit. It's a wonderful thing, and I wouldn't change it for the world. However, two things came up this morning. First, I woke up in pain. My neck and shoulders have that old familiar pain that comes from stress and being on the phone too much. Second, I was too tired to get up early and write.

I'm so in tune to my physical body that I can tell immediately when something is off-kilter. It's not so much pain as tension. There's tightness in my neck and shoulders, my jaw, and upper back that occurs whenever I'm doing too much.

Then I had this sinking feeling, "Oh, my God, I'm putting everyone else before my dreams again."

I got scared that I might be sabotaging my dreams, so I decided to be late for work and write anyway.

Still, the fact that I no longer *want* to get up at five or six in the morning to write scared me enough to get me on my knees. I asked God for clarity and direction. I asked God to help me set boundaries and give me strength to say "No."

There are only two more weeks of school, so things will get better soon. But it's time to let others know I'll be going inward for a while. It's time to get quiet and replenish my spirit again.

I guess the lesson is that we can fall back into our old ways at any time. But if we always do what we always did, we'll always get what we always got. For me, that was stressed-out, with no time for myself, which led to major health problems.

I've heard it said that people with cancer, particularly breast cancer, have trouble saying "No."

Today, I say yes to life and no to stress and overdoing it.

☼ Today's Action | What is your body telling you? Are you listening? Are you still taking time for yourself? Or are you backsliding?

What is your energy level? Maybe it's time to recharge your batteries.

Spend some time today in quiet reflection. Check in and see if you are remaining true to your highest vision for yourself.

Just My Imagination

The editors of *Chicken Soup for the Soul* just called about including "Dharma" in one of their upcoming books. I heard the message on my answer machine last night and nearly died. They've narrowed it down to 200 stories and "Dharma" is one of them.

It's so affirming that people like my work and are moved enough to call me about it. There's nothing like it to keep me going.

Also, a recovery magazine I usually write for wanted an article on "The Lord's Prayer"—whether it's a spiritual or religious prayer. I wrote out my thoughts and sent in my article.

It's astonishing, the speed with which the Universe responds when you put your intentions out there and continue working toward them. Here I am, months later, writing day and night and loving it. You know you're on the right path when there's nothing else in the world you'd rather be doing.

Living your dreams, *letting your heart sing*, is so unbelievably exciting. I've been in accounting for over twenty years and actually enjoy crunching numbers and working on computers. But let's face it, it doesn't come close to living the dream that's been in my heart since I was in seventh grade when I wrote my first short story about losing my grandmother.

This is what I was created for. *This* is my dharma. And to think I owe it all to a very special little kitten of the same name, and cancer. The fact that someday, I might earn a living doing this, well, that's just unimaginable right now. To do something I don't just like, but *love*, would truly be a dream come true.

Four years ago, I didn't think I had the discipline to finish a book, even if I did start it. And then to actually *do* anything with it—never!

My self-esteem wouldn't even allow the thought of me earning a living as a writer to even form. God, forbid I claim it and live it! I can't tell you the amount of courage it took to start. Be prepared, because once you open the door to your heart—to that very special dream that lies in your heart—amazing coincidences begin to occur, and you can never, ever go back to the way things were.

The Universe is responding to my bliss with a resounding, "Yes!" and it is beyond my wildest dreams—*and I'm not even published yet!* I'm just living in that expansive place called *possibilities.*

Today's Action | How has the Universe responded to you putting yourself out there? Is there a quiet excitement building inside of you? There should be, because you are well on your way.

Think back over the last few months at how much courage it took for you to stretch yourself, walk through fears, heal wounds, try new things, set goals for yourself, and begin working toward them.

Share your excitement with your cheerleaders as things bump into high gear during this very exciting time.

Today, revel in the person you are becoming and the new paths that have opened up as a result.

Don't Stop Believing

A stonecutter may strike a rock ninety-nine times with no apparent effect, not even a crack on the surface. Yet with the hundredth blow, the rock splits in two. It was not the final blow that did the trick, but all that had gone before.

We have spent many months stretching ourselves by walking through fears, gaining courage by affirming the positive, healing relationships, nurturing ourselves, and visualizing the possible. By now, some of your dreams are materializing.

Sometimes, our highest vision for ourselves catapults us faster than we could ever imagine. Often, though, it is a long, slow, arduous path, with many hills and valleys along the way. The trick is not to get discouraged.

Creating a *Bliss Chart*, based on what surfaced during your visualizations and journaling crystallizes your dream and keeps you from getting discouraged.

Take a large poster board and with colored markers, draw a grid of six two-inch-high horizontal timelines.

The first four timelines represent the next year in three-month increments. The fifth timeline represents the second and third years, and the sixth line is the fourth and fifth years. This chart gives an overview of the goals you want to accomplish over the next five years. The purpose of the *Bliss Chart* is not only to clarify your goals, but also to mark your progress.

Seeing progress is not always easy. Many times, we work for months or years before any results are visible. Marking your accomplishments on the chart gives you the encouragement you need to continue on the path, regardless of the delays or obstacles encountered.

If your goals change or unexpected twists take you in new and exciting directions, you can always make adjustments, incorporating the new direction into your *Bliss Chart*. The point is to have a visual reference of your dreams.

Within a few days of visualizing my goals, two dreams came true: I sang karaoke the day after I wrote about wanting to sing in front of people and four days after I wrote about wanting to earn a living as a writer, I received my first check as payment for one of my stories. A third dream came true days later when the *Chicken Soup for the Soul* people called to tell me they were considering "Dharma" for publication.

The energy and excitement surrounding my writing is awesome. I actually believe success is possible—even for me.

353

Today's Action	With a poster board and colored markers, design your own *Bliss Chart* based on your dreams, visions, and goals. Flesh out the steps necessary to achieve your goals and anticipated time frames for them.

Amazing Journey

The next step is to take your *Bliss Chart* and fill in the blanks. Determine what steps are necessary to take you to your desired goal by the desired date. Start with the furthest goal, and determine how many months it will take you to reach it based on how much time you plan to devote to this goal during an average week. Mark it on the chart.

Refer back to the journaling you did while visualizing for a general idea of the time frame. Do this with every dream or goal you've fleshed out up to this point. Determine what it will take to get you from point A to point B, a reasonable time frame, and then mark it down. Again, course-correcting is always an option because nothing is written in stone.

Once I realized this book was going to be in the format of a story a day, I knew my goal was 366 stories. I was writing about two hours a day. After a few weeks of doing that, I found I was writing an average of four stories a day. Since I usually wrote five days a week, that was about eighty stories a month. It would take about four to five months to complete the rough draft at that pace. I marked a date on my chart, four months from the day I started, as the date by which I wanted to complete my rough draft.

Since this was just the rough draft, I didn't worry about spelling, punctuation, or grammar. I just showed up on the page every day, ready to write, trusting everything could be organized and polished later.

Some things will happen way ahead of the date you mark on your *Bliss Chart*; others will take longer than anticipated. The most important thing is to have a vision, be committed to taking steps towards it, and flexible as to how it unfolds.

With previous projects I focused on the main goal without giving much thought to the steps necessary to achieve it. Without a clear plan of action, the project usually fizzled before it got off the ground.

With this project I set goals that are a challenge to meet, but because I've also laid out the necessary steps, I get a sense of accomplishment every time I mark one off. This keeps me on track and keeps the dream alive.

At the same time, I keep balanced physically, mentally, and spiritually as I work toward these goals. This ensures I live blissfully in the present moment, not just waiting for some future moment to be happy.

It isn't just about finishing a book. Enjoying each day, living fully, and loving deeply is as important as any tangible goal. Letting your heart sing is as much about inner peace as it is achieving any one dream. Blending the two is what makes the journey worthwhile.

Right livelihood is called so because you are at peace *while* making your contribution.

Today's Action | Align your outer goals with your inner desires. Set them on paper as you envision your future. Fill in details and dates as they come to you. Leave plenty of room for the unexpected. Remember, you can always course-correct as you grow into your vision.

Be Still And Know

If we really enter into genuine solitude, we enter into the center of our being and connect with every other creature in the world.—Father William McNamara

Just as there's a time for high energy and excitement, there's a time for drawing inward.

Taking time for one's self is often thought of as *isolating*. We get shamed for wanting to be alone, when often it is the very thing we need to nourish our soul.

Constant activity and people are not necessary for us to feel alive. I have felt most intensely alive when I am in deep contemplation or meditation.

We need to balance our enthusiastic energy, with our quiet, centered energy. The best way to achieve this delicate balance is by taking time daily for prayer and meditation, and by spending time with nature.

By drawing inward, we retain the energy and focus required for achieving our long-range goals and dreams.

In the stillness, we reconnect with God.

From this quiet, centered place we can *be still and know*.

355

Today's Action | By now, we know what quiets our soul and refreshes our spirit.
Today, spend some time gaining that broader perspective of and deeper connection with life.

Be still and know.

Heartlight

Writing this book would not be possible without a deep commitment to my inner journey. Connecting with God renews my spirit and gives me the strength and energy I need to fulfill my dreams. It also increases the amount of love, joy, and peace in my life.

One way to do this is by connecting with your heart center, the point in your body that is your spiritual heart. When I am in touch with my heart center I am filled with love and able to see the good in everyone.

Close your eyes, take a few deep breaths, then take your right index finger and press the area around your heart. You will know when you locate your heart center because it feels different. It feels open and expansive.

Touching your heart center increases your awareness of the love and power that reside within you. The best thing about this is that it can be done anywhere at anytime—in the midst of an argument, in a traffic jam, when setting a boundary, or even when taking a step out of your comfort zone.

There are many spiritual centers and energy points within the body such as the third eye (our spiritual wisdom) or the solar plexus (our gut). The heart center is where we *feel* our connection with God and others. When we tap into this point, we feel *pure love*. We *feel* God.

The heart center is our spiritual center—our God consciousness. Different religions have different names for it, like the Christ within, the Buddha Self, or the Holy Spirit. What we call it doesn't matter so long as we tap into it, and begin, more and more, to come from this place in our interactions with others.

As you go through your day, touch this point often. Feel your heart expand. Your heart center knows no boundaries. It is all-inclusive. Bring your awareness of your heart center to the forefront by touching it every time another human being crosses your path.

Connect with this point physically, mentally, and spiritually. The love you feel will radiate outward, encompassing all.

Each person has this center. The only thing that differs is our awareness of it and our ability to tap into it. Some of us have constructed ornate castles with motes surrounding our heart center, preventing entrance into the sacred sanctuary within.

Over time, this requires much energy. Tapping into our heart center allows us to pull down our walls, let the drawbridge out, and give open access to everyone.

Experience life through your heart center, blessing everyone whose path crosses yours today.

If you get caught up in the day and forget to touch your heart center, that's fine. When you remember, gently touch your heart center, open up again, and let love flow.

God Loves You

Another way to increase your awareness of your heart center is to mentally say to everyone you see, "God loves you and God loves me." This is an ever-so-gentle reminder that we are all one—no one better, no one less. In God's eyes we are all equal. God resides in each of us to the same degree. Some of us just have thicker walls, so it's harder to see the God within.

When Gary first learned to drive at the age of thirty-four, he thought he was the only one who knew how to drive and constantly muttered to himself about everyone else's driving. It didn't take him long to realize that if you spend an hour or two a day inwardly cursing your fellow man, you are spiritually at war with everyone. There is no room for God in your life when you're in that space.

One day it occurred to Gary, that although his outward behavior had changed, and he didn't act on these thoughts anymore, he was not at peace. He began saying, "God loves you and God loves me," to each person who didn't drive the way he thought they should, affirming that they were all God's children.

Within a few short weeks, everyone drove perfectly. Gary says one of two things could have happened: either everyone learned how to drive correctly and began doing so, or God changed Gary's vision, so that he *saw* everyone was driving exactly as they were supposed to, given where they were in their lives at that moment.

If God loves you and God loves me, the playing field is leveled and we are equal. There is no need for competition or getting ahead of someone.

My experience of life, while in traffic, has always been a good measure of my daily spiritual condition, and I must admit, Gary exemplifies this spirit of love on the road, better than I can ever hope to. And not just on the road. Gary practices this spirit of brotherly love in all areas of his life. And I live with him, so I know.

I work at it and get better a day at a time, but Gary has reached a place of perfect peace and acceptance of all people and circumstances. For me, it's a process. I usually arrive at the same place Gary does. I just take the scenic route, and arrive a little later.

Gary doesn't need to work at it. He *is* love. He's my example of what's attainable. Each day I try to let go into love a little more. I guess I'll have to be satisfied with progress, not perfection.

Spirit In The Sky

A very dear friend of mine, Harlon, died yesterday. He was eighty-seven years old and had seventeen years of sobriety. Imagine that: he thought enough of himself at age seventy to get sober. After a full life as a World War II fighter pilot and a commercial airline pilot for over twenty years, Harlon became an alcoholic when he retired in his early sixties.

After a few years, it became obvious he needed help, and he sought it. He didn't think he was too old to bother. He didn't think he couldn't. He didn't think he wasn't worth it. He went for it and succeeded.

One of his favorite stories was that he didn't know how to pray, so he just asked God for whatever help he needed, always ending each prayer with . . . *but only if it is Your will.* What a humble way to pray.

Being a very private man, Harlon didn't allow many people to visit him in the nursing home he'd called home since he broke his hip four years ago. In fact, it wasn't until after he heard I had had cancer that he allowed me to visit him.

I began visiting Harlon three years ago with a friend of mine, Cindy. We both thought the world of Harlon and always came bearing gifts—balloons, flowers, and chocolates—always chocolates. Oh, how Harlon loved his chocolates. The three of us would sit in his room eating chocolates until the nurses scolded us, saying they would ruin his teeth. Cindy and I figured he didn't have too many years left, so what are a few rotten teeth, in the face of such great pleasure?

The thing that saddens me most about Harlon is that although he had no family, many people cared about him, but he wouldn't let any of them call or visit him. He declined their offers, saying, "I don't want to be a bother."

I also think he didn't want people to see him helpless and in a wheelchair. He wanted to be remembered as the healthy, robust, at times cantankerous, man he used to be. Far from pitying him, though, seeing him so vulnerable just made me feel honored to be allowed into his private sanctuary, honored to bring him joy in his final days.

Although I am sad and will miss him, I am glad he is no longer bound to his wheelchair and bed, suffering. He's back flying among the clouds—piloting the skies—soaring free.

Today's Action | No matter your age, remember you are never too old for anything! Especially love. Don't ever be afraid to let love in. List ten things that bring you joy and ten ways you can let more love in.

Hand Of The Higher Power

I can't tell you for a fact why we're here, but I think it's to become more like God and to joyously celebrate life—and to help others do the same.

Each day, I seek to become more God-like, quieter inside, more loving outside. Some days I fare better than others, but my heart is always the same—I want to be the person God intended me to be. On a good day, I *know* I am that person. I may not have been perfect that day—but I am able to recognize my God essence.

That is a good day. Not the perfection—the noticing. I am *perfectly* imperfect—a flawless child of God. In God's eyes we are all perfect. And that's enough.

I wake up each day, ready to do my best. That's all that is asked. To do no harm is good. To do some small act of kindness is also good. When I help another person on their journey, my heart is full.

That's how I see myself: God's little helper. I am blessed with the desire to be of service. What a wonderful way to live. I've come a long way from the angry girl who hid in the shadows to avoid holding an elevator if I was in a hurry.

Finally, I am able to be of service, not out of unworthiness, or trying to earn God's love—but because my heart is full and I want to share it.

I have learned to take care of myself first—to fill the well—and *then* give to others from the overflow. It no longer feels selfish to say, "I'm sorry, but my plate is full." It's okay. It's the right thing to do. There is a time to honor myself and say no, and a time to give freely. Today, I know what time it is.

Whether I help someone find their dream, give encouragement as they follow it, or help them remove blocks—it's all helping them become more God-like. And as I strive to be the person God intended, I am a living example of what's possible for the next person.

Since I began this journey of finding and following my bliss, I've assisted hundreds of others to do the same. The hand of the Higher Power is everywhere: Changed lives *change lives.*

It's an awesome thing to behold—this huge snowball, gaining momentum, spreading ever outward. Our journeys are like snowflakes—falling ever so gently into a snowy white blanket, our uniqueness blending into Oneness. The great One we all came from and return to.

360

Today's Action | Now that you've made headway toward your dreams, let your life be an example of what is possible for others. Encourage others. Keep your eyes open for opportunities to be a *Bliss Mentor.*

Imagine

The snowflake called Gary has had the most profound impact on my life—mostly because of his commitment to serving others.

In June 1991, after being laid off from work, Gary came home one afternoon, head held high and a spark in his eye, "They are building homes in Liberty City (Miami's Harlem), and I want to be part of it."

I thought: *Great, a long-term project—maybe he won't have to file for unemployment benefits after all.*

Then Gary went on to say, "Habitat for Humanity is looking for volunteers to help them build homes for those in need."

"Volunteers? Honey, don't you think you should concentrate on getting a *paying* job and do something like this when we can afford to?" I asked, alarmed at the thought of another week with only one paycheck coming in.

Gary looked at me squarely, his eyes pleading, "I don't know why, but I really *need* to do this."

Though I didn't agree or understand, I gave in, thinking, *Maybe he will make some contacts in the construction industry. Maybe some good will come of this after all.*

During the Habitat Blitz Build of 1991, Gary worked harder than he ever had worked in his life. He left the house at six every morning and did not get home until after ten at night.

I could not fathom why anyone would push himself this hard—*and for no money!* We were hugely in debt and did not even own a home ourselves, and here Gary was, building a house for someone we did not even know.

If you are not familiar with a Jimmy Carter Work Project, also known as a Habitat Blitz Build, volunteers build homes, from start to finish, *in one week.* Each site consists of ten or more homes, and approximately thirty people work on each house. Building supply stores donate materials, local banks arrange interest-free mortgages, and volunteers work side by side with the homeowners as the homeowners put in hundreds of "sweat equity" hours in labor.

A typical JCWP starts on Monday morning with a slab of concrete, a pile of wood, and a family in need of a home. By Friday evening, that family is moving into the home they helped build.

Gary invited me to the dedication that Friday. In that little auditorium, as the families accepted the keys to their very first home, I finally understood what drew Gary to do this.

Gary had been volunteering at the local homeless shelter for the last two-and-a-half years to help the drug addicts get off drugs, and already knew what I was just learning, "The way out of self-pity is to help someone worse off than yourself. And the way to *avoid* self-pity is to always be helping someone worse off than yourself."

Sometimes, when you cannot see daylight, you take a step forward in faith—and just trust. You trust that if you do the right thing, good will come of it—not always in the way you expect, but good *will* come. Gary never made any construction contacts that week; most everyone was an inexperienced volunteer or from out of town. But he grew as a person. He grew in ways I could not have imagined: in self-esteem, self-respect, confidence, and as a man. He grew spiritually and so did I—just witnessing his growth. He grew in wealth far more than *any* paycheck could have given him.

Here was this homeless junkie from Boston, building homes for people in need, working late into the evening, side by side with an ex-president of the United States, just to make sure they finished the house on time.

Gary still cannot talk about this experience without getting choked up. It is right up there with the day *hope* came into his life.

It is the day he realized *gratitude is an action word.*

> ☼ *Today's Action* | Express your gratitude by doing something kind for someone else, expecting no reward. Your effort can be large or small; with soft eyes and an open heart, look around and see where *you* are needed.

Love Is All Around

Hard work and serving others seems to come naturally to Gary. Me, I'm a different breed altogether. It's not that I'm selfish; it's just that my idea of roughing it is a Holiday Inn.

Coming from two different worlds, Gary and I have been an interesting meld, to say the least.

Physically working until you are sore from head to toe is not my idea of a vacation. So when Gary told me he wanted to use our vacation to drive to Washington, D.C., for another Habitat for Humanity Blitz Build the following June, to say I balked is putting it mildly.

But by the look in his eyes, I could tell it meant a lot to him, so I agreed. If the summer of 1996 was my most carefree summer, the week of June 12, 1992, felt like the most grueling summer of my life, even though it was only a week long.

Up at five every morning, working to the point of exhaustion for twelve hours in the hot sun, before arriving back at the dorms covered with dirt, paint, sawdust, and tar, to stand in line for our dinner was no picnic.

But a Habitat construction site is like no other job site in the world. The love in the air is so thick it's almost palatable. You see it in people's eyes—volunteer and homeowner alike. You feel it in every hammer swing. You smell it in the sawdust and paint.

Not accustomed to this type of work, I got blisters on just about every square inch of my body. Since I wasn't scared of heights and had a good eye, I was assigned to roofing. Grown men would see me up there and come up to the roof thinking, *If she can do this so can I,* only to be sent back down after we had to rip up the shingles they laid and start over.

By the end of the week, I couldn't even hold a hammer, in either hand, much less use it. All the while I'm thinking, *These people are nuts! Why would anyone give up their well-deserved vacation for this?* But I must admit it was more challenging and rewarding than the office work I normally do. And it sure came in handy a couple of months later when Hurricane Andrew hit South Florida, and they needed volunteers to repair roofs.

Even though I go grudgingly, Habitat Blitz weeks have come to hold a special place in my heart. My absolute favorite one, was in June 1997 when we drove to Pikesville, Kentucky, high up in the Appalachian Mountains for Habitat's "Hammering in the Hills." We built a home for Paul and Maxine Williams, two of the nicest people you'd ever want to meet, and their daughter, Delesa, and her two sons, Jeremiah and MacKody.

We met the Williams family on the eve of the Blitz Build, and they were so excited about working on and moving into a brand new home that it was contagious. I actually found myself looking forward to the work. Luckily I was assigned to painting instead of roofing this time, so I had an easier go of it.

Something else happened on this Blitz Build that made it different from all the others—I bonded with the homeowners.

Delesa must be about ten years younger than I am—but meeting her was like finding a long-lost sister. Side by side, we painted their entire house. By the end of the week, I felt so close to Delesa that I shared Dharma's story with her and her family.

They were so touched by it that they wanted a picture taken of all of us standing in front of their newly finished house, with Delesa holding up my little hand-typed story. Gary and I signed our names on the inside of their storage shed, and wrote that they would always have a little angel looking over them. Although we vowed to keep in touch, it was very hard to leave.

Now I *really* "got" it. Selfless service is about giving to another as if they were your own "kin"—because they are—you just don't always realize it.

Right now I feel blessed to be physically *able* to contribute. It wasn't that long ago that I couldn't even walk two blocks without getting tired. Ever so grateful to be alive, my gratitude speaks when I share my bounty with others. Thank you, God, for my life and my ability to serve.

☼ Today's Action | What organizations are close to your heart? Combine your resources with others and find a way to make a difference in your community.

Let It Flow

Today, I join in the flow of life, and say yes to everything. I won't resist a thing. I open and let go of control. If Gary doesn't take out the garbage, I will do it without comment. If I have dealings with a difficult person, I will see their point of view, just for today. If plans suddenly turn upside-down, I will accept last-minute changes gracefully.

364

Today, I won't complain about a thing. I will see that everything is perfect exactly as it is. I will experience life exactly as it is, not wishing anything were different. If someone asks me to do something, I will embrace the opportunity—whatever it is. I will trust God wants me to do whatever is asked of me.

I will not try to control, change, or improve anyone or anything.

As I write this, I think of all the exceptions—all the circumstances I won't, can't, or don't want to *go with the flow.*

Still, I affirm I will experience this one day like this.

I may have to stretch a little to do so, but stretch I will. I may not like everything as it's unfolding, but I will practice complete acceptance and go with the flow of life, for one day.

Today, I will be with the day—exactly as it is.

☼ Today's Action | Go *with* the flow.

On The Road Again

Yesterday, my law firm announced that the senior partners are going their separate ways, and the firm will close its doors in two months.

I am in shock. Ten years . . .

When I put on my *Bliss Chart* that I did not want to be working at this same job in three years, I meant I would be ready to leave in *three years*, not now!

I guess God has other plans.

But, I have bills to pay! Doesn't God understand that I *need* this salary to meet my obligations?

What about Hawaii? I have been planning that trip for nearly twenty years. We traded our timeshare, cashed in our frequent flyer miles, are finally ready to go, and *I don't have a job*! The last thing I wanted to do is go to Hawaii on a budget. I probably shouldn't go at all under the circumstances.

What am I crazy—give up Hawaii? No way! I have wanted this for too long; I think I would rather lose my car. Why couldn't this have happened after I finished my car payments? Things are so tight right now financially. I'm going to be hard-pressed to walk into a new law firm and earn anywhere close to the salary and benefits I've worked up to after ten years on the same job.

How can I be unemployed and run off to Hawaii?

Not going is *not* an option! It was my first regret when I thought I was going to die—I am not giving it up.

That is it—we are going! I *will* see my friend Pixie and make amends to her. I *will* write sitting by a waterfall.

Heck, maybe I'll take my résumé and a suit with me to Hawaii and go on interviews. I always did want to live there. Maybe this is the opportunity I've been waiting for. Do they even wear suits in Hawaii? Do I even want a suit job anymore? Maybe I'll change careers and take up surfing!

Oh my God . . . oh my God . . . oh my God.

I am so scared!

Fear, elation, joy, excitement—FREEDOM!

Emotions are rushing at me. My life feels wide open. This is great!

Maybe we will sell the house and hit the road. I have always wanted to see the U.S.A. in my Chevrolet (Toyota in my case).

We are in our forties—we can't retire yet. I am not a very good waitress—what kind of short-term jobs could I get on the road? Maybe I could write and Gary could do carpentry work and we could travel from city to city seeing all the national parks?

We might have to sell the Harley. Oh, no—not the Harley!

What to do, what to do.

Isn't it ironic that I just wrote about going with the flow yesterday? I guess the Universe is responding big time to my wanting out of this job. It is just so soon. I am glad I did that *Intuition Workout* and got my résumé together.

I feel as if I am standing on a ledge . . . ready to jump off . . . into the unknown. But I am not ready! I am being pushed—pushed off the ledge! I am falling . . . I am falling . . .

But no, I did not fall—I am flying.

I am soaring!

366

 Today's Action | How would you feel if this happened to you? What would you do? Flesh it out—because those are your dreams. Follow them.

The Morning After

I am still reeling. I woke up this morning wondering if it was true. By the way Gary looked at me, I could tell—it was.

My mind is racing. It is still very early and the day has yet to awaken—much like me. The possibilities stretch out endlessly before me. *So does the fear.*

It is going to be important to stay in the moment if I am to maintain some semblance of sanity.

Yesterday, I may have lost my job—but what is happening in this moment? Am I hungry? No. Do I have shelter from the storm? Yes. Do I have two nickels to rub together? Of course I do. In this moment all my needs are met.

I just took a break and enjoyed a nice long walk on the beach. The sun is rising. The day is unfolding much like any other day—yet this day will be different from any that have gone before.

As I write this, in this moment, I am at my sacred place, my centering place: the beach. There is a gentle breeze blowing against my back as the sun warms me. The crickets are chirping, loudly I might add, almost as if they want to be included in my writing. They want to be heard—noticed—and they are. Now, they can delight in the fact that they live on, not only in the moment, but also in the moment captured on this page.

But it was just a moment in time. Now it is gone.

A father and his daughter walk by. She is about two years old and is trying to take her shoes off so she won't get sand in them. She sits down in the sand and tries to master the buckle on her shoe. Some people with an English accent join them. The group is standing nearby talking loudly. Normally, they would disturb my writing. Today, I just brought them into it.

Seeing little girls and their fathers together no longer makes me sad. Now, I know that every father who is a good father to his daughter is helping my father and me to heal spiritually.

Just last week I heard a former drug addict share with pride how the daughter who once would not even speak to him now wants him to walk her down the aisle at her upcoming wedding. Instead of feeling self-pity or jealousy, I was so happy this girl had the father I had always wanted. The healing taking place between them touched me deeply. And I realized once more, that when one father-daughter relationship heals, all fathers and daughters heal.

How loving to embrace what is going on around me. So much more peaceful than wishing it was different.

The crickets, having been heard, stop their continuous chatter. The English tourists move on and I can hear the ocean once more. Either way, I am happy. Did you really mind my writing about the crickets and fathers and daughters, as opposed to lapping waves?

Crickets, or no crickets; tourists, or no tourists; job, or no job; I am reminded to go with the flow and be in the moment.

In this moment, I can be grateful even in the face of great change or loss. I have so much more than most. All of my needs are met.

You can have a sad experience, but it does not have to be your *only* experience. You can also have some pretty wondrous moments. Like this one.

☼ Today's Action | Embrace the moment—whatever it holds.

Every Breath You Take

Once more I am reminded, *God gave me life, that I might enjoy all things.*

Air—the very breath of life. God is in each breath we take. With each intake of air, we breathe in the life force that comes from God. Breathe in God. Breathe out God. We need God's breath, just as the plants need our breath.

Wouldn't it be a kick if we were only here to be the Life Force that plants need? We think we have all these lessons to learn, experiences to experience, possessions to possess, and people to love. What if we are just a good source of carbon dioxide for plants?

I digress. It was just a thought. Back to breathing in God.

Today, be aware of the Divine with each breath you take. Know that this is the breath of Life. It is God. God is in the breath. God is in us—reconnecting us with the entire Universe with every breath we take. God is with us as naturally as we breathe—without our even thinking about it. We can reconnect with God as easily as breathing the next breath.

Every hour, every five minutes, every minute, and every second—whenever you take a conscious breath—think of God. Think of Source. Life Force. It doesn't matter what you call it. Whatever source or energy force we came from—we all go back to, with only our heart centers living on forever.

Our bodies will cease to exist, as will our personalities, but our very essence will live on forever. The difference we've made in the world is already apparent even if we can't see it. If we are parents, that, in and of itself, is an awesome contribution. If, like me, we are not, we find other ways to say, "I was here. I mattered."

And then we slip away. Do not despair. What we counted for will always be unfolding. The endless ripple. We can't begin to trace the moment from whence we came. It is too far back—back to the beginning of time. Even if we trace our roots, there is always further to trace. So it will be, after we are gone.

Two thousand years from now, the world will be different because we have lived, but it is unlikely it will be traced to us. No matter, only the ego wants accolades.

Our essence is happy just knowing we made a difference. Breathe in God and know that. Be that.

And yes, I'm still scared.

 Today's Action | With every breath you take, know that you are of God. You matter. God has a special purpose for you. Breathe it in. Then let go into the breath.

Kindness

Kindness is one of the most incredible ways we can honor God. Kind acts are a way of saying, "Thank you. Thank you for my life. Thank you for all you have given me over the years. I am grateful for all I have and I want to share it with others."

Loving acts expand love. They can be as simple as a smile or as magnanimous as giving of our time and money.

Whenever self-pity or despair come our way, we can shift our feelings by shifting our actions. There is a spiritual saying, "When all hope is gone, we throw ourselves even further into helping others."

I took Winky, my one-eyed wonder kitty, to the veterinarian's office today. She was peeing everywhere, and I thought she probably had a urinary tract infection. As we waited to see the vet, a woman rushed in with a kitten and two small children in tow. The tiny gray kitten had gotten its head caught in a chair the little boy had been playing on and was unconscious.

Everyone was upset as they waited to hear how the kitten was. When the vet came out, she explained that the kitten had swelling on its brain and they would have to keep it under observation for a few days, give it oxygen, and try to keep the swelling down. At this point, they didn't know if the kitten was going to make it.

Then they gave the mother an estimate of the charges—three hundred and fifty dollars—and said that because they had never seen her before, they would need a deposit before continuing with any further treatment.

The woman explained she had no money and didn't get paid until Thursday, but that she could bring some money then. They said the head veterinarian was out of town, and their policies were strict when they didn't know the person, but that they would call other clinics and see if any other clinics could take the kitten.

By now, the mother was visibly upset, "I can't believe you'd turn me away with an unconscious kitten—just because I don't have any money! Where's your heart?" They suggested she call someone to borrow the money. She told them there was no one she could call. They said on a bill that size they would need at least a hundred dollars in order to keep the kitten. The young mother lashed out at her son, "See what happens when you play on the furniture when I told you not to?" At that point he started crying. She immediately told him she was sorry, but that she just didn't know what to do.

One of the assistants had been calling other animal clinics and the Humane Society trying to get treatment for the kitten elsewhere, but was told the funds they normally have for treating indigent animals were depleted.

After fifteen minutes of watching this situation go from bad to worse, I quietly went to the counter and asked if $50.00 would be enough of a deposit for them to keep the kitten. The mother overheard me and said, "I can't let you do that. I don't even know you."

I explained to her that I normally donate to the Humane Society and if their funds weren't depleted and she took her kitten there, she would have been accepting my donation anyway. I further explained I would much rather help someone right in front of me than send a check somewhere else—not knowing how it would be used. I told her nothing would please me more than her allowing me to put my money to good use.

She thanked me profusely and I wrote out a check for $50.00 and left my little Winky to have her tests.

When I called later, the vet's assistant told me that my act of generosity spurred others to do the same and they now had a little fund going that was going to help pay for the kitten's medical bills.

Normally I cringe at bringing my own cats to the vet's because its so expensive these days, but didn't hesitate for one minute when it came to giving freely from my heart. It was the right thing to do—especially considering the financial fear I was in.

Later, when I picked up Winky, I stopped in to see the little kitten that was still unconscious in the little oxygen chamber. It was a tiny pale gray kitten with some Siamese markings. I hope it is going to be okay.

I left with my eyes welled up with tears, but my heart overflowing, too.

Today's Action | Practice small acts of kindness today. A smile, a thank-you note, some flowers, an hour of your time—any kind act from the heart, will do. Reconnect with what is truly important by making another soul's journey just a little easier.

Walking On Sunshine

Søren Kierkegaard, one of the greatest philosophers of all time, once said: *"Above all, do not lose your desire to walk."*

Walking is one of the simplest ways we can reconnect with our Creator, ourselves, and the world around us. Yet most of us walk only if we have to or for exercise.

What about walking just to walk? There's nothing like experiencing the elements firsthand: the sun beaming down on your face, the snow swirling around you, the wind caressing your hair, or the rain pelting your skin, to remind you of your aliveness.

I've been physically active most of my life, starting when I joined a health club at the age of sixteen, began teaching yoga there at seventeen, and became manager by the time I was twenty-one. I remained a member for years afterwards, until my busy schedule pushed me into working out at home. After watching the various videos and workout contraptions collect dust, I had to rethink my exercise plan.

I found I feel healthiest when I am outdoors—walking, running, bike riding, swimming, or playing golf. Lately however, writing seems to take up all my spare time and I don't keep as physically active as I would like. But, tomorrow I'll . . .

Thud! A *huge* foot-long, chartreuse green lizard dropped from a tree, just missing my foot, before scurrying up a burgundy Croton bush.

No, that didn't happen in my house next to the computer. As soon as I saw myself writing about what I was going to do tomorrow . . . I got up, mid-sentence—and went for a walk. If cancer taught me anything, it's to stop putting things off. Today is the day.

That lizard was just too cool! And I would have missed it if I had stayed indoors typing that next line.

I vow, right here and now, to walk outdoors for at least twenty minutes a day—three times a week. This will help clear my head while I figure out what my next move is to be.

And I certainly need clarity, right about now.

 Today's Action | If you've gotten away from outdoor activity, reconnect with your spirit, by including a brief ten- or twenty-minute walk in your day.

Show Me The Way

Part of me longs for the simplicity and quiet of yesteryear. Things were so much easier when I was a child—no job, no bills to pay, no responsibilities, no one to care for, and no balancing act to try and fit it all in.

The appeal of selling everything and running off to Hawaii or somewhere is the shedding of my skin, my responsibilities. But would I just find more, elsewhere?

Would I miss my family and friends? Am I running away? Why can't I find it in myself to just go get another accounting job? I haven't lifted a finger toward finding another job in my field. Yet, financially, I'm not able to just walk away and write for a living.

What else would I want to do to tide me over? I have no idea. I just can't seem to make myself want to go back to the same old grind of crunching numbers. A girl's got to make a living—yet my soul longs to write.

It's all I want to do. Everything else pales in comparison.

So there's my answer. If my bliss and God's will are one and the same—how do I move toward it?

I know at some point, I am going to have to step out in faith—but when? How?

I need to get quiet in order to tap into Higher Wisdom.

I know. I'll spend the weekend at my mother's while she is out of town. Silence and solitude ought to do me good. No telephones. No TV. No "You've Got Mail," just God and me.

I'll create my own little silent retreat—no plans, no rules, no expectations—simply rest and rejuvenation. In the meantime, I'll downshift and get in touch with my quieter side, in preparation. Listening, more than talking.

I'll trust my inner guidance as to what I need and just go with the flow, knowing all will be well.

Today's Action | What can you do to get back to the quiet and simplicity of yesteryear? Can you create it in your life right where you are?

Possibly someone you know is going away, and you could house-sit for them. Maybe a spiritual retreat or a weekend getaway is just what the doctor ordered.

Visualize what you would like, then create it.

In this quiet space, ask God what your next step is to be.

The Right Thing To Do

Money fears are cropping up again. I thought I'd already learned this lesson six years ago.

We'd been together five years, when Gary made the ultimate decision to face his past. I had always known this day would come, but somehow you are never quite prepared for it.

With his drug addiction came many consequences, one of which was trouble with the law. It took a lot of money to support Gary's heroin habit. Stealing, writing bad checks, and dealing drugs were how he supported his habit. As a result, Gary has a three-page criminal record. Not only was he a thief, he was a lousy thief.

Before Gary got clean, responsibility was not his strong suit; he skipped out on most of the charges, never appearing in court at the appointed times. When I met him in 1988, he had been wanted in the state of Massachusetts for seven years. His sponsor told him, "When it bothers you enough, you'll do something about it."

Gary likes to say it only bothered him at certain times, like when the cops pulled him over for a broken taillight. Or when we went to see *The Fugitive* and I elbowed him, pointing at the big screen, and said, "That's you." Or once when I asked him to do the dishes and he said, "Not tonight, honey, I'm tired," and I whipped around and said, "I'll turn you in." Or when we watched the TV show *Cops* and they sang their little ditty, "*Bad boys, Bad boys, what ya gonna do when they come for you?*" Or at three in the morning when I wanted to have sex and Gary would say, "Not tonight, honey, I'm tired," and I'd pick up the phone and say, "I'm dialing, I'm dialing." (That never actually happened, but Gary likes to joke that it did.)

For all those years his past hung over us like a cloud—a source of shame and fear. We'd joke about it to break the tension, but inside we both knew it was pretty serious business.

Then, on September 15, 1993, Katherine Power, after being on the run for twenty-three years, turned herself in.

In 1970, she and a few other "revolutionaries" robbed a bank in Boston. While Katherine waited in the getaway car six blocks away, Officer Walter Schroeder was killed during the heist.

Over the years everyone who participated in the bank robbery was caught, except Katherine. Somehow she managed to stay a step ahead of the law.

Eventually, she started a new life in Oregon. During this time she married, had a son, and opened several successful restaurants under an assumed name, all the while remaining on America's Most Wanted List.

Everything looked normal on the outside, but inside—she could not run from the truth. She took her past with her every where she went—just as Gary carried his. Finally, it must have bothered her enough for her to do something about it.

Gary was in his truck late that September evening when the story broke. Immediately he thought, *That's the right thing to do—for her.* An instant later he realized, *If it's the right thing for her to do, it's the right thing for me to do.*

There and then, he made the decision to turn himself in.

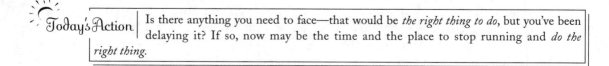

Today's Action | Is there anything you need to face—that would be *the right thing to do*, but you've been delaying it? If so, now may be the time and the place to stop running and *do the right thing.*

I'm No Angel

Intuitively, as soon as I heard the news flash, I knew the effect it would have on Gary. I couldn't have been more right.

Upon hearing the news, he drove to a meeting. By *coincidence*, an attorney in the program, who was originally from Boston, was there. Gary told this attorney, Michael, that he wanted to turn himself in. Michael hooked Gary up with an attorney at his old law firm in Boston. He also told Gary gathering character witness letters might help his case when he went to court.

Armed with this information, Gary came home and said, "It's time."

I knew it was time for him to do the right thing, but by now I loved this man very much and was afraid of losing him. I didn't want him to go to jail. I was scared we would lose everything. And I was afraid our marriage might not survive.

He contacted the attorney in Massachusetts and was told to sit tight; he would see what Gary was up against.

The warrants started coming in. The attorney called and told Gary a cursory check revealed there were six outstanding warrants in the county where Gary had told him he was wanted. I could tell by the look on Gary's face that this wasn't good.

As the weeks passed, and the attorney dug deeper, more warrants started coming in. First nine, then eleven, then nineteen, then twenty-one, until finally, there were twenty-five outstanding warrants for Gary's arrest. He was wanted in three separate counties. Prison looked inevitable.

A hush fell over our household.

No, it wasn't a bank robbery, and certainly no one was physically harmed, but this was no one-time lapse of judgment, either. This was the history of a *career* criminal. We both thought that it was a question of *for how long*, not *if* Gary was going away.

We're going to lose everything. Not that we had a lot, but I really like my security. By now we owned a small two-bedroom house, a car, a truck, and Gary had a small carpentry business that was just getting off the ground.

Our mortgage wasn't huge, but my salary alone couldn't handle it. We discussed our options. We could sell Gary's truck and all of his tools, but the bank owned half his truck. Selling everything wouldn't even cover the attorney's fees. I guess I could get a roommate or take out a loan, but how could I pay a loan back on one salary? And how long would I be willing to live like this? It was starting to get very uncomfortable for me.

For weeks I was consumed with fear—fear of Gary going to jail—financial fear—fear of losing our house and car—everything we had worked so hard for. Then, I had a moment of clarity.

I realized I would rather live in an efficiency like the one Gary lived in when we met, take a bus to work, and be with a man I respect, than to have all the material possessions in the world and be with a man who had no personal integrity.

Finally, I surrendered, "Okay, okay, God . . . I want your will in my life. I trust your plan for our lives."

I got it. I finally understood what Katherine Power must have realized as well: spiritual principles are more important than material possessions.

I just had to let go and trust. I had to be willing to go to any length, not just for my own personal recovery, but for my husband *and* for our marriage.

Today's Action | How important are your material possessions when it comes right down to it? What lengths are you willing to go to *do the right thing* or to help someone else *do the right thing?*
It's something to think about.

376

Through The Fire

Gary took out a loan to pay back the stolen money, cover the attorney's fees, and court costs. Together, we flew up to Boston, Thanksgiving week, November 1993.

His lawyer sent the character reference letters to each county where Gary was wanted. Habitat for Humanity wrote telling what a dedicated, hard-working volunteer Gary was. Camillus House's Brother Harry told of all the drug addicts Gary helped by bringing a recovery meeting to the homeless shelter. Gary had letters from everyone—his sponsees, his sponsor, his boss, even from local prosecutor who said that although very few career criminals ever turn their lives around, she believed Gary was one who had. (Her letter went on and on so much about Gary, that I jokingly told Gary, "She wants you.")

And my mother, the mother who didn't take kindly to the idea of her daughter marrying someone like *that* five years earlier, couldn't wait to write a letter about how trustworthy Gary was.

Hoping these letters would count for something, we walked up the steps into the first courthouse. After much explaining, Gary was allowed to make full restitution, and all charges were dismissed. His probation officer even came up to Gary and said, "So, you're down in Florida . . . . Well, you're doing pretty good. Stay down in Florida." At the second courthouse, pretty much the same thing happened. Gary made good on all the bad checks he had written, paid the court costs, contributed to their victim fund, and all charges were dropped. Everyone seemed genuinely pleased that Gary had turned his life around.

The third county was a whole other story. They had not received the letters. The prosecuting attorney took one look at Gary's extensive criminal record and frankly didn't care how he was doing today. The prosecutor was of the opinion, "You commit the crime, you do the time."

Gary's attorney spoke with the prosecutor privately. Then the prosecutor came over to Gary and said, "Tell me what happened."

Gary proceeded to tell him, "I was dope sick and stole my girlfriend's bank card. And it wasn't $50.00 I stole, it was $420.00. That's the kind of person I was back then, but I'm not that person anymore."

"Yeah, yeah, yeah . . . so you did it. The bank is out that money, so we're going to trial. We'll see the judge in between his scheduled trials, which should be light since tomorrow is Thanksgiving," the tough, no-nonsense prosecutor interrupted, barely glancing at the letters handed to him by Gary's lawyer.

As we walked into the rich, mahogany-paneled courtroom and saw the shackled prisoners sitting to the right of the judge's chambers, the seriousness of the consequences hit both of us. That could be *Gary* sitting there in that orange jumpsuit with his hands and feet manacled.

I got really scared—this time it wasn't about the money at all.

After waiting for the better part of the morning, the judge called Gary's case. The tough young prosecutor walked to the podium, rattled off the charges against Gary and his callous disregard for his girlfriend. You could tell he wanted a conviction.

Gary and I were sitting in the front row of the courtroom, holding hands like two little kids, when all of a sudden, a peace came over me and I *knew* we were going to be okay—*no matter what*. I looked at Gary and could tell he felt the same way.

Then, mid-sentence, the tough young prosecutor's tone changed, "But now, your Honor, Gary is off drugs, he's making a contribution in his community, and he's changed his ways."

All Gary's lawyer had to say was, "I have documentation on that."

The judge accepted Gary's guilty plea and his restitution and gave him one year's probation. All he had to do was stay out of trouble for one year. Piece of cake when you're walking with God.

So I've been through the fire with Gary on something much bigger than losing a job, why am I so scared now?

I guess I forgot I was walking with God.

☀ Today's Action	If you need to go through the fire for something you believe in—remember to walk with God.

Nature's Way

Writing outdoors is just what I need to help me get centered. I feel so close to God when I am outside.

Can you take this book . . . *right now* . . . and finish reading this page outdoors?

A cup of tea or coffee on a patio, balcony, or backyard does wonders to help us reconnect with nature and get centered again.

Doves are cooing, bobwhites are bob-whiting, and wild green parrots are jabbering their heads off.

Karma sits on his throne—the Jacuzzi cover. As soon as I give a call, "Hey, sweetie," he trots over, white paunch swaying from side to side. The backyard is abuzz with activity. I'm just the silent observer.

Karma hops up on my lap for some nuzzling, briefly interrupting my writing, reminding me *he* is "King of the World!" and should be the most important thing in my life (we won't tell him otherwise).

Hot pink bougainvillea peeks over the top of the Jacuzzi, red hibiscus weaves in and out of the gazebo, while palm fronds sway gently in the morning breeze. Backyard bliss among the flowers. No butterflies yet today. Oh . . .

My backyard will probably always remind me of—my little angel—Dharma.

I wonder if he knows he was the catalyst that started this awesome journey? His spirit must be around somewhere, smiling at the good work he did. Bringing me to my bliss and touching so many hearts along the way. My heart warms at the sight of the little clay angel that watches lovingly over his tiny grave.

I miss him.

Karma struts by, swishing his tail in my face, reminding me, "But Mom, I'm here."

Coming out of my reverie, I scratch his head and he is happy.

Spending my days like this—writing among the animals, the flowers, and the birds—there's nothing like it to bring me back to center. I wish I could spend every day like this.

Today's Action | Let nature be your guide. Rest in God's green arms today.

Eleventh Month

Manifesting Your Dreams

Somewhere . . . Over The Rainbow

*M*y dilemma about work is taking the excitement out of going to Hawaii. I'm in financial fear again.

I just don't feel ready to live all out. I like security. I like having a pension plan, health insurance, and paid vacations.

Sometimes I just want to run away. I don't want to make decisions. I just want to go off to Hawaii and forget everything.

I can't believe we're actually going to Hawaii. I've wanted this trip for so long and I *never* thought it would be possible, but here it is.

Three years ago, at my cancer therapist's request, I wrote about the next adventure I wanted to go on and whether I thought it would happen or not:

I would love to spend a month in Hawaii, visiting all the different islands and waterfalls, videotaping the whole trip. I want to fly over the island in a helicopter and near a volcano—not too near—but close enough. I want to hang out in the sun, go diving, and explore all the waterfalls and volcanoes and rain forests. I want to spend time just looking at, listening to and being near the waterfalls. I want to write in my journal sitting beside a waterfall. Of course Gary would be with me, and we'd make love at night under the stars.

And yes, I think I will go on this adventure. Money is all that keeps me from it. Someday, if I live long enough, I may inherit a little bit of money and be able to go then. No, I don't want anyone to die so I can go to Hawaii, but I can't see it happening any other way. I hope I live long enough to fulfill this dream. If I were to become terminal, I would charge the trip on my credit cards and let my life insurance cover it after I die.

Now, here I am alive and healthy three years later, about to go to Hawaii, and no one had to die—I just had to decide I wanted to go more than anything and then make it happen.

We are going to three different islands for a total of eighteen days and the airfare is costing us $98.00 each and that's only because we want to go to an extra island; otherwise it would be free. All we have to pay is the maintenance that we normally pay on our time-share and a few nights in a hotel. So really the trip isn't costing that much, it's just that I want to do so much when I get there. And I can't wait to see my friend Pixie. We talk on the phone all the time now.

I'm getting excited. One of the biggest regrets I had when I thought I was dying is no longer a regret—it's a reality! Where there is a will, there's a way.

If this trip can happen—anything can!

X ☼ Today's Action | Describe your next adventure. Do you think you will actually go on it? What is stopping you? What action could you take to make it happen? (The first thing I did was get a frequent flyer credit card.)

Heaven And Earth

When I first began meditating, I was told to visualize a sacred place—a place of perfect peace.

382

The more I visualized this sacred place, the more real it became.

A waterfall runs through the thick foliage of a rain forest, down a mountain, and then falls into a deep blue, crystal-clear pool, near the ocean's edge.

Large flat rocks surround the natural pool's edge, absorbing the sun. After basking on the rocks in the sun's rays, I slip into the cool water and swim over to where the water is cascading over a grotto and allow the waterfall to pour over me.

The rain forest surrounding the waterfall is thick with palm trees, ferns, and orchids of all shapes and colors. The jungle air is rich with the sweet fragrance of frangipani, jasmine, and plumeria blossoms.

I can hear the ocean lapping against the sandy shoreline where the waterfall flows like a river, into the sea.

Parrots, macaws, toucans, and other exotic birds sing their jungle songs from banana trees swaying gently in the ocean breeze, creating music all their own, in this tropical paradise.

Over the years I've added a sleek, muscular, black panther named Saba, who lies on a ledge at the top of the waterfall, majestically overlooking his kingdom.

I even made up a fruit called pine-raspberry. It's a combination of pineapple and raspberry. It's looks like a pineapple on the outside, but on the inside it's the color of raspberry and tastes alternately like pineapple and raspberry, with some bites sweet and others tart.

Occasionally, I bring Gary to my sacred place, but usually I am alone.

When my writing teacher suggested I meditate before writing—I naturally came here, where I visualize myself sitting by a waterfall, leaning against a palm tree, writing my little heart out.

Although this place is imaginary, it's a combination of Dunn's River Falls in Ocho Rios, Jamaica, and the place where Tarzan and Jane swam in the old Tarzan movies.

In my heart, I've always believed a place like this really exist—a secluded waterfall, off the beaten path, that melts into the ocean.

Maybe I'll find my tropical paradise in Hawaii.

Today's Action | Visualize your place of perfect peace. Imagine a place that is as close to heaven as you can get here on earth. Know these moments of bliss are yours whenever you desire—simply create them in your own mind.

God's Eyes

I have but one relationship—with God. God may be disguised as my husband, my dog, or the person driving me crazy. Or God can come to me as the wind and the weather. Truthfully, everything and everyone is a manifestation of God in different forms. My goal is to always be in relationship with God through everything I do.—Barbara De Angelis, Ph.D.

The hardest place to practice spirituality is with our loved ones. Why is it so difficult? I guess because we are at ease enough to let it all hang out. They see the real us—*or do they?*

I think there's a deeper us—a Higher Self—*our True Self.*

This Self doesn't need to be right, in control, or to win. This Self loves all—unconditionally, even the wounded. We all have our broken places—remnants from that severed pipeline that we rebuild as we reconnect with God.

This Self is able to see through God's eyes to the wounded child within each person and come from love in all interactions, *even the people we live with.*

Whenever Gary and I bicker or become sarcastic with one another, we acknowledge what we are doing and recommit to do better. Neither of us wants to be hurtful, so it rarely takes long for one of us to realize we are off track and to course-correct.

Financial fear is one of my biggies with Gary. So I try to practice generosity whenever I am in financial fear. After a while it becomes second nature to donate money when I think I don't have enough or to treat Gary to a nice dinner when I've just lost my job.

It's all about trusting in the abundance of the Universe and coming from Love—*our True Self.*

Today's Action | Are there people in your life whom you do not treat as lovingly, gently, and with respect as you would like? Pull your mask down and let them see your *True Self.* Look beyond their walls to their *True Selves* and see the child within—the one that gives and receives love freely and easily.

Re-commit to come from love in all you do. Sometimes that means behaving the opposite of how you feel, trusting it will become second nature in time.

Peace Of Mind

If peace of mind is the goal, it matters not the source of the disturbance, only that it be resolved.

Even when someone else is at fault—we can make the first move toward reconciliation. If fear is disturbing our peace of mind, we can walk through the fear or simply transcend our fears by trusting God.

That sounds easy, doesn't it—*transcend your fears by trusting God.*

Tell that to someone who has just lost a job or been diagnosed with cancer, or whose relationship is breaking up.

Last night at Satsang I heard a story that I know was meant for me.

A woman whose baby had just died begged God, "Please. Please God, let my baby live!"

God told her to go to every hut in the village, some two hundred, and collect a mustard seed from every home that had not been touched by death. The woman came back empty-handed—with not one mustard seed.

She then handed her baby to God, realizing as great as her loss was, so too, was the loss of every other villager.

"Life is difficult."

M. Scott Peck's *The Road Less Traveled* opens with this profound statement. The premise being that once you accept that life is difficult—it ceases being difficult.

We seldom like hearing, "Acceptance is the answer to all of my problems," but with acceptance comes peace of mind. And if peace of mind is the goal, acceptance is the path.

Once we accept something, deeply accept it, we can change—either our actions or our attitudes. Until then, we are too busy *resisting* to effect any lasting change.

If we remind ourselves, *peace of mind is the goal*, we will intuitively know how to handle every situation.

Today's Action | *Peace of mind is the goal.* Pull that statement into your consciousness, repeating it often throughout the day.

In This Moment

Why is peace of mind the goal? For our comfort? Yes, comfort is usually a by-product of living that intention, but more importantly, when we have *peace of mind*, something magical happens. God is.

We experience God in the peace of our own minds. When our minds are not jumping frantically from one thought to the next, when we are at peace, we experience God-consciousness.

God sees all, knows all, is all. God knows the bigger picture—how tragedies turn to triumph, how people pull together and draw closer to God during a crisis, and how everything, absolutely *everything*, unfolds for our highest good.

When we experience *God-consciousness*, this knowledge becomes our knowledge.

In the quiet, peaceful moments when our mind is still, we glimpse *Truth*.

Tragedy strikes all human beings at one time or another. The way to ease suffering is to keep one eye on the bigger picture through *God-consciousness*.

Difficult situations hone us, make us stronger, build character, and compassion. Resistance builds bitterness. Acceptance of what is, and rising to meet its challenge, builds wisdom.

Perseverance, especially in the face of the unknown, is the mark of a courageous soul.

Today's Action | Rest in the knowledge that everything is unfolding according to plan, according to a *Higher Purpose.* Trust that.

Don't Worry, Be Happy

Last night Gary and I went to see David Helfgott, the critically acclaimed pianist, in concert.

By some fluke (*Godincidence*) we got third-row seats at the last minute and witnessed one of the most moving performances I have ever seen.

For those of you who don't know, David Helfgott suffered a mental breakdown and was institutionalized for more than ten years. With the help of his wife, he made a startling comeback, which was depicted in the award-winning movie, *Shine*.

Sitting center stage at his piano, rocking back and forth, Helfgott played *the* most exquisite music. Talking to himself under his breath as he played, Helfgott was totally immersed in the moment. Watching him so lost in his music, you couldn't help remember that he was not of *this* world—but it made you want to be of his world.

Aside from his brilliant playing, the most noticeable thing about this man is his guilelessness and unabashed love for what he does. With each piece he finished, the audience roared. Every time the audience clapped, Helfgott left the piano, took a bow, and another, and another. His childlike enthusiasm made the audience applaud even louder, at which he beamed even more.

He truly has the heart of a child with no pretense or fear, only joy at doing the one thing he was meant to do—play the piano. When the applause became thunderous after his last encore, he jumped up and down—absolutely tickled to death we liked him.

I have never witnessed anyone so completely *live* their bliss. And wouldn't any one of us love the accolades that were showered on him? But most of us would be too sophisticated to show how much we loved the attention. Yet, here's this grown man, beaming from ear to ear as he looked out at the audience. It was akin to Sally Fields saying, "You like me. *You really like me*," upon receiving her Oscar for *Norma Rae*. Or more recently, John Cameron declaring, "I am king of the world!" after picking up his Oscar for *Titanic*.

Both were pooh-poohed afterward for their enthusiastic display of emotion. There's this code of silence, where no one is supposed to admit they want to be liked and accepted. We are supposed to act cool, as if we don't care, one way or the other, whether we get any validation or recognition—when deep inside, it's what we crave.

I can't tell you how refreshing it was to see a grown man drop to the floor at the end of his performance, and sign as many programs as were handed to him, with the intensity of a child coloring a coloring book.

Instead of growing up and becoming more mature, we should grow down and become more childlike.

For all our intelligence, wisdom, and spirituality—they say no one is closer to God than a child. And no one was closer to God last night than David Helfgott.

Heaven Knows

It looks like I might have a job when I get back from Hawaii.

There is an opening for a customer engineer with my law firm's legal accounting software provider. They like my legal and accounting background and that I'm already familiar with their software. I'm not sure how qualified I am for the position; they normally hire people with more technical backgrounds. Still, the interview went well, and they asked me to get in touch when I get back from vacation. The financial opportunity is fantastic, and I would be teaching people to use software I have been using for years. As long as they could teach me basic programming and troubleshooting, I think I'd be fine.

388 I love learning new computer programs and think training people would be right up my alley. Maybe this is why I wasn't motivated to find a job in accounting.

My old job wants me to stay as long as I can to help close the firm, so I'm not sure how it's all going to work out. I hate being up in the air. I wish I knew what the future held.

I'm pretty excited about the possibility of a job in computers, but a small part of me feels like I might be selling out.

For whatever reason, I am too scared to pursue my writing full time right now. I like the security of a steady paycheck, but I have this nagging feeling that this job is *my* will—not *God's*.

I guess only time will tell.

For now, it's off to Hawaii.

Today's Action | Sometimes you just take the next step; more will be revealed.

♡

Anytime You Need A Friend

My friend Pixie met us at the airport in Maui and welcomed us with fresh leis. The plumeria blossoms smelled heavenly.

And Pixie, well, what can you say about someone who is fast approaching forty, who you haven't seen since they were a teenager. She looked the same, slim and tan with dirty blond hair, yet different. She is a storeowner and mother now, not the carefree kid I last saw eighteen years ago. We had so much catching up to do. Gary and I picked up our Jeep and followed Pixie to our hotel, and then made plans to go to her house the next day.

Driving through Maui, I was overcome by the mountainous terrain. You can really envision this island coming up from the earth's center, with its crater-shaped beaches littering the shoreline and volcanic mountains looming in the distance. I'm so used to Miami's long, flat stretches of white, sandy beaches that these gray and black, crescent-shaped beaches were just too cool. Everything is so thick and lush, even in the cities. I'm in paradise.

My mouth fell open every two minutes as we drove from sea level up into the mountains, taking in the most amazing views. Waterfalls are everywhere! And I do mean everywhere. Mountainous cliffs fall right into the sea. Surfers grab every surfable wave. I've never seen anything like it. My camera and video camera never left my side; God forbid, I miss one minute of this perfection.

I could write a book about this trip alone! Suffice to say, they were the most incredible eighteen days of my life.

When the time was right, I told Pixie what I'd done so many years ago that I was so ashamed of. She forgave me and graciously accepted my Limoges cat box as a token of my sincerity. We talked for hours, catching up on her family and mine, and everything that transpired over the last eighteen years. I had my friend back. There was no awkwardness, no grudges, just two friends making up for lost time. It was wonderful.

While we were talking, Pixie admitted that she missed her relationship with her brother Ronnie, my first boyfriend. Messed up on drugs, he had stolen from the family and broken their trust with his vain attempts at getting clean. As far as Pixie was concerned, the damage was irreparable.

I explained to her about drug addiction and how it changed us into people we didn't want to be, caused us to do things we never meant to do. I told her he seemed like he was getting his life together when I visited him last year. I suggested telling him what bothered her might clear the air between them and help repair the relationship.

Coincidentally, Ronnie called Pixie from Florida later that very same night with some awful news. His girlfriend died unexpectedly, and he was beside himself with grief. Pixie's heart opened and she was able to be there for him.

They talked for hours. Instead of the usual wooden conversations, Pixie told Ronnie how it felt being on the receiving end of his drug addiction for all those years. Ronnie never knew how much pain he had caused her and was deeply sorry. Honestly broaching long-avoided subjects instantly relieved the tension between them, and they began rebuilding their relationship.

Later, Pixie told me our earlier conversation sparked a healing between her and Ronnie. She was amazed that we had that conversation on the very day he called. I felt blessed to be part of their healing. It's the least I owe them.

Today's Action | Delight in the healings that are taking place and will continue to take place.

While You See A Chance

The amends with Pixie was just the beginning of our trip of a lifetime.

While on Maui, we took the "Trip to Hana"—a four-hour drive that winds through over four hundred waterfalls, passing the most magnificent scenery along the way.

We set out early from the sunny side of Maui and drove some eighty miles along the coast and through the rain forest to the western side of the island. Normally, it's a half-day trip, but because I wanted to take pictures of *every single waterfall*, it took us all day. We found a little guest cottage for $40.00 and spent the night in the rain forest.

Believe it or not, we found a Twelve-Step meeting, right in the middle of the rain forest, where, as one of the members put it, "I haven't smoked any weed in over thirty years." There was also a teenager at the meeting, just days out of detox. Silly me, I didn't think Hawaii had problems like that. Except for the constant rain, I felt right at home. I guess you learn to live wet. Great place to visit, but I can't imagine living there.

On our way to see some of the most famous waterfalls in the world, *Seven Sacred Pools*, Pixie told us to be sure and stop at her favorite out-of-the-way waterfall: *Blue Pools*.

She didn't remember exactly how to get there because it's been years since she last visited Hana, but told us to ask a local for directions, because it wasn't on any map. (Can you believe it? When you live in Hawaii, you actually take waterfalls for granted!)

To get to *Blue Pools*, we drove over two miles of dirt roads and crossed over a couple of streams before coming to a halt at a third stream that emptied right into the ocean. It was too wide and deep to cross in our Jeep, so we got out and carefully waded across; we didn't want to lose our footing and be swept out to sea.

After crossing the stream, we walked to the point and saw the most incredible waterfall *ever*—coming right out of a fifty-foot cliff and falling into a pool surrounded by rocks, *right on the edge of the ocean*. Wow—just like the waterfall in my meditation!

The best part was that, unlike the rest of the Hana trip, where we shared Hawaii's liquid beauties with dozens of other tourists, we were the *only* people at this waterfall!

The next morning we explored caves by a black-sand beach before hiking through a bamboo forest on the edge of *Seven Sacred Pools*. Finally, we made our way around the island back to our little hotel on the beach.

After a few days in Maui, I said to heck with Hawaii on a budget, took a step out in faith, trusted we would always be provided for—abundantly, and cashed in my IRAs—making this *truly* the trip of my dreams. Luaus, sightseeing by helicopter, volcanoes at sunrise, and snorkeling with sea turtles completed our Maui trip, *tourist style*.

Now, I really have *no regrets*!

☀ Today's Action | What is the best vacation you've ever been on? Why? Where have you always wanted to go, but thought you couldn't because of time or money constraints? Design your ideal trip and find a way to make it happen.

Almost Paradise

After a week in Maui, we flew to the quietest Hawaiian Island—Molokai. If you want to get away from it all and do absolutely nothing—Molokai is the place to go.

Gary and I slept late every day, lounged around the pool, took long walks on the beach, and watched waves pound the shoreline. It was too rough for swimming, so we watched surfers instead.

A week in Molokai was just the break Gary and I needed. One night we even took a blanket out to a secluded beach and spent the night under the stars. It was so romantic. The city lights of Honolulu sparkled in the distance. The moon was full, and the stars winked knowingly against the midnight sky. We lay twenty feet from the ocean's edge, where waves undulated against the shore. Shooting stars set the mood for romance.

Mesmerized, we gave in to the seduction of Hawaiian nights and made love on the beach. Then we fell asleep as the full moon turned deep orange and slipped off into the ocean, setting for the evening.

Magical is the only way to describe our trip. It was everything I'd ever hoped it would be and more.

The next day we went to the other side of the island and a local took us hiking through his family's property to another, yes another, gorgeous waterfall. This one fell some two hundred feet straight down sheer crater walls. We ate sandwiches, fresh guava, and coconut at the foot of the waterfall. Tropical paradise doesn't begin to describe it.

Hawaii is truly heaven on earth.

Today's Action | Where is your most romantic vacation spot? Have you been there yet? Would you like to go again? Maybe you'd like a risqué romantic night like Gary and I had. What is stopping you? Plan your idyllic getaway. Flesh out the details. Then let your wildest dreams come true.

Sacrifice

There is another reason we chose to visit Molokai—the leper colony on the Kalaupapa peninsula on the northern tip of Molokai.

Six years ago, I read this in *Sacred Journey of the Peaceful Warrior* by Dan Millman: "Ultimately, it comes down to service. Jesus said, '*Whoever would be the greatest among you is servant to all.*' This, Dan, is the way to the heart, the path up the inner mountain. And mark my words: One day you will serve others not out of self-interest or guilt or social conscience, *but because there's nothing else you'd rather do.* It will feel as simple and pleasurable as seeing a wonderful film that makes you feel happy and wanting to share it with others."

In the form of a fictional tale, Dan told the story of Father Damien, who served among the lepers sent to live in isolation on this tiny peninsula, surrounded by the tallest sea cliffs in the world. For years, I didn't know that Father Damien or this place really existed. It wasn't until I planned the trip that I found out lepers were indeed separated from their families and sent off to Kalaupapa to die. Father Damien heard his calling and went to live among the lepers. He ministered to them until he died, some sixteen years later, after contracting leprosy himself.

Today, to visit this isolated piece of Hawaiian history, you must get special permission and be escorted by a Kalaupapa resident. Gary and I made the arrangements, hiked down sixteen hundred winding steps, from cliffs to sea level, and took a journey neither of us will soon forget.

Although leprosy is now curable and no longer contagious, it still exists. Many people with Hanson's disease, as it is now known, choose to live on the peninsula though they, thankfully, are no longer forced to. Our guide was one of the residents/patients, as was the woman who ran the community museum and library.

The two-hour hike down and then back up the cliffs left me bruised and aching, my knees painfully swollen. Yet after seeing firsthand the horrors some people must face in life, I found I could not complain about anything. Although these people do not feel any less blessed than I do, which is amazing in and of itself, I left feeling ever so grateful for the freedom I take for granted, daily.

Their humble, joyful nature was inspiring, and their stories touched me deeply. But what struck me most was the courage displayed by these people and the humility of those who served them. Seeing the sacrifice some made left me with a burning desire to do more to make a difference in someone's life.

About a third of the way down the stone steps to Kalaupapa we ran across a makeshift altar, carved into the rocky cliff. There was a small statute of the Virgin Mary, a cross, some flowers, some Hawaiian gods, and a single black poker chip. When we flipped the poker chip over, it read, "Nine Years."

Those in recovery know what that means. For those not familiar with it—it stands for the amount of time someone has been abstinent from their addiction. Many fellowships use these poker chips as mile markers. This was an NA, a Narcotics Anonymous one. Someone managed to stay off drugs for *nine years* and was in Hawaii paying homage to the ultimate servants—those who cared for lepers. I can almost bet they left that poker chip there out of gratitude, for the life they've been afforded due to the Twelve Steps, and the

393

service inherent in those fellowships. If it weren't for those who have gone before us, no one would have been there to light the way.

Gary and I feel the same way.

If I can help one person heal their pain and find the courage to live their dreams, my life will be a success. I can think of no greater joy than sharing my experience with others through the written or spoken word. I feel grateful to have found a way to make a contribution, while thoroughly enjoying myself.

Today's Action | How do you serve others? Does it bring you joy? Discern what it is you really enjoy, then find a way to help others in the process.

These Are The Sweetest Days

The final leg of our journey was four days spent on my favorite Hawaiian island. Kauai is quainter than Maui, yet not as secluded as Molokai, with its seaside villages scattered along the single road separating beach from rain forest.

A helicopter tour gave us the lay of the land. Our first day in Kauai was rather windy and the helicopter came a bit too close to the green cliffs of the Na Pali Coast for my liking, but we managed to enjoy the breathtaking views in between dips. After the helicopter trip, we picked up a couple of hitchhikers and drove to Waimea. The teenager hitchhikers were part of a missionary church group and a delight to share the afternoon with. We traipsed all through the Waimea Canyon, which is the largest canyon in the United States with the exception of the Grand Canyon. I, of course, had to go off the main path to marvel at a waterfall running through the red clay desert. Imagine that—a waterfall, right in the middle of the desert? It was just too cool.

As we climbed higher, the desert turned into lush tropical rain forest. From an elevation of more than five thousand feet, we had the most incredible view of canyons, valleys, cliffs, and mountains. Waterfalls cascaded down walls hundreds of feet high. It was breathtaking. At the end of a brief rain shower, we were treated to a double rainbow that ran from one expansive end of the canyon to the other.

On our second day, after chasing waterfalls all day, we watched the sun set at the famous Ke'e Beach and dined in a wonderful little tropical café. The next day, we went horseback riding to a private waterfall and ate a gourmet lunch by the water's edge. Gary and I went swimming and then kissed in a grotto under the waterfall as water cascaded over our heads—something I had always dreamed of.

On our last day, we hiked to another secluded waterfall where we lay on the rocks, sunbathed, and listened to rushing water, just like in my meditation. In the afternoon, Gary napped, and I wrote in my journal.

I was in heaven. If I died right then and there, I would die happy.

Thank you, God, thank you, God. Sometimes, I feel undeserving of such joy, yet here it is. They say true joy is a by-product of right living, so I must be doing something right. Bliss. That is the state I am in—*bliss*. (And I thought I was in Hawaii.)

 | What is bliss for you? Find it. Follow it. Live it. Be it.

Starting Over

Funny, I always thought I wanted to live in Hawaii. Now I don't think so. As beautiful as it is, I'd miss my friends and family too much. I didn't even go on any interviews; it just didn't make sense once I was there. It turns out I wouldn't trade my loved ones or the life I have for all the beauty in the world. What a nice place to come back to—home—literally and figuratively.

I got the job!

I start on Monday. I am so excited. Who would have thought I'd be starting over at forty? They're going to train me for customer support, programming, installations, and how to teach clients to use the accounting software I've been using for the last ten years. It is such an incredible opportunity.

It is a small company, around forty employees, but they are on the cutting edge of legal software technology. They install their software all over the country, so I'll be traveling, which I love, and working in a service-oriented business, which I think I'll love compared to working with numbers for the last twenty years. And to think I used to hate the thought of working with people.

To top it all off, with salary and bonuses, I'll be earning two to three times what I earned at my old job. I am a little nervous, learning a new career and all. Plus my old firm wants me to help them close shop. Who knows how long that will take? But it looks like I'll work both jobs for a while.

I guess if I am completely honest, I am afraid that between the two jobs, I will have to put my writing aside. And if I do that, even for a short time, I am afraid it may get shelved for good.

God, please do not let me lose sight of my bliss.

Maybe if I am lucky I can work here for two or three years until my car and credit cards are paid, and then, God willing, my book will take off and I can write for a living— my ultimate dream.

Wish me luck.

☼ Today's Action | Sometimes major changes are necessary at midlife—just don't lose sight of your dreams.

Borderline

Sometimes I question my sanity. I prayed to get this job (*only if it were God's will, of course*), and now that I've landed it, I'm too exhausted to do anything else.

I hope this is only temporary, because for the last six weeks I've hardly written a word. I've been closing down my old firm at night and on the weekends and trying to learn an entirely new career by day. I *love* working with computers and helping people, so I just know this is the job for me, but the pace is unbelievable.

Did I mention that I was so stressed working both jobs that I fell and broke two of my ribs while cleaning my Jacuzzi?

I had to let my old firm go last week so I could focus on my new career, my writing, and healing my aching body. They are furious with me. One of the senior partners even asked if I really broke my ribs; he wanted to know if the fracture showed on X rays! The office manager even tried to guilt-trip me by saying, "Debbie, you just can't leave them high and dry, after all they've done for you."

I mean, *they* closed the doors on *me*!

It's been over a month since they actually closed the doors, and although I offered to help, I can't be expected to continue doing the ongoing work forever. Enough is enough. At some point, the accountants were going to have to take over anyway. My ribs just named the time: *Now!*

I hope things start to settle down now, because I'm fried—mentally, emotionally, spiritually, and physically. I haven't even had time to go to the beach or meditate and that's not like me.

God, please help me get back on track.

☀ Today's Action | If by chance you get off track, pray for guidance.

Higher Love

Tonight, at my meditation meeting, a man gave a definition of spirituality that I had never heard before. He said, "Spirituality is being able to see the good in every person and situation."

That's *exactly* what spirituality is.

Seeing the God Self, Higher Self, or Christ Self within each person is the most spiritual way to envision another person.

When I can look at someone I don't particularly like and see how they are a gift in my life, or when I can see the lesson in a difficult situation, while in the midst of it, *then* I have arrived.

I'm certainly not there yet. Judgments constantly enter my mind about the way others behave, think, and speak—from their driving skills—down to their beliefs and opinions.

After years of meditating, I realize I am powerless over my *initial* thoughts; they come and go at will. What matters is whether I *dwell* in those negative judgments or not. What thoughts do I entertain, take to dinner, and go to bed with? Which thoughts or judgments go round and round in my head?

The ideal place to be in relation to my thoughts is detached enough to notice them and wise enough to let them go. Rising above my judgments, I can see the *good* or *God* in every one and every thing. This is my spiritual goal.

I can't imagine ever actually reaching this goal.

Right now, I have trouble seeing the good in some of our clients. As far as finding the good in my work situation, that's difficult too, but I keep trying. I'll probably always have judgments of people and experiences, but it's nice to have something to work toward.

Spiritual progress is about moving *toward* the solution.

If someone cuts me off in traffic today, my initial reaction may be to mutter, "Jerk" under my breath. But if I am living in the Spirit and have *peace of mind as the goal*, my next thought will be, *God loves you and God loves me.* Recognizing our equality once again, I let go of all judgment.

I guess it depends on my level of awareness. Some days I am more conscious than others.

398

Today's Action | Look around and see God's beauty everywhere. Focus on the good in all you see. Then look in a mirror and see the beauty within.

She Works Hard For The Money

Things are hectic at my new job and I feel inadequate. I didn't absorb enough during training because of working both jobs and dealing with my broken ribs.

The job is so high-tech and high-gear it is hard to adjust to, but very rewarding. I receive validation from my peers, my bosses, and customers all the time, something I never got at my old job. And I really enjoy the firm and my co-workers.

It has been two months since I stopped working at my old firm, but I still feel as if I am working two jobs, since I spend most nights and weekends inputting and editing the stories for this book. I love doing it, but there is little time left for me, so I am tired a lot. My mentor says it is like that when you're making the transition from the life you have to the life you want.

I hardly see Gary. And to think of all those years I complained about his working on Saturdays. Now I'm happy if he works on Sundays too, so that I can write. He is so supportive. I am one lucky woman.

Two people from my department have been on the road nonstop for a month and two others quit, so we are very shorthanded. The stress is unbelievable. As response time increases, so does customer irritability. Tempers are short within the department as well, and often no one at all is available to help me help clients. It's very frustrating.

I leave the house at seven in the morning and get home around seven at night. I tell myself everyone does this. Commuting an hour to and from work is the American way, isn't it? I am so tense when I come home; Gary has to massage my neck the minute I walk in the door. I can't wait until the other customer engineers get back in town.

Maybe if I stay at my mother's house more? She lives close to my office. Maybe that will help. Something has got to give. I just don't know how much longer I can take it.

God, where are you?

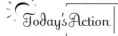 When all else fails—pray.

No Matter What

A friend of mine, Ed, speaks of growing up with a punishing God. It was hard for him to pray to this God and difficult, if not impossible, for him to trust this God. A friend asked Ed, "If your son did something horrendous and asked for forgiveness—what would you do?"

"Forgive him, of course." Ed replied.

"No matter what he did?" his friend asked.

"No matter what," Ed replied emphatically.

Ed's friend suggested he meditate on *that* concept of God.

This completely turned around how Ed viewed God.

As a father Ed knew his love for his son was constant and unconditional. From that moment on, Ed began thinking of God as the loving father he had always wanted and was trying to be.

Although I am not a mother, I am someone's child, and I know my mother's love has always been constant and unconditional. No matter how rebellious I was as a teenager, often screaming at my mother, "I hate you! I'm going to go live with my father!" my mother always forgave me and loved me anyway.

Though my mother was far from perfect, she loved me *no matter what*. Nothing I could do could turn her away. She may have hated what I said and did, but she always loved *me*. She may have disciplined me, but she never turned her back on me. A parent's love is the kind of love you can trust.

I can only assume that since my Creator created me, my Creator's love for me must be as unconditional as that of my earthly parents, and certainly more perfect.

❀

As my mind races with thoughts of what to do, I draw closer to Source, knowing this is the only way.

In my heart, I know God has not forsaken me—I just have to trust and be open to his will. Right now, I'm just not sure what it is. So I'll continue checking in and asking for help.

On My Knees

God has always answered every one of Gary's prayers.

Starting when Gary asked God to help him stay off drugs, and then on December 3, 1988, *hope* came into Gary's life in the form of eight hundred other addicts, showing him what was possible for them was possible for him, if he but followed in their footsteps. He did. And eleven years later that prayer is still working in his life.

Then, there was the time when Gary was still testing this Higher Power by praying for specific things, like for God to put the woman who had just turned him down at the dance into his life—and nine months later *we* were married.

Seven years later, instead of praying for a specific outcome when I was having my breast biopsied, Gary prayed that we would be able to handle the outcome, whatever it was. And handle it we did, but *only* through the love and strength of that God we had come to believe in.

Gary's most heartfelt prayer was two years ago, when he asked God to bring his dying mother an angel.

Suffering from emphysema since her early forties, Gary's mother spent the last fifteen years of her life wheeling around an oxygen tank everywhere she went. Doing her best not to let the disease slow her down, she went for coffee every day with her friends, bought thoughtful little gifts for her family and friends, and even helped raise her granddaughter, Leah, before Gary and I tried our hand at it.

Each year, her health declined and her visits out of the house were less frequent, until at the end she could no longer climb the stairs of her third-floor walk-up.

Gary visited and called as much as he could. And I know his mother's prayers were answered when Gary got clean nine years before. She no longer had to stay up nights worrying about him or skimming the obituaries for his name. She was *very* proud of how he had turned his life around.

401

One Friday afternoon, Gary's brother beeped him from Boston. As is usually the case, an out-of-town beep in the middle of the day is cause for concern. Gary's brother told him their mother was fading fast and to come quickly.

We arrived around midnight and went directly to the hospital. The whole family was gathered around Charlotte's hospital bed. Noticing everyone standing around her, Charlotte asked, "Am I dying?" There was silence, so I spoke up quietly, "You're very sick, but we don't know if you are dying or not. We're here because we love you very much and want to be with you."

Gary and I spent the next four days in his mother's hospital room, taking turns sleeping in the spare hospital bed, feeding her ice and calming her whenever her breath became too labored. We played her favorite music—Frank Sinatra and lyrical Celtic melodies on her little CD player. Dim lights, hushed voices, and music playing softly in the background gave the hospital room a mystical churchlike feel to it.

One night, when everyone was present, Charlotte expressed wisdom and insight way beyond her sixth-grade education. We were all amazed, as she gave each person a bit of personal advice to keep with them always. As sad as it was, it was also the most beautiful thing I've ever witnessed—the love surrounding this woman—and the fact that we were all able to be there, letting her know how very loved she was.

By Monday, Charlotte seemed to be getting better, so Gary and I flew home.

Gary talked with his brother or stepfather every day about his mother's condition. Tuesday Gary and I went to a meditation meeting where they just happened to play the same Celtic songs we had listened to all weekend with Gary's mother.

On Thursday evening, she took a turn for the worse and was suffering horribly. At about ten o'clock Gary knelt by our bed and asked God to send his mother an angel and to please end her suffering. Ten minutes later, Gary's sister-in-law called to tell him his mother had just passed away. She died at the exact moment Gary was praying for an angel to come and take her.

We flew back up north for the funeral—sad, but comforted by the fact that we had witnessed a beautiful healing in that little hospital room in Salem, Massachusetts. It was truly a magical experience.

Yes, people die, but often, wondrous beauty surrounds the passing from this life to the next. Like when Dharma died, taking my fear of death with him. God can handle all my fears—if I let him.

I'll never forget Charlotte's last words of wisdom to us, *Be kind, and don't forget to love each other.*

Simple, yet profound.

I'm Looking Through You

I want to drink. I want to numb out. I want to lie down and never wake up. I just don't want to go on anymore. I can't take it. Exhaustion descends on me like a heavy, gray cloud.

I wanted this job so bad. Now, I've never been more miserable in my life. It's three in the morning, I'm at my mother's house trying to cut down on the commute time and get more sleep, but here I am wide awake.

I like the firm. I like the people I work with. Most of the clients are decent, but the stress of the never-ending line of calls waiting and constant problems is tough. We're always behind, and clients constantly complain about how long it takes for us to get back to them. Is it like this in every service industry?

Sometimes I wish Y2K would just blow up all computers and we could go back to a simpler life. I never lost any sleep over the good old pegboard system.

I feel trapped. Yesterday, I had to put a thousand dollars into my car to fix the brakes, and my car won't even be paid off for another eight months. Until then I'm stuck—my expenses are right up to my income. I can't even look for another job—I mean when would I interview—6 A.M.?

I'm on call nights and weekends one week out of every six. I guess that's not the end of the world, but I am so tired and feel so inadequate without other customer engineers to help me. This is my week, and I couldn't do it last night. My boss was upset with me—but I had to pick up my car.

I'm not paralyzed by fear, but I feel I have no other choice, at least until some of my bills are paid. Then, maybe I could afford to take a job for less money.

Every night when I leave for the day and the mirrored elevator doors close, it just breaks my heart to see that girl's pleading eyes staring back at me. Where is that fun-spirited Debbie I used to know? I used to be happy most of the time, now I feel dead inside, like I have the weight of the whole world on my shoulders. What happened?

What happened to my dream?

I am still inputting stories, but I can only work about ten to fifteen hours a week on the book, so progress is very slow. Sometimes I want to give up.

Despair fills my heart. This job takes so much out of me. I have no time or energy left for friends, sponsees, my recovery program, exercise, or meditation. I work, write, and fall into bed.

God, I don't know what to do. I don't even know the person staring back at me in the mirror anymore. Please help me.

☀ *Today's Action* | The in-between stage can be pretty rough at times, but don't *ever* lose faith.

We Gotta Get Out Of This Place

"... if it's the last thing we ever do."

Last night I told Gary I want to lie down and go to sleep—*forever.*

The voices in my head say I will never make it as a writer; I might as well accept that I have to stay at this job.

If I can just hang in until my credit cards and car are paid, then I can find another job. When I told Gary my plan to try to hang in there at least another eight months, he said, "Debbie, if it were anyone else, I would say leave when you can afford to, but I have watched your spirit be *crushed*, right before my eyes. If I were you, I'd quit tomorrow."

Easy for him to say—he used to live on cardboard boxes! Gary is comfortable when he is in debt. *I am not!*

I just realized another reason why I can't quit—I can't get back on Gary's health insurance until the next open-enrollment period in six months. I certainly can't be without insurance with my medical history. I guess I have to find a way to hang in there.

I will go to lunchtime Twelve-Step meetings and work on changing my attitude. It will work out. I can do this.

They just awarded me "Employee of the Month" at my job. Normally, the recognition would thrill me, but at this point, I don't care.

I avert my eyes when I get in the elevator; I don't want to face the girl in the mirror anymore. Leaving the garage I think to myself: *Well, I am out of hell for the day.*

Last night I broke down crying and told the women in my Thursday night group, "I feel as if I am in prison and I'm not sure I can make it to the end of my sentence."

Two of the women in the group are as miserable at their jobs as I am. Terry, our resident grandmother, works in a check-cashing store, but really wants to help troubled teens. Someday, she hopes to go back to school, but right now her hours are too long.

Angel, a legal secretary, as a result of reading the first few hundred stories in this book, stumbled on a dream of her own. She wants to open a boutique/coffee bar for bikers, where they can hang out, drink coffee and soda, and buy accessories in a clean healthy environment, instead of going to a bar.

Both told me I should "Quit, immediately." Today, they both realized they are suggesting I do what they themselves are afraid to do. We all committed to take *some action, any action* that will move us of out of our current situations and closer to our dreams.

"Girl, there's a better life for me and you."

 Today's Action | If you are stuck, commit to taking action, *any action*, to move you out of your prison. The real bars exist only in our minds.

Can't Find My Way Home

I got my résumé together, bought a newspaper, and have decided to look for another job. Somehow, I'll find a way to go on interviews.

I took a personal day off today because I am so exhausted—mentally and physically, but for some reason, I can't seem to find the motivation to send out my résumé. What's up with that?

Not knowing what else to do, I began re-reading the stories in this book.

It's obvious my spirit soars when I spend time in nature, but now I have no time. I believe stress contributed to my getting cancer, yet here I am working in the most stressful environment imaginable. I'm a huge proponent of living each day as if it were your last, yet five days out of every week, I am doing something that makes me wish I were dead. What if this *were* my last year? Is this how I'd want to spend it? No, absolutely not! Yet fear of the unknown has me paralyzed.

My mom wrote me a beautiful letter encouraging me to trust God and follow my heart. She ended the letter by saying: *You've overcome so much worse than this so wonderfully—my special, special gal—I love you—Mom.*

I was really touched. This is the kind of love and support I've always wanted from my mom. It reminded me how far we both have come and how much strength my mother has passed on to me over the years. *I love you too, Mom.*

Well, instead of going on interviews, I am going to the beach to spend some time with God.

Today's Action | Where are your sources of strength? Spend time there today.

A Ray of Hope

After some introspective time with God at the beach, I was led to call my brother Brent, the chef in Colorado. I told him how miserable I was at my job, and that I didn't know what to do. He reminded me of his humble beginnings.

Stifled creatively at his job as executive chef of a well-known restaurant in Aspen, Brent wasn't sure what direction to go in, so he prayed and asked for help. After much indecision, he walked away from his very cushy job and opened his own restaurant in Steamboat Springs.

He wasn't even sure how he was going to pay the mortgage on his condo that month, yet he borrowed fifty thousand dollars to get his restaurant off the ground, and put another twenty thousand on credit cards. Three years later, he has expanded the seating in the restaurant, bought the building, and is doing fabulously.

Still not sure how he *actually* made the leap, I asked, "But how did you find the courage to walk away from your safe, secure job? How did you deal with the financial insecurity?"

Brent said, "When I was trying to decided whether to go back to the big hotel chains, stay where I was, or open my own restaurant, a friend asked me, 'What would you do, if you could do anything in the world—and the outcome didn't matter?' Without hesitation I told him, 'I'd open my own restaurant.' My friend then said, 'Then let's forget the other ideas and focus on how to make that one dream happen. Because the outcome is *always* in God's hands.'"

There's my answer—place the outcome in *His* hands.

Still, I'm scared.

I told Brent, "I just don't know . . ."

Brent asked me, "Has God ever let you down? Has he ever not carried you? Have you ever gone hungry? For forty-one years God has held you in the palm of his hand. What makes you think he would drop you now?"

It's just that so few writers ever make a living writing. They say one out of every four thousand submitted manuscripts gets published each year. What makes me I am that one? What makes *me* any different?

I don't know . . . *but I am.*

I am at that stepping-off place, yet I don't feel quite ready to make the leap.

I just don't have enough faith.

Then I thought of someone who did.

I called my brother, Deacon, and asked him to tell me Sarah's story one more time.

God's Hands

After a very difficult pregnancy, on September 18, 1991, my brother's wife Bonita went into labor. She wasn't due until the end of December.

Born three-and-a-half months early, the baby was so tiny my mother and I assumed she probably wouldn't make it, so we flew to Kentucky knowing Deke and Bonita would need our love and support—now more than ever. After trying to have children for more than eight years, this pregnancy was a miracle, in and of itself.

Arriving in Louisville, my mother and I went straight to the hospital to see how everyone was faring. Bonita was out of the woods, but the baby girl she had given birth to weighed one pound, five ounces. The doctors gave the baby less than a five percent chance of making it. The full impact of what the doctors said didn't hit me until they led me to the Neonatal Intensive Care Unit.

I scrubbed with a stiff brush, put on a mask and gown, and went in to see the baby.

She was in an incubator and could not wear clothes because her paper-thin skin couldn't handle touch of any kind. Her lungs, ears, and eyes were all underdeveloped. Machines breathed for her and monitored her little heartbeat. Tubes stuck out of every conceivable place, and monitors covered her tiny body.

Her body wasn't much bigger than the palm of my hand and her legs were no thicker than my middle finger. She looked like a little doll—not a baby at all. My eyes filled with tears at the sight of her.

I couldn't imagine what my brother and his wife must be going through, spending day and night in the hospital not knowing whether their baby would make it through another spiked temperature or code blue. Every day was touch and go.

Although the doctors were adamant about giving false hope to families in this situation, there was a bulletin board by the nurses' station with the birth weight of the premature babies born there, along with follow-up pictures of their first, second, and third birthdays.

I asked my brother how they were doing and he said they were fine—because they *knew* God was going to take care of their baby. He *knew* everything was going to be just fine. I told Bonita I couldn't fathom a faith that deep. She told me, "God has not brought us this far to let us down now."

I shook my head at how calm they were. Concerned, but calm. There was a peace about them that comforted all who came to visit. And we were supposed to be comforting *them*.

Everyone was praying for the little girl named *Sarah Hope*. And everyone had *hope* that God would carry this little one through.

Five percent, that's just a number. This little baby was going to make it against *all* odds. Bonita's and my brother's faith never wavered. From day one, they *knew* their daughter, *Sarah Hope*, was going to make it.

And make it she did.

Today, Sarah Hope is a happy, healthy, fun-loving seven-year-old. To me it's a miracle. To my brother and his wife: they knew from the start that Sarah was in God's hands, and they trusted God implicitly.

Today's Action | To heck with the numbers. You can make it whatever the odds. Remember . . . *with God, all things are possible.*

God Will Make A Way

The term *right livelihood* keeps coming to mind.

After talking to my brothers, I did a 180-degree turn and called my husband's insurance company, "What would happen if I quit my job . . . do I have to wait until the open-enrollment period or can I just switch from one group insurance plan to another?" They said if it was due to loss of coverage, I could come back to my husband's insurance plan the same day the other coverage ended.

Hmmm.

Next, I called my old firm's pension administrator, asked how much money I had in my pension fund, and what the penalty would be if I took the money now, as opposed to rolling it over into another 401k. After taxes and penalty, there would be enough money to pay my car and credit cards, enabling me to write for about a year without having to work.

Am I crazy to even think of this? The very thought makes my stomach flip-flop.

My safe, secure, levelheaded friends think I am insane to consider cashing in my pension fund. Even my oncologist said, "Isn't the point of retirement money, *retirement*?" I guess that sometimes you *do* have to go crazy, before you get sane.

As I contemplate the insane, my brother's words keep ringing in my ears, "Focus on what you *can* do. And remember the outcome is in God's hands."

I asked Gary what he thought and he said, "Debbie, what do you think God's will is for you?"

The small quiet voice within answered, "Writing."

Gary looked at me, eyes filled with love and compassion, and said very quietly, "Then you know what to do."

The following Thursday I gave notice.

 | Feel the fear, take the next right step, and trust God will make a way.

Overjoyed

The miracles surrounding this decision are astounding. The night before I gave notice, I shared at the meeting near my office that I was finally quitting the job from hell. Everyone was happy for me; they had seen firsthand how miserable I had been these last few months.

The woman sitting next to me leaned over after the meeting and said, "I don't mean to be rude, but would you mind if I interviewed for your position?" Mind? I was ecstatic! I felt horrible leaving them so short-handed.

The same day I gave notice, this woman e-mailed her résumé, came in for an interview, and was hired the next day. Not only is she more qualified for the job than I am, she lives less than five miles away.

It is going to be great for both of them. After all, this woman studied computers in school. Leaving them with a good replacement made giving notice so much easier. Everyone wins. My hell may very well be her heaven.

That was the first sign that God was thrilled with my decision and assisting me in every way.

Next, I got a fortune cookie that read, "You will travel far and wide, both business and pleasure." I can actually see myself on the road, signing books, and visiting national parks—just like I fleshed out on my *Bliss Chart*.

How cool! I see this book helping people all over the country—to truly live their bliss—*full time*.

And today, eleven days after giving notice, I received final confirmation from God that I am on the right track, in the form of a letter from the editors at *Chicken Soup for the Soul*. They selected "Dharma—My Little Angel" out of more than five thousand stories to be in their upcoming book *Chicken Soup for the Unsinkable Soul*. I mean, is the Universe responding to my decision, or what!

It feels like God is actually excited for me.

In fact, when I got a little fearful after giving notice and started second-guessing my decision, a deep, resonant voice from within said, "*But if it is from Me—why worry?*" One more time, God found a way to reassure me that I made the right decision.

This is just too cool! I can't stand it! It doesn't seem possible that I could live the life I have always wanted to, that I could be a full-time writer, but here it is. No other life seems possible anymore. This is just too good to be true—to make a living doing something I love so much—I guess dreams really can come true.

And the energy around this book is unbelievable! Everyone who's read it so far is re-evaluating their lives and beginning to move toward their dreams. People are interviewing for new jobs, going back to school, going into business for themselves, and leaving unhealthy relationships behind. They see that what is possible for me is possible for them. What is possible for us is possible for you.

Today's Action | Keep your eyes on God. Keep focused on your dreams. Doors *will* open.

Free Girl

Yesterday was my last day on the job. Dianne, the receptionist who is so talented with arts and crafts, said as I was leaving, "Remember, tomorrow is the first day of the rest of your life." Another friend called me this morning welcoming me to the same.

I don't think the reality of what I've done has fully set in yet, but it feels awesome not to have to wake up at the crack of dawn to drive across town to a job that sucks the very life out of me.

My heart flutters with excitement and fear every time I think about what I've done. Some people think I am courageous. Others are inspired by my actions. And still others think I'm crazy.

Me, well, all I can say is that the day I gave notice, I beamed at myself as the mirrored elevator doors closed. The gleam is back in my eyes. My face positively glows. Looking at myself, I thought, *she's back*. Until that moment, I hadn't realized how far away I had slipped.

I *know* I made the right decision, one I was not ready to make seven months ago when my old law firm first closed. I needed to go through what I went through. Sometimes that's just the way it is.

Dianne thinks I needed to be at this job for these last seven months to light the way for her. She calls me her mentor and just did her first arts-and-crafts show. People are beating down the door to buy her exquisite handmade gifts. She can't fill the orders fast enough, and is amazed by the response. I'm not—I can tell a fellow bliss traveler when I see one. You should see her face light up when she talks about doing it full time. Someday. Someday soon.

As Dianne talks about her six-month plan of action to leave her job of eleven years, I smile a satisfied smile. It's so rewarding to know I've played a part in Dianne's becoming courageous enough to follow her dreams. These last seven months have been worth it just to see this.

Thank you, God. Thank you, God, for this *first* day of the rest of my life. I will use it well.

Today's Action | Review your plan of action, your *Bliss Chart*. How are you doing? Dreams don't always unfold exactly as planned, but I bet you've been able to mark off a few things already. The point is to put your dreams out there; then allow *God's* will to unfold.

Right Through You

While arranging to pick up my pension money, I spoke with my old boss today—the one who didn't believe my ribs were really broken.

He had heard what the money was for, and began telling me about his nephew who is writing a screenplay. He said, "I can't wait until he's finished with this silly notion and gets back to the business of practicing law. He is wasting such a good education."

I couldn't help thinking, "This man has no clue. He just doesn't get that there's more to life than making money—like cultivating relationships, enjoying nature, or helping others. I guess he can't fathom people being happy with a simple life, doing what they love."

Then he asked, "What makes you think you can earn a living writing? Do you have a publisher? Have you ever been published?"

I've learned when people ask questions like this, they're just itching to burst your bubble. I didn't finish my answer, "*Chicken Soup for the . . .* ," before he laughed in my face. *Scoff all you want*, I thought, quickly changing the subject back to getting my check, not wanting to waste another minute with a bliss stealer.

Secretly though, I can't wait until this book is published, so I can send him a signed copy.

On the other side of the coin, a really cool thing happened yesterday. The owner of the software company I just left asked me to outline what it takes to be a customer engineer, what causes burnout, and how the company could help prevent it. I took it as a major compliment that he wanted my input and really respected his desire to improve the high turnover rate in the software support department.

I spent a few hours recording my observations and took the liberty of adding a section on what the employee could do to help prevent burnout. The head of Human Resources read my comments and responded via e-mail, "Fabulous! I know if all these suggestions were implemented, our company would be a roaring success."

Responses like this help me see that maybe I needed to take that little detour, in order to help this company be the best it can be. It also affirms my writing ability and vision, something I can certainly use after talking to a bliss stealer.

I spent half the day writing and feel back on track.

414   Now, *this* is how I want to live!

Today's Action | Avoid or discount bliss stealers at all costs. Focus instead on those who can support your vision.

I'm Free

I still can't believe I don't have a job!

I have *always* worked—since I was fourteen years old—except for two brief periods. The first was when I was in my early twenties. I had been working two jobs trying to earn enough money to get my own place (after a run of bad luck—I had ended up back home—*again*), when I met this very wealthy man, Carlos, through a friend of mine. He wined and dined, champagned and cocained me, until finally I gave in and allowed myself to be a kept woman. The fun soon turned into a nightmare as I sold my self-respect for drugs and money. Within in two months I ran back home and started saving for that apartment again.

The second time I didn't work was during the seven months I underwent chemotherapy. That started off as a nightmare, but somehow I managed to have some fun in between treatments.

So, my only frames of reference for not working leave a bad taste in my mouth. Now, I voluntarily quit my job, but no longer fill up my time with partying or have endless doctor appointments to go to. What am I going to do with my time?

I know—spend lots of time writing; but really, how much can a person write?

I feel undeserving of this opportunity. I *should* work at least part time. Says who? The little voice inside that is still fearful of living large.

Ever since I can remember, I've longed for the opportunity to write *full time*; now here it is, and I'm scared to death. I even woke up at six this morning, though I no longer have to. I guess working is a hard habit to break.

But I *am* working!

Right!

No matter how much time I put into it, I don't think I will ever consider writing work. I enjoy it way too much.

I'll just think of it as an extended vacation—a leave of absence—a sabbatical.

It's hard to believe, but I guess I really do have an opportunity to realize my dreams, instead of living another nightmare.

Who would have thought?

Today's Action | Believe in and affirm your dreams. Life doesn't have to be a succession of nightmares— you really *can* live your dreams—whatever they are. *"I'm free . . . and I'm waiting for you to follow me."*

My God Is An Awesome God

As we come into the final stretch, how are you doing with your goals? Are the dreams on your *Bliss Chart* coming to pass? Has this year been a transformational year? What new insights have you gleaned about yourself? Do you feel more connected to the world around you? Is your heart more expansive? What healings have taken place? What fears have you walked through? Is your heart overflowing with gratitude? Do you have a clearer picture of your purpose here on earth? And, most importantly, is your heart singing?

Do you feel your life shifting? Isn't it wonderful?

You are closer than ever before to who you really are.

Isn't God's power awesome? Think back on all the synchronicity, all the *Godincidences*, that occurred over the last few months. Isn't it exciting when the Universe responds so personally to your desires, making your way easier?

As I near the end of my first big dream—writing a book—I am filled with exhilaration and doubt about my new path. It is vital that I embrace all of my emotions as well as maintain contact with my cheerleaders and mentors. Many artists have been known to sabotage their success just as they are on the verge of achieving it.

So much fear is kicked up that it's not uncommon for someone to buy into the doubts and insecurities, close up, and return to their old familiar, safe life.

> **Today's Action** | What feelings crop up as we near the end of our journey together? Excitement? Fear? Joy?
>
> Share your feelings with one of your cheerleaders or mentors. Allow them to honor the new, more-courageous self you have created. It's through your desire, excitement, and perseverance that this new person has emerged. Look in the mirror and celebrate the new you. You've earned it.

The Point Of No Return

Now that you are grounded in the daily actions laid out on your *Bliss Chart*, it's important to know that the closer you are to doing the things you think you cannot do, the more terrifying things seem. This is a natural reaction to living outside your comfort zone.

When fear creeps in, we may be tempted to return to our old life. I've had five offers of work since I quit. Some were part time, stress-free, and convenient to where I live, but I don't want to go backward, I want to go *forward*. I don't want a safety net. I want to give writing my all and trust it with every fiber of my being.

Once I opened up to greater possibilities for my life, there was no turning back. Just the act of discovering my heart's desire did not make it painless to move toward it, but the pain of not living it is far greater than the fear of moving forward.

Any steps I take lay the groundwork. It's all practice; there's no such thing as failure and no time is wasted. I spent two years writing about cancer. Recovering from it was my whole life. Now, cancer has become just part of my life, enabling me to write from a much broader perspective than just a cancer survivor.

Since I never published anything about my cancer recovery, does that mean those two years were wasted? Absolutely not! This book could not have been written if I hadn't spent two years building my writing muscles, developing my skill, and honing my craft. It was a necessary part of the process.

If your bliss is planting and pruning a beautiful rose garden, you're not going to throw in the trowel because one rose bush dies, you learn and grow—blossoming along with your rose garden.

Today, each step I take toward my dreams increases my self-esteem. As my self-esteem increases, so does my ability to walk through fears. With each fear I walk through, I become more courageous. As I become more courageous, I am less fearful. When fear ceases to run my life—I cannot help but follow my dreams.

All I have to do is follow my heart.

Today's Action | Stay on the path. Follow your heart. Most of all, never give up. Just learn and grow— learn and grow.

417

Twelfth Month

Living In A State Of Bliss

I'm Still Standing

*a*s I near the end of my beginning, it's important to reflect on my growth, for there have been many memorable touchstones, cornerstones, and milestones.

The first that come to mind are the touchstones—the painful lessons.

It still amazes me that you can have a desire so deep it reverberates in your bones, yet fear can keep you so stuck that you take little or no action toward it.

This year the dabbling stopped. I became a committed writer. I didn't base whether I wrote or not on how I felt, or whether I felt inspired, I just did it. Regardless of how I felt, I woke up every morning, two hours earlier than usual, and wrote—flexing and strengthening my writing muscles daily.

The index cards, the great processor of all feelings, were the initial catalyst. And boy, did they kick my butt. But work they did. My mentor told me that in his sixteen years of working with others, he has found no more effective way to feel, deal with, and move through feelings than working with the index cards.

Painful as the feelings were, the cards are so thorough that it's unnecessary to revisit the memories again. Over the last year, I have worked with many people. Some wanted to be writers or felt blocked creatively, and others just wanted to heal their pain. Every single one of them has faced their demons and moved on to create happier, healthier lives.

From my own painful memories of sexual abuse, to grieving about not being a mom, to having cancer and losing my breast—not one of these issues holds any weight on me today. It took about a month of working with the cards, and then I was done. I guess only time will tell if there is any residual pain, but so far, just as my teacher said, "When you're done, you're done."

Just for today, I am at peace with my past and the trials I've faced. Today, I know that everything happens for a reason, and I wouldn't change one single thing, because everything that transpired led me to where I am today, and I *love* where I am today.

A touchstone is something you rub to remind you of the pain, so that you never have to repeat it again. The cards have been my touchstone. By rubbing my pen on them, I was freed from the bondage of my past.

Once clear, I am ready to face today, and the adventures that lie ahead.

If, for whatever reason, you skipped the cards earlier, reconsider working with them. You cannot imagine the blocks they will remove—you can only experience it. (Refer to *The Wall* for more details.)

And in case anyone wants to know: you can pick up the cards at any time, to process any emotions that come up. So, whenever fear, doubt, or insecurity crop up, say, "Thanks for sharing," and *write* them away.

The Best Is Yet To Come

Cornerstones mark major turning points—we can actually see where we turned the corner or took a new road. The decision changes the course of our lives.

For me, the first one was June 18, 1988, when I made the decision to stop killing myself with drugs and alcohol.

420   The next major cornerstone was June 2, 1995, when the words "It's cancer" sent my life into a tailspin, from which only finding my true purpose could help me recover.

Another huge one was March 15, 1998, when I committed to working with a published author, my mentor. By this point, I knew what my bliss was and had been dabbling at it for over two years. However, floundering around on my own made this journey difficult at best.

The day I decided that my dream deserved my financial backing was the day my life shifted. Writing became *the* most important thing in my life. Every other decision was based on how it affected my writing.

Would this take away from or add to my goal? Would this impede or enhance my growth as a writer? How will this class affect my writing? Instinctively, I knew I would be leaving my accounting career someday and would need to gain more confidence as a speaker, that's why I dropped an accounting class and signed up for public speaking.

My biggest cornerstone to date officially began today, July 15, 1999—my first day writing full time for a living.

I can't tell you how major this decision was, but you can probably guess.

The future is a blank slate, as I get ready to live a life I can't even imagine. All I can do is hold on for the ride of my life.

Today's Action | Look back over the major turning points in your life. Did things happen to you (like cancer), or did you take risks (like quitting a job)? What would you change if you could? Or do you see these cornerstones as invaluable contributions to where you are today?

Reason To Believe

Lastly, my favorite: milestones, the actual shift, or achievement.

When I received the magazine's initial edited version of "Dharma," and realized that the integrity of the story was more important than money or being published, that was a major milestone. When I was willing to say "no" to a sure thing because it distorted the facts, that's when I *knew* I was a writer.

It was a defining moment in my life.

It is interesting, though, that I don't count my first time being published for money as a major milestone. Instead, what stood out for me was the inner awakening surrounding the experience. Outward recognition or financial success doesn't necessarily determine milestones. To me it is much more important to ask, "Does it have value?" "Did you enjoy doing it?" or "Did it help someone?" rather than, "How much did you earn?"

So many of my friends kept asking about the "Oprah phone call," like it was supposed to be the most exciting thing in my life. Don't get me wrong, being on her show would have been great, but distracting, I think, to my own writing at that point. So, I took the call as just what it was—someone who reads hundred of letters a day said *mine stood out*. As a writer, I needed that kind of validation much more than being on television.

Another major milestone was the day I decided to quit my job—not the day I gave notice or my first day as a full-time writer, but the day I made the decision to go for it.

It was exhilarating. I was flying high, my feet barely touching the ground. I *knew* it was the right decision.

Talk about life-changing experiences!

Now that I think about it, all of my important milestones were internal shifts: moments in time where my whole outlook on life changed. The external validation is just God's way of reassuring me that I am on the right path.

421

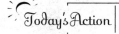

Flashdance . . . What A Feeling

This is just too cool. I now have time to go to the beach, pray, meditate, and exercise to my heart's content. I have more time to write than anyone could possibly want. It is delightful. I can tell I am going to get spoiled.

As I began my usual Saturday routine, I laughed aloud. I realized I didn't have to arrange my vitamins for the week anymore. I can do this any day of the week or just take them at my leisure.

Living the life you have always wanted is a surreal experience. Although it has only been a few days, I can't get over it. As floored as I was when I lost my breast is exactly how I feel about having quit my job. I have done it! It is not something I am thinking of doing—or something I might do in the future—it is a done deal.

Now, I am not only master of my time, I am master of my life.

This is how God intends that we live—happy—doing what we love, every day. It feels so right. My only regret is that I did not do it sooner.

As with most things, they happen when they are supposed to, and not a moment before. I wasn't ready until I was ready.

When you are ready, nothing, absolutely nothing, can stand in your way.

It feels great to be back to my old self.

God is probably wondering what took me so long.

Today's Action | What does "having it all" mean to you? What is stopping you?

In The Light

One of the reasons I meditate before writing is to get in a right-brain state so I can write without allowing the critical, left side to edit as I go, creating choppy, overanalyzed work.

The best time for me is first thing in the morning, when I'm still in a semi-subconscious state. I meditate for fifteen minutes, then emerge, pick up the pen, and write as fast as I can, always keeping the pen moving.

Ideally, there will be no crossing out, although that rarely happens. In fact, as I started this page, I was not even finished with the first sentence before I went back and crossed out the number at the top of the page, correcting it.

Catching myself editing, I had to chuckle; correcting myself is so ingrained. It takes great discipline to get and stay in a relaxed right-brain state. It is not my normal state. Practice will allow going with the flow to become my normal state.

Continuous movement of pen across paper, regardless of spelling or punctuation, helps override the need to edit as I go. Mistakes can be corrected later. The point is—I want to write so fast and go so deep that I get to the original thought—the deepest essence of what I have to say.

423

This is true for anything. We want to be so immersed in our acting, painting, gardening, singing—whatever—that we totally lose ourselves in the moment. We are so fully in the moment we experience *bliss*.

Bliss is being so fully in the moment that you are one with God. Lost in the moment. Immersed. So connected to the experience you are one with the experience. You are no longer doing anything. You just are.

Wow, what an experience!

Writing this page as fast as I did is as close to it as I've come in a long time.

It's nice to get back to my essence.

Not working sure does agree with me.

☀ Today's Action | Engage yourself so fully, in what you love, that you totally lose yourself in the moment. *Be* the dirt. *Be* the canvas. *Be* the words. Immerse yourself to the point of forgetting yourself. Reach the point of no separation—where the doing and the being become one.

Grace Changes Everything

When we are in a state of bliss our lives are fully integrated. We experience a deep connection with God. We are in tune with ourselves and at peace with others. We know our place in the world and are content.

We know and honor ourselves and aren't afraid to risk in love or life. Life is constantly expanding for us and is enjoyed as one great big adventure.

Once you surrender to love and become immersed in the moment—that is all there is—Bliss.

This is the life I have always wanted. I can't believe I actually created it for myself. I am still in the world with all its daily clamors, yet they don't penetrate my reality anymore. Those of you who have found your bliss, and are following it, know what I am talking about. Anyone in the process of taking that leap of faith, *this* is what awaits you, just around the corner.

Excitement, joy, abundance, peace, and contentment are the rewards of living your heart's desire. This *is* God's will for us. That, and soaring spirits and full hearts.

Living each day fully, loving God, ourselves, and all we come in contact with is what God desires for us.

Removing our blocks, God let us know we are loved and supported if we but open our eyes. The Universe *always* responds with our highest good.

Inherent in every lesson is growth for our soul. However painful or hard the lesson may be, the gifts are proportional. My biggest challenges—drug and alcohol addiction, relationship problems, infertility, cancer, and loss—have been my greatest teachers. I would not trade one moment of pain.

The love and joy in my heart is sweeter because of the pain and sadness I've experienced. If I felt joy all of the time, I would be unable to fully appreciate it. For it is in the contrasting emotions that I experience gratitude.

I am blessed, not as much with the specifics of my life as with my attitude and outlook on life. Over time, focusing on the good and practicing gratitude have become my nature. I no longer need to work at being grateful. More often than not, it just comes.

Bliss is where I reside most of the time.

Sometimes, I don't feel worthy of this much joy. The pain and suffering are but a distant yet necessary memory bringing me to this moment, this one singular moment in time, when our hearts become one through the written word.

Running On Empty

When your heart is full and overflowing with gratitude, it cannot help but flow out to others. I believe this is God's intention for us: to spread love to others, through our actions.

When we do kind acts out of love and an honest desire to help others, rather than from a sense of duty, we are richer for it. I used to help others because it was the right thing to do. Subconsciously, I was trying to earn God's love or to prove my worth. I meant well, but had never learned how lovable and special *I* was, so I came last on my list.

Eventually, after years of putting others first and neglecting myself, my health suffered. I was emotionally, physically, and spiritually bankrupt one more time. Out of necessity, I drew closer to God and sought answers as to why my life was in the state it was in.

Cancer was my turning point—my hitting bottom, if you will. Regardless of the cause of my cancer, I used the experience to heal my life, and put myself first in a healthy way.

Sure, it felt selfish, but I trusted that would go away as my self-worth improved—or rather my *recognition* of it—because my actual worth has always been limitless in God's eyes.

From this place of taking care of myself first, dreams were born. I finally had the time and the energy to ask, "What makes *my* heart full?" Instead of just helping others find their unique purpose, I began asking, "What is *my* unique contribution?"

I was afraid I was near the end of my life, only to find it was but a new beginning.

From this full space, this physically rested, emotionally healed, and spiritually connected place, I can finally live as God intended—*giving from overflow*—not *running on empty*.

You Can Relax Now

Prepare for the holidays at a leisurely pace. Think simplicity. Think quality time, rather than quantity of presents.

If this were your last holiday with your loved ones, the size of the new toy or the brightness of a new outfit would matter far less than the quiet moments spent together sharing love.

Lately, I've been suffering from severe headaches and dizziness. Concerned, my oncologist scheduled a series of tests to check things out.

It's funny how once you've had cancer, it never strays too far from your consciousness. Headaches become possible brain tumors. Cramps turn into colon or stomach cancer. Bone pain means the cancer has metastasized. The possibility of cancer's return is an ever-present cloud floating nearby.

Since the occasional thoughts of recurrence are a reality, I view these thoughts as time to check in and see where I am in the grand scheme of things.

Am I on track regarding my *Bliss Chart*? Am I taking care of myself? Am I spending time with God and nature? Am I still walking through fears? Am I living each day as if it were my last? Am I spending quality time with friends and family? Am I relaxed and happy as I go through my day? Am I right with God, myself, and others? And most of all—am I living my bliss? Am I doing that which I love: singing my heart's song, instead of fearing my potential?

These questions seem to get more attention when you've had a brush with death—for that I am grateful. It allows me to think of my brush with the great beyond as a gift from God, which saved me years of wasted time and energy.

Today, I follow my intuition—no matter how strange. Today, I see miracles in coincidences. I choose joy over duty. I embrace my gifts—instead of denying them. And I truly treasure love and friendships. I wouldn't trade places with anyone.

I am finally living as I believe my Maker intended. I am authentic—finally!

I am at peace.

 **Today's Action** | Check in: Are you living *exactly* as you would like? Give yourself permission to live this one day as if it were your last.
To heck with shopping, to heck with the dishes—they can wait.
Instead, go for a walk with someone you love.

Dawn Is A Feeling

I am not normally a morning person, but getting up in the wee hours of the morning these past few years has brought me in touch with a very special time of day. A quiet expectant energy abounds as the Universe gives birth to a new day. The birds haven't started singing. The sun is still sleeping. My husband is still sleeping.

Although I haven't seen him yet, it is comforting to know he is there—always close at hand. I am wearing his favorite blue-denim shirt, which, fitted for his 6'1" frame, is quite large for my tiny 5'3" one. But that, in itself, is comforting.

Gary and I are truly blessed—mostly with full hearts. Some people find it hard to believe we never fight. It doesn't seem possible—but we really are that content and happy most of the time.

Last night someone was talking about taking the easier, softer route, rather than taking the harder road of doing the right thing. Gary and I have learned that doing the right thing *is* the easier, softer way. There is no clean up, no guilt, no lies, no regrets. The seemingly harder path is inevitably the easier, richer one in the long run.

Life has taught me:

Joy is a by-product of following your heart.

Wisdom is a by-product of listening to your intuition.

Peace is a by-product of doing the right thing.

Happiness is a by-product of living fully and loving deeply.

Gratitude is a by-product of seeing the gift in everything.

Love is a by-product of sharing your time, energy, and blessings abundantly with others.

Contentment is a by-product of living the above way of life—the easier, softer way.

And bliss . . .

Bliss is a by-product of living so fully in the moment that you are one with it.

When I See You Smile

Waiting in the car yesterday, while Gary returned a video, my eyes connected with the woman in the car next to ours. She was sitting in the back seat of a very old, run-down car that had seen better days. I sensed she felt like that car looked.

Our eyes met.

I smiled.

All at once, her face lit up.

We never exchanged a word—we didn't need to. Instead, we exchanged our hearts—for a moment. During that one brief moment, we shared our suffering, our pain, our sadness, our hopes, our dreams, and our love.

In that instant I *knew*.

I *knew* that we truly are one and the same, in spirit.

Little things, like smiling at an unsuspecting stranger, can change the world.

It is such a simple thing—yet profoundly powerful.

Today's Action | Connect with God through your smile. Then see God reflected through the eyes.

Against All Odds

Okay, this might seem really strange, but I'm going to tell you anyway.

Yesterday morning Gary and I watched the movie *Amistad* about a group of African slaves' legal fight for freedom.

Former President John Quincy Adams, played by Anthony Hopkins, was instrumental in helping their cause, passionately addressing the Supreme Court on their behalf. At the time, seven out of nine Supreme Court Justices were slave owners themselves. Yet John Quincy Adams was able to help them see beyond their own actions, to what was right and just.

It was a very powerful movie, which Gary and I continued to talk about even after returning the video. During our discussions, the question came up as to whether John Quincy Adams was our second President's son or nephew. For some reason I remembered them as uncle and nephew. So Gary and I had one of our friendly little debates about who was right.

He asked how we could find out, and I said I would check the Internet later.

By the time we finished running our errands, we forgot all about our debate and went about our day.

Late last night about ten-thirty, Gary complained of dire hunger pains and was rummaging through our empty-day-before-grocery cupboards, searching for something—*anything*—to eat.

I remembered an old box of oatmeal and yelled to Gary that there was some instant oatmeal on the bottom shelf.

Five minutes later, Gary came preening into the bedroom proudly displaying an empty oatmeal packet. It seems they have little trivia questions on each one—what they call "Fun Facts." The answer on the back of the envelope was "John Adams and John Quincy Adams," with the question being, "What Presidents were our only father-son team?"

Now, I ask you what are the odds of that?

Normally, it would never occur to either of us to have oatmeal at that hour, much less read the packaging. And to find that obscure fact on the very day we were pondering the same question—I mean *really*—what are the odds of that?

We both started singing the *Twilight Zone* theme, thinking *how bizarre.*

Then, I had this wild thought about being surrounded by an intelligent, interactive, loving creative energy—that is totally connected to our every thought, word, and deed—that responds in much the same unbelievable at-your-fingertip way, to our every need—be it large or small.

No, I don't think God put that answer on the oatmeal pack after we discussed the question, I know it was already there. But the amazing set of circumstances that brought Gary to the package, and led him to read something he has never even looked at before, on the very day we were talking about it—well, I just think it is astounding.

You may think us silly, but we are both delighted at the speed and manner in which the Universe responds to our every need.

By Your Side

Every time I listen to this song, I can't help but think of God singing it to me.

I spent the first thirty years of my life relying solely on myself, and then something miraculous happened and I came to believe in this awesome Power that I now call God.

Though there have been many trying times in my life, every single time I have needed extra strength, courage, or comfort—I could rely on God, and somehow *feel* his presence.

Even now, as I walk this path of bliss, I always get the help I need. Whether it is in the form of amazing coincidences like yesterday, or the right person or book put in my life, at exactly the right moment, the answers always come.

Sometimes, I am aware of God through an inner knowing, and others times I have an overwhelming feeling that I am not alone. There is *always* an unseen Presence or Power by my side.

When little Dharma died, God used that loss to bring me the peace I had been searching for but had found so elusive.

Last night someone said, "Things happen; *I* attach the meaning." It's true; I have choices as to how I experience each situation. It takes a particularly God-centered or spiritual person to search for the lesson or the good in *all* things. Yet, this search for the good brings us closer to God, closer to the idea that there is a purpose and plan for our lives. Searching for answers leads us away from thoughts of a meaningless existence.

I don't think we could survive if we truly believed it was all for naught. We were designed not only with a unique purpose for our lives, but an innate desire to find it.

Many people spend the first part of their lives acquiring material possessions, chasing financial success, and trying to gain a sense of security. This doesn't satisfy us for very long though, because of that built-in longing for something more, something from which we can only run for so long.

Whether we use chemicals, working too much, busyness, food, sex, shopping, gambling, relationships, or something else, in the end we are left with a void that only God can fill.

God *is* by our side. We just need to slow down long enough to really know this. God walks at a much slower pace, and sometimes it takes paralyzing fear, or tremendous loss, to slow us down enough for God to catch up.

 Today's Action | Walk, drive, and talk a little slower today. Allow God to catch up.

Rain On Me

Speed is necessary to attain material things. Calm is necessary for gaining things spiritual in nature.

Until I learned this, I was always rushing everywhere—rushing to work to get more money to buy more things, rushing home to enjoy the things, then rushing back to work to get even more stuff.

It wasn't making me happy. That great job with the huge salary would probably have killed me before I had the chance to enjoy any of the material rewards.

Now, I work at achieving a state of calm, believing the spiritual to be more lasting than the material. In doing so, I am always graced with more than I need. I trust this as I let go of my need for speed.

There used to be a bumper sticker that read: "The person with the most toys wins!"

Thank God, we, as a nation, are moving beyond that way of thinking. We used to think that our basic physical needs had to be met *before* we could seek spiritual fulfillment. Now, we realize it is those very basic spiritual beliefs that sustain us through our trials on the physical plane.

The more appropriate bumper sticker might be: "The person who realizes that there *is* no winning, wins!"

That belief takes away all competition, all comparison, and all judgment.

People *are* getting it—that if I cut you off on the road—I am cutting myself off from God. If I don't let you in in traffic—I am not letting God in.

Any lack or pain one person suffers—we all suffer.

432 Yesterday, during my morning walk, I could see it begin to rain a few blocks from me. Watching the oncoming rain, my first inclination was to outrun it. Realizing that was impossible, I surrendered and got soaked.

As the rain ran off my body, I lifted my arms up to the heavens and asked God to wash away all that stood between us, particularly my impatience while driving.

Leaning my head back, I caught raindrops in my mouth like I used to when I was a child.

I felt cleansed.

It was a perfect moment.

I was sure I would ascend to perfection and never struggle with impatience or any of my other defects of character again.

Instead, I settled back down to earth in all my humanness.

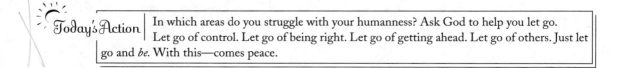

Today's Action | In which areas do you struggle with your humanness? Ask God to help you let go. Let go of control. Let go of being right. Let go of getting ahead. Let go of others. Just let go and *be*. With this—comes peace.

Jesus Is Just Alright With Me

Sometimes when I fall short of my ideal for myself or don't know where to turn, I reflect on the question put to readers by author/minister Charles Sheldon in his book *In His Steps*: "What would Jesus do?"

Back in 1988, Gary began asking himself, "What would a good person do?" when he first tried to turn his life around. Questions like these guide me back to truth—back to what I know is good, just, and right. Even though I, myself, am not a Christian, I take comfort in thinking about what a great leader such as Jesus might do.

In 1896, *over one hundred years ago*, Dr. Sheldon asked his congregation to ask themselves, "What would Jesus do?" before beginning any endeavor during the course of the next year. He then records, in the form of a novel, how various towns' people were affected by applying this simple, yet probing question to their lives.

From "the newspaper editor awakening to the opportunity to do great good for his neighbors even though his job is endangered" to "the heiress realizing spiritual fulfillment is within her grasp, even at the cost of bitter family opposition" to "the executive facing up to community responsibility in his business dealings"—each of them recount the spiritual transformation of their lives as they base their decisions on the question, "What would Jesus do?" and then accept the challenge to walk, *In His Steps*.

So, when Gary asked me a few weeks ago, "What do you think God's will is for you?" and I responded, "Writing," how can I not use the gift my Maker gave me?

I honestly don't know what Jesus would do in my situation, nor do I truly know what God's will for me is in every situation. But I believe, as the philosopher Thomas Merton once said, "We will never truly know whether something is God's will or not. But the *desire* we have in our hearts to do God's will, is certainly pleasing to Him." So I do my best to try to live as I believe God would want me to.

As I sit here typing my little heart out, I know I have made the right decision.

Today's Action | What are your guiding principles? What motto do you live your life by? Is your desire to please your God and leave the world a little better off for your having lived?
You may find it helpful to symbolically bring God into your life by wearing one of those woven bracelets that read: "WWJD." Or find some other reminder to help you bring the God of *your* understanding into your day and into your life.

Somebody's Out There Watching

After finishing that last story, I took a break and went for a walk. I'm house-sitting for my mother this weekend while she is out of town. My plan is to write all weekend, with no distractions, and finish the book.

As I returned to my mother's house after my afternoon walk, a car passed me whose front license plate read: "WWJD."

Now there is no way the lady driving that little white car could possibly have known that less than an hour earlier, I wrote a little story about "What would Jesus do?"

I know it shouldn't, but I swear the Universe astounds me! At times like these, I have to laugh out loud. It's so clear God *is* watching me. He is so close as to hear my every thought, secret wish, or darkest fear.

God is present in times of trial and suffering, gently comforting us and helping us through challenges. God is with us during our triumphs, celebrating our high points with us. And God is with us on ordinary days, such as today, pointing the way with little reminders like "WWJD." He let us know he is close by, should we want to rest in his company.

I wish I understood the nature of these *Godincidences*, but all I know is that once you open up to them, they happen all the time. I almost said, "I wish I understood the nature of God," but that is so clear—*how can I not see his loving, caring nature?*

I mean, that car passed within ten feet of me! And I was actually debating whether to leave the "WWJD" story in the book—afraid it might be perceived as too Christian or too religious—even though I mean it in the most spiritual sense.

My face lit up when I saw those four little letters magically appear in front of me. It was almost as if God wanted to say hi and bless the work I'm doing.

I still stumble over the word *work* in relation to my writing. I just can't think of writing as work. And I still can't fathom making a living doing something I love, but here I am.

I've been told I have the talent, discipline, and passion necessary to make it as a writer. I don't know whether that's true or not, I just show up, do the footwork, and trust the rest to that magical God, who constantly finds new ways to remind me of his ever-loving presence.

Colors Of The Wind

I don't want to get to the end of my life and find that I have just lived the length of it. I want to have lived the width of it as well.—Diane Ackerman

This quote embodies the very essence of *letting your heart sing*—living a rich and vibrant life—experiencing its multitude of textures and rainbow of colors.

Can you hear the forests' song—the gentle swaying of trees and rustling of leaves? How about the rich fragrance of night-blooming jasmine or long-stem roses? Doesn't their aroma delight your senses? When was the last time you watched the sun rise or set, in all its glory? Do you remember the sticky feel of cactus or milkweed juice between your fingers? And when was the last time you bit into a juicy peach or plum, and let the nectar drip down your chin?

435

To experience the width of your life is to move slow enough to savor all the assaults on your senses. To be centered enough to delight in answering a small child's questions, rather than brushing them off in annoyance.

Often, we only experience life at this depth after we've had a brush with death, our own or that of others. We don't appreciate what we have until we are in danger of losing it, and sometimes not even then.

Maya Angelou describes it well when she writes, "Because of our routines, we often forget that life is an ongoing adventure."

Cancer was my wake-up call because I wasn't living as fully as God intended, until I was faced with losing it all. Life ceased being an adventure. That's not to say I wasn't happy. For the most part I was, but my childlike sense of awe and wonder was gone.

As I live my bliss, my experience of life deepens daily. Now, I wake up every morning, excited—especially since I quit my job.

I mean, who wouldn't? Talk about feeling like a little kid. School's out—*forever*!

This afternoon, my friend Angel and I are taking her nephew, JJ, on an airboat ride through the *river of grass* known as the Florida Everglades. At 8 A.M. this morning, I had no plans for the day, and now there's a great adventure ahead. I've wanted to do this for years. In fact, it's an *Artist Date* I never got around to. I can't wait.

JJ probably thinks he's going with two adults. Well, I have news for him—there will be three kids on that boat—even if two are over thirty.

With outstretched arms, I embrace all of God's abundance.

Today's Action | What is your experience of life? Has your sense of adventure returned? If not, what could you do to bring more spontaneity into your life?

Do you need to slow down to regain some of your lost energy? Or is it time to get out and get moving?

If you wake up with a sense of joyful expectancy about the day ahead—you are already *letting your heart sing.* If not, go inward and see what's preventing you from having the rich, vibrant life you deserve.

436

Circle Of Life

We had the coolest time on the airboat; it lasted much longer than I thought it would, and they took us all through the Everglades.

Twin Cadillac engines and two gigantic propellers that looked like huge fans powered our airboat. Taking off like a high-speed jet, we skipped across the water like a skimmed stone. Gliding over the lily pads, we drove right into miles of tall grass, as if racing a car through a wheat field. It was fantastic!

Angel, JJ, and I took turns sitting on the edge on the boat. Wet stalks of grass hit our hands as the airboat raced by. The captain of the airboat, affectionately called "the bald guy," was a real hot dog. From kissing wild alligators to eating tequila worms from the inside of lily stalks, *I mean he did it all.*

We stopped on an island, in the middle of nowhere, and watched an Indian wrestle an alligator. Then, he hypnotized it, so that it was as gentle as a sleeping baby, simply by covering its eyes. Not a trick I would try myself anytime soon, but I was adventurous enough to taste some alligator tail (I liked the homemade lemonade better). Then, we topped off our meal with a cherry seed-spitting contest (I won).

Majestic white storks stood straight and stiff as arrows, keeping keen eyes out for whatever dinner might be lurking in the murky water. Blue herons flew overhead with their expansive wingspan reflecting on the water, as they glided gracefully over the glade.

It was like going back in time. Back to when Florida was first settled and most of the land was marshland, like what now constitutes the unique ecosystem known as the Florida Everglades. Nothing but water and grass stretch out for miles and miles in every direction. One canal alone was over forty-seven miles long.

There's nothing like a day in the Everglades to bring you back to nature and remind you of a simpler way of life waiting to be lived again. Except for those damned mosquitoes! They're not around much in the daytime, but I wouldn't want to be caught dead out there at night. They say nothing can keep them away. Your choices are to endure hundreds of mosquito bites or dive into the water with the alligators. Two choices I think I'll pass on, as I put the top down in my convertible and drive back to my nice air-conditioned house awaiting me in the suburbs.

Some things in life are a little *too* simple for me.

Today's Action | Visit a place of natural beauty that you haven't been to in a while. Revel in the exquisite splendor surrounding you.

Listen To Your Heart

I just got off the phone with Maggie. After spending the better part of a year rethinking her decision to become a nun, she has decided to go ahead with it.

Not sure if she was running from responsibility and her issues with self-image and intimacy, Maggie decided to remain in the world and work through her uncertainties.

First, she became financially responsible and began balancing her checkbook instead of guessing, sometimes incorrectly, what her balance was. Next, she bought a car and made regular monthly payments on it. Then she got a personal trainer, began kickboxing, and quit smoking. (Watching her get in shape encouraged me to take Tae-Bo, making me stronger and more physically fit than ever.)

She also pulled away from religious life a bit, in order to gain some perspective. During this time, she also explored some of the things she would be giving up: dancing, karaoke, parties, and dating.

After finding out she *could* be financially responsible, take care of herself, and get into great physical condition, Maggie realized, this was all well and good, but her heart still longed for the quiet simplicity of convent life.

Maggie believes she is meant to be a nun. Now, it is no longer a tortuous call—but something she embraces.

Once ready, everything fell into place, much like my decision to quit my job and follow my bliss. Maggie knows she has choices. She can do anything she wants to. This is her choice, her bliss.

When Maggie speaks of her love of God and her desire to serve, and the calling she feels deep in her soul, you know this is what she is meant to do. She is as *in love* with serving God in the church as I am with serving through my writing.

She thanked me for allowing her to find her own way, instead of imposing my beliefs or opinions on her. Even when she asked, "What should I do?" I asked, "What do *you* really want to do? What do you think *God* wants you to do? What is your *heart* telling you?" The answers usually came while we were still on the phone.

Intuitively, we each know what our own path is to be. Going inward and getting quiet, we can discern what our path is. We can seek guidance outside of ourselves when the situation permits, but ultimately the decision rests with us.

We need to be true to ourselves above the judgment of all others, for it is only in this way, that we will truly know whether we are following *God's* will.

Today's Action | God's will for us resides in our very own hearts. Are you following your heart yet?

The Hand Of God

Terry, the grandmother in our Thursday night group, was just fired!

Don't spend one minute feeling bad for her. She was called away for a family emergency; her daughter-in-law had to have an emergency C-section because the baby was stuck in the birth canal, and Terry wanted to be there in case anything happened. Thankfully, mother and baby are fine.

Her boss, however, did not agree with her decision. He told her that her priorities were out of order and suggested she pick up her last paycheck.

Normally, I wouldn't be so happy about someone being fired, but in this case, I think it is the best thing that could possibly happen to Terry.

Working six days a week at a job she hated depressed Terry to no end. She was fighting a losing battle, trying to balance caring for her teenage son, her daughter, and grandchild, all of whom live with her, with a job that required too much of her time.

Even Terry thinks being fired is a blessing in disguise. She says God did for her what she couldn't do for herself, and only weeks after she voiced in our *Bliss Group* what her ideal job would be. God is just too cool. Seems like he's got his hand in everything.

439

The first thing Terry is going to do is find out the schedule for GED classes in her neighborhood. Then she'll work her next job around that schedule, since getting her high-school diploma is the first step in working toward her dream of being a children's counselor.

Out of the blue, Terry got a call from AutoNation USA offering her a job. She had applied there months ago, but never heard back. Now, less than a week after being fired from a job she hated, a job she loves lands right in her lap. She'll be earning more money, working fewer hours, *and* the hours will allow to her return to night school. She can now follow her bigger dream of helping children.

Is God cool, or what!

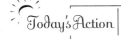 Today's Action | If you were fired today, what would be your first step toward *letting your heart sing*? Why wait?

One Way Or Another

Angel's news is almost as exciting as Terry's.

As exciting as *getting fired,* you ask? It's funny how bliss seekers see opportunity where others see calamity.

Within one week of Angel telling the group how miserable she was at her job, her doctor told her that she might have carpal tunnel and have to be re-educated for a new career.

Most people would be devastated if told their career of eighteen years may no longer be an option. Angel was bursting with excitement when she called me with the news. I mean she is upset about her wrist and the pain it causes her—but she *totally* sees this as a God thing.

She was going to be hard-pressed to walk away from the kind of money she was making, to follow her dream of opening a boutique, but now it looks like she may qualify for both disability and vocational rehabilitation, which makes following her bliss all the easier.

You may remember Angel as the biker in our Thursday night group. But far from your typical biker—Angel collects porcelain dolls. She has a room in her house, "the pink room," dedicated to this hobby. Another dream of Angel's is to learn how to make these delicate dolls herself. Coincidentally, her mother met a woman last week who teaches porcelain doll making. Angel is on her way, right now, to find out more about life as a doll-maker. With this health issue, so many doors are opening that Angel isn't sure which dream she wants to follow.

It seems when one door opens, they all open.

Terry and Angel were the two women in our *Bliss Group* who told me I should quit my job *immediately*, but were too scared to do it themselves.

Be very careful when putting your dreams and desires out into the Universe. It really *is* listening.

Today's Action | Remember that list you made back at the beginning of this book of things you love doing? How many things on the list have you tackled this past year? Is it time to venture out again and try your hand at something new?

Hold On

When I met Sari, she was very sad about having just lost a baby through miscarriage. Being pregnant was the most wonderful experience she had ever had, and now that she knew she *could* get pregnant, she wanted to try again.

She had tried in vitro fertilization twice already and wasn't sure if she was going to be able to do it again. In vitro fertilization costs between $8,000.00 and $10,000.00 per try, and insurance doesn't usually cover it. Fortunately, Sari's mother was able to help and paid for the first two in vitro attempts.

In vitro fertilization is risky, with only one in four attempts at pregnancy making it to term, but Sari's mother saw how much it meant to her and agreed to pay for one more round.

This time Sari had an allergic reaction and spiked a high fever. Subsequently, the in vitro did not take, and she was crushed one more time. Although I only did artificial insemination, not in vitro, I know what it's like to have your hopes and dreams shot to pieces every time you get your period.

The emotional roller coaster can be a huge strain on any marriage, but Sari and her husband are committed to having a child and seem be handling things well.

After three unsuccessful in vitro attempts, everyone told them to give up, that it must not be God's will. Or that maybe they should try adoption instead.

For whatever reason, Sari felt she would be successful if she tried one more time. After discussing it with her husband, they decided to go into debt in order to try again. They did, and held their breath, until the dreadful day when her period came, yet again.

After four attempts, anyone of sound mind would have said enough is enough, what are our other options, but not Sari. Even in the face of horrible odds, and many failed attempts at getting pregnant this way, she wanted to try *one more time*.

In recovery circles, there's a saying, "Insanity is doing the same thing over and over expecting different results." Everyone who knew Sari thought she was crazy to try again.

As her sponsor, I always advise Sari to follow her heart. Because I know, sometimes, you just have to do what you have to do. Playing it safe may keep some people from taking the very risk that would make their dreams come true.

As of this moment, Sari is one very pregnant woman, albeit a bit in debt, but pregnant nonetheless. I guess the fifth time is the charm.

Based on her commitment alone, I know she is going to be a great mother.

I wish I had the determination Sari had to have pursued motherhood the way she did. But I guess I have what it takes when it comes to pursuing my dream of being a writer.

Sometimes, to truly let your heart sing, you have to be willing to go to any lengths—possibly even do what others consider quite insane—like putting close to $20,000.00 on a credit card to have a baby—or quitting a well-paying job to write full time.

| Today's Action | No matter what the odds, no matter what others think: go the distance—live your heart's desire. |

Hard To Say I'm Sorry

And you remember my great aunt, Fi?

Well, if it were up to me, my whole family would be having a barbecue at her house today. However, it's not up to me, and the healing that I had hoped and prayed for, has not taken place—yet.

I haven't lost hope. I still remember my great-grandmother Gammy's last request and would love, more than anything, to help bring *peace in the family*.

There is a softening though, on both sides. Starting with my aunt reminiscing about that summer trip she took with my mother. Then, just this week my mother told me Jackie said, after reading a letter to the editor that her sister Fi wrote last week, that it was *very* well written.

That may not seem like much to you, but my mother and I were both taken back by my grandmother's comments. First, that she saw who wrote it and read it anyway, and second by the fact that she would give the sister she hasn't spoken to in over twenty years such a compliment.

Me, I always focus on progress rather than perfection. The outcome isn't the perfect one I had hoped for, but there is progress. Those twenty years didn't happen overnight, so it may take more than a year to bridge the gap.

Aunt Fi and I talk on the phone regularly and write each other in between phone calls. And that's more than we had four years ago. It always thrills me to get a letter in the mail that has her big, expansive handwriting on it. So, one relationship—ours—has been healed.

Whenever I get anxious about the future, and whether or not a healing will take place while my grandmother, great-aunt, and mother are still alive, I remember how much humility and courage it takes, and that not everyone is capable of putting aside being right, in favor of what's right.

At this point, my job is to pray for all concerned and to do my best to extend love and understanding to all.

❀

Somehow, a copy of this manuscript made its way into a state prison. Here are excerpts from an inmate's letter:

443

5/2000

Dear Deborah,

My name is Saree and I am incarcerated with Rochelle who has been sharing your book with me. The first night we read about Gary and all his support through your fight (and winning) against cancer. We laughed and cried. Then we read about your workshop and read the words to "Hero," and cried again. We both were so touched by your story regarding if only four people could live and your assertiveness regarding your self-worth. The next day, Rochelle and I were sitting under a tree and "Hero" came on the radio. It touched my soul.

A little about myself: I'm 36, Jewish, and come from an upper-class dysfunctional home. Last Sunday, after reading more of your book, I had an emotional breakthrough and wrote a letter to my mother, offered forgiveness and asked for hers. I felt the weight of the world lifted off my shoulders. It freed me. Your Aunt Fi should try it. If she has, I haven't gotten to that part yet. I felt the letter allowed me to move forward in my spiritual and emotional growth. Without your book, this would not have happened. Thank you. Saree

Saree and her mother are now speaking regularly and rebuilding their relationship. One more time God used someone seemingly worse off than me to give me hope. Maybe, someday, this will happen in my family.

☀ Today's Action | During the course of this last year, what healings have taken place in your life? Are there more to come? If so, pray that everyone finds the courage and humility necessary to face and heal the past.

Teach Your Children

Writing by the lily pond and waterfall in my mother's backyard, I am at peace. The gentlest of breezes blows through the jasmine bushes, soothing my soul. A deep purple lily is beginning to open. I was sure I saw purple yesterday, but by the time I came outside, the green bulbs were closed tight. Wondering if I only imagined that bright purple splash, I came out early this morning to investigate, and here it is, on the verge of opening.

Most people wouldn't trade their changing seasons to have the nonexistent winters that we have in South Florida, but having been born here, this is the only winter I know. The warmth of winter and year-round blossoms lay in balance against the heat of our summers.

The miracle is, as my friend was saying the other night—to see the good in everything—to blossom where you are planted. And today, I am planted by this lovely backyard waterfall.

It has long been a dream of mine to create a waterfall in my own backyard. Someday . . . Until then, I have this one. And of course Hawaii—I'll always have Hawaii.

When I think back to just a few short years ago, when Hawaii was but a dream, when writing was but a dream, when fighting for my life was the only reality I knew—I am amazed at how my life is unfolding. My heart *is* singing. Amazing—truly amazing.

One of my most treasured gifts, my love of nature, was passed down from my great-grandmother, to my grandmother, to my mother, and finally to me.

I remember Gammy taking my small hand and leading me through the neighborhood, naming every tree, bird, and flower we saw—quizzing me later. What an education! Here, some thirty years later, I still remember the huge oak and ficus trees, the shedding

Melaleuca and gumbo-limbo trees, and can still tell a blue jay from a blue bird, and a dove from a lovebird.

As much as I love computers, I thank God we didn't have home computers when I was a child, and that our time in front of the television was limited. It gave us a chance to be outdoors, with nature.

| Today's Action | Make a commitment to teach a child about nature—firsthand. |

Garden

Sitting in my mother's garden, I am reminded of a few lines from one of my favorite poems:

God's Garden

The Kiss of the Sun for Pardon

The Song of the Birds for Mirth

One is Nearer God's heart in a Garden

Than anywhere else on Earth

— D.F. Gurney

When we are connected to the earth, we can't help but feel closer to God. When we feel closer to God, we can't help but feel closer to all living creatures, great and small. This connected feeling awakens our gentle nature and softens our hearts.

I agree with Theodore Isaac Rubin's sentiments, "Kindness is more important than wisdom, and the recognition of this is the beginning of wisdom."

Inviting kindness to blossom in our hearts hastens our journey toward bliss. Kindness is the essence of love. Our hearts long to be open and loving toward all of mankind.

To truly love deeply, the vision of that love must be carried beyond our loved ones, beyond our community, beyond the people who are like us and who believe like we do. Openhearted love sees all as one. To truly let our hearts sing, we need do more than just what we love; we need to know that *we are all one in spirit*—regardless of race, creed, or religion, and act accordingly.

Connecting with nature helps us reconnect with our universal heart.

Today's Action	Plant a tree, some herbs, or some flowers as a reminder that your bliss is a living, breathing, evolving entity.

We All Shine On

Hilda is single and loving it. After months of tortuous pain, she has finally emerged on the other side stronger and more independent than ever. She drives all the time now and is finally learning to live by her own lights, not in the shadow of another person.

Melissa passed the Florida bar exam and is earning a six-figure income with the firm she clerked at over the summer, so she is ecstatic. And although living with her mother was difficult at times, Melissa is grateful her mother was able to be there for her. Not too many mothers would quit their jobs, move from their home, and take care of your child for three years, while you follow your dream.

Even with all she has been through, Melissa is not giving up on love. However, she is learning to take her time and improve her picking skills.

Melissa sees not having a relationship right now as a gift. She's able to focus her attention on her new career and on her family. As a result, she is getting wonderful recognition at work and has become close with her daughter and mother. What a wonderful time for family healings and for dreams coming true.

I am grateful for her example; Melissa quitting her job three years ago helped me find the courage to do the same when it was my time.

My grandmother Jackie is still going strong. Now that I'm not working, we take long walks on the beach together every week. I now have plenty of time to spend with my family and friends. I wonder how I ever found time to work before.

⚜

Patricia and her father keep in touch and are rebuilding their relationship, a bit slower than she would like, but they are making progress. Her prayer now is that things heal between her sister and father. I guess like me, with my family, she'll have to practice patience.

Today's Action | During this last year, have you created more space in your life for those who matter most, your friends and family?
In the end, time spent with our loved ones will be our most cherished possession.

447

If I Could

My mother called last week to let me know she finished reading the first half of this book, and although she thinks I'm a wonderful writer, she didn't think she was portrayed in the best light.

I had begun to feel the same way and wondered if I could tell the whole truth without hurting her. It turns out she is not upset about the things I wrote so much as by what I neglected to say.

Did I tell you that seven years ago my relationship with my mother fell apart while we were on vacation together? I had been stuffing so much hurt and anger for so long, that eventually, I just closed up and stopped talking to her.

My mother was distraught and said she would do anything to make things right between us. Realizing I was afraid of the intensity of my emotions, I told her we might need a third party to help us. My mother said, "I'll do whatever it takes."

We spent three months in therapy. During this time, I was able to tell my mother how it felt growing up in our household, how living with my stepfather affected me, and how much it hurt when she said, "If I had to do it all over again, I would not have had children."

Week after week, my mother patiently listened to my pain and anger. Her willingness to listen healed our relationship—she never once negated my truth. This was one of the biggest gifts she has ever given me.

The therapist helped me understand how it felt to be a child raising children, and I have an unbelievable amount of compassion and admiration for my mother now. I think she did pretty well considering she was sixteen when she started.

Today I consider my mother one of my best friends, and her house is my oasis anytime I'm in need of emotional healing. Whenever I'm hurting, I know I can go home for a *mom hug*.

Every year I send her mushy cards on her birthday and on Christmas, telling her what a wonderful mother I think she is. Though she always denies the sentiments, I think she really loves getting these cards.

She didn't want me to write any more about her. She says my stories make her cry.

But, Mom, I need you to know that, in great part, I owe who I am to you—and I love who I am, so thank you. Thank you, for allowing me to be me.

Today's Action | Our mother and father are two of the most important relationships we will ever have. Have we made our peace with them? Have we told them how much we love them? Have we thanked them for the whole of who we are?
If we haven't done this recently, today is as good a day as any.

In The House of Stone And Light

Those who do not know how to weep with their whole heart do not know how to laugh either.—Golda Meir

To let your heart sing is to experience all the richness that life has to offer—the painfully bitter moments—as well as the profoundly joyful ones.

People tell me I wear my heart on my sleeve. You can always tell exactly how I am feeling. I take that as a compliment. I've also been told that it is not spiritual to be angry, that fear is lack of faith, and crying is a sign of self-pity.

Frankly, I think the fact that I am totally immersed in my emotions is one of the most spiritual things about me. It gives me such a deep experience of life. I would not want to change this about myself for all the tea in China.

I laugh heartily when I am happy, cry from the depths of my soul when I am sad, and vent like a banshee when I'm angry. Because they are God-given, I am never closer to spirit than when I am lost in my emotions.

Next time an overwhelming emotion threatens to overtake you, let it. Really feel whatever comes up. There was a time when I was afraid that if the floodgates opened, they would never close. I found just the opposite to be true.

When we allow ourselves to experience the full range of our emotions, even our anger or grief, we open to joy and beauty beyond belief. Our heart expands as we breathe deeply into our emotions, allowing ourselves to *be* with them, all of them.

What an incredible way to experience life—fully awake, fully alive.

449

Today's Action | Dive in. The water is fine. That deep pool of emotion is just waiting for us to dive into it—splashing down, spiraling upward—creating ongoing ripples, before settling back into a calm reflecting pool.

Mornin' Mr. Radio

Journeying into the past, we healed old wounds, freeing ourselves to live our bliss. Our hearts and minds opened and our dreams awakened. Endless possibilities stretch out ahead. Traveling deep into our hearts, we have become more compassionate.

We learned forgiveness of others frees us. We experienced an interconnectedness that comes only from living fully in the present moment. Throwing caution to the wind, we are living our dreams.

Our inner child has come out to play. The spirit of fun and whimsy lives within us again and the song in our hearts overflows into our lives, lifting us.

Following our hearts, we realize there is nothing to fear. God's will for each of us *is* our very own heart's desire.

As our lives deepen, our smiles broaden and we experience *bliss*.

We now know that we are not alone with our doubts and fears. As others live their dreams, hope enters our lives, and we gain courage. Courageously walking through our fears, we transcend them. We *can* become who we really are. We already *are* who we really are, but now we can see it.

Our families and friends notice the change in us—our lighter step, our adventurous spirit, our newfound inner strength. We are different than we were at the onset of this journey—somehow more ourselves.

Our lives have changed according to our vision for ourselves. As our vision continues to expand, so does our experience of life.

We have seen the miracle that is God, through the countless, unexplainable coincidences occurring around us all the time—the *Godincidences*. As we mark off our goals on our *Bliss Charts*, we see that *we really do create our own reality*.

We learned valuable lessons and are grateful for them all—even the painful ones, for we know that is when we grow most. We are ever so thankful the Universe responds to our every thought, wish, and prayer. And most of all, we are grateful our lives crossed this path of bliss, for it was just what we needed, right when we needed it.

Looking back over the last year, write about your lessons and insights, the fears you have overcome, the little miracles that have occurred, the healings that have taken place, and the person you have become.

As you marvel at how much your life has changed in the last year, vow to make a similar difference in someone else's life by passing on what you have learned.

My Place In This World

I have never written a book that was not born out of a question I needed to answer for myself.—May Sarton

When I started writing this book, I had no idea it would end with me raising the bar even higher for myself, by quitting my job and becoming a writer, *full time.* Had I known at the beginning that I would lose my job of ten years, and shortly afterward give up all the security I had ever known, I might never have started this journey.

When you surrender to a Higher Will for your life—you lose control of your life—at least your illusion of it.

Yet I would not change a thing. I believe my law firm's closing was God's way of doing for me what I could not do for myself. I was too comfortable to live all-out, until I had no choice but to stay miserable in my new job or go for it, *all the way.*

At the onset of this journey I thought I had an answer to pass on; what I found was that I had a question to live: *What is the meaning of my life? Am I living the width of it? Am I truly living my dharma?*

Who would have thought that one tiny orange tabby could have such a profound impact on someone's life. Yet here it is. I guess I was ready. Once I overcame my fear, that is.

Angel still doesn't believe that her dream of opening a boutique could ever *really* happen. She says this as she checks into the availability and rent of various locations, and as she designs her logo and begins fleshing out her fashion ideas on paper.

I think she is where I was four years ago when I began working on my first book—going through the motions—but not believing that I had what it takes to see my dream all the way through.

It's okay if you don't believe that your dream will become a reality. Just take the next right step, and then the next one after that. When fear paralyzes you—be with it, until you are ready to do the *irreducible minimum*, and get moving again. That's how I've done it and that's how you will—one step at a time—one fear at a time—one dream at a time.

Amazingly, the most devastating experience of my life—cancer—turned into the greatest blessing.

Today's Action | Realize that you, too, are an incredible person, capable of miracles. Allow this book to do for you what Dharma did for me: Awaken you to your life's purpose and give you the courage to *let your heart sing*.

Always

As I read the sign my friend Patty painted for me, "Believe in the Magic of Your Dreams," I think back to the one who believed in my dream even before I did.

I hold the rock he gave me for inspiration in my lap, right now, as I write the final stories. The smooth oval-shaped rock, given to me by *my rock*, says simply, "Create."

Gary is the one person who has stood by me from the beginning. From putting up with my ditziness in early recovery, through the PMS years (at close range), through the fearful years of cancer recovery, right up to now, as I sing my song—reawakening to and reclaiming the life I was meant to live.

When Gary gave me this rock, three years ago, my eyes filled with tears—it was shortly after I had left him, thinking our paths were too different and that we no longer wanted the same things.

Having fought so hard for my life, I wanted to share it with someone who had time to live life fully—not just work and serve others. When Gary made the decision to serve less and spend more time with me—well, that was the best gift he has ever given me. Then, when he gave me this rock with the single word "Create" etched on its surface—I knew that he knew my heart, with all of his.

Together, we have created what Gary refers to as a glorious life—one that I would not trade for anything—a far cry from where we were a few short years ago, when I cried myself to sleep singing, "I Can't Make You Love Me."

In this life there is room for both of us to follow our dreams, as Gary's finished carpentry business expands, and I give up my day job.

Gary, a gifted carpenter, does each job as if God were the customer—because in essence God *is* the customer. I guess that is why he is in such high demand.

And me—well, I write for God, too. It is my gift to God, for giving me a second chance at life, and a thank you, for putting Dharma in my life.

I could never fully express what writing this book has meant to me—I can only hope and pray that God has used me well to bring you closer to your heart's song.

Today's Action | Create.

Epilogue

My Heart Will Go On

If there is one thing I learned from Dharma's death more than anything else, it is that we do go on—forever. Dharma resides forever in my heart, as I will in the heart of everyone I touch, and you will in the heart of everyone you touch.

This book is the child I never had—my firstborn—the scariest since I had no previous experience. But once the birthing process began—*life* began. And life is a beautiful sight to behold. This is it. This is my mark—what I leave behind—*my dharma.*

I know God uses me in many ways—but when I am lost in the moment living my bliss—God and I are truly one. As I do that which I love, God smiles down upon me. Every story is a song, every song a smile, and every smile pure joy.

Creation, whatever its form, is how we all live on.

"Aren't you afraid of dying?" I ask Gary in my little girl voice.

"What if I knew, without a doubt, that when you die you go back to be with God again? How could I be scared?" Gary responds in his gentle way.

"Won't you miss me if I die?" I press on in my usual way.

"Of course I would be sad, because I would miss our life together. But you know me, I would be off volunteering for Habitat for Humanity in your memory before you know it."

Scrunching up my face, I look questioningly up at his, wanting more.

Gary finishes reassuringly, "In my heart I would know you were safe and at home, *waiting for me.*"

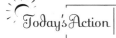 Today's Action | Treasure those you love, leave this world a better place for your having lived, and most of all—open your heart and sing your song at the top of your lungs!

Bibliography

Anonymous. *A Stonecutter May Strike* . . . . (n.p., n.d.).

Anonymous. *Courage To Be Me (The)* . . . . (n.p., n.d.).

Anonymous. *I Asked God for All Things* . . . . (n.p., n.d.).

Anonymous. *My Commitment To You* . . . . (n.p., n.d.).

Anonymous. *Priorities* . . . . (n.p., n.d.).

A Course In Miracles. Tiburon, Cal.: Foundation for Inner Peace, 1975.

Cameron, Julia, and Mark Bryan. *The Artist's Way.* New York: G.P. Putnam's Sons, 1992.

Gurney, D.F. *God's Garden.*

Jeffers, Susan, Ph.D. *Feel the Fear and Do It Anyway.* New York: Ballantine Books, 1987.

Millman, Dan. *Sacred Journey of the Peaceful Warrior.* Tiburon, Cal.: HJ Kramer, 1991.

———. *Way of the Peaceful Warrior.* Tiburon, Cal.: HJ Kramer, 1984.

Mother Teresa. *A Simple Path.* New York: Ballantine Books, 1995.

Naparstek, Belleruth. *Cancer—Guided Imagery.* Los Angeles, Cal.: Time Warner AudioBooks, 1993.

———. *Chemotherapy—Guided Imagery.* Los Angeles, Cal.: Time Warner AudioBooks, 1993.

Peck, M. Scott, M.D. *The Road Less Traveled.* New York: Simon and Schuster, 1978.

Piper, Watty. *The Little Engine That Could.* New York: The Putnam Publishing Group, Platt & Munk, Publishers, 1930.

Rosanoff, Nancy. *Intuition Workout.* Fairfield, Conn.: Aslan Publishing, 1990.

Sheldon, Charles M. *In His Steps.* Spire Books, 1984.

Copyright Acknowledgments